phati'tude
LITERARY MAGAZINE
VOL. 3 || NO. 4 || WINTER 2012

a publication of

The Intercultural Alliance of Artists & Scholars, Inc.(IAAS)
a New York nonprofit organization

Gabrielle David
Editor-in-Chief

Jennifer-Crystal Johnson
Managing Editor

Rebecca Kaye
Associate Editor

Nancy Mercado
Guest Editor

**Karen Chau
Kevin Tobar Pesántez**
Editors

Adam Wier
Senior Translator

**Amanda A. Cunniff, Jane Losaw
Joanna Morales, Amy Savage**
Translators

Lorraine Miller Nuzzo
Art Director

F E A T U R E S

D1230910

FEATURING ARTWORK & PHOTOGRAPHS
Miguel Ángel, Wanda Benvenutti, Pablo Delano, Marcos Dimas, Diana G. Hernandez, Elvis Irizarry, Ivelisse Jiménez, George Malave, Soraya Marcano, Renny Molenaar, Marlis Momber, Rafael Colón Morales, Jose Antonio Vazquez/Tontxi, Kukuli Velarde, Manuel Adolfo Villalobos

phati'tude Literary Magazine is published quarterly (Winter, Spring, Summer and Fall), ISSN: 1091-1480; ISBN-13: 978-1468013139; ISBN-10: 1468013130; Copyright © 2012 by The Intercultural Alliance of Artists & Scholars, Inc. (IAAS). All rights reserved. Printed and bound in the U.S.A. No part of this book may be reproduced or transmitted in any form or by any means, electronic or mechanical without permission in writing from the Publisher. The views expressed by authors do not necessarily reflect the opinions of the editors of ***phati'tude Literary Magazine***, the Board of Directors of the IAAS, donors or sponsors. Single issue: US$18/$20; Annual subscriptions: US$65; Int'l-Canadian: US$75; Institutional US$110; Int'l-Canadian: US$140. We offer special discounts for classes and groups. The Publisher cannot guarantee delivery unless notification of change of address is received. Visit our website at www.phatitude.org. Manuscripts with SASE, letters to the editor and all other correspondence to ***phati'tude Literary Magazine***, P.O. Box 4378, Grand Central Station, New York, NY 10163-4378; or email editor@phatitude.org. Cover Art: Goñi Montes (*see* p. 310).

CONTENTS

REPORTS FROM THE HOMELAND

INTERVIEWS

ESSAYS ARTICLES

SHORT STORIES

ARTWORK PHOTOGRAPHS

PROSE POETRY

EDITOR'S NOTE

GABRIELLE DAVID

"Even if we were to agree that being 'Latino' implies someone who feels separate from the American mainstream simply because of their culture, language and innermost sense of being, should this be of intrinsic literary significance?"

Gabrielle David, founder and editor of *phati'tude Literary Magazine*, is a writer and multimedia artist who has worked as a desktop publisher, photographer, visual artist, video editor and musician.

WHAT'S IN A NOMBRE? *Writing Latin@ Identity in America* sets out to investigate the diverse cultural identities of writers of Spanish decent by bringing together an amazing range of voices that we felt had been unfairly lumped into the category of "Hispanic" and "Latino."

Producing an issue about Latino literature first required grasping the meaning of an ethnic label that is so strategically incorporated and reformulated in our daily lives. Titles and social labels can take on a life of their own beyond the immediate realm of those who coin them or those to wh0om they are initially applied. We recognized, from the outset, the importance of examining and exploring the evolution of a population that has continued to break the boundaries of historical demarcation and defy its status as a homogenized ethnic group. Understanding this flourishing of cultural identities would help us to better understand who U.S. Latino writers are and what they are writing about. What follows represents the results of our investigation into the individual voices that lay behind "Hispanic" and Latino" labels.

The terms "Hispanic" or "Latino" continue to be a source of contention because the former implies a connection to ancient Spain and its language while the latter represents a single nationality that is in fact the myriad nationalities and ethnicities of Latin America. "Hispanic," a reference to "Hispania," the name by which Spain was known during the Roman period, was a term adopted by the Nixon administration and added to the census questionnaire in 1970 as a way to identify people who speak Spanish. Eventually, it has come to be used as a marketing term to brand government initiatives, as well as products and services, directly to the Spanish-speaking community.

However, many people have come to reject the label outright because of its connection to the former colonial superpower that was Spain during the fifteenth and sixteenth centuries. They deemed this Eurocentric label to be willfully ignorant of their indigenous Amerindian, Caribbean, African, and, in some cases, Asian cultural roots. Most importantly, some resented a term created by a government that did not have their best interest at heart.

During the 1960s and 1970s, Mexican-American activists in California and Puerto Rican activists in New York had other ideas in mind. The term "Chicano," which is thought to have originated as slang to describe immigrants and refuges from the Mexican revolution, later evolved to define the champions of Mexican-American civil rights and artistic voices. "Nuyorican," once used as a derogatory term by native Puerto Ricans when describing their U.S.-born counterparts, was later embraced by poets, artists, writers and community activists located in or around New York in the mid-1970s. As activists from both coasts joined the civil rights movement for political and

social reform, "Latino" was quickly adopted as a progressive alternative to the state-imposed bureaucratic label, "Hispanic."

While the term "Latino" has quickly been absorbed into American society (in 1997, the U.S. government adopted the ethnonym "Hispanic or Latino" to replace the single term "Hispanic"), the community remains split in its use. Clearly, these terms have, over time, become strongly associated with various grades of class and color and played a larger role in how people describe themselves and each other. For example, the term "Hispanic" is often associated with a white, affluent, socially and politically conservative demographic while "Latinos" align themselves with their indigenous roots, which consist of a liberal working-class community of activists and artists who are advocates for the poor. Of course, this theory is not set in stone. Since poll findings vary from different regions of the country, there is no clear cut answer as to its use and why.

These terms become even more convoluted for people who are not "Hispanic" or "Latino" and the question of political correctness comes into play. When Sonia Sotomayor was nominated to the Supreme Court, the *New York Times* published an article, *"Hispanic? Latino? Or What?"* (June 9, 2009) querying the proper use of such hotly debated ethnic labels and decided to use both under certain circumstances. The Los Angeles Times, however, decided to use "Latino" exclusively (*Reader's Representative Journal, "Usage: 'Latino' Preferred over 'Hispanic',"* July 28, 2011) because they felt it was "the appropriate choice over Hispanic, in keeping with the practices and sensibilities of residents of our region."

While these two terms continue to fight for space, in the end, most

people generally choose to describe themselves by their country of origin, and if by chance you call someone something they don't want to be called, they'll certainly correct you. Then again, there are others who don't really care what they are called, either way, and argue it's an insignificant disagreement that has been totally blown out of proportion. Yet, the argument still persists within and outside of the Hispanic/Latino community.

One thing is certain: The invention of the "Hispanic" and "Latino" labels has forced a group of people to be counted as a minority. It erases the differences between the historically oppressed populations of Mexicans and Puerto Ricans, exiled communities such as Cubans and Dominicans, as well as newly arrived immigrants from Central and South Americas. It has distorted perceptions of these communities and arguably has deepened the ignorance of the average person about the "real" culture of these populations. This blurring of distinctions has had negative implications for the people who were born in the U.S., for arriving immigrants, and even for the average American, whose lack of knowledge about the world beyond U.S. boundaries is strengthened by labels that stereotype people from various countries and ancestries into one seemingly homogenous group.

But we cannot ignore the fact that we live in a world of labels. So when it came time to choose which term to use, we chose "Latino." Why? We felt the term Latino best exemplified what we wish to convey in this issue; that is, Latinos are a multiethnic, multicultural group of individuals who may or may not have been born on U.S. soil and who may or may not speak Spanish. We chose to acknowledge the relationship that U.S. Latinos have with Latin America as opposed to Spain because we believe U.S. Latinos' cultural back-

ground is closer to the former. In short, our aim is not to "advocate" for the adoption of one term over the other or even to repudiate the use of ethnic labels. Instead, we hope that our in-depth examination of this term will help readers to reconsider their notions of who Latinos are, the role they play in contemporary American society, and how their voices are reflected in American literature.

To the question of our spelling of "Latin@" for the title of this issue, well, we kind of discovered it along the way. While I'm not really certain when its use began in this context, if we are to believe that women and men deserve social equality, then we should think seriously about how to reflect that belief in the language we use on a daily basis. So instead of using the traditional use of masculine plural ("o" ending) as the all-inclusive plural form, we've adopted the ampersat (at-sign) as a gender-neutral substitute that represents both men and women.

It was this lengthy discussion of identity that became the premise of this issue, and team *phati'tude* understood this to be our biggest challenge. In trying to figure out the theme of this issue, we asked the questions: What is Latino literature? How do we define it? Who are the writers out there? What are they writing about? What happens when writers contributing to American literature are pigeonholed (either by others or themselves) as writers of Latino literature? This eventually led to the naming of the issue, *¿WHAT'S IN A NOMBRE? Writing Latin@ Identity in America? ¿Qué hay en un nombre?* What's in a name? Slowly the theme became not just about how others see Latinos but, perhaps more importantly, how they see themselves and each other through literature and art.

This led to yet another question, that is, what is a Latino writer? Even if we were to agree that being "Latino" implies someone who feels separate from the American mainstream simply because of their culture, language and innermost sense of being, should this be of intrinsic literary significance? The truth is not every Latino writer has to be a self-aware Latino; there are probably many writers of Latino heritage who feel trapped or stifled by an obligation to write as one. Not every writer experiences being a Latino as a blessing nor as a hardship. Some experience their "Latino-ness" as a defining part of their internal or external struggles as human beings and citizens, and others less so. It would be easy to say that Latino literature is drawn from assimilation and exile, the migratory experience, life in el barrio, racism, or that it represents a specific style such as "magical realism," but this is nothing more than a set of expectations that has been placed on them or that they have placed on themselves. While Latino literature reflects the distinct immigration experiences of discrete

groups, there really is no authentically "Latino" way of expressing oneself, and it should not preclude anything. The only limit is the political expectations and prejudices that others have about Latinos and what they are supposed to write about.

Having said this, Latino writers, in spite of their prolificacy and influence, sadly enjoy less academic recognition than their European-American counterparts in the Western canon. Although Latinos hailing from a diverse selection of countries with unique opinions, insights and experiences have earned national and international recognition, they remain largely overlooked in popular culture. While familiar names such as Pablo Neruda and Gabriel García Márquez enjoy "household name" status amongst literary types, plenty of readers are missing out on lesser-known writers with some amazing things to say and share.

Taking all of this into consideration and attempting to address some of the questions raised above, we set as our goal to re-affirm, celebrate and introduce readers to Latino writers from a U.S. perspective. By no means is this issue complete, nor is it meant to be, but we have created a collection that includes some of the older, established writers alongside the newer and lesser-known voices that represent the different cultures thriving beneath the umbrella term of "Latino." The authors here have courageously shared their stories with us through interviews, essays and poetry, where language, culture, history, religion, and gender issues are explored against the cultural backdrop of American culture. We are certain that literary aficionados, students and teachers alike will enjoy reading *¿WHAT'S IN A NOMBRE?* because they'll discover within these pages Latino writers enriched with a unique literary and cultural perspective that contributes greatly to the tapestry of American culture.

I want to express my gratitude to our guest editor, Nancy Mercado, for not only having worked tirelessly to help make this issue a success but for her personal courage, friendship and support. This issue would not be possible without translators Adam Wier, Jane Losaw, Joanna Morales, Amy Savage and Amanda A. Cunniff, students from the finest language programs in the nation, who donated their time and effort to translate much of the works included in this issue. A shout-out to Kevin T. Pesántez, our editorial intern, who did everything from transcribing interviews and assisting with translations, to proofing, editing and fulfilling writing assignments for publication. Of course, many thanks to team *phati'tude:* Jen Johnson, Rebecca Kaye, Karen Chau and Lorraine Miller Nuzzo, who continue to give one-hundred percent to the cause and assist me in my last-minute fits. ▣

O F N O T E

The Legacy of Piri Thomas

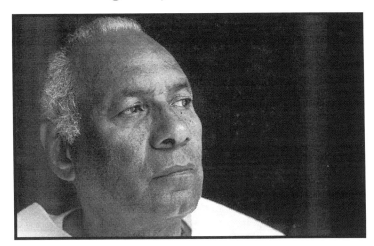

Piri the Flowmaster
Poet par excellence
Love of my life
Keeper of my heart
Your marvelous gifts to the world
were only a prelude
to those you gave to me.
Your song will live forever.

HEN I FIRST READ PIRI THOMAS'S BOOK, *Down These Mean Streets,* I was 20 years old, and a junior in college. Little did I know then that I would end up married to the man 21 years later. Initially I was skeptical of the book's author being a Puerto Rican because who had ever heard of a Puerto Rican with a name like Piri Thomas? However, after I read it, so much resonated with my experience growing up as a *gringa* in Puerto Rico from 1947-1964 that I knew Piri's spirit must have originated in Puerto Rico.

We met in San Francisco in 1984 while he was still married to Betty Elder Thomas. Betty was terminally ill and wanted to do many things before she died; my networks provided them that access and the activities they sought.

After Betty died in 1986, Piri began looking for a *compañera* who also would be his partner in work. I ended up being that person, and we were married in 1988. According to a friend in New York, "He went out to California and reinvented himself!!" He had books, stories, poetry, plays, years of experience, all waiting to come to life again after taking care of Betty. We put our heads together and developed programs and itineraries for colleges back east and schools in the Bay Area. We went to prisons, juvenile halls, middle schools, high schools, graduations, labor conferences, political rallies,

(cont'd.)

S U Z I E D O D T H O M A S

THE LEGACY OF PIRI THOMAS
Suzie Dod Thomas

(cont'd from pg. 11)

fundraisers, colleges and universities, senior centers, you name it, Piri was there. The Bay Area's progressive community at large embraced Piri. It was not just the Puerto Ricans, not just the Latinos.

For me, his work was of extreme importance. I would watch a restless classroom of kids settle down to the point of hearing a pin drop once Piri started talking. He had a way of creating unity in the room, of uniting everyone's heartbeat into one rhythm. After he was finished, you could see the kids settle into an identity, universal, global, local, individual, all at once. Piri had a way of helping young people locate themselves in a matrix, with self-worth at the center, surrounded by individuality, cultural roots, responsibility, community, and above all, love.

Seven Long Times and *Stories from El Barrio* were reprinted. We made two CDs of music and poetry, produced by Greg Landau, raising the bar on the quality of recorded spoken word. A film about him, *Every Child is Born a Poet,* was made, which took 10 years to finish and is a masterpiece by Jonathan Robinson. We were busy.

Piri was sidelined by a stroke in early 2008, not long after a trip to New York, where one of his last gigs was with Capicu Poetry in Brooklyn. He also took me to see the play, *Celia,* by Candido Tirado, which we loved.

He continued to mentor a few people and see selected friends his last 3-1/2 years as much as he was able.

Piri used his experiences, his moral authority from having spent seven years in prison, his writing talent, and, above all, his exquisite "gift of gab" to change lives. He had changed his life and was continuing to change and grow, so therefore his listeners could, too. It was a powerful message, and it worked.

It was very gratifying to work with Piri. The countless letters that poured in after a gig were his "medals." His plaques of appreciation and other awards covered several walls in his office. We wanted everyone to feel like we were making a difference; that was important to both of us. He seemed to be working off an old debt to God and to his mother. He had told God that if S/He got him out of prison, he would put his hand back into the sewer and help others climb out. And I think he did just that. From time to time he would also ask his mother, "Did I do OK, Ma?"

SUZIE DOD THOMAS is a translator, editor, and writer. She has been a member of the editorial board of the journal *Social Justice* since its founding 40 years ago. She lives in El Cerrito, California. www.socialjusticejournal.org

Let us grow your book

2 Leaf Press

www.2leafpress.org

artscenetoday .com

the new forum for emerging artists

online art competitions + exhibitions

videos + show lists + artist resources

ast merchandise

exhibition catalogues

www.artscenetoday.com

THIS & THAT
RANDOM THOUGHTS & IDEAS

The Problem of Being Bilingual, Bicultural

WAS BORN AND RAISED in El Paso, Texas/Cd. Juárez, Chihuahua, right on the U.S./Mexico border and consequently have been bicultural, bilingual for almost all of my life, heir to two muses who speak in two tongues, Spanish and English.

One would suppose that that such a gift from the gods would be an unmitigated blessing, but as it has long been noted, all gifts from the gods are double-edged swords. I have found that in the literary world of these United States it seems that the ones who least understand bilingualism are editors and critics

Being completely bilingual means that not only does one express one's self in two languages but, more crucially, thinks and perceives in them both. I have been writing my work simultaneously in both Spanish and English for a very, very long time, such that each work stands an integral whole in the two tongues.

Even so, for many years, I had thought it necessary to only submit the Spanish versions to Spanish publications and only the English versions to English publications, and this avoided all problems.

(cont'd pg. 16)

RAFAEL JESÚS GONZÁLEZ

Sins of Omission

AS A CATHOLIC SCHOOL KID, I learned all about sin. Committing a Mortal Sin could send me straight to hell, and Venial Sins would earn me a few years of burning in purgatory before being allowed into heaven. Even thinking bad stuff was sinful—and for boys, ogling girls and pondering the nasty became a repeat offense.

At first, I thought a person had to do something in order to sin. But then the priests explained another important concept: failure to do something that can and should be done is also a sin, a Sin of Omission. It wasn't until I became a government worker and observed our political process that the importance of this concept became clearer. Consider the following mortal examples:

(cont'd pg. 17)

T E R R Y S A N V I L L E

Afro-Spanglish Culture in Harlem and East Harlem

"Africa's blood runs through Cuba's veins
When you think about negroes who imitate whites
Who imitate us (Africans throughout the diaspora)
You must ask yourself who's doing who
In whose culture do we live . . ." (Ted Wilson, "Slo' Dance")

FROM NINETEEN-FIFTY-TWO to nineteen-fifty-seven, baseball was the dominant sport in the lives of my friends and in Harlem and, to our knowledge, everywhere in New York City. It was even true, from our point of view, all over the country. As a male resident of central Harlem, you would attempt to play the sport to the best of your

(cont'd pg. 18)

T E D W I L S O N

THE PROBLEM OF BEING BILINGUAL
Rafael Jesús González

(cont'd from pg. 14)

(cont'd from pg. 14)

Except that it felt fragmented to me; my poems on the page in only one or the other of my two tongues seemed truncated to me. And for some time now, I have submitted my work to editors in both Spanish and English explaining to them that neither version is a translation of the other, as I did in my email to Gabrielle David, Editor-in-Chief, and Nancy Mercado, Guest Editor of *phati'tude Literary Magazine's* Winter 2012 issue *¿What's in a Nombre? Writing Latin@ identity in America*, and that if it was accepted for publication, it be published in both English and Spanish (neither version to be printed in italics.)

I must say that no editor has yet refused to publish my work in both Spanish and English, but in spite of what I thought was a clear explanation, all too often, the Spanish version is set in italics alerting the reader that "this is in a foreign language" (as if the reader were not bright enough to recognized it as a language foreign to him or her if he or she was monolingual in English) and implying that the English is a translation of the Spanish. But neither language is foreign to me, and in my poems, neither is the Spanish or English a translation of the other, but its equivalent and/or variant as the case may be, an integral perception as it manifests itself in two tongues.

It is, in a word, a matter of identity, and I believe that this is at the crux of the problem. I am both Mexican and U.S. (I do not say "American" because American is anyone or anything from Alaska to Patagonia and to say Mexican-American is a redundancy at best) if not politically, certainly culturally. Indeed, *¿What's in a Nombre?* By any other name, says Willy, the rose would smell as sweet, but would it?

That question aside, what is *Writing Latin@ identity in America* (read U.S.)? What is Latino/a? I write these thoughts at the invitation of Gabrielle David, editor of *phati'tude,* and they stem from our discussion on my poem "Ave de Barro Negro/Bird of Black Clay", accepted by Nancy Mercado for publication, whose English version was modified by a "translator" commissioned by *phati'tude*. Though I happen to write in both "Standard" Spanish and "Standard" English, the question came up as to what is "Standard"? And what is a "Standard" language for a "Latin@" in the U.S.? Not going into the history of languages (I would say European languages), a social-linguist would find the problem of a "Standard" language a thorny one at best linked as it is to empire and the imposition of the conqueror's language upon the conquered and/or enslaved, to the problems of class, and, certainly in the U.S. (and throughout Latin America), race.

"Our policy," Ms. David wrote, "is to provide accurate Spanish translations that avoid Spanish dialect and stick to as close to a standard Spanish as possible. This means avoiding Mexican-Spanish, Puerto Rican-Spanish, Cuban-Spanish (and so on), so that Spanish translations can be read and enjoyed by everyone." My hackles rose. Who is everyone? Mickey Mouse? The question is a serious one, especially in light of such egregious educational policies as Bush II's cynically named "No Child Left Behind" (essentially carried on by the Obama administration), whose intent is to impose "standard English" which in effect makes education a privilege of the already entitled, those already "standard-ized" into the "mainstream," emphasizing as it does not education but testing and leaving out great parts of the population, many of whom are faced with poverty, economic coercion into the military, and being put in jail.

When we require a "Standard" language, we speak of standardizing not only meaning but standardizing an identity. Is there a "standard" Latin@ identity? To require such would be to involve class and, given the history of the European conquest of the Americas and the attendant institution of slavery, race. There is not one but various Latin@ identities and these require Mexican-Spanish, Puerto Rican-Spanish, Cuban-Spanish (and so on.)

I speak of a variety of identities and a wide multicultural-ism in a world that is becoming globalized, a multiculturalism that threatens the conservative soul, triggers xenophobia, and is anathema to fascist philosophy. It is not a theoretical question as we are seeing in what is even now happening in Arizona where ethnic studies have been outlawed by the state; classes and even schools have been closed; books are banned and confiscated, even torn out of students' hands; professors and teachers have been hounded— even when it has been established that students at schools that have ethnic studies graduate in larger numbers than those in schools that do not.

The issues are real and serious and how we confront them is crucial to our survival as a democracy and a just society. Language is not a trivial matter, and every language, however varied and amalgamated, is of utmost importance to an identity. A language names and identifies; it gives a name, a nombre to the speaker—and writer.

And as for translation into English, Spanish dialects may be difficult to translate, but there are English translators who speak or are familiar with at least one of their own English dialects, slang, argots, jargons which are useful for trans-lating the "feel" of Spanish dialects, and with some effort, the reader can figure it out. And this introduction into, this figuring it out of non-standard dialects, is intrinsic to forming a democracy in a nation that is made up of a multiplicity of

cultures and subcultures in a globalized world.

As for the problem of being bilingual, bicultural, it is the problem of maintaining one's identity in a society dominated by a conservative bias that would insist on the assimilation of all other cultures and identities, one common language, one parochial loyalty, one world-view, one dominant empire based on a predatory cosmology and economic system that sees the Earth and its varied peoples as only resources to be exploited for profit and domination. 🔲

RAFAEL JESÚS GONZÁLEZ was raised in the bicultural/bilingual environment of El Paso, Texas and Cd. Juárez, Chihuahua, Mexico. His poetry and academic articles have appeared in reviews and anthologies in the U.S., Mexico, and abroad. González published his poetry collections, *El Hacedor De Juegos/The Maker of Games* (1977-78), and *La musa lunática/The Lunatic Muse* (2009). http://rjgonzalez.blogspot.com

SINS OF OMISSION
Terry Sanville

(cont'd from pg. 15)

- **National Health Care.** Our country experienced run-away medical and insurance costs that deprived millions of life and the pursuit of happiness. Yet we continue to debate this issue while poor and middle-class people die. President Clinton tried to institute reforms in the 1990's but failed. President Obama has made progress. But these modest gains are already being challenged. How many more years will go by before we experience meaningful relief?

- **Global Climate Change and Clean Energy.** For years we've known that carbon-based energy forms are finite and that their use pollutes land, water and air, leads to global climate change, and involves us in volatile Middle-Eastern affairs. Yet our government still provides petrochemical companies with an oil depletion allowance (billions of dollars in tax breaks) while only lip service is paid to clean energy development. Continued support of old technology (e.g. support for drilling of the East Coast, the Gulf Coast, Alaska, and oil shale deposits) only increases the severity of this particular sin of omission.

- **Real Estate, Banking, and Investment.** Personal and corporate greed and our desire to blindly let the good times roll with minimal government safeguards contributed to the current economic downturn—that now requires massive taxpayer bailouts—funds that could have paid for public health care. Was the myth of our so-called free market system so strong that we allowed our-selves to be suckered into a hands-off approach? Will we let it happen again?

- **Natural Disasters.** Growing up in the 1950s, I remember newscasts about floods along the Mississippi and hurricanes battering the eastern seaboard. They will continue to occur. But we wait to respond to natural disasters rather than taking meaningful preemptive steps to reduce or eliminate their impacts. What will happen when the next great earthquakes hit the New Madrid fault in the Mid-West, the Oregon and Washington Coast, or California? Will yet another President fly over a scene of destruction in Air Force 1 and wring her hands? I'd rather have meaningful and sustained hazard-reduction programs than more flights!

- **Immigration.** In 1964, the U.S. ended its long-standing guest worker program with Mexico (The Bracero Program). But the demand for cheap labor continued to grow. We now have millions of hard-working, tax-paying souls involved in the agriculture, construction, and service industries who are part of an illegal shadow workforce, one that we depend on but complain about for a variety of sometimes hateful reasons. How long will families live in these shadows before our country creates an equitable solution? Es muy estupido. ¿No es verdad?

- **Unemployment and Education.** When economic times are tough, the loss of jobs hurts millions of people. But if our country and planet are to survive, economies and cultures must evolve to become sustainable from an environmental perspective. Yet every proposed change is couched in terms of jobs lost, as old sectors die off, rather than in terms of opportunities gained. Why haven't we insisted that our government and our educational institutions better prepared our populace for shifts to greener industries and services? Why can't we get ahead of the game, become leaders in these sectors?

The result of these and other sins of omission is that our country and possibly the planet will struggle through turbulent times, with the outcome uncertain. Unfortunately, we Americans sometimes punish public officials at the polls for taking positive action to change the status quo. And so many politicians sit on the sidelines and carp at those pursuing initiatives, I suspect because sins of omission are less damaging at election time.

Personally, I would prefer a government that takes actions to achieve a desired objective and fails over one that

fails because of inaction. But then I grew up Catholic, and a sin is a sin, whether it's one of omission or commission. We're all accountable for both types. ▨

TERRY SANVILLE writes full time and lives with his artist-poet wife (his in-house editor) and one plump cat (his in-house critic). He may be contacted at tsanville@sbcglobal.net.

AFRO-SPANGLISH CULTURE
Ted Wilson

(cont'd from pg. 15)

ability from the age of three up. From stickball in the streets, played with broom handles and rubber balls, to lots with or without grass, which afforded us the opportunity to play with bats and baseballs, the kind the pros used.

We taught each other how to play and organized ourselves into a ragtag team with aspirations to whatever the next level might be. Some of our group had older brothers who played in an organized league. Some of these older fellas became our mentors and began teaching us the finer points of the game. They saw our potential and after two years of discipline, practice, and learning the best way to hold the bat, field the ball and run the bases, placed our team in the PAL (police athletic league). Our coaches got us to the point where we would have serious practices on our own when they could not be there. When the season started, they made sure one or more of them would be at the game.

In '55 something interesting happened: We played a team from an East Harlem precinct. We had played teams from precincts all over the city, however, this was our first time playing a team in this particular precinct. The team was made up as expected, of all Spanish-American (Hispanic/Latino) ballplayers. They reflected the makeup of the community which was called Spanish Harlem. The various hues went from very fair skin to, what we called in the Negro community, light brown skin. The only standout was a little fellow whose complexion was dark. He was so dark he was on the edge of black/brown or what we, in our ignorance would say, he was "burple".

As I got older, I found this complexion less common among African Americans in the south than Cubans and Puerto Ricans. What stood out to us was his fluid Spanish and denial of being called Negro or Colored. At one point in the conversation he referred to himself as white. His name always stayed with me: Oscevedo. He had very thick hair in great abundance. He was an outstanding athlete. The idea of being linked to or considered an American Negro was repulsive to him.

Like that baseball team from the East Harlem precinct, many musicians of Latin music bands ranged, in complexion, from fair to brown skin. In the latter 50s Latin music (which included Mambo, Cha Cha, and Merengue) became the rave as dance music. When I say it was the rave, I mean among American Negroes in Harlem first and then, later on, throughout the boroughs. So on a social level, a relationship between Hispanics and Negroes started developing. Some of the best dancers to Latin music in the city were Negroes. They could step with any of their Latino brothers and sisters. In turn, some of the musicians, especially horn players, were American Negroes.

As teenagers we formed clubs, not gangs. We paid dues and saved our money, rented dance halls, hired bands and kept them working with regularity. There were numerous teenage and young adult clubs; consequently there were dances every weekend. This gave some of the new bands popularity. We printed tickets, fliers, and posters and distributed them in all the neighborhoods. The standard was to have continuous music, so we needed to have three to four bands per dance. The more bands each club had, the greater the popularity. We grew quickly from the neighborhood ballrooms to the Hotel Diplomat, Riviera Terrace Ballroom, to Manhattan Center ballrooms.

Some of the young fellas in the neighborhood on the edge of Central Harlem, like 113th and Lenox, both north and south, would rehearse in each other's apartments or community centers during the winter and show off their skills in the neighborhood parks during the summer. This resulted in a more in-depth relationship developed between, primarily Puerto Ricans and Negroes, a fair amount of whom were from the Caribbean. Many of these bands were, what we might call, mixed with Negroes and Puerto Rican/Cubans playing together. During the summer, at 110th and Lenox Avenue the City Parks Department funded Latin band concerts right on the lake. We came from the north end of Harlem and folks came from the east, west, and even the Bronx. Most of the Spanish speaking-folks were "Ricans," or what we now called Nuyorican and some were Cuban. There was an amalgamation that was happening without a big to-do. Black folks would frequent the Palladium, particularly on Sunday night.

Beginning in September, we would give our first "Back to School" dance. Eventually, we worked our way up to the Grand Ballroom at the Manhattan Center. We had bands like Tito Puente who became known as El Rey (the king), Tito Rodriguez—who many felt would have had that title but he passed away too early— and Joe Cuba who had a large following. It was these teenage clubs that gave the Palmieri brothers (Charlie, then Eddie) their start in music and their popularity. Johnny Pacheco came along with the Pachanga and folks were doing the Pachanga and the Charanga by 1961 and 1962

Around the same time, there was a brother named Kako. He was a brown-skin fellow who was kicking it at the Club International, in the Bronx. One of the teen clubs discovered him, and he hit Manhattan like a storm. There were a number of Black youngsters who learned to play the congas and timbales and made music their career. This led some of them into African drums and a deeper education in the religious culture. Three of the most respected musicians from East Harlem were Louis "Sabu" Martinez (July 14, 1930 -January 13, 1979), who was an American conguero and percussionist. A prominent player in the Cubop movement in the 1950s, Martinez appeared on many important recordings and live performances during that period and recorded several Latin jazz albums, now recognized as classics of the genre.

Another great musician of the time was Candido Camero who, now in his nineties, continues to have a sure touch on the congas and has retained his unique sound. Born in 1921 in a Havana barrio called El Cerro, Candido was initially a multi-instrumentalist. A switch to bongos and congas led to a six-year spell with the CMQ Radio Orchestra and a residency at the famed Cabaret Tropicana. Heralded as the father of the technique of coordinated independence, Candido had further accomplishments. For one, he pioneered the use of two congas and later three, whereas in the past congueros were content with a single drum. Then there was Machito who died on April 19, 1984. Born as Francisco Raúl Gutiérrez Grillo, Machito was an influential Latin jazz musician who helped refine Afro-Cuban jazz and create both Cubop and Salsa music. Machito was raised in Havana alongside the singer Graciela, his foster sister. In 1940 New York City, Machito formed the band, The Afro-Cubans, and along with Mario Bauzá as musical director. They brought Cuban rhythms and Negro big band arrangements together in one group. He made numerous recordings from the '40s to the '80s, many with Graciela as lead vocalist. Machito changed to a smaller ensemble format in 1975, touring Europe extensively. He brought his son and daughter into the band and received a Grammy Award in 1983, one year before he died. Machito's music had an effect on the lives of many musicians who played in The Afro-Cubans over the years and on those who were attracted to Latin jazz after hearing him. George Shearing, Dizzy Gillespie, Charlie Parker and Stan Kenton credited Machito as an influence. An intersection in East Harlem is named "Machito Square" in his honor. All of this speaks to the topic of the African diaspora that runs through the culture of so called Hispanic/Latino, British, French, Dutch West Indies, and U.S. African-Americans.

Unfortunately, the trans-Atlantic slave trade has exploited each of us and continues to keep all of these various cultures in the same box, resulting in third place a/k/a third world or under developed groups. It is very difficult, in a lot of cases, to call these cultures nations because they do not fit the definition. Like all of us from the diaspora, due to the brainwashing of Oscevedo the little ballplayer, we hated our Black selves. What we hated most was our African-ness. It ran the gamut from brown to dark chocolate. As in the case of the island of Hispaniola, where we have two countries, one side colonized by the Spanish and the other side colonized by the French, and because of the difference in each colonizer's language and customs we, as kidnapped Africans, find ourselves in denial and rejection of what (in the end) we all are and where we all come from. Is language then or, dialect within the same language, a valuable commodity on the world market? Is complexion or hair texture of some extraordinary value?

When we start to look closely at each individual culture which ought to be respected in its own right, what we find is that the best of who we are comes from where we originated. The foods we eat, or certainly the preparation of them, have a distinct similarity. Our body movements and rhythms are equally so. Some of our greatest thinkers and warriors are responsible for whatever achievements we have made, in spite of the overwhelming odds and unfair play which we have been experiencing over decades. Even our infinite view of the Creator, the Universe and similarity in ritualistic worship, regardless of name, has no relevance, since our language has been altered on both sides of the Atlantic.

In this second decade of the twenty first century, we as African peoples need to look at how we can slowly weave a tapestry that speaks to our sameness. Just as we discovered in the 1960s there is no such place as Negro-land. We could not be Negroes and when we speak of colored people we must put an (S) on it because we are speaking of the diaspora-plus. The same is true for language. I may speak English because I developed in an English colony. However, we are not English, and solely because the erroneous terms of Hispanic/Latino have been put upon our various cultures due to the Spanish language derived from the Spanish colonizer, this does not make us "Spanish." The same is true for the French, Dutch and Portuguese. Language does not make us who we are. Similarly, there is no such place as the West Indies; consequently there is no such thing as a West Indian.

We must remove the walls created and climb out of the box. The blood of Africa runs through Cuba's veins and throughout the whole diaspora. Let the music play hard and fast in order to get the reparations due us for the work of our ancestors. But first we must repair ourselves. ◻

TED WILSON is the author of *Slo Dance,* a collection of prose and poetry, and the recently published chapbook, *Senses & Shadows*.

BOOK REVIEWS
EXPLORING LITERATURE

Breaking Ground: Anthology of Puerto Rican Women Writers in New York 1980-2012
Edited by Myrna Nieves
Editorial Campana, 2012
http://editorialcampana.com
432 pp.; ISBN 13: 978-1-934370-16-2
Language: English and Spanish
Reviewed by G. David

SINCE THE 1960s the number of Latina writers has grown considerably, adding a new spice to the U.S. literary panorama and to feminine/feminist literature. Their work has been an important contribution to other previous works by third world women and other ethnic writers in the United States. *Breaking Ground: Anthology of Puerto Rican Women Writers in New York 1980-2012,* uniquely explores the development of Puerto Rican women writers by presenting a wide spectrum of poetry,

(cont'd pg. 26)

La Voz Latina: Contemporary Plays and Performance Pieces by Latinas

Edited by Elizabeth C. Ramírez, Catherine Casiano
University of Illinois Press, 2011
www.press.uillinois.edu
$60.00; 368 pp.; ISBN-13: 978-0252036224
Reviewed by Kevin Tobar Pesántez

ELIZABETH C. RAMÍREZ and Catherine Casiano present a whirlwind of Latina playwrights in *La Voz Latina*. At times this collection may seem chaotic in selection but in the end all of this diversity blends into a wonderful hue accompanied by a sharp critique and representation of Latina theatre. The book covers an extensive span of topics and the editors have selected a group of prominent, passionate, and eclectic Latina playwrights from 1980 to present. Ramirez and Casiano draw myriad amounts of knowledge from past anthologies of Latina (cont'd pg. 27)

The Other Latin@, Writing Against a Singular Identity

Edited by Blas Falconer and Lorraine M. López
University of Arizona Press, 2011
www.uapress.arizona.edu
$22.00; 184 pp.; ISBN-13 978-0816528677
Reviewed by Jose Israel Lopez

FOR THE LAST DECADES, a narrative of Latino identity in the U.S. went something like this: Migration from Latin nations created the conditions for enclaves of Mexicans, Puerto Ricans, Cubans, Dominicans, South Americans (Colombians and Ecuadorians) and Central Americans (Nicaraguans and Salvadorians), in different regions of the U.S. Their mere presence and increased numbers pressed the need for a supra-national Latin@ identity.

This narrative frames itself in the exquisite modernist Gran Combo song "El Caballo Pelotero" (Author Bobby (cont'd pg. 28)

In the Shadow of Al-Andalus

By Victor Hernández Cruz
Coffee House Press, 2011
www.coffeehousepress.org
$16.00; 140 pp.; ISBN-13: 978-1566892773
Reviewed Rebecca Kaye

N *IN THE SHADOW OF AL-ANDALUS,* Victor Hernández Cruz illuminates, through evocative poetic narrative, the interconnectedness of countries and cities across the Atlantic; from Puerto Rico to Morocco, from New York City to Mexico City, from Cordoba to Amsterdam. In his introduction to this poetic pilgrimage, Cruz specifies the importance of the "shadows" cast by Spain as both an ancient superpower and a lasting cultural influence: "I am in the shadow when I am in Morocco . . . and I am in that same shadow when in Puerto Rico, through language and culture."

(cont'd

Camino del Sol: Fifteen Years of Latina and Latino Writing

Edited by Rigoberto Gonzalez
University of Arizona Press, 2010
www.uapress.arizona.edu
ISBN-13: 978-0816528134
$24.95; 368 pp.: ISBN-13: 978-0816528134
Reviewed by G. David

N 1994, LUMINARY CHICANO WRITER Ray Gonzalez helped launch the Camino Del Sol series, a vehicle of Latino literary voices that is published by the University of Arizona Press. Since its founding, the Camino del Sol series has established itself in both the Latino community and the publishing world as it garnered awards for its outstanding writing. This anthology, *Camino del Sol, Fifteen Years of Latina and Latino Writing* edited by Rigoberto González, is a generous volume that features poetry,

(cont'd. pg. 30)

The Oxford Book of Latin American Poetry

Edited by Cecilia Vicuña, Ernesto Livon Grosman
Oxford University Press, 2009
www.oup.com/us
$49.95; 608 pp.; ISBN-13: 978-0195124545
Reviewed by G. David

IN RECENT YEARS, ANTHOLOGIES have become the bedrock of the literary industry. They are used as teaching tools and as historical touchstones. But as we peruse these comprehensive anthologies, one cannot help but become aware of the highly subjective forces standing behind the contributions of individual scholars, and editors that each bring to the table their own point of view, including the collective will of an editorial board and publisher. Thus, a comprehensive anthology of a specific genre of literature is always more than the sum of its literary

(cont'd. pg. 31)

The Chicano/Latino Literary Prize: An Anthology of Prize-Winning Fiction, Poetry, and Drama

Edited by Stephanie Fetta
Arte Público Press, 2008
www.latinoteca.com/arte-publico-press
$00.00; 320 pp.; ISBN-13: 978-1558855113
Language: English and Spanish
Reviewed by G. David

LITERARY AWARDS HAVE ALWAYS been a bone of contention in the literary world. For years, the National Book Awards, Man Booker Prize, The John Newbery Medal, National Book Critics Circle Award and the covetous Pulitzer Prize, excluded people of color. The African American, Native American, Latino, Arab and Asian communities created their own awards, providing a venue for authors that may not otherwise be discovered. Such

(cont'd. pg. 32)

Puerto Rican Poetry: An Anthology from Aboriginal to Contemporary Times

Edited and translated by Roberto Márquez
Univ. of Massachusetts Press, 2007
www.umass.edu/umpress/
$80.00; 490 pp.; ISBN-10: 1558495614
Reviewed by G. David

N *PUERTO RICAN POETRY: An Anthology from Aboriginal to Contemporary Times,* editor Roberto Márquez provides a wide-ranging and comprehensive collection of Puerto Rican poetry that dates back to the era of conquest and colonization to contemporary poets on both the mainland and the island.

The motivation behind *Puerto Rican Poetry* came in no small part from Márquez's students when he realized that available material was restricted to the contemporary era, with no sense of an historical context, and in many cases

(cont'd. pg. 33)

Bordering Fires: The Vintage Book of Contemporary Mexican and Chicano/a Literature

Edited by Cristina García
Vintage, 2006
http://vintage-anchor.knopfdoubleday.com
$13.95; 304 pp.; ISBN-13: 978-1400077182
Reviewed by Rebecca Kaye

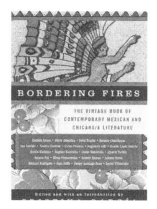

READ *BORDERING FIRES: The Vintage Book of Contemporary Mexican and Chicano/a Literature* from cover to cover on an Amtrak train-ride from Boston to New York. *Bordering Fires*, edited and with an introduction by Cristina García, is a compilation of some of the most interesting and influential works by Mexican, Mexican-American, and Chicano/a writers of both past and present. When one thinks of a literary anthology the

(cont'd. pg. 34)

THE PRESIDENT LOOKS LIKE ME
& OTHER POEMS
BY TONY MEDINA

ISBN 978-1-933491-94-3
cover illustration copyright © 2012 by Mansa K. Mussa

The election of Barack Obama as the first African-American President of the United States marked a pivotal point in the history of a nation often preoccupied with race, color and identity. Millions of people around the world have been inspired by Mr. Obama's historic victory and his personal story of determination and success—especially children of color.

In *The President Looks Like Me and Other Poems*, Tony Medina celebrates the diversity that President Obama symbolizes through poems that are multicultural in scope and wide-ranging in style. With distinctly urban settings and an urban flavor, this collection covers a myriad of themes including childhood, family, friendship, identity, spirituality, social justice and hip hop. Medina's poems realistically capture the impact of what it means to be young in a complex world. Yet, they also offer hope—hope that resounds more prominently when a child of color can say, "the president looks like me."

AVAILABLE FROM JUST US BOOKS, INC—SEPTEMBER 14, 2012
http://justusbooks.com 973.672.7701

BREAKING GROUND

(cont'd from pg. 20)

poetic prose and fiction produced in the past few decades. These 46 *Puertorriqueñas* in this groundbreaking collection represent the literary works of writers of various ages who lived in New York or were born and raised in the city. While many of these writers write in English, Myrna Nieves, a professor at Boricua College in New York City, compiled a full bilingual edition that includes an acknowledgement, introduction and biographies in both languages.

Breaking Ground is organized in alphabetical order by the author's names. Each chapter opens with a photograph and biography in both Spanish and English. Besides providing a section of photo credits, and permissions at the end of the book, Nieves also includes a section that provides contact information (email addresses and websites), making the writers accessible to readers. As Nieves states in her introduction, the premise of the book comes from her years of producing The Boricua College Winter Poetry Series, which she co-founded in 1988. During her years as curator, Nieves found that the "literary production of Puerto Rican women writers was distinct and impressive" and "became aware of the need to expand these efforts in order to present a larger group of writers and to document in some way their artistic, cultural and social contributions to the City of New York."(19).

Nieves' desire to create a space for Puerto Rican women in this context is both admirable and complex, especially when it comes to issues of homeland and nationality. *Puertorriqueñas* from the island possess a cultural identity that derives more directly from their status as citizens of a U.S. commonwealth and from their bicultural linkages with New York City, even though their socioeconomic subordination mirrors that of other U.S. minorities. Puerto Ricans on the mainland also experience firsthand the negative and positive duality of split national and cultural identities. In general, islanders and mainlanders alike bear the weight of the statehood issue (whether or not to promote the Commonwealth of Puerto Rico's absorption into the Union as a state) which has divided the Island's inhabitants for decades. Ultimately, the essence and complexities of Puerto Rican culture and identity, the mainland and the island, have prompted an intense sense of place among the writers in *Breaking Ground,* where *Puertorriqueñas* document their role in the artistic, social, political and intellectual history of New York City.

Since Nieves' prerequisite for inclusion in this anthology was that the writers had to have lived in New York for

at least ten years and be "active in the cultural scene," it would be easy to peg this as a "Nuyorican" collection but it's clearly much more. While there is a distinct New York beat found throughout the book, it cannot nor should not be pigeonholed as "Nuyorican," a term often used as a literary genre or an ethnonym that, for all intent purposes, has pretty much ignored women. *Breaking Ground* offers a different kind of beat, packed with fierce passion or quiet meditative tones, urban rhythms, poignant humor, and unique, sometimes visionary styles.

Upon further examination, the writers in this anthology take things one step further: they emphasize the metaphorical possibilities of the cultural and historical through the eyes of a *Puertorriqueña* with varying viewpoints, themes and symbols. For example, the spirituality of Alba Ambert, the playfulness of Maria Arrillaga and Lydia Cortés, and the frank revelations of Magdalena Gómez, come to mind. In a narrow sense, they often refer to the racial and cultural fusion of being Spanish, Taíno and African, a natural syncretism that has, for better or worse, makes them "different." Besides definitive intersections with ethnicity and class, such syncretism stands in multicultural opposition to the monocultural language and society of the dominant U.S. intellectual canons and discourses.

What Nieves endeavors to do is to "break ground" by challenging the prevailing monomyths both of U.S. culture and of phallocentric Latino arts and letters by emphasizing the gendered aspects of being a Puerto Rican woman and her relevance not only in Puerto Rican society, but in mainstream America as well. This foregrounding of gender in all aspects of cultural experience and the repositioning of these women's subjectivities into this anthology adds to the richness of American literary production too long identified primarily in masculine terms.

While familiar names such as Sandra Barreras del Río, Giannina Braschi, Sandra Maria Esteves, Nicholasa Mohr, Esmeralda Santiago, Luz María Umpierre-Herrera and Lourdes Vasquez make an appearance in this anthology, Nieves also throws into the mix spoken word poets such as Stephanie Agosto, María T. Fernández (a.k.a. Mariposa) and Caridad de la Luz "La Bruja," providing a cutting edge and youthful perspective that helps round out what is clearly an inter-generational collection. Only one minor disappointment in this collection is that a small amount of works written in Spanish were not translated into English.

It's no secret that U.S. publishers have lagged considerably in publishing bilingual editions, however in recent years, a number of small independent presses have taken up this cause with the belief that translation expands and

deepens our world in countless indescribable ways. In that regard, *Breaking Ground* accomplishes two things: (1) it provides a sprawling, multitudinous canvas that continues the important positioning of *Puertorriqueñas'* voices in the American literary discourse; and (2) as a bilingual edition it enters the world stage as definitive, credible scholarship. Overall, *Breaking Ground: Anthology of Puerto Rican Women Writers in New York 1980-2012* is a collection worthy of anyone's personal library, and a fantastic teaching tool for high school and college students alike. ▢

MYRNA NIEVES is a writer, cultural activist and educator. A founding member and professor at Boricua College, she was director for twenty years of its Winter Poetry Series. Recent published works include *Viaje a la lluvia, poemas* (2002) and co-editor of the collection of poetry and prose *Tripartita: Earth, Dreams, Powers* and the anthology *Mujeres como islas* (2002).

LA VOZ LATINA:

(cont'd *from pg. 21*)

writers and playwrights while also making sure to include an incisive and clear voice. In the shadow of all of the plays in this collection this voice is continuously reminding us of the cultural, sociological, and anthropological aspects of theatre, which give impetus to the community building forces it has. While the individual plays have allowed for distinct types of Latinas/os to have a voice this anthology has allowed for these works of art to come into a greater dialogue with each other about the ever-changing Latina/o identity.

The book contains six sections: (1) "Creating a Performance Voice: Themes of Family, Religion, and Community," (2) "Chicanas and Chicano Teatro: Staging Identity," (3) "La Indígena/The Indigenous: Staging Myth, (4) "Race Matters," (5) "Where is Home and How Do We Get There?," and (6)"Commentary on Latina Theatre in the United States." The first five sections contain a total of eleven plays and the last section contains two pieces of commentary. Each section has an introduction followed by the plays. Each play-text is accompanied by short sections that introduce "The Playwright," followed by an "About the Play" section. Additionally we are given the "Artistic Vision," which consists of a brief interview of the playwrights by the editors of the anthology. Lastly, before the play-text itself, we are given the "Production History" and contact information of the playwrights.

In the exploration of family, religion, and community we are graced with the most produced Chicana/o play during the late 1980s, *Roosters* by Milcha Sanchez. This play, touching on issues of machismo, feminism, and love, incorporates a magical realism that runs through the playwright's veins and is translated into a powerful work that floats off of the paper

for readers. In the same vein, Cherríe Moraga talks about the central theme of the family in her play *Waiting for Da God.* This depressing, yet uplifting, play deals with issues of loss in various perspectives, family, and transformation. Through deaths, failures, and dementia we are able to see out of Moraga's very real and personal lens. In *The Path to Divadom, Or how to Make Fat-free Tamales in G minor,* Diane Rodriguez tells us a story of a changing recipe for changing times. We are met with the values of upholding tradition and at the same time are faced with a head on, satirical, and "big ole" challenge to tradition. Yareli Arizmendi's *Who Buys Your Shoes?,* a dramatic-comedic monologue for six takes form in characters as distinct as a chubby teenage Chicana girl to a Chicana lesbian who is also a rape survivor. All of her characters in this prescient play speak not just for Chicanas but also for all Latinas.

Insofar as the indigenous is concerned, Celia Herrera Rodríguez's *Cositas Quebradas: Performance Codex* exemplifies the broken parts that Latinas/os are. She reminds us though, in her harrowing and ritualistic language, that we all belong to a huge mythological and indigenous past. This is something that is often forgotten but that the Colorado Sisters remind us of in their play *Mimixcoa—Cloud Serpent.* In a dreamlike journey through time and memory the Sisters lead us back to our origins while traversing centuries of shame that plague the Latina/o subconscious. When looking at race Josefina Báez leads us through a non-linear expedition in which we find ways to decolonize our selves through or bodies and with movement. Touching upon the major issues that plague the Dominican discourse (misogyny, homophobia, negrophobia among many) Báez truly proves that race matters in her play *Dominicanish.* On the other hand while Evelina Fernández presents us with a more traditional play, *Luminarias,* she breaks traditional Latina roles. Whereas most of the time the Latina plays the victim in this daring and truly modern play Fernández creates more positive roles wherein issues of self-hatred, hatred of Anglos, and mistrust of other cultures are played with.

Lastly, this question of *Where is Home and How Do We Get There?* Carmen Peláez offers us two short plays *El Postre de Estrada Palma* and *My Cuba.* In these plays, we are met with stories of grandparents in exile and a character on her way to Cuba. Both of these stories, filled with longing and comedic relief, offer us doorways into the memories that constitute the home of Cuba that was left behind by so many long ago. In Carmen Rivera's *La Gringa* we are encountered with the hilarious return of a second-generation Nuyorican to the homeland of Puerto Rico. This tale of reconnection and light humor is juxtaposed intensely with the last play in this anthology, *Another Part of the House* by Migdalia Cruz. In this reworking of Federico García Lorca's *La Casa de Bernarda Alba,* Cruz brings to life soul-searching and traumatic

episodes of a grandmother forcing her granddaughters into subversive acts that translate the tragedy of this play.

In the last section of this book, the two commentary pieces by Kathy Perkins and Caridad Svich challenge us with questions of the significance and future of Latina/o theatre in the U.S. In the end, *La Voz Latina* gives a refreshing point of view on issues that matter most to the Latina/o community. Although we do not see a huge diversity among the nationalities/origins of the playwrights, we are met with strong and influential Latina voices that speak for the whole community at once through their works. Ramírez and Casiano have allowed for us to have an incredible insight into this world along with the challenges it faces in the coming times. ▢

ELIZABETH C. RAMÍREZ is the fine arts specialist administrator with the Edgewood Independent School District of San Antonio, Texas, and the author of *Chicanas/Latinas on the American Stage: A History of Performance.*

CATHERINE CASIANO has assisted Elizabeth C. Ramírez with numerous dramaturgical projects and is an attorney practicing family and criminal law with indigent Latina/o populations in San Antonio.

THE OTHER LATIN@

(cont'd from pg. 21)

Capó). In the song, an outstanding horse is a baseball player recruited by the New York Yankees because of his batting prowess. Lo and behold, he comes to bat with three men on base and hits a home run. Everybody comes to the plate (three runs) but the Yankees need him to score the fourth run to win, and he stays still. He is asked to run the bases and he responds, "Si yo corriera estaría en el hipódromo" loosely translated "If I could run I would be in the racetrack." A (male?) Puerto Rican horse that cannot run, that plays for the "imperialist," most recognizable sport franchise, the New York Yankees, that actually fulfills the promise of "making it" by hitting a home run in the clutch and—oh so close!—cannot become a full Yankee because "his" identity is split between a horse and a baseball player. The Latino narrative skirts the trap, identity/assimilation, essence/contingency, colony/metropolis, nation/exile, culture/bi-culture, Spanish/English, barely. The first part of the dyad is always more progressive and authoritative than the second. Tradition (racetrack horses or baseball), Community (Puerto Rican from the Island or the New York Yankees), Language (Spanish or Yankee) sitting comfortably side-by-side waiting for effacement by dislocation, by exile, by otherness or the Lacanian big O.

The series of, mostly, autobiographical essays compiled in *The Other Latin@, Writing Against a Singular Identity* responds and expands this narrative with a plurality of experiences and writings. Tradition, community and language do not sit well as foundation for authorship or writing. The authors defy monolithic discourses of Latin@ traditions, communities and languages, by embracing and answering multicultural families, sexual identities, dislocated places and Americana meta-narratives. Form structures their writings: poetry, crime stories, testimonies, short stories, philosophical essays; content fills up their vessels: prejudice from the larger community, prejudice from their own families, prejudice from their own culture, gay love, gang violence, female detectives, and Western or Latin@ metaphysics.

In their introductory essay, editors Blas Falconer and Lorraine M. López propose that Latin@s are not a homogeneous group. They argue that even Latin@s are complicit in this push for homogeneity creating illusory solidarity for the sake of future political power.

The place of a Latin@ writer is problematic too. Carla Trujillo states: "being a Chicana and a woman has its perks. As most writers are prone to do, I observe everything around me. When I am rendered invisible or insignificant, I am privy to information that wouldn't be uttered in other company." The locus of the writer is problematized. Where is the author? Who is the audience? May I use Spanish or indigenous languages? Tradition, Community and Language is questioned, fractured.

Alex Espinosa wants to be a Coyote, not the ones that smuggle *paisanos* but someone resembling Huehuecoyotl, the Aztec God of music and song; a shape-shifter, a singer, a storyteller, not a Chicano writer, but an American writer and an educator writing for immortality. The privilege of being educated is to be able to educate, to write, to endure.

Teresa Dovalpage questions the use of Spanglish, not the code switching but the English forced into Spanish: la troca (for truck), parquear (for parking). She fears losing skills with language—Spanish or English. There is an advantage of writing in English and Spanish. To whom am I speaking/writing to? What are the politics of publishing?

Helena Mesa, not writing about Cuba, finds her connection with Cuba through her father. She talks about Cuban poetry as "political poetry draped in an elegiac tone. I think of lyrics exploring place through memory and the imagination. I think about narratives that capture a sense of displacement and exile that often rock the speaker between the two shores of loss or longing." She quotes Sandra Castillo:

> Trapped by geography
> You lean against a Ford Fairline,
> An odd, left-over '50s we never knew,
> Out of time, out of sequence.

The poet is detached from this elusive reality, detached in space and time. To be sure, the exile poet is not so much at loss. She borrows from its immediacy (family, friends, books

and other writers). She borrows from those who came before her (ancestors, cultural traditions of herself, her surroundings, and other writing traditions). Sometimes, she borrows from the ones that are pregnant with stories, metaphors and legends, creating abstractions that bridge descriptions and narratives.

Judith Ortiz Cofer ruminates about living in English or not living in Spanish. She calls it "My Word Hunger." She becomes aware when she speaks fluentl "Southern English" at her house in Georgia or when she visits her mother in Puerto Rico. She states:

> "I usually spend the time at her (mother's) house reading books by contemporary Puerto Rican writers such as Rosario Ferré, Ana Lydia Vega, Carmen Lugo Filippi, and many others, and marveling at the beauty of my native tongue, especially when it sings at the hands of a talented wordsmith. I fall in love with its cadences, its music. Spanish is a delicious language, *miel en la boca,* and I often feel like an onlooker at a banquet, kept out of the festivities mainly because of a speech impediment. *Pero en mi vida,* I had to choose a tongue to serve me, and it had to be English. But I can dream in Spanish. *¿No creen?*

Ortiz Cofer has access to Spanish; she is 'hungry" for an unbroken connection to her mother, to her father, to her dreams and to her *corazón.*

Steven Cordova writes about HIV and about his teacher Rachel Hadas in a poetry workshop at GMHC (Gay Men's Health Crisis). He writes about acronyms: PWA (Person with AIDS), HIV, AIDS, GMHC. He writes about shouting and grief. He writes about activism: Act Up (AIDS Coalition to Unleash Power). He writes about life and death. The noble and combative Act Up's logo: Silence equals Death becomes more metaphysical in Hadas' hands:

> ... danger's hardly tyranny by silence.
> It's hard to shut us up while we draw breath.
> If anything can guarantee our silence
> Death can. But silence doesn't equal death.

Silence does not equal death. Writing immortalizes (a la Kundera). The desperate, and very real, balancing act of people with AIDS in the 80s and 90s transforms itself into poetry.

By way of metaphysics, Gina Franco in The Child in the House takes us to Latino poetry and a deconstruction of Western narratives. Christianity, language, culture and logocentrism (the idea that we have access to truth by way of reason and written language) are difficult to contest. One contests them by identifying and dismantling the oppressor in American culture, and she acknowledges this by "wielding her sword at abstractions" at history, government and patri-

archy. Poetry is a point of dissension. What is to dissent? To live in dualities, at a distance, in opposition and to sustain the differences instead of accepting the hierarchical nature of the first term: right/left, north/south, soul/body, you/me.

This essay bisects Latin@ identity. On the one hand, every identity is a construct. It always leaves out the particularities of the concept. Biography enters the stage, not as a correction but as the only moral solution. On the other hand, Christianity and metaphysics are the pervasive and omnipresent traditions in bracketing off Latina identity. It is the universal. Every biography has been here before.

The child lives in a stucco house in Stargo, Arizona but thinks about the terror of Abraham's sacrifice of his son Isaac. Franco does not care about the angel's intervention. She imagines the child's mind wondering about the father's offering. Is Franco intimating a similar offering for Latino poetry? We do not know.

The Other Latin@ is a pleasant amalgam of biographies of self-proclaimed Latin@ writers. The writers capture not only their biographies but also their crossing paths with "schools of thought," immediate masters, Latin@ traditions and their dislocated experiences. It takes us to a series of bifurcations of otherness. The reader is left with the impression that one can pluralize Latin@ experiences ad infinitum. And of course, one can!

To be sure, some of the essays, Lucha Corpi's "Chicano/a Crime Fiction," and Urayoán Noel's and Blas Falconer's "New York Puerto Rican tradition," allude to some literary tradition. These traditions embed the authors' writings in the shoulders of ancestors. There is something very encouraging about these narratives: It is recognition of Latino literary traditions.

The strength and the weaknesses of these essays are given by their pluralizing aspirations. This plurality differentiates until everybody has an original Latin@ story to tell; that is their strength. However, this plurality also questions the allegiance to any tradition, which is their weakness, because it neither questions the homogenizing force of tradition, nor expand its limits.

I had a wonderful experience reading these essays, although I would have hoped for them to delineate further readings. There is always an imagined community! ◼

BLAS FALCONER is the author of *The Foundling Wheel* (forthcoming, Four Way Books, 2012). He is an associate professor at Austin Peay State University, and a poetry mentor for the low-residency MFA program at Murray State University.

LORRAINE M. LÓPEZ's recent books are the novel, *The Gifted Gabaldon Sisters* (Grand Central Pr., 2008), and the short story collection, *Homicide Survivors Picnic* (BkMk Pr., 2009. She teaches in the Master of Fine Arts Program at Vanderbilt University in Nashville, and she is an associate editor of the *Afro-Hispanic Review.*

THE SHADOW OF AL-ANDALUS:

(cont'd from pg. 22)

The rich visions that result from these shadows of acculturation are expressed in Cruz's collection—from the "orgasms of the Sahara" to the "blue vastness" of the Caribbean—as the author's imagination meanders along city streets, over bodies of water, across centuries and continental divides. Through the poems, Cruz describes himself as finally free "to untangle" long-standing cultural and historical "knots" and examine the intricate "layers of weaving" brought about by the passing of centuries, changes of regimes and systems of belief, and the evolution of multiple cultural identities.

As such, awe at the depth and scope of history is an ever-present theme in the collection: "We are still standing with our mouths / wide opened in disbelief at what / has happened, a mystery even unto / ourselves." Cruz attempts to unravel some of this mystery in his poetic vision as prehistoric, biblical, and exotic elements are interwoven with the portrayal of modern cities. In "Manhattan Transfer," for example, dinosaurs inhabit the metropolis, occasionally "popping out of windows:"

> wondering if the day had turned to night
> and if the stars had fallen into the East River,
> or if it was going to rain blood.

In this passage, Cruz transposes biblical events (which supposedly occurred in Egypt thousands of years ago), and dinosaurs (which existed hundreds of millions of years ago) to the streets of modern-day Manhattan—thereby transforming that which is relatively new and known with that which is ancient and not entirely knowable.

The "Exotic" is another element of the perpetual transposition of *In the Shadow of Al-Andalus*—exotic in the sense of originating in a distant country as well as exotic in the sense of intriguing, magical—and excitingly strange. Indeed, many of the poems, such as "Dawn in the Tropical Zones," offer up a view of hazy islands, where the very air seems to shudder and fog "as if the trees were smoking cigarettes."

But the overall vista is not always as serene as it first appears: Cruz makes mention of "panoramas of compost" in these "destructive paradise[s]." At once fascinating and vibrant, the beautiful landscapes of Cruz's writing—whether ancient or modern, urban or island—seem tinged by unknown dangers and can turn threatening from one line to the next: the palm trees go from lazy, innocuous "smokers" to an overwhelming "green color coming to eat you, under an all-blue sky."

This apparent instability of the physical landscape is heightened by Cruz's depiction of countries and cities over decades and centuries. In this sense, the poetic vision of *In the Shadow of Al-Andalus* becomes composite—and even apocalyptic—as the reader is made to bear witness to "the beginning and the end of cities."

The overload of cultural topographies in Cruz's writing spills over into the very language in which the poetic sentiment is expressed. In *In the Shadow of Al-Andalus*, cultural transfusion is omnipresent, resurfacing on a linguistic level as well as a descriptive one. Cruz has long been lauded for his experimental style in which he mixes English and Spanish lexemes. Once again, *In the Shadow of Al-Andalus*, Cruz glides effortlessly (almost subconsciously) between English and non-English, academic and regional dialect, lyrical and stunted, familiar and foreign. In being dual—and even multiple—this use of language more truthful to the constantly changing cultural and linguistic outpourings of the countries on Cruz's poetic atlas.

The fact that Cruz's special blend of poetic language has the ability to capture such a variety of cultures stems from its polyglot nature. At once familiar and strange, the words sing the same song in different tongues and still speak "the same meaning." In Victor Hernández Cruz's collection we hear "the layla lo lay of mountain songs" as well as the slick beats of city streets. "Once I knew a city that I now dream in another country," speaks the poet. In many ways, *In the Shadow of Al-Andalus* is preoccupied with the perpetual existence of the immigrant, the migrant, the refugee, the descendant of rich ancestry that dreams of a place that no longer exists except in the individual's imagination and memories.

And it is at the interstice of imagination and memory that *In the Shadow of Al-Andalus* lives and breathes. The poems came out of the author's personal quest for a written history that reflects his intricate cultural identity and yet, they come to represent the expatriate's cry, the exile's song, and the descendant's lullaby that echo over centuries. ◪

VICTOR HERNÁNDEZ CRUZ is an award-winning Puerto Rican-born poet who began writing at fifteen, and published his first highly acclaimed collection of poetry, *Snaps* (1969), the year he turned nineteen. The author of ten books of poetry, he is considered one of the original Nuyorican writers.

CAMINO DEL SOL

(cont'd from pg. 22)

fiction and nonfiction works by established writers, award winning and first-time authors. The book is divided into three sections and aptly titled: (1) "Poetry," (2) "Fiction," and (3) "Nonfiction," with "Source Credits," "About the Author," "About the Contributors," Bibliography," and "Index of Authors" appearing at the end of the book. In his Introduction, González provides a history of the Camino del Sol

series that is interwoven into a brief yet insightful history of Latino publishing in the United States: the authors, trends, sub-trends, categories, and publishers, the obscure as well as the well-known, the distant past as well as the future that appraises the state of American literature written by Latinos. While the writers in this collection are primarily Chicana/o, this collection creates a benchmark for the series and serves as a great introduction to the world of Latina/o literature.

Established writers appear alongside emerging writers throughout the book. González presents this "smorgasbord" of works from existing books that Camino Del Sol has published, so the full works are readily available to readers interested in reading more. The "Poetry" section consists of some really fine writers, such as Francisco X. Alarcón, Rane Arroyo, Blas Falconer, Maurice Kilwein Guevara, Juan Felipe Herrrera, Rita María Magdaleno, Demetria Martinez, Pat Mora, and Virgil Suárez, who have been on the scene for quite some time, and do not disappoint.

Stand-outs (at least for this reviewer) include Richard Blanco, Lisa D. Chávez, and Dixie Salazar. Blanco sets the tone of his "Cuban-ness" in the poem "When I Was a Little Cuban Boy": "O José can you see . . . that's how I sang it, when I was / a cubanito in Miami, and América was some country / I the glossy pages of my history book, someplace / way north, everyone white, cold, perfect" Or Chávez, whose sardonic wit challenges the historical, and turns it into the hysterical with lines like "Step right in, ladies and gents, step / right in and see the conjuror of the new / century, sample the wonders / he unveils. Years will wink past with a snap of his fingers; his magic / lantern will reveal the glories / of the century ahead, splendor / spread before you like a vast / unsettled plain" from the poem "The Conjuror of the New Century."

In Salazar's "Piñon Nuts," as Blanco grapples with being Cuban, Salazar tackles her "American-ness" cancelling out her "Mexican-ness": "We begged him to teach us Spanish / but he wouldn't. Here in the heart / of America, skin tones / and tongues were homogenous / as milk from purebred cows."

In the "Fiction" section of this collection, readers are treated to works by Fred Arroyo, Kathleen de Azevedo, Stella Pope Duarte, Christine Granados, Jack Lopez, Patricia Preciado Martin, Ana Consuelo Matiella, Brauilio Muñoz and Serbe Troncoso. The characters and plotlines are primarily centered around glaring examples of "otherness"; belonging to two diametrically opposing worlds that play tug-of-war between being American and "Other," never able to fully melt in America's so-called melting pot.

The final section is "Nonfiction"—usually not for inclusion in a "literary" collection, but certainly a welcome change in this collection—like a gift wrapped in a big red bow. Kathleen J. Alcalá's "otherness" is further complicated by her being Jewish and Mexican, ". . . Jews who didn't know Hebrew, Indians who don't pray to the morning star." Ray González talks about home and borderlines, the constant challenge of dealing with an "us against them" mentality, while Luis Alberto Urrea comically yet deftly talks about growing up between two worlds: white, Protestant and Mexican that memorializes his family in such a way that makes them endearing to the reader.

In this bleak era of ethnic studies banning, Camino del Sol provides renewed hope for educators and professors who seek a text that will bring them both the familiar and established voices of the past, and the emerging and vibrant voices of the present. More importantly, it provides readers an invaluable resource that allows them to discover new names and learn new works on their own terms, making it an excellent addition to anyone's literary collection.◻ `

RIGOBERTO GONZÁLEZ, an award-winning author and editor, was born in California and raised in Mexico, is the author of eight books and the editor of Xicano Duende: A Select Anthology of Alurista's Poetry. He is Associate Professor of English at Rutgers-Newark, the State University of New Jersey.

THE OXFORD BOOK

(cont'd from pg. 23)

works and, therefore, always more difficult to calculate than anyone might imagine.

Oxford's latest entry into a crowded field of specialized anthologies, The Oxford Book of Latin American Poetry, presents a largely rich and complex tradition of literature that is an ambitious collection of works drawn from three major sources: the world of Aztlán, the mythical homeland of the Aztecs prior to Cortez; the Spanish heritage of the national homelands of the writers; and the intersection of these two with Anglo and African culture. These influences create persistent themes, the most common of which are social protest and exploitation; the migratory experience; self-exploration or self-definition, including the exploration of myths and legends; and life in the countryside as well as the barrio (the traditional Latino district of the city).

The editors, Cecilia Vicuña and Ernesto Livon-Grosman present a fresh and expansive selection of Latin American poetry. This 608 page anthology is organized in chapters for each poet in chronological order and begins with a brief biography of the poet. In addition to "Acknowledgements" and "Preface," each editor provides separate introductions. A "List of Translators" and "Source Acknowledgements" appear at the end of the book.

Beginning with obscure oral and visual works that date back many centures to twentieth century writers as diverse as Rubén Darío, Jorge Luis Borges, Pablo Neruda, Gabriel García Márquez, Octavio Paz and Mario Vargas Llosa, *The Oxford Book of Latin American Poetry* presents more than 120 poets with many new translations commissioned for this volume. Of the pre-twentieth century poets represented in this anthology, more than a third are anonymous, and write in non-European languages and/or in combined drawing and writing systems. These earlier selections prepare readers for the visual poetics, oral poetry and indigenous forms that later appear in the twentieth-century selections, showing readers that poetry is more than just words on a page.

The Oxford Book of Latin American Poetry represents the geographical regions of Mexico, the Caribbean, Central and South America, the Caribbean and South America, where Romance languages (i.e., those derived from Latin)—particularly Spanish and Portuguese, and indigenous languages of the Americas and variably French—are primarily spoken. This is more than a bilingual anthology, the works presented herein have been translated from Quechua, Guarani, Mapundungun, Nahualt and several Mayan languages, including Yucatec, K'iche', and Tzotzil, in addition to Spanish and Portuguese. In that regard, it is probably one of the most inclusive anthologies published today.

As more works of this scope publish in the U.S., questions have arisen as to how best present translations and remain mindful of the ever-swelling page count that comes with it. In the case of *The Oxford Book of Latin American Poetry,* the editors chose to run the original works under the English translation as run-on prose using slashes for line breaks. Some critics object to this because they believe it marginalizes the original text. As the editors reiterated in their introduction, the purpose of this volume is to present these works to an English audience. Coming in a little over 600 pages, if the editors had chosen to publish the translations using the traditional side-by-side presentation, it would come at significant cost, reducing the number of contributors considerably. While ideally the works should be presented equally, when one reviews the table of contents, you can see why the editors came up with this less-than-ideal solution.

Of course, the argument of who was included and not included in this volume challenges the subjectivity of the editors. But there will never be an anthology that will completely satisfies scholars, teachers and students alike. In the case of *The Oxford Book of Latin American Poetry,* it is such a huge undertaking and really the first of its kind. It will be interesting to see what improvements editors Vicuña and Livon-Grosman will address in future volumes to come.

As we move away from the study of an isolated American poetry and toward the teaching of as more inclusive poetry of the Americas, *The Oxford Book of Latin American Poetry* provides a unique look at Latin American literature as an academic discipline and a recognized category in the world book market, offering new ways to look at a poetry as diverse and complex as Latin America itself. ▣

CECILIA VICUÑA is a poet, artist and political activist born in Chile. The author of 16 books, her poetry has been translated into several languages. *Templo e'Saliva / Spit Temple*, a collection of her oral performances, edited by Rosa Alcalá is forthcoming by Factory School Press. She performs and exhibits her work widely in Europe, Latin America and the US, and currently lives in both New York and Chile.

ERNESTO LIVON-GROSMAN, born and raised in Buenos Aires, has edited and translated several anthologies and poetry collections in both English and Spanish, and produced and directed

THE CHICANO/LATINO LITERARY PRIZE
(cont'd from pg. 23)

is the case with the Chicano/Latino Literature Prize. Established in 1974, this annual competition is awarded by the Department of Spanish and Portuguese at the University of California.

In over thirty-five years, the Chicano/Latino Literature Prize has clearly demonstrated the wealth and vibrancy of Chicano/Latino creative writing in the United States. Awards are given for novels, short story collections, drama and poetry. The prize winners have been—to name a few among many—accomplished authors as Ron Arias, Cherie L. Moraga, Demetria Martínez, Gary Soto, Helena María Viramontes, and Francisco X. Alarcón. It seems fitting to publish a compilation that celebrates a rich history of Latino literature, *The Chicano/Latino Literary Prize, An Anthology of Prize-Winning Fiction, Poetry and Drama,* which offers a compilation of over a quarter century of writing (1974-1999), consisting of a wide sampling of thoughts and ideas from multiple generations of Latino Writers, many of them Chicano.

Stephanie Fetta has written an extensive introduction that discusses the works of key figures, and what follows are the works of second- and third-place winners, as well as honorable mentions. Presented in chronological order, the works are varied in subject, style, and take form in multiple formats and multiple languages. Familiar names pop up, alongside lesser-known writers such as Mary Helen Ponce, Wilfredo Q. Castaño and Benjamin Alire Saénz with some pretty engaging literature. An author and chronological index of prize-winners, as well as author biographies appears at the end of the book.

With this impressive diversity of voices goes a caveat: not all of the winners are published in this anthology, due to lack of permissions or accessibility. Another drawback is that the editor Fetta chose not to translate those works in Spanish, which is disappointing for those of us who do not read Spanish. Excerpts of longer works, which raise expectations for characters and plots, feel incomplete, and what's worse is that many of these writers have not published, so what you see is what you get. To her credit, Fetta handles some of these short-comings like a pro, creating a landmark collection of prize-winning fiction, poetry, and drama that paints an historical and aesthetic panorama of Chicano letters. Many of the pieces in this anthology are considered to be foundational texts of Chicano literature, and those that are not as widely recognized deserve more serious study and attention.

Literary prizes are the last stage of the mainstream curation stage that starts with agents, then to publishers, then to reviewers, and then to awards panels. For many readers, a literary prize gives them the confidence to buy or borrow a book because they think that it is a fairly reliable indicator of quality. *The Chicano/Latino Prize* offers something more, an historic collection that presents a panoramic view of the concerns, styles, and artistry of twenty-five years of Chicano/Latino writing. A highly recommended addition to anyone's personal or academic collection, *The Chicano/Latino Literary Prize* is a testament to U.S. Latinos' literary accomplishments. 🔲

STEPHANIE FETTA is an Assistant Professor of Spanish at The College of Arts and Sciences, Syracuse University, New York. She is the translator of the book-length study by Spanish Anthropologist Francisco Checa, *Spain and Its Immigrants: Images and Stereotypes of Social Exclusion,* and has published several articles in the United States and abroad.

PUERTO RICAN POETRY

(cont'd from pg. 24)

ignoring form and lyrical expression. In this 490 page volume, Márquez presents the work of 64 poets from both the U.S. and Puerto Rico, with many of the poems appearing for the first time in English. He also includes previously inaccessible selections from Puerto Rico's tradition of popular verse forms—*coplas, décimas,* and *bombas*—produced by anonymous writers.

The anthology is organized into four historical periods: (1) "Book One: Before Columbus and After, 1400-1820," which explores the genesis of Puerto Rican poetry from the eyes of aboriginals and conquistadors; (2) "Book Two: The Creole Matrix: Notions of Nation, 1821-1950s," reflects Puerto Rican consciousness, Spain and U.S. intervention;

(3) "Book Three: Critique, Revolt, and Renewal"; and (4) "Book Four: Of Disporas, Syncretisms, Border Crossings and Transnationalizations: An AmeRican *Sancocho*." Instead of listing biographies in the back of the book, Márquez presents biographical profiles of each poet as an introduction to their work. A detailed "Chronology" of the history of the island showing readers how poetry has informed the work, appears at the end of the book.

What immediately captures readers' attention is "Book One" because it provides the groundwork into the early development of Puerto Rican poetry. Here, Márquez painstakingly explains the Taino-Arawak communities input vis-à-vis an oral tradition, followed by existing works by the conquistadors (Spanish colonists, including the soldiers and church layman from the Catholic church) the *jíbaros* (mountain-dwelling peasants), which grabs the reader's attention. In "Vox Populi," Márquez explains and then presents the different forms and styles of poetry—*coplas, décimas, turtelos, bombas, plenas, guarachas*—that flourished during this era, including their origins and the mixing of these elements indigenous to the people on the island.

"Book Two" concentrates on works by Creoles *(criollos),* a person of Spanish descent, born in the New World as opposed to Spain, with some Amerindian ancestry. The poetry before the Spanish American War (1898) sets the tone for Puerto Rican poetry today as we know it that addresses the indigenous with the Spanish, and the fight for independence. It is ironic that many of these Puerto Rican writers, who came from some of the island's wealthiest families, were fed up with the injustices of the Spanish Crown and territorial displacement. This section explodes with poetry written by the likes of Maria Bibíana Benítez, Lola Rodríguez de Tió and José Gautier Benítez, Francisco Gonzalo Marín, Luis Lloréns Torres, Luis Palés Matos, Clemente Soto Vélez and Julia de Burgos, allowing readers to enjoy these works in one shared space under an historical context, which makes these works ever more meaningful.

When the Americans invaded Puerto Rico during the Spanish-American War in 1898, many members of the Puerto Rican literary class welcomed them believing that eventually Puerto Rico would be granted its independence. Instead, Puerto Rico was declared a territory of the United States. By the time readers get to "Book Three" and "Book Four," one has developed a sense of how much Puerto Rican poetry is tied to the island's history and the struggle for independence. The poems in "Book Three" are from poets on the island, while "Book Four" are Puerto Ricans poets living in the U.S., a true *sancocho* (stew) of intergenerational poets. Many writers began to focus on the conflict between traditional "Hispanic" culture and the increasing Americanization

of the island. While both groups evoke patriotic themes throughout their work, the poets, particularly those in the U.S., tackle poverty, racism and the struggle maintaining cultural identity in a foreign land. While most readers are perhaps more familiar with the U.S. poets, it's interesting to learn about the poets on the island as well as observe the growth and development of Puerto Rican poetry from both the island and the mainland in the same study.

Some have argued in the Puerto Rican literary community that certain poets were left out or that both the Spanish and English versions of the poems should have been published side-by-side in this anthology. Although no one anthology can truly capture the vast works of contemporary Puerto Rican writers, this collection is a first step in the right direction. And while there is merit in publishing both Spanish and English versions, Márquez's goal (as he indicates in his introduction), sets out to provide a comprehensive collection on Puerto Rican literature in English, so American students can learn more about Puerto Rican literature. *Puerto Rican Poetry: An Anthology from Aboriginal to Contemporary Times* manages to do just that and more, providing an in-depth understanding and appreciation of the genesis and exploration of Puerto Rican literature.

ROBERTO MÁRQUEZ, a Puerto Rican born and raised in Spanish Harlem, is a translator, editor, essayist, and literary critic. His latest work, *A World among These Islands: Essays on Literature, Race, and National Identity in Antillean American,* was published in the fall of 2010 by the University of Massachusetts Press. He is the William R. Kenan Jr. Professor of Latin American and Caribbean Studies at Mount Holyoke College in New York.

BORDERING FIRES

(cont'd from pg. 24)

words "easy reading" do not always spring to mind, however, the rare humor, diversity and magical nature of the writing in *Bordering Fires* made reading on—page after page—not an option but a delicious necessity.

In her wonderfully informative and succinct introduction, García defines being Mexican, Mexican-American, or Chicano/a as being part of "grandly diverse and complex communities with multiple allegiances and multiple hyphenated identities." Indeed, García maintains that there no longer exists such a thing as a purely Mexican or Chicano/a identity, and the seemingly "simple" aim of the collection is therefore "to showcase the preoccupations and sensibilities of a wide range of people with historical commonalities" who exist on "all sides" of "multifaceted" and "pliant" borders.

As such, the collection includes short stories, creative nonfiction and selected poems by such esteemed writers as Alfonso Reyes, Gloria Andzaldúa, Sandra Cisneros, Xavier Villarrutia, Octavio Paz, Ana Castillo, and Ignacio Padilla. The stories range from lyrical and magical to humorous, from journalistic and unflinchingly unsentimental to excruciatingly intimate. They represent the works of authors spanning decades and national borders; some of whom are categorized as "early influences" whose "unmistakable imprint" has already been made on Mexican Literature, while others are "new departures" who have yet to claim a literary legacy but nonetheless have the stunning quality of an instant classic.

All of the works in *Bordering Fires*, regardless of genre and time period, share the same preoccupation with real and imagined "border lands." And yet, like beautiful, "disordered clock[s] striking all hours in a disordered room" (Ramón López Velarde), none of the works approach the "interstices of culture and identity" in quite the same way. While some authors focus on geographical and ethnic borders, others examine the more elusive limits of identity, sexuality, sanity, and language.

Much of the women's writing represented in *Bordering Fires* deals with such sexual and linguistic border lands and exposes bias and internal gender politics within Mexican, Chicano/a and Mexican-American communities. Ana Castillo's poem "Daddy with Chesterfields in a Rolled Up Sleeve," for example, examines and questions gender roles in relation to the child narrator's cultural upbringing by playing with traditional notions of machismo and femininity.

Similarly, in her story, "Never Marry a Mexican," Sandra Cisneros reveals the internal discrimination and hierarchies that exist *within* Mexican communities on either side of the Mexican-American border. Cisneros' narrator also betrays a type of sexuality that is deeply rooted in language and race; while she categorically chooses white lovers, her ultimate pleasure is to hear them speak to her in Spanish: "I liked when you spoke to me in my language. I could love myself and think myself worth loving." Cisneros' narrator seems to experience a wonderful sense of empowerment and true selfhood when she is addressed in her own language by those who are ethnically different because in speaking to her in Spanish they are simultaneously recognizing and valuing her ethnic and linguistic identity.

This sense of coming into one's own upon embracing one's true cultural self is also present in Elena Poniatowska's "Introduction from: Here's To You Jesusa" when the main character experiences a simultaneous awakening of nationalistic and female selfhood:

"I get stronger…I'm growing, I'm finally going to be a woman." What was growing, although it may have been there for years

was my Mexican being, my becoming Mexican; feeling Mexico inside me, the same one that was in Jesusa.

Interviewing an old, poverty-stricken woman named Jesusa brings the narrator closer to her own Mexican identity and thereby reinforces in her a powerful sense of her own strength as both a woman and a *mexicana* that had previously lain dormant within her.

One of the pieces featured in *Bordering Fires* which is most vocal on the issue of cultural, sexual, and linguistic traditions of silence is Gloria Anzaldúa's "How to Tame a Wild Tongue." In this vociferous piece which combines storytelling with memoir and essay, Anzaldúa discusses the issue of linguistic bias both within and outside of American Latino communities or, "how quickly one can be judged for the way one speaks Spanish." Anzaldúa stipulates that Latinos living in America have unwittingly absorbed the American bias to the Spanish Language: "because we internalize how our language has been used against us by the dominant culture, we use our language differences against each other." Anzaldúa also stresses the importance of one's language in establishing one's ethnic or cultural identity: "If you want to hurt me, talk really badly about my language. Ethnic identity is twin skin to linguistic identity— I am my language."

Feeling as though one is linguistically and culturally misunderstood is a problem that resurfaces again and again throughout *Bordering Fires.* As the narrator of Cisneros' story muses, "I have such an urge to communicate and no language with which to form the words." In this sense, many of the works in the collection seek a common ground: a language and method of storytelling—a voice—that best corresponds to a specific condition or way of life (*un leguaje que corresponde a un modo de vivir*).

The resulting works that come together to form *Bordering Fires* exist in the "lively borders" of multiple cultural and linguistic identities as well as in the "slippery places owned only, and temporarily, by the imagination." As such, this fine collection is not just an excellent anthology for scholars and enthusiasts of Chicano/a Literature but—as I came to realize, somewhere between Boston and New York's Penn Station—*Bordering Fires* is that rare book that we as readers can come home to, regardless of where we have come from or where we are going. ⬛

CRISTINA GARCÍA is a Cuban-born American journalist and novelist. Her first novel, *Dreaming in Cuban* (1992), received critical acclaim and was a finalist for the National Book Award. She has since published *The Agüero Sisters* (1997) and *Monkey Hunting* (2003), *The Lady Matador's Hotel: A Novel* (2010) and has edited books of Cuban and other Latin American literature.

WHAT'S IN A NOMBRE?

Writing Latin@ Identity in America

WHEN I PROPOSED PUTTING together a "Latino" issue of *phati'tude Literary Magazine* to Gabrielle David, I didn't think selecting the writers and artists would be such a difficult process; difficult because there are so many forms of "Latinos" in the United States. Although I emailed and made phone calls to a myriad of artists for inclusion in this issue, I nevertheless ended up with many more of Puerto Rican descent. Attempting to include a balance of the variety of "Latino(a)" writers and artists in one magazine (or any single publication, especially one based on the East Coast) is a daunting, if not impossible, task. That said, it's been a pleasure and an honor gathering a selection of such a distinguished assortment of writers and visual artists for this issue.

Witnessing our kinships and the vastness of our differences, our complexities and variety have been educational and exciting. Classifying us under one heading is like arriving at the Unified Theory of Everything. Race, ethnicity, cuisine, language, politics, sexual preferences, art forms, social structures, geography—all play pivotal roles simultaneously in making up who we are. What's more, each classifier on this list accounts for varying percentages of composition between distinct groups: one group may lean more towards considering itself by race than by geography, while another may label itself principally by common geography and so on. Additionally, this often happens within single ethnic groups as well. For example, some Peruvians may identify as white and consider their dominant language to be Spanish, while others consider themselves as indigenous and possibly speak either Quechua or Aymara.

It has also been intriguing and, at times, disheartening to see the attempts being made to place all of us under a catch-all phrase. I remember when I first heard of the term "Hispanic" and the uproar this triggered because of what the term implies as well as what it excludes: white, Spanish dominant, of a higher economic class. While on the other hand, the label "Latino" carries other connotations: dark complexion, English dominant, lower class. Clearly it benefits the government to lump us all together for the purposes of Census taking, thus the redistricting of the country, the allocation of Congressional representatives, of public services and the like. However, classifying all of us by one invented term eliminates who we are in particular and our individual cultural richness. The Census is also used as a tool for posterity, a record kept for the future. Similarly, the elimination and move to absorb many Puerto Rican and Chicano Studies departments—into Latino or Latin American or even Spanish departments—throughout the U.S. is another attempt at not only homogenizing us but at "erasing" entire ethnic groups. This is the imposition of the "melting pot." It psychologically disables, redirects, and eventually disintegrates a group's sense of pride and history, and ultimately individual nations.

The imposition of the "melting pot" also results in our fixated attention on, frantic search for, and categorical assertion of our distinct identities within the U.S. Herein lies our separation. Those "Latino" groups who are single-minded about their unique culture and language are often discriminatory against other kindred groups. Ultimately both situations, our complete absorption into the dominant culture as well as our separateness from it and from each other, serve to sustain the empire (the status quo) and to fulfill its objective to divide and conquer, while those in power remain in power.

Our focus should be on celebrating our vibrancy as distinct and kindred communities our incredible amalgamation of voices and images, histories and prospects, colors and triumphs over the most damaging of circumstances. We are and have always been in the United States, and, for better or worse, we're a slice of its history and future. Without denying who we are, without competing against one another for the illusive, "piece of the American pie," within these pages we come together to assert who we are, to learn from one another, to support each other in our uniqueness and ultimate contribution to American life. These are some of the things that you, the reader, might experience. Hopefully, you'll come to understand the extraordinary contribution "Latino(a)" literature and art has made, and is making, as part of the American canon. From one of the cornerstones of American literature, William Carlos Williams who was Puerto Rican, to Sandra Cisneros, a Mexican-American and recipient of the Pen Award and the Lannan Foundation Literary Award, to Junot Diaz, an author born in the Dominican Republic and recipient of the Pulitzer Prize, to Kukuli Velarde, a Peruvian-born visual artist and winner of the USA Knight Fellowship by the Knight Foundation, "Latinos" in the United States are part of the American canon, not a fringe element but an integral feature of the American narrative.

I would like to thank, first and foremost, Gabrielle David for giving me this opportunity and for her support; a big thanks to Dr. Myrna Nieves, who was instrumental in getting us the Esmeralda Santiago interview and advised me throughout this process, and to Dan Shot, a great friend and advisor. Thanks also to the Boricua College, Bronx Campus faculty and staff for their support and to all of the writers and visual artists who heeded the call. Your works are reflections of us—a marvelous multitude of courage, drive, and humanity. ◻

N A N C Y M E R C A D O

where do U.S. Latinos come from?

WHO ARE U.S. LATINOS? Who are Chicanos, Nuevos Mexicanos, Cubanos, Nuyoricans, Boricuas, Tainos, Quisqueyanos and Dominicanyorks? And where do they come from?

Although Latinos in the U.S. see themselves as members of a unified group, there remains this assumption that all Latinos are alike when nothing could be further from the truth. Each group has retained, whether from Mexico, the Caribbean, or Central and South Americas, a strong sense of ethnic identity regardless of the length of time they have lived in the U.S.

While Latinos come from countries that are former colonies of Spain, each country has a distinct culture, language, and flavor to that of their indigenous landscape, including a built-in, complex relationship with the U.S., whether born on American soil or as immigrants. Through interventions, occupations and colonialism, the Mexican American and Spanish American Wars, Trujillo and Batista dictatorships, the Cuba Revolution, socialism, communism, the "banana republics" and more, the U.S. has had a tremendous effect on Latinos and their place of origin, which, in turn, has impacted their culture and literature.

Identifying as a Latino gives these writers a sense of community and shared purpose, but it also gives them the freedom to acknowledge their specific heritage as integral parts of their social, cultural, emotional, and intellectual experience. At the same time, it helps them to appreciate the cultural, emotional, and intellectual characteristics that define other Latino writers in varied and unique ways. What brings them together as "Latino writers" is as interesting as what makes them different and unique.

So it's no surprise that Latino literature contains infinite possibilities that segue into historical and cultural aspects of a Latino community in the U.S. Whatever journey the poets and writers have undertaken, people often find themselves reading ideas about history, religion, music, cultural myths, politics, poverty, racism, immigration and exile that are forged by the origins of their distinct geographical spaces. Unfortunately, most of us do not know or fully understand where this comes from. Well, it comes from a place called "home."

So we decided to respond to this question of "Where do Latinos come from?" by informing readers of their origins, to highlight some basic differences and connections, which we hope will ultimately inspire you to learn more about these great Latino writers with some insight of where they come from. ▨

R E B E C C A K A Y E & G A B R I E L L E D A V I D

Mexican/Chicano

THE MEXICAN NATIONAL IDENTITY fuses the cultural traits of indigenous pre-Columbian origin with those of European, particularly Iberian, ancestry. This particular type of multi-ethnic nationalism was forged after the Mexican Nation achieved independence from the Spanish empire in 1821. But today's Mexican identity is still reflective of the many Amerindian and European conquests going back as far as the Olmec, the Teotihuacan, and the Toltec Peoples. While most Mexicans speak Spanish, this diverse cultural heritage is still evidenced

(cont'd. pg. 42)

Puerto Rican/Boricua

THE PEOPLE OF PUERTO RICO represent yet another cultural and racial mix. When the Spanish conquistadors arrived on the island, they forced the indigenous Taíno people into slavery. The Taíno population was almost completely decimated except for a few Amerindians who escaped to remote areas of the island and who would eventually intermarry with poor Spanish farmers and became known as *jíbaros*. Much of the unique Puerto Rican cultural identity stems from a long history of slavery on the island;. Aside from the slaves who were

(cont'd. pg. 43)

Cuban

VARIOUS ETHNICITIES COMPRISE THE CUBAN PEOPLE. Aside from the indigenous Native American population, nearly all Cubans or their ancestors immigrated within the past five centuries, coming from Europe, Africa, and even North America. The current Cuban population is a mixture of the descendants of the original Spanish settlers and descendants of the slave population imported from Africa during the eighteenth and nineteenth centuries. In addition, there is a sizable Chinese population, who are descendants of the Chinese workers that came to Cuba in the second half of the nineteenth century.

(cont'd. pg. 44)

Dominican

TAÍNO POPULATIONS INHABITED THE ISLAND of Hispaniola (now shared between the current-day nations of the Dominican Republic and Haiti) since the seventh century A.D. until the arrival of Columbus when the site became the location of the first European settlement in the Americas. As with many other former Spanish colonies, many Dominicans can trace their ancestry to slaves imported by Spanish plantation owners. It is estimated that approximately 90% of contemporary Dominicans are of West African descent, but the ethnicity of Dominicans remains a much contested issue. For most

(cont'd. pg. 45)

South American

THE INHABITANTS OF SOUTH AMERICA represent one of the most diverse populations in the world in terms of ancestry, race, and ethnic and linguistic groups. From country to country, within the twelve independent countries that comprise South America (Argentina, Bolivia, Brazil, Chile, Colombia, Ecuador, Guyana, Paraguay, Peru, Suriname, Uruguay, and Venezuela), ethnic composition varies greatly but generally includes large populations of European-Amerindian (or mestizo), black, mulatto, South American and Asian people, varying greatly in ethnic makeup as well as cultural heritage.

(cont'd. pg. 46)

Central American

CENTRAL AMERICA, LOCATED in the southernmost, isthmian portion of the North American continent, connects with South America on the southeast and is considered a subcontinent. It consists of the seven states of Belize, Costa Rica, El Salvador, Guatemala, Honduras, Nicaragua, and Panama, each possessing its own racial, linguistic, cultural and ethnic identities: white, mestizo (European-Amerindian), black, and Native American. For example, Costa Ricans are of primarily Spanish ancestry with minorities of various Western and Northern European ancestries, Nicaraguans represent the

(cont'd. pg. 46)

WHERE DO U.S. LATINOS COME FROM
Mexican

(cont'd from pg. 40)

today in the 62 different linguistic groups indigenous to Mexico. Today, there is a considerable Mexican diaspora, with an estimated 22% of the Mexican People living in the United States. According to the 2010 U.S. Census, there are an estimated 32,000,000 people of Mexican origin living in the United States, making them the largest Hispanic group in America.

Mexican Americans have developed a rich and varied literary tradition—ranging from border ballads and protest poetry to novels and journalistic exposés. While Mexican literature can be traced to the sixteenth century, the genesis of Mexican American literature begins in earnest after the Mexican-American War in 1848, when the U.S. annexed Texas, New Mexico, Arizona and California of what had once been Mexico. By the mid-nineteenth century, some thirty years after Mexico's independence from Spain, the literature, both oral and written, of the Spanish-speaking Southwest was not remarkably different from that created in the Mexican heartland. But by the late nineteenth century, easily the most popular literary form among Mexican Americans was poetry, much of which appeared in the hundreds of Spanish-language newspapers that proliferated in the Southwest. Much of the poetry was lyrical, generally in the prevailing Spanish and Latin American styles and, in some cases, purely political. While most of the newspaper poetry was anonymous, as a body of work it provides invaluable insight into the collective consciousness of the Mexican American community.

During the early twentieth century, Mexican American literature began to take shape as a distinctive part of the literary culture of the United States. A great deal of literary energy was expended in chronicling the American takeover of the Southwest, a considerable portion of it by prominent southwestern Mexicans who had supported American annexation only to feel betrayed and discarded. Mexicans who lived on the land before it became part of the United States in 1848 faced a different set of issues because they became an ethnic minority through the direct conquest of their homelands.

In fact, anti-Mexican lynchings, mob violence and other forms of intimidation (which ran rampant from the 1840s to the 1920s) resulted in Mexicans being murdered, displaced from their land, and denied access to natural resources, a fact that has long been overlooked in American history. Mexican American writers launched their literary missiles not only at Anglo land-grabbing but at a series of practices that immobilized their people at the lower rungs of the socioeconomic ladder.

Among American ethnic groups, Mexican Americans occupied a curious position, being neither immigrants—the United States, after all, had absorbed them—nor a minority in many of the Southwestern communities they inhabited. When the U.S. entered World War II, it greatly accelerated the process of Mexican American acculturation. For one thing, the War stimulated the movement of Mexican Americans into large cities where military industries were badly in need of labor. And the high levels of Mexican American participation in the military significantly reduced cultural isolation. Like other forms of ethnic expression, Mexican American literature received a boost from the Civil Rights movement of the 1960s when Mexican Americans made the name "Chicano" (once meaning "poorest of the poor") theirs as a way to empower themselves through unity. During this period, Chicano publishing houses were established to produce literary works by Chicano writers; many are still in existence today.

As with most labels, the Mexican American/Chicano experience is not homogenous. Besides encompassing Mexicans who are U.S. born or are immigrants, Mexican Americans find themselves continuously negotiating a border territory where competing languages and cultures encounter each other: migrants and natives, Tejanos and Mesitzos, Hispanos and Indian, the periphery and the core, which has managed to coalesce and come together over the years into a potent mix of a transcultural literature.

In the twenty-first century, Mexican American students have had to protest the elimination of Mexican American Studies courses in Tucson, Arizona. It's more than a little ironic that the same Arizona Legislature that spearheaded a ruthless, racially charged campaign against illegal immigrants also banned K-12 ethnic studies classes on the grounds that they promote hatred and division. However, it is evident with the recent ruling in the Tucson Unified School District—which also banned several prominent books and made the Mexican American Studies program illegal—that Mexican American/Chicano literature has become a force to be reckoned with. As Mexican American/Chicano literature continues to focus on themes of identity, discrimination, culture, and history, it has truly validated the Mexican American experience and Chicano culture in the United States, creating a voice of social critique and protest. ▣

Select List of Mexican American Authors: Oscar Zeta Acosta, Francisco X. Alarcón, Alicia Gaspar de Alba, Kathleen Alcala, Rudolfo Anaya, Gloria Anzaldúa, Jimmy Santiago Baca, María Ruiz de Burton, Rafael C. Castillo, Ana Castillo, Lorna Dee Cervantes, Denise Chávez, Sandra Cisneros, Ray Gonzáles, Rigoberto González, Juan Felipe Herrera, Rolando Hinojosa, Demetria Martínez, Cherríe Moraga, Américo Paredes, Gary Soto, Tomás Rivera, Benjamin Alire Saenz, Luis Omar Salinas, Esteia Portillo Trambley, Luis Alberto Urrea, Luis Valdez, Alma Luz Villanueva, Helena Maria Viramontes.

WHERE DO U.S. LATINOS COME FROM
Puerto Rican

(cont'd from pg. 40)

imported from Africa (Sudan, Senegal, Guinea and Sierra Leone), many other ethnic groups were brought to work on the island's plantations or simply emigrated to flee certain political situations in their homelands. Today's rich and vibrant Puerto Rican cultural identity represents the merging of all of these identities.

During the Spanish-American War (1898), Puerto Rico was invaded by the United States, and in the outcome, Spain ceded Puerto Rico (along with the Philippines and Guam) to the U.S. under the Treaty of Paris. Initially under military rule, in 1917, Puerto Ricans became U.S. citizens, effectively making Puerto Rico a "colony" of the United States. In 1952, Puerto Rico negotiated "Commonwealth" status with the U.S. that cleverly avoided any permanent decision of independence while at the same time firmly linking the two economies.

When the U.S. took control of Puerto Rico, the island was already marked by 400 years of Spanish colonial rule. Puerto Rico, along with other colonies in the Caribbean, was an important agricultural base for international markets. (Ironically, the Spanish almost granted the island independence in 1898, but with the arrival of U.S. troops during the Spanish-American War that same year, the island became a war prize and was transferred to U.S. military control.) Throughout Puerto Rico's occupation, a movement has thrived aimed at obtaining independence for the island, first from Spain and then from the United States. This movement is not localized to one group of individuals or even one organization throughout the years but represents instead the events and activities of dozens of groups and organizations and thousands of individuals that share the common goal of advocating, supporting, or seeking political independence for Puerto Rico. The nature of Puerto Rico's political relationship with the U.S. remains a subject of ongoing debate by Puerto Ricans, the United States Congress, and the United Nations.

Following on the heels of the success of the New Deal, the U.S. undertook a massive reform of the island's institutional and economic structure, called "Operation Bootstrap," during the late 1940s and 1950s, which prompted the largest migration of Puerto Ricans to the U.S. Today, it is estimated that over two million Puerto Ricans have settled primarily in Central Florida, Chicago Metropolitan Area, and New York City, accounting as the second largest Latino group in the U.S.

Puerto Ricans on both the mainland and the island, commonly refer to themselves as "Boricua" (from the terms "Boriken" or "Boriquén," derived from "Taíno" a sub-group of the Arawak People). Over the years, a new identity emerged within and alongside the Boricua identity, that of "Nuyorican," a portmanteau of the terms "New York" and "Puerto Rican" that refers to the members or culture of the Puerto Rican diaspora located in or around the New York City metropolitan area or their descendants (especially those raised or still living in the New York area).

Puerto Rican literature evolved from the art of oral storytelling from the Taíno Indians. Once the Spanish took over the island, written works by the native islanders of Puerto Rico were prohibited and repressed by the Spanish colonial government. Only those who were commissioned by the Spanish Crown to document the chronological history of the island were allowed to write.

It wasn't until the late nineteenth century with the arrival of the first printing press and the founding of the Royal Academy of Belles Letters that Puerto Rican literature began to flourish. The first writers to express their political views in regard to Spanish colonial rule of the island were journalists. After Puerto Rico was ceded to the Americans in 1898, writers and poets on the mainland began to express their opposition of the new colonial rule by writing about patriotic themes.

From the 1940s, a distinction can be drawn between the literature that is written and published in Puerto Rico and the literature produced in the United States. These two branches of the same tree have developed simultaneously, providing a representation of the complex experience of Puerto Ricans. It was not until the 1960s and 1970s when a consolidated literature written by and about Puerto Ricans in the U.S. began to flourish. This new literature, widely described as "Nuyorican literature" (even though some authors, like Piri Thomas, did not identify as part of the movement) has a deep concern for the social and economic situation of Puerto Ricans that also explores an identity crisis that has emerged for second-generation Puerto Ricans in the U.S.

In the past few decades, a more diverse number of Puerto Rican writers have written from a different perspective on Puerto Rican identity, including the role of the island as an important element of their cultural past and the need to find a new "home" or identity as Puerto Ricans in the U.S. Puerto Rican identity is, for these writers, something that is being continuously explored and redefined all the time, but it is also something new and full of life and energy as a product of the interaction of cultures on American soil. Still, the recurrent concerns, such as racism, ethnic stereotyping, social discrimination and isolation, and lack of respect

and understanding by mainstream society, continues to flow in much of the work. ▣

Select List of Puerto Rican Authors: Miguel Algarín, Alba Ambert, Fred Arroyo, Naomi Ayala, Giannina Braschi, Judith Ortiz Cofer, Zoé Jiménez Corretjer, Victor Hernández Cruz, Martin Espada, Sandra María Esteves, Aracelis Girmay, Tato Laviera, Julio Marzán, Tony Medina, Jesús Papoleto Meléndez, Luis Palés Matos, Nicholasa Mohr, Urayoán Noel, Willie Perdomo, Pedro Pietri, Miguel Piñero, Yolanda Arroyo Pizarro, Louis Reyes Rivera, José Rivera, Esmeralda Santiago, Mayra Santos-Febres, Piri Thomas, Luis Lloréns Torres, Luz María Umpierre, Irene Vilar.

WHERE DO U.S. LATINOS COME FROM
Cuban

(cont'd from pg. 40)

In addition to this rich multi-ethnic composition, the modern-day culture of Cuba is thought to be greatly influenced by Western European traditions brought over by the early Spanish settlers as well as the other numerous European immigrants arriving much later, including Portuguese and French immigrants as well as immigrants from countries in the Middle East: Lebanon, Turkey, and Palestine, representing the largest group of Hispanics of European ancestry. Today, Cuban Americans form the third largest Latino group in the United States.

Since the sixteenth century, Spain at one time claimed and controlled territory in North America that is now the states of Louisiana, Florida, parts of Georgia and Mississippi, as well as New Mexico, California, and Texas (which was part of Mexico). Since Cuba was also a Spanish colony, Cuban immigration to the U.S. has had a long history, with Florida having the most prominent Cuban American community due to its close proximity to Cuba.

At the end of the Spanish-American War (1898), Cuba was handed over to the United States in 1899. Unlike Guam, Puerto Rico, and the Philippines, the United States did not annex Cuba because of the restrictions imposed in the Teller Amendment, so Cuba gained formal independence from the U.S. in 1902 as the Republic of Cuba. Under Cuba's new constitution, the U.S. retained the right to intervene in Cuban affairs and to supervise its finances and foreign relations, making Cuba an "economic colony." The United States assumed territorial control over the southern portion of Guantánamo Bay under the 1903 Cuban-American Treaty, which granted it a perpetual lease of the area, an act considered illegal by Cuba's current Cuban government.

Since its independence, Cuba experienced ongoing social and political turmoil that ultimately led to the Cuban Revolution and culminated to the overthrow of Fulgencio Batista in 1959. This political upheaval created new waves of Cuban immigrants to the U.S. as the new government allied itself with the Soviet Union and began to introduce communism. From 1960 to 1979, hundreds of thousands of Cubans fled their homeland and began a new life in the U.S. Initially, many of them were from the educated upper and middle classes. Another large wave occurred during the early 1980s with the Mariel boatlifts. Unlike immigrants from other countries, Cubans are considered exiles and are granted special status to gain permanent residency, which has become a source of friction between Cuban Americans and other Latino immigrants.

Cuban literature began to find its voice in the early nineteenth century. The major works published in Cuba during that time were of an abolitionist character. In time, Cuban literature (often referred to as an "exile" literature) would become one of the most prolific, relevant, and influential literatures in Latin America.

The Cuban Revolution brought forth three distinct groups of writers to the U.S. The first group consists of writers who came to the United States as adults, who write in Spanish and whose main, though not sole preoccupation, lies in their testimony and condemnation, if not outright vilification, of the Castro regime. The second group constitutes the 1980 Mariel boatlift writers, and the third group consists of young writers born in the U.S. or who arrived as young children or teenagers from the Mariel boatlift. Coincidental are writers whose families immigrated to the U.S. prior to the Cuban Revolution and who happened to be writing at about the same time as the others.

The year 1990 marked another historical moment of extraordinary change on the island. The dissolution of the Soviet Union brought on Cuba's so-called Special Period of economic hardship. As Cubans prevailed, albeit haphazardly, the overriding message was that intellectuals, poets and writers had an oral obligation to the revolutionary cause and therefore should neither engage in divisive politics nor create works without significant political content within the revolution. While several writers and artists managed to thrive in this environment by spouting revolutionary rhetoric, many disappeared or left the country. As a result, there has been a so-called Cuban "boom" among authors who were born during the 1950s and 1960s and forced into exile due to censorship by the Cuban authorities during the 1990s. Some well-known names include Daína Chaviano (U.S.); Zoé Valdés (France); Eliseo Alberto (Mexico); Pedro Juan Gutiérrez (Cuba); Leonardo Padura (Cuba); Antonio Rodríguez Salvador (Cuba) and Abilio Estévez (Spain).

While many Cuban American writers have centered their works around Cuba and being Cuban, a third and fourth generation of writers have come to the fore that are changing the dynamics of Cuban American literature. Their perspective is critical of the Cuban communities (principally Miami and Union City in New Jersey), without conceding anything to the Cuban government. They are redefining themselves within the boundaries of American society but are not characteristically a defender of all things Cuban, merely seeking the right to a Cuban/Cuban American space in the midst of American society. It is to be noted that under Cuban law, children of Cubans born abroad are considered Cuban Citizens.

The experience of Cuban immigration has been both internally and externally divisive. Cuban Americans find themselves the exception rather than the rule when discussing the larger Latino immigrant experience since their experience is of exile. Within the community, they are divided politically, linguistically, generationally and culturally, including the relative degrees of direct experience they may have had with the island or living in Cuban American communities, as well as dealing with the larger mainstream culture of the United States. It is largely on the borders between these divided spaces of experience that an emerging generation of Cuban-exile writers write to build bridges between generations, ideologies and cultural experiences, even though it may never coalesce into one voice or one language.

Although most of the Cuban American writers who have risen to prominence over the years have been white, there remains a multicultural group of writers from Cuba that have been ignored. For example, while Afro-Cuban poets such as Nicolás Guillén and Lydia Cabrera brought to light the African foundations of much of Cuba's culture, Cuban writers such as Nancy Morejón, Evelio Grillo, Soleida Ríos, Domingo Nicolás Alfonso, Alberto Guerra Naranjo, Ahmel Echevarría Peré and Victor Fowler Calzada are a handful of Afro-Cuban poets that are not known outside the Cuban diaspora. This is to say that Cuba is not one-dimensional, nor is it just black and white; it is many things, many flavors and rhythms yet to be explored. ▢

Select List of Cuban American Authors: Mercedes de Acosta, Reynaldo Arenas, Nilo Cruz, Carmen Agra Deedy, Carlos Eire, Roberto G. Fernández, Gustavo Pérez Firmat, María Irene Fornés, Paula Fox, Cristina García, Carolina Garcia-Aguilera, Oscar Hijuelos, Carolina Hospital, Robert Lima, Rosa Lowinger, Pablo Medina, Ana Menéndez, Achy Obejas, Alex Abella, Jorge Reyes, Antonio Sacre, Virgil Suárez, Alisa Valdes-Rodriguez, Armando Valladares

WHERE DO U.S. LATINOS COME FROM
Dominican

(cont'd from pg. 41)

of the Dominican Republic's history the national body has been defined as "non-black" despite such prevalent black ancestry. Much of this can be attributed to dictator Rafael Trujillo's policy of ethnic cleansing of Afro-Dominicans and Haitian immigrants. Today, the ethnic composition of the Dominican population is estimated to be 73% multiracial, 16% white, and 11% black, with the majority of Dominicans self-identifying as multiracial with European, African, and Taíno ancestry. A large Dominican diaspora exists largely in Puerto Rico, Spain, and the United States.

The Dominican Republic has been engaged in the struggle against the political oppression that has held Hispaniola in its grip since 1492 when this island—now known as Haiti and the Dominican Republic—became part of the then nascent Spanish empire. Since then, Dominican literary text has served as an instrument of protest against abuses by governments concerned with exploiting the people and the land, including the historical realities of a nation that has suffered from a particularly disturbing history. While Hispaniola was first settled by Spaniards, it also passed under the colonial rule of England and France. As the native inhabitants were obliterated, Africans were brought over by force to work the plantations. Dominicans came to share their Caribbean island with Haiti, a country that invaded and annexed the Dominican Republic during the nineteenth century.

From 1930 to 1961, Dominican life was profoundly affected by the brutal dictatorship of Trujillo. His assassination in 1961 marked the start of a period of political uncertainty in the Dominican Republic that ended when U.S. paratroops intervened by order of President Lyndon Johnson (under the pretext of eliminating Communist influence in the Caribbean), which led to the election of former Trujillo aide Joaquin Balaguer to the presidency. Those who opposed or had reason to fear the new regime and violence, came to the U.S. in notable numbers.

Because of extended periods of U.S. occupation and American cultural and political hegemony in the Caribbean basin, Dominicans have obtained more than a passing familiarity with American culture and the country to which they immigrated to. By the 1980s, immigration to the U.S. from the Dominican Republic rose to unprecedented levels because of limited employment opportunities and poor economic conditions.

It is somewhat difficult to determine at what precise moment a body of Dominican literature with an identity of its own began to take shape. As with other Latin American countries, Dominican literature emerged from the Catholic clergy and an educated class that challenged Spain's rule and the injustices of various despotic and corrupt governments that dominated the island. By the nineteenth century, the Dominican Republic experienced a time of nation-building and after Trujillo's death, literature both on the island and in the United States began to flower. From Dominicans living in the U.S., a new body of literature, sometimes written in English, sometimes in Spanish or a combination of both, had begun to emerge.

In recent years, Dominican American writers have captured the public's attention. Notably, writer Junot Díaz drew on his life and the Dominican American experience generally in authoring *Drown* and *The Brief Wondrous Life of Oscar Wao,* the latter of which won him the Pulitzer Prize for Fiction in 2008, making him the first Dominican American and the second U.S. Latino in history to win the Pulitzer Prize. Julia Alvarez is the nationally-recognized author of *In the Time of the Butterflies* and *How the García Girls Lost Their Accents.* Nelly Rosario, born in the Dominican Republic and raised in New York City, also won critical acclaim for her debut novel *Song of the Water Saints.* Angie Cruz's explosive first novel, *Soledad,* burns with as much narrative ambition as social criticism. Collectively, their works have helped to inaugurate a generation that is neither fully Dominican nor American, forging a sort of "Dominicanyork" identity, akin to the likes of Chicanos and Nuyoricans. Their stories portray the problems of inner-city life, racism, becoming an outsider in one's native country for having lived abroad, memories that invoke the taste and smell of the island, the intersection between Dominicans' colonial views and the contemporary U.S., and in some cases, the dream of returning home.

Dominican American literature constitutes a provocation against the official history of either the Spanish-Dominican or the U.S. political context that occupies a significant place in American literature. It is a body of literature that is constantly breaking boundaries and redefining itself as a traveling literature that circulates between the U.S. and the Dominican Republic that's being published and read in both English and Spanish around the world. ▣

Select List of Dominican American Authors: Julia Alvarez, Léon Félix Batista, Rei Berroa, José Carvajal, Angie Cruz, Junot Díaz, Rhina P. Espaillat, Daisy Cocco De Filippis, Franklin Guitérrez, Ana-Maurine Lara, Dagoberto López, Juan Matos, Marianela Medrano, Félix Darío Mendoza, Loida Maritza Pérez, Juan Rivero, Carlos Rodríguez, Alexis Gómez Rosa, Nelly Rosario, Miriam Ventura, Sherezada Vicioso.

WHERE DO U.S. LATINOS COME FROM
South American

(cont'd from pg. 41)

South America has a history that spans a wide range of cultural forms. For over one thousand years, independent cultural development was interrupted by the Spanish and Portuguese colonization drive of the late fifteenth century and the demographic collapse that followed, yet the continent's mestizo and indigenous cultures managed to remain distinct from its colonizers. Through the trans-Atlantic slave trade, South America (especially Brazil) became the home of millions of people in the African diaspora, and the mixing of races led to new social structures. The tensions between colonial countries in Europe, indigenous peoples and escaped slaves shaped South America from the sixteenth through the nineteenth centuries. With the revolution for independence from the Spanish crown during the nineteenth century, South America underwent even more social and political changes, among them nation-building projects, European immigration waves, increased trade, colonization of hinterlands, wars about territory ownership and power balance, the reorganization of Indian rights and duties, liberal-conservative conflicts among the ruling class, and the subjugation of Indians living in the states' frontiers, that lasted until the early 1900s.

South America, like many other continents, became a battlefield for the superpowers during the Cold War in the mid-twentieth century. During the 1960s and 1970s, the governments of Argentina, Brazil, Chile, and Uruguay were overthrown or displaced by U.S.-aligned military dictatorships, which detained tens of thousands of political prisoners, many of whom were tortured or killed. Throughout the 1980s and 1990s, a wave of democratization came through the continent, and socialist democratic rule is now widespread. Despite the move to the left, South America remains largely capitalist and is enjoying its best years of economic growth. ▣

WHERE DO U.S. LATINOS COME FROM
Central American

(cont'd from pg. 41)

Central America's greatest Afro-Latin descent, while Guatemala boasts the largest percentage and plurality of individuals of Native American descent.

Following Christopher Columbus's discovery of the Americas for Spain, the Spanish sent numerous expeditions to the region, and they began their conquest of

Maya lands in the 1520s. In 1540, Spain established the Captaincy General of Guatemala, which extended from southern Mexico to Costa Rica, and thus encompassed most of what is currently known as Central America, with the exception of British Honduras (present-day Belize). This lasted nearly three centuries, until a rebellion (which followed closely on the heels of the Mexican War of Independence) in 1821.

The original nations of Guatemala, Honduras, El Salvador, Nicaragua and Costa Rica formed the ill-fated Republic of Central America before setting off on their separate paths. They have since been joined by the countries Panama and Belize (formerly known as Honduras).

Panama, situated in the very south of Central America on the Isthmus of Panama, became a key conduit for international maritime trade. Honduras was contested between the Spanish Empire and the British Empire, a dispute that continued after the independence of Guatemala, who considered Belize to be a Guatemalan department. It was declared a British colony and given the name British Honduras in 1871, gaining independence as Belize in 1981.

A Snapshot of Central and South American Literatures

Since the literary history of Central and South Americas is vast and space constraints make it difficult for us to go into great detail about the literatures of each country, for the purposes of this essay we are providing instead a brief snapshot of overall literary achievements of each continent, followed by a brief list of their American counterparts.

Beginning in the 1530s, the people and natural resources of South America were repeatedly exploited by foreign conquistadors, first from Spain and later from Portugal, England, France and Holland. These competing colonial nations claimed the land and resources as their own and divided it into colonies. During the early centuries, Central and South American literature continued literary currents and traditions of Spain, written mainly by Spanish intellectuals and *criollos*.

Much of the region gained independence from Spain in 1822. In South America, a few countries, such as Panama, Guyana, Suriname, Trinidad and Tobago would not gain independence until the twentieth century (French Guiana remains an overseas department of France). The new independent nations began a process of Balkanization and several civil wars and wars with neighboring countries, while post-independence literature was controlled mainly by the Catholic Church, the government, and landowners.

Although the United States instituted a quota system during the 1920s (which lasted until 1965), immigrants could and did move quite freely from Mexico, the Caribbean (including Jamaica, Barbados, and Haiti), and other parts of Central and South America. When the U.S. began constructing a canal in Panama to facilitate trade, the U.S.'s continuous political, military and economic interference in the region due to the Monroe Doctrine (1823) (considered by many to be an economic and military invasion of Latin America) inspired a literature that challenged the status quo. In the following decades, events have served as detonators of the region's literature, characterized by social issues, political unrest and protest.

Both Americas became a battlefield of the Cold War during the late twentieth century. Following the 1959 Cuban Revolution and the local implementation in several countries of Che Guevara's foco theory (revolution by way of guerrilla warfare, also known as *focalism* or *foquismo*), the U.S. waged a war in South America against the "communist subversives" by systematically helping to overthrow democratically elected governments perceived at the time as becoming left-wing or unfriendly to U.S. interests.

Examples include the 1954 Guatemalan coup d'état, the 1973 Chilean coup d'état, support of the Nicaraguan Contras, the training Salvadoran officers, or encroaching in Honduran (Belize) politics. Many middle- and upper-class Panamanians and Hondurans began immigrating to the United States in search of better opportunities, considered by many as the first large wave of Central American immigration.

Literature from Latin America rose to prominence globally during the late 1960s and 1970s. Often called the "boom period" in Latin American literature, there were several factors that attributed to its phenomenon. First, major changes were taking place in how history and literature were approached in terms of interpretation and writing. Moreover, the development of cities, the coming of age of a large middle class, the Cuban Revolution, the Alliance for Progress, an increase in communication between the countries of Latin America, the greater importance of the mass media, and a greater attention to Latin America from Europe and the United States all contributed to this "boom."

As writers such as Julio Cortázar (Argentina); Gabriel García Márquez (Columbia); and Mario Vargas Llosa (Peru) entered the international literary mainstream (first through publishing houses in Europe and later, works translated into English and published in the U.S.), they adopted a political tone in their writing that informed the world about Latin America's social and political realities.

Cold War cultural politics played an active role in disseminating their work in the United States, with universities, book and journal publishers, philanthropic organizations, cultural centers, and authors coordinating their efforts to bring Latin American literature to a U.S. reading public.

These Latin American authors were greatly influenced by European and American authors of the generations preceding them, especially those who experimented with novelistic structure and chronology. More importantly, the "boom" brought about a new genre of writing coined "magic realism" or "magical realism" because these Latin American novels tended to blend magic and dream-like features with an attentiveness to everyday reality.

By the early 1970s, the Boom began to dissipate as the hope that had initially surrounded the Cuban Revolution was replaced with disillusionment, which culminated for many when the poet Heberto Padilla was arrested in Cuba in 1971 for openly criticizing the government. Sixty intellectuals who had supported the Revolution, including García Márquez, signed an open letter to Fidel Castro demanding Padilla's release. Throughout the 1970s, many of the Central and South American left-wing governments fell under repressive and violent military dictatorships. Still, the success of the Boom forever changed the way Latin American culture and arts are perceived around the world and opened the door for many new writers. Authors from this region have won some of the most prestigious literary awards in the world, including the Nobel Prize for Literature: Mario Vargas Llosa (Peru, 2010); Gabriel García Márquez (Colombia, 1982); Pablo Neruda (Chile, 1971); Miguel Ángel Asturias (Guatemala, 1967) and Gabriela Mistral (Chile, 1945). The Boom was a critical and commercial success.

Significant legal and illegal immigration to the United States began during the 1980s when civil wars in Nicaragua, El Salvador, and Guatemala, combined with already weak economies, created an exodus to the U.S. When civil war broke out in Guatemala in 1979, it was the longest and most destructive war in Central American history. When the war ended in 1996, over 100,000 people died, thousands disappeared, and roughly a million people were left homeless or forced to flee the country.

After the defeat of the Sandinista government in Nicaragua during the 1990s, the era of "nationalist literature" gave way to the emergence of a post-national and postwar literature. Although Central America was plagued by economic strife and political violence, its literature has evolved to reach its current place in Latin American literary history. Yet despite its rise in recognition, the writers remain relatively unknown outside their countries of origin. Many writers, some very renowned, work in foreign universities and live in exile, either forced or voluntary, include writers such as Rubén Dario (Nicaragua); Miguel Ángel Asturias (Guatemala), winner of the Nobel Prize in literature in 1967; Sergio Ramirez (Nicaragua); Dante Liano (Guatemala); Ernesto Cardenal (Nicaragua); Augusto Monterroso (Guatemala); Claribel Alegría (Nicaragua); Rigoberta Menchu (Guatemala) and Blanca Castellón (Nicaraguan).

During the first decade of the twenty-first century, South American governments have drifted to the political left, with socialist leaders being elected in Chile, Uruguay, Brazil, Argentina, Ecuador, Bolivia, Paraguay, Peru and Venezuela. Despite the move to the left, South America for the most part still embraces free market policies, and it is taking an active path toward greater continental integration. Overall, contemporary literature in South America is flourishing. It is vibrant and varied, ranging from the best-selling Paulo Coelho (Brazil) and Isabel Allende (Chile) to the more avant-garde and critically acclaimed work of writers such as Diamela Eltit (Chile); Luisa Valenzuela (Argentina); Ricardo Piglia (Argentina); Roberto Ampuero (Chile); Jorge Marchant Lazcano (Chile); Edmundo Paz Soldán (Bolivia); Jorge Franco (Columbia); Víctor Montoya (Bolivia); César Aira (Argentina) and Fernando Vallejo (Columbia).

Most Central and South American writers in the United States are somewhat disconnected from the "typical" American immigrant experience and do not readily identify as "South American" or "Central American" writers but rather, identify with their country of origin. As a result, specific literary genres such as "Columbian American" or "Ecuadorian American" have not been established along the lines of, for example, Cuban American or Mexican American literature in the United States. Thus, identifying and tracking writers based on origin and under this category has been difficult. Below is a sampling of American-based writers from Central and South America. ▣

Select list of Central American Authors: *Guatemalan American:* Omar Castañeda, Francisco Goldman, Victor Montejo, Alberto Rios, Sylvia Sellers-Garcia, Hector Tobar. *Nicaraguan American:* Francisco Aragón, Yolanda Blanco, Blanca Castellon, Francisco Mayorga, Christianne Meneses Jacobs, Horacio Peña, Danilo Lopez Roman, Silvio Sirias, Gabriel Traversari, Daisy Zamora. *Salvadoran American:* William Archila, Sandra Rodriguez Barron, Daisy Cubias, Jose B. Gonzalez, Leticia Hernandez-Linares, Rene Colato Lainez, Ruben Martinez, Marcos M. Villatoro.

Select list of South American Authors: *Colombian American:* James Cañón, Iris Gomez, Maurice Kilwein Guevara, Jaime Manrique. *Ecuadorian American:* Antonio Farias, Fernando Iturburu, Ernesto Quinonez, Ivón Gordon Vailakis. *Peruvian American:* Daniel Alarcón, Marie Arana, Paul Cuadros, Gabriela de Ferrari, González Viaña.

an emphatic attitude towards contemporary literature, born
from the need to change a static mindset on the written word

Calling all
poets,
writers
and lovers of
the written word.

Check out the
new online
destination
where literature
rules.

Where voices with
diverse perspectives
are welcome.

And new ideas
are encouraged.

phati'tude *(n)* an emphatic
attitude towards literature.

be part of

phati'tude
LITERARY MAGAZINE

submit poetry, stories,
essays and articles to post on
our website & printed literary magazine

list your literary event on our calendar

submit videos and audio clips of your work

let us have your thoughts and comments

join the conversations on our forums

check out our links and resource

sign up for newsletter

purchase merchandise

volunteer your time

organize an event

make a donation

contact us at:

editor@phatitude.org

www.phatitude.org

LATINO CARIBBEAN WRITERS born or raised in the United States are at the vanguard of a literary movement that has opened up a new field in literary history and criticism. The movement, both Hispanic and North American in character, is helping to bring the two cultural groups and their literature together. The body of writing produced gives meaning to postmodern and postcolonial concerns and expresses the aspirations, disillusions, and sense of acceptance and rejection felt by Chicanos, Puerto Rican Americans, Cuban Americans, and Dominican Americans, to name the four largest Latino communities. Writing sometimes in Spanish but mainly in English, they speak both to Latino and all North American readers.(1)

In recent years, there has been a proliferation of Spanish American literature written in the United States. These Hispanic writers, born or educated in their countries of origin, left for economic or political reasons and took up residence in the United States. Authors such as Reinaldo Arenas (Cuba), Luis Rafael Sánchez (Puerto Rico), Luisa Valenzuela (Argentina), Laura Esquivel (Mexico), and Isabel Allende (Chile) write about their homelands. But as their stay in the United States becomes more permanent, these and other authors tend to incorporate a North American perspective into their works. Equally significant, they are also narrating their experiences in the United States and thus contributing to an existing body of Latino literature written by Chicanos such as Rudolfo Anaya, Sandra Cisnero, and Gary Soto; Puerto Rican Americans such as Nicholasa Mohr, Piri Thomas, and Tato Laviera; Cuban Americans such as Oscar Hijuelos, Gustavo Pérez Firmat, and Cristina García; and Dominican Americans such as Franklin Gutiérrez, Junot Díaz, and

(cont'd. pg. 52)

Dance *Between* T*wo* *Cultures*

A Conversation About Latino Literature

DANCE BETWEEN TWO CULTURES
William Luis

(cont'd from pg. 50)

Julia Álvarez, who live and write in New York, Los Angeles, Miami, Newark, and other cities that have acquired a distinctly Latino character.(2)

Political events have helped to promote Latino Caribbean literature. During the turbulent decade of the sixties, organizations such as the Urban League, the National Council for the Advancement of Colored People (NAACP), and the Black Panthers, as well as the Young Lords Party, drew attention to the plight of blacks, Hispanics, and Latinos in the United States. Latino Caribbean college students, many of them the sons and daughters of immigrants, were instrumental in creating and developing Latin American or Puerto Rican Studies programs throughout New York and other northeastern states. This was also the case with Chicano students in the Southwest. In search of an identity, they demanded relevant courses about life in Puerto Rico, the Dominican Republic, Cuba, Mexico and other Spanish-speaking countries and, equally important, about their own experiences in the United States. The newly created courses were different from traditional offerings insofar as they decentered the dominant perspective and incorporated an understanding of the lives of those being studied. The enthusiastic efforts of college students on U.S. campuses were paralleled by community activists and organizers who sponsored events to promote ethnic awareness and literary and artistic expressions emerging from the barrios and ghettos.

Latino Caribbean literature written in the United States has profited from the publicity received by the novel of the so-called Boom of Latin American literature, which during the 1960s brought Latin American literature to the attention of world readers.(3) North Americans who read Latin American writers in translation have also uncovered works written in English by Latinos living in the United States. Like their Latin American counterparts, the works written by Latinos also refer to the Hispanic experience, but within a familiar North American context. Similarly, Latino works written in Spanish and those in English translated into Spanish have made the Hispanic American culture accessible to the Spanish-speaking world.

My definition of *Latino*, which reflects the lives of those born or raised in the United States, differs from the one used by other scholars and by politicians.(4) Whereas the general tendency is to use the terms *Hispanic* and *Latino* interchangeably, I prefer to be more specific about the words' referentiality. *Latino* is a reappropriation of the nomenclature *Latin*, as in Latin American. The usage of Latin in the U.S. context is meant to distinguish those who reside in Latin America from those who live in the United States. But Latins or Latinos growing up within the North American society are unique because they have experienced a tension between the culture of their parents and that of the United States. Those raised in metropolitan areas such as New York, Chicago, Miami, and Los Angeles were subjugated by the dominant culture and political establishment. They, in turn, developed a culture of resistance and a language that mediates between their parents' identity and the culture of their present reality. Their sacrifice and effort to establish a distinct identity contributed to an awareness of the Hispanic community throughout the United States.

The definition I propose for *Latino* is different from the broader term *Hispanic*, which refers to those born or raised in their parents' country of origin. *Hispanic* in North America does not have the same meaning in Spain or Spanish America. In the United States it can refer to those who travel for political or economic reasons to the United States. For the most part, Hispanics are Spanish speakers, and English is their second language. Although North Americans may view them also as being Latinos, their experiences in the United States are markedly different from those born or raised and educated in the Anglo-American environment. They, for example, have not been exposed to the same pressures as their U.S. counterparts. This is not to diminish the difficulties many Hispanic immigrants experience when traveling north, but to establish cultural referents that give Hispanics and Latinos meaning to their lives and experiences. It would be incongruous to group Hispanics from privileged families who have superior educational opportunities, traveling to the United States to pursue a postsecondary education, with Latinos living in the ghettos of East Harlem or East Los Angeles, attending inferior schools and lacking the economic, social, and political support necessary to overcome the limitations of their existence. Richard Rodriguez recognizes the difference between the two terms, and he was able to profit from opportunities others so desperately needed:

> The policy of affirmative action, however, was never able to distinguish someone like me (a graduate student of English, ambitious for a college teaching career) from a slightly educated Mexican American who lived in a barrio and worked as a menial laborer, never expecting a future improved. Worse, affirmative action made me the beneficiary of this condition.(5)

Hispanic and Latino Caribbean literature written in the United States can be studied by country of origin and

genre, but more appropriately should be divided into two main categories. The first consists of works by writers who were raised and educated in their native countries and later emigrated or were forced to flee to the United States. While in the United States, they continued to write in the vernacular, mostly about themes pertaining to their island of provenance. Some traveled to the United States for brief periods; others stayed longer. Regardless of the reasons for going to the United States or length of time spent there, the writers' presence in the United States has had a lasting effect on their lives and works.

The second category includes Latino writers who were born or raised in the United States and who for the most part write in English. As a group, Latinos write an ethnic and racial literature that responds to concerns about their isolation within a dominant culture that has denied them an identity, and access to mainstream U.S. society. For these writers, their parents' country of birth is a distant memory. They compose a literature that searches for their own identity and origins in the United States.

Hispanic and Latino Caribbean literature written in the United States is receiving much deserved attention. However, it is not new. It began as a literature of exile that can be traced to the first half of the nineteenth century when Cuban, Puerto Rican, and Dominican intellectuals, seeking political asylum from the Spanish colonial government, traveled to and resided mainly in the northeastern part of the United States. New York became the center of operation against Spanish dominion over the islands and emerged as an important intellectual and publishing center for Hispanic Caribbean authors. Newspapers and journals contain the political and literary aspirations of generations of intellectuals fighting for their countries' independence and include the works of figures like Cirilo Villaverde, Enrique Piñeyro, and José Martí, of Cuba, Ramón Emeterio Betances, Eugenio María de Hostos, Francisco Gonzalo (Pachín) Marín, and Arturo Alfonso Schomburg, of Puerto Rico, and Gens. Narciso López and Máximo Gómez, of the Dominican Republic.

The number of Hispanics traveling to the United States increased after the Spanish-Cuban-American War of 1898, into the first decades of the twentieth century. After the Foraker Law of 1900, which made Puerto Rico a territory of the United States, and in particular the Jones Act of 1917, which gave Puerto Ricans U.S. citizenship, Puerto Ricans began to leave their native island to reside in New York City. Many of these immigrants joined their Cuban counterparts and worked as cigar makers. Later, after Operation Bootstrap went into effect during the 1940s and 1950s, Puerto Ricans migrated in greater numbers and were employed in New York's garment district.

The Puerto Ricans were soon joined by a large wave of Cubans, who were forced to leave their homeland shortly after the triumph of the Cuban Revolution in 1959. This group of professionally trained upper and middleclass exiles sought refuge in San Juan but also in Miami, Newark, and New York City. Cubans arrived in four migratory waves: first, from 1959 to 1962; second, from 1965 to 1972; third, in 1980, as a result of the Mariel boatlift; and fourth, from 1989 to 1994, as *balseros*.(6) They added to a notable presence of Hispanics and Latinos in the United States, which continues to increase.

Dominicans are the newest members of a Caribbean population living in the United States. Their numbers rose as they began to leave their country concomitantly with the first two waves of Cubans, a period corresponding with the end of the Trujillo dictatorship in 1961 and the U.S. invasion of the Dominican Republic in 1965. But it was not until the 1970s and 1980s that the Dominicans became a noticeable presence in Latino communities. Like the Puerto Ricans, Dominicans fled their homeland to escape declining economic conditions.

Hispanics and Latinos living in the United States have indeed altered the cultural, racial, and linguistic complexion of North American society and are becoming a significant force to consider in this country's electoral campaigns. By the turn of the century, Hispanics and Latinos have become the largest minority in the United States.

Although Chicano, Puerto Rican, Cuban, and Dominican communities make up most of the Latino population in the United States, people of Spanish descent have inhabited the North American continent before the founding fathers transformed the British colony into an independent nation, living in territories that would later he incorporated into the growing United States. There were Spaniards living in the Southeast, on the peninsula that later became the state of Florida, and Mexicans in the Southwest, on land that encompassed the current states of Texas, New Mexico, Nevada, Utah, Arizona, Colorado, Wyoming, and California, and recognized as Aztlan, originally settled by the Aztecs. It is not uncommon for government officials and North Americans in general to consider all Hispanics or Latinos, with Spanish surnames, to be the same, and there are important similarities among them.

As a region, the Spanish Caribbean islands share many similarities in geography climactic conditions, history, culture, religion, diet, music, language, and economy.(7) However, their differences in development have led to varying political and economic conditions among these nations: Cuba as a Communist country, Puerto Rico as a colony of the United States, and the Dominican Republic as a struggling democracy.

When Hispanics migrate to the United States, native differences are reinforced and others are created. They speak a "foreign" language many do not understand, and because of barriers in communication widespread attitudes toward foreigners, stereotypes are created, promoted, and generalized. Hispanics with limited access to the political, educational, and economic systems in their homelands believe that in the United States they can have freer vertical movement. Once they arrive, these immigrants find that they cannot achieve those goals without encountering unexpected obstacles. Those who grew up under privileged conditions in their country of origin are dismayed when in the United States they are treated in a manner that denies them the status to which they were accustomed. Moreover, the racial situation on the mainland makes Afro-Hispanics understand more clearly that discrimination exists in their country of origin, and the racial prejudice in the United States forces many Hispanics and Latinos to seek refuge in African American culture.

Historic events vary the experiences of Hispanics from the same country. For example, there are significant distinctions between Puerto Ricans who migrated to the mainland during the turn of the century and those who arrived in the 1940s; Cubans who fled Castro's island in the early stages of the revolution and Marielitos who arrived in 1980; and Dominicans who escaped the Dominican Republic before the downfall of Rafael Leónidas Trujillo Molina and those who migrated after the U.S. occupation of the island in 1965. And just as there are differences between Puerto Ricans living on the island and those residing on the mainland, there are noticeable ones between Cubans from Miami and those from New York. More likely than not, Cubans living in New York have more political common ground with Puerto Ricans and Dominicans living in the city than they do with their compatriots from Miami.

But for many Anglo-Americans, the differences are negligible. Hispanics, whether born in the United States or abroad, from privileged or low socioeconomic classes, economic or political exiles, black or white, are grouped into a single category and viewed as Hispanics or foreigners. Even in classical times, Pliny the Elder's study of the monstrous races reveals that the differences travelers encountered, whether real or imaginary, when venturing outside Europe tended to reinforce European culture and identities. In the postmodern and postcolonial period, travelers do not have to venture outside the United States; rather, travelers and foreigners occupy the same geographic setting. Separating Hispanics and Latinos from mainstream society is essential for preserving and reinforcing U.S. (European) national and racial identity. All Hispanics, whether living in crowded cities or in the suburbs, and blacks more so than whites, have been adversely affected by the dominant society. In some respects, they are treated as if they were members of Pliny the Elder's monstrous races. Regardless of the differences among them, Latinos share the same marginal experience in the United States, one that inevitably brings them together.

Generally speaking, Cubans have fared better than other Latino groups. As political refugees of a Communist regime, they have been welcomed with open arms. Cubans are exiles who may not return to their homeland, and an increasing number of them are putting the past behind them, accepting their destiny in the new environment. Their transition has been smoother. In comparison to other Latinos, white Cubans have reached a higher level of education. Puerto Ricans have fared the worst, in part because a large number of them are dark-skinned, less educated, and poor. Their situation is paradoxical. On the island, Puerto Ricans are subjected to a colonial status, on the mainland they do not escape a postcolonial condition, and they confront cultural and racial discrimination. Their double alienation, on the island and mainland, underscores Puerto Rican minority status and cultural identity.

Although it is true that some Latinos have made gains, the majority has not. Even those who have been able to transcend their parents' economic and educational situations continue to face cultural resistance from Anglo-Americans, who on the one hand demand homogeneity and conformity and on the other do not allow Hispanics to forget they are foreigners. Each of these attitudes is somewhat shortsighted. Latinos are ethnically, racially, and culturally diverse and can best understand both U.S. and Hispanic cultures and mediate the interrelationship of these two parts of the world. The Hispanic presence in the United States serves as a barometer of tolerance or intolerance of North American society and culture.

Latinos and their culture are engaged in a metaphorical dance with Anglo-Americans and the dominant culture. The dance suggests a coming together of the two and influences the way they dance, to the same tune in the same dance hall. Though the dance refers to Latino and U.S. cultures, it is not restricted to one dance or one partner; on the contrary, it includes others, such as African Americans and their culture. Once the two partners engage in the dance, both will change; neither one will ever remain the same.

Latinos will ultimately influence all aspects of life and culture in the United States. This is already evident in entertainment, music, sports, literature, and politics, with such controversial issues as bilingual education, the

English-only movement, affirmative action, and California's propositions 187 and 206. The influence is also evident in higher education, as more and more Latinos enter the university and, with African Americans, impact the traditional offerings.

Latino literature and culture have affected the way we perceive Latin American and American studies. The migratory and exile experience of Hispanics in the United States is related to the internal circumstances of each Latin American country and to U.S. attitudes toward it. With regard to the Caribbean, the longstanding interest the U.S. government has had in acquiring politically or economically one or more of the Caribbean islands has directed foreign policy. The U.S. government's desire to intervene in other countries has made the notion of borders more fluid, allowing people to migrate with relative ease. Likewise, the type of relationship the United States has with its neighbors to the south is not totally independent of the way Latinos are treated in the United States. In some respects, Latinos also influence how the general public and government officials perceive Latin America and provide a counterdiscourse on their countries' conditions.

American studies programs do not concentrate on all of the Americas, but rather the United States. Even so, Hispanics have lived in territories that were later incorporated into the United States, like Florida and states in the Southwest. U.S. studies do pertain to the study of the Americas insofar as the cultural, ethnic, and racial complexities of the New World are also represented in the lives of Latinos living in the United States. Hispanics have been from the beginning an integral part of U.S. history, but their presence is barely perceptible in the curricula of American studies programs.

Latinos also influence the direction of African American studies programs. The interrelationship between black Latinos and African Americans points to the black presence in the diaspora, leading to comparative studies of slavery and race relations in Latin America, the Caribbean, and the United States. Most of the African slaves were taken to Brazil and the Caribbean, and very few to the United States. Racially speaking, countries such as Cuba, the Dominican Republic, Uruguay, Peru, Costa Rica, Nicaragua, and Mexico have a significant black population. Politically speaking, the issue of race and difference encompasses much more. It provides insight into history not from the victors' perspective, but from the victims'. And as more writers publish their works, literature departments, such as Romance languages, Spanish and Portuguese, English, and comparative literature, will adjust their course offerings and study the current reality of Hispanics and Latinos. Equally important, a study of Latinos stimulates cross-disciplinary communications across colleges and universities, a requisite, according to François Lyotard, for a postmodern education.(8)

Latino literature will certainly figure prominently in postcolonial studies and have a shaping influence on past or present literary theories. Latinos living in the United States are subjected to a multilevel postcolonial existence. As a British colony, the Unites States fought successfully for independence and has "written back" to the center. But this once peripheral country has also become a center.(9) The United States is an imperial country in the traditional sense: Puerto Rico continues to be its colony; and in the modern sense: Latin American countries are affected by decisions made in Washington. Whereas Spanish America was a colony of Spain and also "wrote back" to the imperial center, the United States has replaced the Spanish presence and continues to have a say in the economic and political systems of the region. Latinos are caught in a double bind, between the imperial influences of the U.S. and Spain (represented by the cultural dominance of their parents' country of origin). Within the Latino context, postcolonial studies indicate the presence of the periphery in the center. Latino literature incorporates the dynamic relationship between the center and the periphery and, equally important, between the periphery and the center. This is most viable in the language in which some writers choose to write, which speaks simultaneously to their marginality and centrality.

I also draw upon the postcolonial debate. It is with Latinos that postcoloniality assumes another dimension, one that is relevant to U.S. criticism; the lives of Latinos gain significance, not with the colony, but within the colonizing country. In essence, both colony and colonizer, oppressor and oppressed share the same geographic time and space. Latino works provide a counterdiscourse to the discourse of power, one that questions and uncovers the strategies the dominant discourse masks as "truths."

As it is widely known, anthologies play a crucial role in the formation and promotion of the canon. There are already a representative number of anthologies in Spanish and English on Chicanos, Cuban Americans, Puerto Rican Americans, or Dominican American writers, and a few transcend any one particular group and highlight the writings of many Latino authors. These and other anthologies were compiled to reach a Latino and North American public and speak eloquently to the presence of Latino culture in the United States. It is too early to talk about a Latino canon, but anthologies and the present study will pave the way.

There are only a handful of book-length studies on Latino Caribbean literature. For the most part, they concentrate on one aspect of this literature, either the Cuban, Dominican, or Puerto Rican. Eugene Mohr's *The Nuyorican Experience: Literature of the Puerto Rican Minority* (1982), whose subject is Puerto Rican American literature, has the distinction of being the first on any of the three literatures. (10) As the title suggests, he focuses exclusively on Nuyorican literature and provides a useful overview of important works, from Bernardo Vega to the present. Of more academic rigor is Juan Flores's *Divided Borders: Essays on Puerto Rican Identity* (1992), a collection of essay that considers Puerto Rican popular culture as resisting the pressures to assimilate into the dominate culture. The presence of Puerto Ricans in New York allows him to reinterpret island literature as well as understand the one that is unfolding in the city. His latest study, *The Diaspora Strikes Back* (2008), considers the impact cultural remittances on the mainland have on country of origin. (11) Regarding Cuban American literature, Gustavo Pérez Firmat is the only critic of stature to treat the issues of that community. In *Life on the Hyphen: The Cuban-American Way* (1994) he looks at the translational properties of Cuban American literature, popular music, and other aspect of culture. Pérez Firmat had begun to explore this idea in the *Cuban Condition: Translation and Identity in Modern Cuban Literature* (1989).(12) If Flores privileges New York as the source for Nuyorican literature, Pérez Firmat does the same with Miami and Cuban American culture.

Of a broader perspective Illan Stavans's *The Hispanic Condition: Reflections on Culture and Identity in America* (1995), which expands on Pérez Firmat's position.(13) Stavans looks at Hispanic society as represented by Chicanos, Cubans, Puerto Ricans, and Central and South Americans, and he inserts himself into the same tradition. As a Mexican who identifies with Latino issues, Stavans gives the term a symbolic quality that goes beyond the parameters I have outlined.

Gloria Anzaldúa's *Borderlands/La Frontera* (1987) continues to be the most profound study of Chicano or Latino literatura and culture.(14) A hybrid book that mixes fact and fiction, myth and reality, poetry and narrative, the past and the present, Spanish and English, queers and heterosexuals, Chicano and Anglo cultures, and other binary opposites, it proposes the physical and metaphorical borderland as a third space for articulating a new and different discourse on identity.

Flores and Miriam Jiménez's *The Afro-Latino Reader* (2010) is the first book to gather and give coherence and meaning to the writings of authors of Afro-Hispanic descent living on the mainland.(15) No full-length study on Dominican American literature exists.

I have found no study that gives a cogent overview of Latino Caribbean literature written in the United States. Although I do not consider myself a literary historian, I saw the need to fill a void in literary history, which I did in my book, *Dance Between Two Cultures: Latino Caribbean Literature Written in the United States* (1997).(16) At the time it was the first book to provide a representative narrative of Hispanic Caribbean and Latino literature in the United States from a historical, social and political viewpoint. With the growing influence of Hispanic culture as indicated by Peruvian author Mario Vargas Llosa's recent receipt of the Nobel Prize for Literature, as well as the increasing popularity of Latino culture in the United States, undoubtedly the significance of Latino literature will continue to increase in years to come. The recent period already includes two Pulitzer Prize winners: Oscar Hijuelos for *The Mambo Kings Play Songs of* Love (1990) and Junot Díaz for*The Brief Wondrous Life of Oscar* Wao (2008).(17) This observation is even more pertinent when considering that with Hispanics and Latinos the United States has become the second largest Spanish-speaking country in the world.

Simon Bolívar's discourse of the Gran Columbia, a unified Spanish American continent forged by his liberation movement against Spanish colonialism, has become a reality. It was kept alive by José Martí, and in the twentieth century by Che Guevara and, in a different way, by the Organizations of American States and the Pan-American Union. Above all, Bolívar's discourse has been recontextualized not in Latin America, where national boundaries continue to exist, but in the United States, where Puerto Ricans, Cubans, Dominicans, Mexicans, and Chicanos, but also Venezuelans, Peruvians, Chileans, and many other Hispanics live, study, and work, keeping their traditions alive. At the same time they also combine their cultures with those of African Americans, Native Americans, and, most important, Anglo-Americans to produce a new concept of Latino, race and identity. In this regard, the United States is truly a postcolonial and postmodern nation. 🔲

This essay is an excerpt from my book, *Dance Between Two Cultures: Latino Caribbean Literature Written in the United States* (Vanderbilt University Press, 1997), which has been updated and revised for this issue of *phati'tude Literary Magazine*.

WILLIAM LUIS is the Gertrude Conaway Vanderbilt Chair in Spanish at Vanderbilt University in Tennessee. His has published numerous papers, written, edited and coedited several books, notably, *Lunes de Revolución: Literatura y cultura* (2003); *Culture and Customs of Cuba* (2001); and *Dance Between Two Cultures: Latino Caribbean Literature Written in the United States* (1997). He serves as editor of the *Afro-Hispanic Review*.

WORKS CITED

1. I have chosen to use the terms *Cuban American, Puerto Rican American,* and Dominican American for the sake of consistency and to differentiate between those born or educated in the United States and those born or educated in their country of origin. I am aware that whereas Cuban Americans are relatively willing to accept their "hyphenated" experience in the United States, Puerto Ricans are less so. Like other ethnic minorities, Puerto Ricans are proud of their culture and nationality and do not consider themselves part of the mainstream North American experience. But the experience of Latinos in the United States has changed them in a profound manner so that they are indeed different from their counterparts living on the islands. In many respects, looking at their heritage involves examining not only the present conditions in the homeland but also the past and their childhood in the United States. For instance, in his *AmeRican* (1985), Tato Laviera focuses specifically on the Puerto Rican experience in the United States, as one interpretation of the title suggests. In addition, the usage of the dual terms allows me to present those groups alongside other ethnic minorities in the United States. Classifications such as African American and Native American are widely accepted. Although I use the terms *Nuyorican* and *Dominicanyork*. they are limited to the New York experience.

I would also like to clarify that I use the term *Latino* to refer to Hispanics born or raised in the United States and *Spanish American* or *Hispanic* to refer to those born or educated in their country of origin. For a full discussion of these terms, see chapter 8, *Dance Between Two Cultures: Latino Caribbean Literature Written in the United States* (Vanderbilt University Press, 1997).

2. Although I recognize the important role Chicano writers play in the development of Latino literature and that as a people they are treated in a manner similar to that experienced by Latino Caribbeans, their history and literature are beyond the scope of this book. Instead, I have decided to focus on writers from Cuba, Puerto Rico, and the Dominican Republic, countries that share a common location, history, and culture and whose people have also contributed to Latino literature in the United States. For an understanding of Chicanos see, for example, David T. Abalos, *Latinos in the United States* (Notre Dame: University of Notre Dame Press, 1986).

3. See, for example, Emir Rodriguez Monegal's *El boom de la novela latinoamericana* (Caracas: Editorial Tiempo Nuevo, 1972) and my two volumes of *Modern Latin American Fiction Writers. First Series* (Detroit: Gale Research, 1992) and with Ann Gonzalez *Modern Latin American Fiction Writers. Second Series* (Detroit: Gale Research, 1994).

4. Even the informed critic Juan Flores does not distinguish between Hispanics and Latinos, instead grouping them all together. When referring to Hispanics or Latinos, his studies do not differentiate among the more specific groups of Latinos and exclude Cuban Americans by omission. They are mentioned only once in passing. See *Divided Borders. Essays on Puerto Rican Identity* (Houston: Arte Publico, 1993). In contrast, others such as Denis Lynn Heyck, whose anthology focuses on Mexican Americans, Puerto Ricans, and Cuban Americans, go as far as including in the definition Amerindians as well as the Spanish discoverers and conquerors of the New World. This is the case in her "Chronology of Latino Events," which starts at 10,500 B.C., with "Humans inhabit Americas from Alaska to the tip of South America." See *Barrios and Borderlands: Cultures of Latinos and Latinas In the United States* (London: Routledge, 1994), xiii-xviii. For a detailed discussion of this term, see my chapter 8.

5. *Hunger of Memory: The Education of Richard Rodriguez. An Autobiography* (Boston: David R. Godme, 1982), 151. Also cited by Flores, *Divided Borders,* 211. Although it is not my intention to criticize affirmative action, a program with many positive qualities, I do want to show how U.S. government agencies and culture fail to distinguish between Hispanics and Latinos.

6. Holly Ackerman defines *balseros* as "persons who have escaped from Cuba in small boats, on homemade rafts (balsas), or on inner tubes, in an effort to reach the United States." She adds: "They have left in sizable numbers since 1959 and form two distinct cycles: 1959-1974 and 1989-1994." "*The Balsero Phenomenon,* 1991-1994," in Cuban Studies 26. ed. Jorge Dominguez (Pittsburgh: University of Pittsburgh Press, 1996), 170. During the period from 1991 to 1994, 45,575 rafters were saved by the Coast Guard. Though not all rafters were allowed to enter the United States, a sizable number have. There are some writers among them, and soon there will be a corpus of works that will merit serious study.

7. See Antonio Benitez Rojo's *The Repeating Island. The Caribbean and the Postmodern Perspective,* trans. James Marannis (Durham, N.C.: Duke University Press, 1992).

8. See *The Postmodern Condition: A Report on Knowledge,* trans. Geoff Bennington and Brian Massumi (Minneapolis: University of Minnesota Press, 1984),

9. See Bill Aschroft, Gareth Griffiths, and Helin Tiffin, *The Empire Writes Back: Theory and Practice in Post-Colonial Literatures* (London: Routledge, 1989).

10. *The Nuyorican Experience: Literature of the Puerto Rican Minority* (Westport, Conn.: Greenwood Press, 1982).

11. See Flores, *Divided Borders* (Houston: Arte Público Press, 1992) and *The Diaspora Strikes Back* (London: Routledge, 2008).

12. *The Cuban Condition: Translation and Identity in Modern Cuban Literature* (Cambridge: Cambridge University Press, 1989).

13. *The Hispanic Condition: Reflections on Culture and Identity in America* (New York: HarperCollins, 1995).

14. *Borderlands/La Frontera* (San Francisco: Aunt Lute Books, 1987).

15. *The Afro-Latin@ Reader* (Durham: Duke University Press, 2010).

16. *Dance Between Two Cultures* (Nashville: Vanderbilt University Press, 1997).

17. *The Mambo Kings* (New York: Harpercollins, 1990), and *The Brief Wondrous Life of Oscar Wao* (New York: Riverhead Trade, 2008).

Reflections on Being Latino in America and in American Literature

D URING THE WEEK OF October 21, 2009, I watched segments of the Cable News Network show "Latino in America," hosted by the Afro-Latina TV news reporter Soledad O'Brien. Although I was happy to see that the show did its best to embrace the incredible diversity of U.S. Latino heritage, I was disappointed that the show promoted certain stereotypes—such as, for example, the stereotype of Latinos as Mexican or South American immigrants who have crossed the border illegally. Illegal immigration is an issue of concern for many Americans from different ethnic groups. The subject is complex and deserves a nuanced and compassionate approach. However, it seems to me that when it comes to discussing U.S. Latino identity, the

(cont'd. pg. 60)

REFLECTIONS ON BEING LATINO
Lyn Di Iorio

(cont'd from pg. 59)

experiences and characteristics of Latinos born in the U.S.; or whose families have been here for generations, should be given at least as much focus as the stories of those who are "illegal." Indeed highlighting the illegal immigrants and their stories seemed to underline somehow that "Latino" in America is in itself some kind of illegitimate identity. I don't think Soledad O'Brien—who often writes and speaks with pride of her own Cuban American mother—really understood that her show accomplished just this ambiguous and hardly positive definition of what it is to be Latino in the United States of America.

Of course, even when one highlights the variety in the stories of Latinos born in the United States, there is a complexity that attaches to U.S. Latino identity, which does not attend the identities of many other U.S. ethnic groups. Italian Americans, German Americans, Polish Americans, Swedish Americans, and Irish Americans, for example, all have a history of immigration leading to homogenization in the so-called melting pot, which ends up producing subjects who may have Swedish or Italian last names but who generally grow up speaking only English and identified mainly as Americans with no more than a nominal attachment to their European origins.

The relationship of U.S. Latinos to their Latin American or Caribbean places of origin, even after a generation or more, is more complex. The United States in the 1840s articulated the concept of Manifest Destiny emphasizing the expansion of frontiers at the obvious expense of bordering territories belonging almost exclusively, with the exception of Canada, to former colonies of Spain. Since then, the history of Latino identity has been marked by the conflict over the border with Mexico as well as the U.S. neocolonialist and colonialist ventures into Latin American and Caribbean territories. Moreover, Mexican Americans specifically can claim—because so many colonies of New Spain became eventual states of the United States—that their presence in the United States predates that of those of Americans of other ancestries. In the case of Puerto Ricans, who have been citizens since 1917 whether they reside in the continental United States or on the island itself, the fact that the island is essentially a colony of the U.S., and one of the world's last remaining colonies, points to a gross inequity. It is an inequity comparable to that of African American segregation; namely, there is a whole colonial territory filled with U.S. citizens who actually do not have the same rights as other U.S. citizens.

Interestingly, the uniquely American injustice towards African Americans articulated in the famous Supreme Court decision of *Plessy vs. Ferguson* (1896), which made African American "separate but equal," was mirrored by the less well known, but just as damaging, 1901 U.S. Supreme Court decision in *Downes vs Bidwell,* which declared that "citizens of territories can be subject to laws and regulations that are not constitutionally applicable to other citizens of the United States." In the case of *Downes vs. Bidwell,* Puerto Ricans who reside on the island of Puerto Rico are considered "separate but equal" citizens by virtue of the fact that Puerto Rico is a territory. *Plessy vs Ferguson* condoned racism and thereby created a state of psychic "double consciousness" for African Americans, as noted by the African American writer W.E.B. Dubois shortly thereafter in his seminal work "The Souls of Black Folk" (1903). Some African Americans may still suffer from double consciousness, but the situation of African Americans was vastly ameliorated by the 1954 U.S. Supreme Court decision in *Brown vs. Board of Education,* which struck down *Plessy vs. Ferguson.* Just so, the decision in *Downes vs. Bidwell,* condoning unequal treatment for "other citizens of the United States," must be struck down. Now that there is a Puerto Rican Associate Justice sitting on the United States Supreme Court, perhaps *Downes vs. Bidwell* will one day receive both the scrutiny and the judgement it deserves.

U.S. Latinos are closer, in terms of physical as well as psychic proximity, to their geographical areas of origin than other ethnic Americans. These areas of origin can claim either to have been taken over by the U.S. at some point or to have colonial and neocolonial histories with the U.S. So, then, it is not surprising that Latinos cannot so easily leave behind originary identity and language. Likewise "becoming American" is not the grand narrative for Puerto Ricans, for example, that it has been for other ethnics. Puerto Ricans are born American despite the fact that the status of the island is in question. So, because the relationship to the originary identity persists, often even after generations, Latino identity is complex in a way that mainstream America often misunderstands. In the remainder of this essay, I wish to address the complexity attendant on being Latino in the U.S. by focusing on the literature written by Latinos in the United States and largely in English.

One of the complex elements that manifests particularly in the literature written by Latinos in the United States is the question of language and precisely the relationship that Latinos take up regarding both English—their ostensibly "new" language—and Spanish, the originary language. In my first published book I approached this idea by positing something I called "Killing Spanish." This phrase came

to me because it was a translation of a phrase used very often in Puerto Rico to make fun of Nuyoricans, i.e. those Puerto Ricans of second, third, or even more removed, generations who lived in New York and who returned to the island of Puerto Rico on vacations, during which they often attempt to speak Spanish. But often when they speak Spanish with island locals, the locals make fun of their English-inflected accents or the fact that they no longer can speak Spanish fluently. Puerto Ricans on the island will say of Nuyoricans speaking Spanish: *¡Están matando el español!* They are killing Spanish! Or a local might actually say to the face of one of these tourists on a street in the tourist strip of El Condado: *Chico, no mates el español:* Buddy, don't kill Spanish!

When I called my first book *Killing Spanish* (2004, 2009), I was not writing a critique of the way Nuyoricans, or other U.S. Latinos, speak Spanish. On the contrary, I wanted to engage precisely with the idea that Nuyoricans—not just New York Puerto Ricans but in a sense "New" Puerto Ricans and U.S. Latinos—were creating something entirely new. "Killing Spanish" is a metaphor for how an identity, which Puerto Ricans on the island mislabeled as "impure" is in my opinion the grounds for a radical creativity. Something is killed—Spanish—but from that killing emerges things that are new: Spanglish, U.S. Latino identity, U.S. Latinos of all colors and ethnicities who speak English first but who still locate themselves in some sort of relationship to their Latin American and metaphorically "Spanish" origins.

However, "Killing Spanish" is not just a metaphor for a creative relationship to Latin American identity and the Spanish language that reverses and plays with conventional ideas about language, identity, and purity. It also refers to a dynamic that I see in many books by U.S. Latinos writing in English in which characters born in the Latin American or Caribbean country or island of origin—or sometimes merely returning to the country of origin—die, are murdered, or go mad. They are closer to the origin, for which Spanish is a metonym. The texts kill off these characters who either represent the Latin American or Caribbean origin or return to it. Protagonists in those same novels grapple with what it takes to become American. In the Dominican-American Loida Maritza Pérez's novel *Geographies of Home* (1999), for example, female characters closer to the origin either die under mysterious circumstances or go mad.

For example, take the brief but very important story in *Geographies of Home* about Annabelle, a young woman in a rural town in the Dominican Republic whose father rapes and impregnates her. This episode seems to function as a kind of allegory for how patriarchy in the Dominican Republic damages and ultimately destroys Dominican womanhood. Annabelle dies mysteriously in a thunderstorm. Her would-be suitor, the father of the Dominican family in the book, who is interestingly known throughout the novel only through his parental role as Papito (or little Father), understands Annabelle's terrible situation, but just too late to save her from it. The idea that Dominican patriarchal norms create ruinous conditions for Dominican women seems to persist even after Papito immigrates to the United States and rears his family there. One of his daughters, Marina, goes mad and another one, Rebeca, not only becomes involved with a Dominican man who viciously abuses her and their children, she enables the abuse, and mourns the abuser once he is dead. The book exemplifies my idea of "Killing Spanish," not through any treatment of the language issue but by literally killing off a woman metonymically related to the Latin American and Caribbean country of origin. My logic is this: Pure Spanish is closer to the land of origin, and so are characters born there or who are recently immigrated and speak English with an accent or don't speak English. Annabelle's death is both a sign of the origin's harmfulness but also a sign that something is being sacrificed so that a possibly more vibrant Latino identity can be born in the United States.

The idea that a newer, freer, and more dynamic Latino identity comes into being in the United States is borne out in *Geographies of Home* through the experience of yet another one of Papito's daughters. Iliana becomes more Americanized and seems to escape the dark fates of her sisters Marina and Rebeca and the island woman Annabelle. Although Iliana too suffers a rape, her ultimately more positive fate arises from the fact that, as a highly educated woman, Iliana has the resources to create some distance from her impoverished and very traditional family who seem to emblematize the harmful and rigid patriarchalism stemming from the Dominican Republic. In this sense, the originary identity, represented by Annabelle and her rape, is killed off with the death of Annabelle. However, an identity that incorporates the origin in a fundamental way is born in Iliana who, in the text, is depicted as being in some ways like her ancestresses back in the Dominican Republic.

Iliana is represented as being gifted with the capacity to hear "voices" that speak to her supernaturally. This particular representation is one example of how a U.S. Latino novel such as *Geographies of Home* is linked to Latin American magical realism. This technique, so closely identified with Alejo Carpentier, Gabriel García Márquez, Jorge Luis Borges, Isabel Allende, and other famous Latin American writers, appears so sporadically—and in a sense is put in such doubt by life in the United States—that I think it too also is "killed." Iliana loses her ability to hear voices

almost as soon as this ability appears. I interpret this to mean that in this text Latin American magical realism—as a recognizable dynamic and style conveying a particular image of Latin American reality—cannot ultimately survive.

Geographies of Home is written largely in a realistic style that I call "dirty realism" in order to emphasize that the book focuses largely on the grittiness and poverty of life in the big city for working-class U.S. Latinos. Geographies of Home is for the most part indebted to a realism that has dominated American literature since Theodore Dreiser's Sister Carrie. The magical realism in Geographies of Home appears sporadically and cannot overcome the text's American realism. Here is another example: The family's mother, Aurelia, desperate to help Rebeca, the abuse victim, performs a ritual associated with Afro-Caribbean magical practices. Aurelia, who was born in the Dominican Republic and whose mother was a priestess of unspecified Afro-Caribbean practices, slowly wishes Rebeca's husband dead as she plucks feathers from a chicken. She is successful in killing her target. But killing the man does not save her daughter Rebeca or bring Rebeca closer to the family. Magical realism appears only twice in the text. The second time it appears, in the guise of Aurelia's spell using the chicken, it works but only from Aurelia's motherly perspective. It fails from the perspective of the Americanized daughter, Rebeca. Yet again something associated with the Latin American origin is killed off.

The Dominican American Junot Díaz's novel The Brief Wondrous Life of Oscar Wao, which won The Pulitzer Prize in 2008, presents a variation on my idea of "killing off the origin" or "killing Spanish." A focal character, Oscar, who has become a comic book reading, Dungeons and Dragons-dazzled dork fails to find happiness until he travels back to the originary land, the Dominican republic, where he thinks he finds love in the arms of a prostitute. Despite repeated warnings from a local military man, who is the prostitute's lover and main client that he, Oscar, will be killed if he refuses to stop the courtship, Oscar persists in staying in a country in which death has been promised to him. Not surprisingly, he is killed by the military man. However, the story of Oscar is told by his friend, and in some respects his double, another U.S. Latino, Yunior. Yunior lives to tell the story in an innovative lexicon composed of English, Spanglish, Spanish, and pervasive references to The Lord of the Rings and many other books beloved to dorks of all nationalities and persuasions. My idea of "Killing Spanish" is applicable to Díaz's novel in the sense that Oscar, who has traveled back to the origin and wishes to identify with it, is killed off. His death becomes a warning to Yunior, the tale's narrator, and to U.S. Latinos in general about the dangers of returning to the native land.

However, interestingly, in Díaz's text "Killing Spanish" emerges vibrantly in terms of the actual language in which the book is written. It is written in an English mixed with many phrases in Spanish and Spanglish. Not only is Spanish killed, but English is killed too. The result is a polyglot, excessive, and often hilarious linguistic skein that shows how rich and vibrant U.S. Latino literary discourse is. In Díaz's first book, a collection of short stories called Drown, the character in one of the stories refers to "my busted up Spanish," and thus directly to the idea that Dominican Americans (in this case) "Kill Spanish." But the use of Spanish in The Brief Wondrous Life of of Oscar Wao shows that the Spanish words add so much richness to the narrator's mostly English language discourse that the Spanish words sometimes acquire new meanings because of their juxtaposition with English. And the English words gain meaning because of the Spanish words that put pressure on the English language. For example, right at the beginning of the novel, Díaz introduces the word "fukú." This word is an African-inflected Spanish word used by Dominicans to refer to a kind of curse. If a person suffers an injury, or something bad happens, a superstitious Dominican might say it was because of a "fukú," a spell or curse. However, instead of limiting himself to just the idea that the word is the ones Dominicans use for "curse," Díaz riffs on and expands the meaning; the fukú transforms into the "curse of the New World," a curse Christopher Columbus's discovery introduced, and slavery and other new world realities made even more vile. "Fukú" becomes the word for the condition of colonial and postcolonial suffering in the new world, but Díaz's perspective on this suffering remains wry and humorous. Hilariously, English is "killed" or reinvented in this context, too, as "fukú" also sounds like "fuck you." Columbus initiated a colonial/postcolonial "fuck you" in the Americas that in Díaz's creative vision both curses and blesses its victims.

Like Loida Maritza Pérez and Junot Díaz, I believe that it is important to creatively and pragmatically engage with something or someone—place, a person, a language—that you imaginatively had already discarded, or killed off. You thought to psychically or physically abandon or leave behind that place, that people, that person. Now you realize that you must engage again, in ways that are creative, or practical, one or both. Creative—the explanation and analysis about something as seemingly trifling to people who are not academics or creative writers as the repeated killing off of characters in novels, and how those characters come to metaphorically represent language, ethnicity, and race. Practical—the struggle in actions and

words to end the colonial status of Puerto Rico and to turn that ambivalent territory into a place with a recognizable identity, whether it be as a state of the United States or as a nation. One has to engage at least creatively and hopefully at some point, also practically in the matter of this unresolved colonial status and psychic identity. Talk about it. Better—make a decision about status that will definitely improve the material and psychic situations of island Puerto Ricans.

In my book *Killing Spanish,* I initially examined the threat of Other to self within the psyche from an opposite perspective to that described above. In examining the Puerto Rican writer Rosario Ferré's major works in chapter three of *Killing Spanish,* I noted that, in arguing for statehood for Puerto Rico in her 1998 New York Times opinion piece, Ferré observed that Puerto Ricans themselves have become the Other. They have adopted the subjectivities of the mainlanders from the United States whom they once feared. That is, Puerto Ricans are hybridized; they are citizens of the United States as well as Latin American and Caribbean. They might seem monstrous in their rich subjectivity to Latin Americans and to mainlanders from the United States, but this kind of complex subjectivity is in fact becoming both a norm and an advantage in today's globalized world. I want to suggest that Puerto Ricans are good examples of subjects who absorbed the once feared Other, their so-called colonizers, into their psyches. I also want to suggest that Americans on the mainland are starting to wrestle with the fact that we too will one day absorb the Other. We too will soon be . . . the Other America.

In this context then, in the context of the idea of the threat that the Other poses to the self, I want to emphasize that the killing off of the character representing the island of origin is in a way a killing off of the self as Other. Something in the self dies so that the self can function in another context, the context that Richard Rodriguez in *Hunger of Memory* (1983) has called "public" and which he says for U.S. Latinos involves using English, not Spanish, in order to wield agency and power. The character who dies usually seems to embody the idea of originary identity: a character who lives on the island or in Latin America and therefore metonymically is related to the origin, a character who is often a mother, or a character who often speaks Spanish as a native language. Hence, the idea of the killing off of Spanish, an aspect of the self deemed as originary.

This leads to the idea of allegory. I believe that many novels written by U.S. Latino writers tend to be allegories examining the fragmentation of U.S. Latino/a and Caribbean identities. For if the mother is identified often with land and language, with traditional practices and beliefs in these texts, the father is frequently, although not always, identified with ways of being that are modern and sometimes neocolonial. For example, in *Geographies of Home* the mother is identified with Afro-Caribbean religion and practices, and the father is associated with Adventism, brought to the Dominican Republic by American missionaries.

What replaces this killed-off Spanish for U.S. Latinos? English of course. In the cityscapes, and increasingly in suburbia, Americans of Argentinian, Colombian, Costa Rican, Cuban, Dominican, Honduran, Mexican, Puerto Rican, Salvadoran, and Venezuelan heritages speak their naturalized, California, East Coast, newscaster-sounding, Midwestern, or ghetto-tinged, English; or as the case might be. Americans of Latin American and Caribbean descent in the U.S. favor English. We might say that Father English dominates Mother Spanish. Or that English is the public language and Spanish the language of intimacy, private phone conversations, shrieking arguments buffered by walls and doors and distance; the language that comes down in bits and pieces, fragments that no longer mean what they meant back there but mean even more when used in such fortuitous forms. In which case "killing Spanish" really means that that broken "killed off" language is alive and well, spoken in forms and ways that purists decry and misread. The recurrence of dead mother figures and double characters in books by U.S. Latino writers suggests that Spanish, in point of fact, while killed, is not killed off.

Spanish returns in fragments, ghostly sounds, growls from the street. I want to evoke the passionate intensity with which one destroys one identity, not so much to let another one come into being—American as opposed to Latin American—although that of course is a possibility—but to reconstitute that original identity in a different way, to deface, fragment, mix, miscegenate, lace over it like a feathery green fungus, tear at a façade that vaunts an identity that seems too slippery smooth. Being Latino in the United States of America in this context always preserves the trace, then, of what was killed off, the Latin American origin. We reconstitute these images, ideas, figures, memories into new and stronger identities, identities that engage the corpses, and their specters, from the past. Such is my endeavor, and that of Cristina García, Rosario Ferré, Loida Maritza Pérez, Edward Rivera, Piri Thomas, Junot Díaz, Yxta Maya Murray, and many other U.S. Latino writers. What is killed off in the self never dies. ◻

LYN DI IORIO is a professor at The City College of New York and The Graduate Center of the City University of New York. She grew up in Puerto Rico. She is the author of the novel *Outside the Bones* (2011) and *Killing Spanish: Literary Essays on Ambivalent U.S. Latino/a Identity* (2004).

ON THE PASSING OF A
MAJOR REVOLUTIONARY POET
Louis Reyes Rivera

I AM COMPLETELY FLOORED and shocked by the news of the sudden passing of the great poet Louis Reyes Rivera. Louis was an unsung hero and a true revolutionary poet. A bridge between the African, Pan-American and Latino Diaspora, Louis was in the tradition of Luis Pales Matos and Nicolás Guillén in that he identified with his African roots. He was a major poet of the post-Black Arts and Nuyorican traditions who, as publisher and editor of Shamal Books, published many of the poets who came of age directly after the Black Arts generation. He first published poets like Sekou Sundiata, Rashidah Ishmaili, Sandra María Esteves, Baron James Ashanti, Safiya Henderson-Holmes, and Zizwe Ngafua to name a few. He even published the work of his father-in-law, the great John Oliver Killens.

Louis was a tireless cultural worker who mentored and fostered many writers into print as editor and workshop instructor. He was also a radio talk show host who explored the socio-political and cultural work of artists of all disciplines. Louis led a band called The Jazzoets at the famed Sistas' Place in Bedstuy Brooklyn that included Ahmed Abdullah, Atiba Kwabena Wilson and Ngoma Hill. It was also there where he held countless workshops helping to publish numerous writers to the selfless neglect of his own work. A college professor for many years, Louis was a historian who held court in and out of the classroom and held his students (and disciples) transfixed with his encyclopedic

(cont'd. pg. 66)

T O N Y M E D I N A

LOUIS REYES RIVERA
Tony Medina

(cont'd *from pg. 64*)

knowledge of African, Caribbean and African American history and politics.

When I first started reading my work in the New York City poetry and activist community, it was Louis and the great Pedro Pietri who I first read with in one particular venue in Harlem hosted by S.E. Anderson. I was so nervous that I was reading with two of my main poetic heroes, but the two of them embraced me and welcomed me into the fold after reading for the first time what became a signature poem, "Capitalism Is a Brutal Motherfucker." I was welcomed among the most radical and dynamic poets who were throwing down since the 1970s, and that they were also two Black Puerto Rican communists that came out of similarly impoverished backgrounds as I did was a major jolt to my sense of self and confidence as a young, emerging political poet. Of course, I read all of Louis' books and was excited for the major work he recently completed and was about to publish, which is a jazz epic in poetry entitled *Jazz in Jail.*

Louis was an incredible spoken word artist as well. He would read these long epics totally from memory and completely and utterly blow up the spot, leaving a giant hole in the stage. After a big reading we had at Borough of Manhattan Community College, CUNY, I asked him how he memorized all of that. He said, "I always look for the music in the poem." 'Til this day, I could never memorize such lengthy poems.

Louis was truly an amazing artist whose work has not garnered the attention and acclaim it deserves. But in the activist and cultural communities, particularly in New York and among those poets of his generation and mine who are in the know, understand that Louis Reyes Rivera is a major poet and writer. His keynote speeches at The Black Writers Conference at Medgar Evers College, CUNY, in the 1990s alone, have influenced a new generation of poets, writers and activists who found in his work and commitment an example of an artist and witness of the utmost integrity and dedication to the people.

Rivera (l) with Medina (c) and artist John Abner (r) at Amiri Baraka's 75th Birthday Celebration at The Schomburg Center in Harlem, 2009. PHOTO: Lamont B. Steptoe Copyright © 2009

Louis was honored July 23, 2011 at the Harlem Book Fair by his community of artists and activists for his contributions to literature and art. Organized and hosted by long-time friends and fellow poet-activists, Gary Johnston, publisher of Blind Begger Press and Layding Kaliba, poetry editor and co-publisher (with founder Carolyn A. Butts) of *African Voices,* Louis was paid tribute by Amiri and Amina Baraka,

"We really lost a true giant and a tireless cultural worker . . ."

Sonia Sanchez, Ted Wilson, C.D. Grant and Tony Mitchelson, among other friends, colleagues and literary luminaries.

A child of the Marcy Projects in Brooklyn, Louis was known as "The Janitor of History." He was an artist who so identified and championed the working class and oppressed everywhere. This was made clear in his seminal volumes of verse *Who Pays the Cost?* and the epic *Scattered Scripture*, which I hold dear and find myself dipping into every now and again.

I had the honor of working with Louis on the anthology *Bum Rush the Page: A Def Jam* that was published by Random House. We were invited to edit the book by one of his mentees, the poet, editor, filmmaker and creator of *Def Poetry Jam,* Bruce George. In those weeks and months we worked on *Bum Rush,* Louis would make the trek each day from Brooklyn to my crib in Harlem, and we would spend the better part of the afternoon reading and sifting through poems while he would tell me these great stories of the poets and the scene from back in the day, that good old behind the scenes literary gossip and oral history where you really learn beyond any old academic workshop environment. One such anecdote was the story he told me after my prompting of how he met his wife and life partner Barbara, who is the daughter of the great novelist and activist John Oliver Killens. I was transfixed as he told me Nikki Giovanni, who was her dorm mate at Fisk University in the 1960s, introduced him to Barbara. Like a griot, he unfolded literary history to which

he was a major stitch in the fabric. I had a front row seat to a seldom heard and relatively unknown story of Black literary history.

Those were some good times, and I am profoundly proud that I got to work with such a seminal professional and tie my name to his in literary history. We put together what we felt was a revolutionary and wide-ranging collection of contemporary poetry that we tried, to the best of our ability, to make as inclusive and representative (in terms of generation, ethnicity and aesthetics) as possible.

The last time I saw Louis was at Amiri Baraka's 75th birthday celebration at the Schomburg in Harlem that was organized by the poet Ted Wilson, whose first book of poetry Louis recently published. We sat next to each other, and he looked as good as ever, and it did not seem as if he aged from the time we worked together on *Bum Rush* nearly ten years earlier. He read an excerpt from his newly completed manuscript, *Jazz in Jail.* I remember him being very excited about this new work and how he wanted it to be published by a major press that would give it the attention and care it deserved.

My deep sense of grief and condolences goes out to Louis' wife Barbara, their children, his family, friends and comrades in the struggle. We really lost a true giant and a tireless cultural worker whose every breath and movement in this capitalist beast of a stolen land we call America was his undying dedication, devotion and love of the people. Louis' work will carry on in the books he left us and in the Louis Reyes Rivera Lifetime Achievement Award founded by poet and activist Shaggy Flores (another of his mentees) for The Voices for the Voiceless, a poetry festival and conference that is close to fifteen years now.

There is a profound difference between an image and an example: Influence is more important than fame. Louis' influence will live on in the work he did as a student activist in the 1960s helping to organize Black and Latino Studies in the City University of New York, in the numerous recorded images of him throwing down with his powerful poetry of lyrical flow, in the work he did for literary journals such as *phati'tude,* in the many interviews he gave and panels he moderated and participated on, and above all, in the countless students he touched with his words and wisdom.

Godspeed, my friend, big brother and comrade. You leave behind giant shoes to fill! I can hear you now shouting out at us from the Spirit World —*MANTECA!!!!!!*

TONY MEDINA, two-time winner of The Paterson Prize for Books for Young People, is the author/editor of sixteen books for adults and young readers, the most recent of which are *An Onion of Wars* and *The President Looks Like Me and Other Poems.* He is the first-ever Professor of Creative Writing at Howard University.

Poetry, you see, is as old as breath itself. For when human beings across the planet simultaneously uttered that first initial sound, they gave rise to the same echo heard in the wail of every newborn child. The sound of that cry might be onomatopoeic, but its meaning is quite literal. "I am here, now!" This is the essential affidavit that serves as testament inside every person's compulsion to give voice to the voice, as condition urges vision, vision provokes thought, and thought pronounces the name of God: "I matter, too!"

Thus the birth of the word, the root of every language. Poetry. The strength of the people. The finest manifestation of craft, content and intent in every written and oral expression. The basis upon which all other literary genres have evolved. From poetry, not only the lyric, but as well drama and narrative, the expository and the thematic, the didactic and the ideological as root to all our scripture, sacred and profane.

It began as a blending of sound (the rhythm), sense (the experience), and color (the given image). A voice raised in celebration of itself. Chant and dance, music and tone, mystery and miracle forged into the embodied literature of people passing it on, by speech and sight, to each subsequent generation, asking and answering the fundamental question: How do we live? And is that the same as how we want to live or what we mean when we say there's something we're supposed to do?

— Louis Reyes Rivera, 2002
phatLiterature,
A Literary TV Show

Remembering
Louis Reyes Rivera
1945-2012

SHOCKED AND STUNNED. Those are the words that come to mind every time I go back to the moment I heard of Louis Reyes Rivera's sudden passing. He was a friend and a mentor, always chastising me to do better and more, to own it, to push the boundaries and limits of the publishing and literary worlds. Our friendship began through Jesús Papoleto Meléndez, when I asked him to participate in the literary programming I had developed at the Langston Hughes Community Library & Cultural Center during the early 1990s. The literary series was the precursor to the creation of *phati'tude Literary Magazine,* of which he also participated in, in both its publication and promotion.

Louis was also an avid supporter and an eager participant of our television program, *phatLiterature,* and when I was in fundraising despair, he single-handedly encouraged me and helped save our first African American Literary Festival held February 2011 at the Langston Hughes Library. He also helped launched our reading series, "Real Poetry, Real Talk," at the Bowery Poetry Club, participating as a headliner in May 2011. He has left an indelible imprint in our *phati'tude* programming and will be sorely missed in every sense of the word, both personally and professionally.

My heartfelt sympathies to his wife Barbara, his children, siblings, cousins, family, friends and colleagues. To the many students, mentees, and lovers of poetry he touched with his words, always remember that Louis left a lasting impact on us all with his wisdom, his character and his ability to inspire others. We will continue to honor him and the legacy he has left us through the good works we have left to do.

— Gabrielle David
Executive Director,
The Intercultural Alliance of Artists & Scholars, Inc.

Rivera (r) with co-host José Angel Figueroa (l) , on *phatLiterature*, Episode No, 3, "Poet-to-Poet: The Image & the Spoken Word,' featuring Rivera, Stephanie Agosto and Pedro Pietri. PHOTO: The IAAS Copyright © 2002

Rivera on *phatLiterature*, discussing his favorite topic poetry. PHOTO: The IAAS Copyright © 2002

Sharon Dennis Wyeth with Rivera participating in a panel discussion at phati'tude's 1st Annual African American Literary Magazine at the Langston Hughes Library, February 26, 2011. PHOTO: Veronica Caceido Copyright © 2011

Rivera running a workshop at phati'tude's 1st Annual African American Literary Magazine at the Langston Hughes Library, February 26, 2011. PHOTO: Veronica Caceido Copyright © 2011

Rivera (r) talking to panel moderator Jon Sands (c) and writer Rachel Hadas (l) at the "Real Poetry, Real Talk" reading series at the Bowery Poetry Club, May 2011. PHOTO: Veronica Caceido Copyright © 2011

Rivera discussing his poetry at the "Real Poetry, Real Talk" reading series at the Bowery Poetry Club, May 2011. PHOTO: Veronica Caceido Copyright © 2011

reports from the homeland

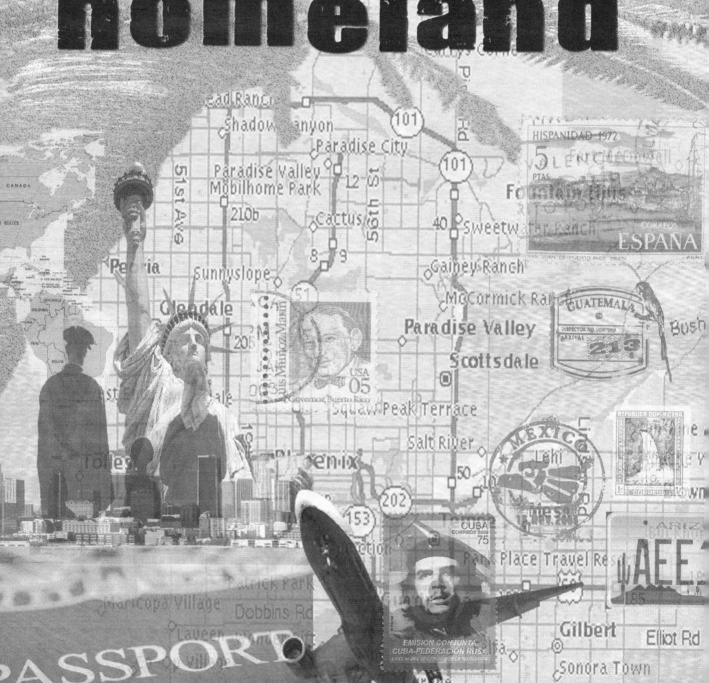

WHETHER IMMIGRANTS TO THIS COUNTRY, children of immigrants, or second or third generation, I am sure that every Latin@/Hispanic person has gone through myriad instances of identity crises; this is expected. Of course we all have those moments where we think, *I am the only person who understands what I am going through!* but as we get older we realize that there is an endless community of people just like us: Latin@/Hispanic in the U.S., and confused. In this incredible array of essays we are introduced to writers who clearly demonstrate what is truly at the heart of our identity: diversity.

REPORTS FROM THE HOMELAND is a collection of memoiristic essays by Meg Petersen, José Angel Figueroa, Adriana Páramo, Gizella Meneses and Andrea O'Reilly Herrera. We did not find these essays, they found us, and we were amazed how much common ground they share as each writer imparts personal stories about who they are and where they come from.

Regardless of the fact that we are diverse and we know it, confusion was okay then and is still okay now. In the Dominican Republican there is a palpable difference in the way blackness is defined and Meg Petersen, in her essay *Racial Categories and the Dominican Diaspora*, honors this, by not only giving us a history of the construction of race in this country but by citing various examples of high school students, women, and even the personal example of her own children.

Race and identity are an extremely important issue to our abstract struggle, but at times that continuous fight can become very real. As vivid as a "rose, sighing while melting inside," José Angel Figueroa delineates his memories of coming to the U.S. from Puerto Rico. He really leads us through the motions in his essay *Noo Jork: From an Island to an Inner City*; from being picked on in school for his accent to being told only to speak English to eventually becoming aware of the American war against his cultural heritage, José shows us how poetics became his *pana* (my favorite line!). Andrea O'Reilly Herrera also finds solace for her identity crisis in silky lines of poetry. If Andrea's parents, being Cuban immigrants, identify themselves as American then where does this leave her? Perhaps in the constantly shifting landscape that we all seem to inhabit. When she writes to us of how we are gypsies, deprived of ever knowing our homelands firsthand, I immediately took a look away from my computer and had a long deep moment with myself. I have always felt that way, as I know many Latin@/Hispanic people who don't know their homelands have, and Andrea hits that issue right on the head in her dreamy yet incisive essay, *Una Cubanita Pasada Por Agua*.

Gizella Meneses takes us through what seems like a trans-historic journey between her personal childhood and her great aunt's dietary travail in a hospital. With morbid wit Meneses gives us the Ecuadorian perspective of being lumped into the "Hispanic" category. On a personal level, I identified with this immensely since I am Ecuadorian as well. I love my Boricuas, Dominicans, Puerto Ricans, and Mexicans but unfortunately if you are something else besides these nationalities/cultures in this country you are immediately lumped into them. Gizella caustically demonstrates for us in her essay, *What's a spic?* that — from child to sickly great-aunt — we might be all destined to eat tacos, regardless of where we're from.

In the end we are left with the every day problem of pronouncing a name properly. I always grew up listening to my mom vehemently correct people on the pronunciation of her name. In an effortlessly witty romp Adriana Páramo gives us a very real account of what it's like for someone who is looking for a job and who, therefore, can't take the first chance to jump on someone for pronouncing their name wrong. The vibrant imagery of her essay, *Hey You, Dr. Paloma*, reflects Adriana's innate musicality (perhaps this comes from her being Colombian . . . or not) in telling a story. From a brief history of the Klu Klux Klan in Florida to her journey through the academic world of a community college, Páramo does justice to the rightful pronunciation of her name in this essay.

Confused yet? I am. From Puerto Rican rebelliousness to Ecuadorian food snobbery, from Dominican race confusion to Cuban gypsy-like endeavors we are thrown into a dizzying world of identity. The following essays will truly emphasize and elucidate the meaning of the title of this issue of *phati'tude,* ¿What's in a nombre? We may never know. But perhaps, through sharing these amazing works and strong voices among each other, we can get a little bit closer to understanding the multi-faceted, vibrant, insuppressible identity that we share as Latin@/Hispanic people.

K E V I N T O B A R P E S Á N T E Z

Some Other Race:
Racial Categories and the Dominican Diaspora

MEG PETERSEN

WHEN I WAS LIVING in the Dominican Republic, I once spoke with a young man born to Dominican parents who had been raised in the US. He was in college studying sustainable energy and intended to return to the DR after graduation. When he learned I was a writer, he showed me a work by a hip-hop poet about which he was very enthused. He asked me about how I happened to be in Santo Domingo, and I told him I had lived there before, with my Dominican husband, and had returned on a Fulbright grant with my three half-Dominican children. He started telling me he didn't feel he fit in Santo Domingo, at least partially because he identified with black hip-hop urban culture, and people in the DR did not see themselves as black.

(cont'd. pg. 74)

Noo Jork:
From an Island to an Inner City

JOSÉ ANGEL FIGUEROA

I STILL REMEMBER THAT FIRST DAY. It was 1952 and Mama was proud to announce we had finally arrived at our new island called The Bronx. We got off the economy flight with splintered shopping bags and—half-panicky—*mi familia* walked through of the airport like some sort of rainbow. I was that skinny dark suit and purple shirt with the thin black tie, red socks with rings around the heels and, at that age, always hungry for bubble gum drops. Tall, lanky Carlos stood out the most since his rooster's pompadour made him look cocky. And Ruben was the chubby *jíbaro* who loved reading Gene Autry and Roy Rogers comic books and who never got used to wearing long-sleeve shirts 'cause

PHOTO: George Malave
Copyright © 2012

(cont'd. pg. 78)

Hey You, Dr. Paloma

ADRIANA PÁRAMO

WHEN I GOT THE phone call from the local community college, I was too broke to consider the wording of the offer being made:

"Are you still interested in the humanities position?" the Arts and Letters secretary asked.

"Yes, absolutely, yes," I said into the receiver as I scribbled the word "humanities" on a piece of paper.

"The class starts tomorrow," she said, "Three hour session, 6:30 to 9:30 p.m. Still interested, Dr. Palano?"

I noticed how she said my name, Palano, not even close to Páramo. Had I not been busy counting on my fingers how many hours I had to prepare my first lecture, I would've corrected her.

(cont'd. pg. 81)

Una cubanita pasada por agua

ANDREA O'REILLY HERRERA

Inhabited Woman

three women reside within me
 spooning and nesting
 pushing and pressing
vying for my attention.
all three peer
with unwavering gaze,
as though from a single pair of almond-shaped eyes.
the third raises our brows in Pyrenean arches,
as she transforms us into a garden of dusting powder and cologne.
then unannounced, the first appears in profile—
her lavender skirts spread out around her like a framboyán.
with small, porcelain hands,
she pulls at the nylons that fold around our ankles and knees—
impatiently discards the modern, choosing instead
a circle of scarabs on linen,
cameos and pearls.
all the while, I sense the second present,
hidden among the shadows between two shores,
riding the dark waves of my hair,
across that endless white beaches and tourmaline seas
that unite us and divide us.
three women reside within me.

(cont'd. pg. 87)

What's a spic?

GIZELLA MENESES

LAST MAY I BROUGHT MY 99-year-old Ecuadorian great aunt, Leonor, to the hospital after a dizzy spell hurtled her off the couch and landed her on the parquet living room floor. Her morning caretaker called my mom at home, and we rushed over, beating the paramedics by a full 60 seconds. Fortunately, there were no broken bones—only a minor flesh wound conspicuously spanning the width of her forehead. We finally coaxed my great aunt to take a ride in the ambulance and have a medical professional examine her at the neighborhood hospital in Lincoln Square. Since she didn't have any gunshot wounds and was easily intelligible in Spanish, her only language, we spent the greater part of the afternoon and evening at her bedside, gazing at row after row of baby blue, paisley-printed curtains, whose endeavor of obscuring voyeuristic attempts proved insufficient. After our assigned medical professional reviewed the MRI report, Leonor was finally admitted.

(cont'd. pg. 89)

SOME OTHER RACE
Meg Petersen

(cont'd from pg. 72)

I thought about my own children, who, having been raised in the States, also identify themselves as black and struggled to understand what this meant in a Dominican context. This young man, about the same age as the oldest of them, faced similar issues about where he fit in the racial cultural mix that makes up a transnational/trans-racial identity.

Racial identity is a painful puzzle I have long been trying to solve. Do we have the right to claim an identity that makes sense to us in a world that seeks to define us by how we look? How can we resist identities imposed upon us by others? My ex-husband struggled with being labeled as black when he came to the U.S. to study. He expended a lot of energy trying to explain that he was not African American. An American woman I knew when I lived in the DR 20 years ago once told me Dominicans didn't understand race and didn't know they were black. She positioned the American way of looking at race as right and true. Dominicans, however, have long defined race differently. So what happens to ideas about race for the large numbers of Dominicans who have immigrated to the United States since 1965? What effect will they have on long established patterns of racial identification and interaction in this country? The cross-border movement of both Dominicans and North Americans with their opposing ideas about race has the potential to disrupt concepts of race in both countries, and bring about positive change.

Dominican concepts of race bear some similarity to other former Spanish colonies in the Caribbean—Cuba and Puerto Rico—but they developed in a unique context, mainly due to the fact that the Dominican Republic shares the island of Hispaniola with the Republic of Haiti. Both sides of the island were colonized by European powers and both developed the sugar industry, which, after the destruction of the native population, required the importation of large numbers of Africans who were enslaved and made to work the plantations. Hispaniola was the first place in the New World to import enslaved Africans, as early as 1502 (Gates). By the early 1600s, however, as Torres-Saillant explains, the sugar industry in the Dominican Republic had collapsed and the colony had fallen on hard times. There was so much poverty that it was no longer tenable to maintain a slave system. While slavery continued, the distinctions between the master and the slave disintegrated as the economy moved to cattle ranching. There was little differentiation in roles, and rigid racial boundaries broke down, leading to much racial mixing (6). The mulatto became the predominant ethnic type in the Dominican Republic.

In 1805, slavery was abolished in the black Republic of Haiti. Haitians declared themselves to be black by decree at that time (Gates). Haitians invaded the Spanish side of the island, and forcefully unified it in 1822 under Haitian rule, abolishing slavery in the Dominican territory (Moya Pons). However, Dominicans recognize February 27, 1844 as their Independence Day, for this was when the Dominicans expelled the Haitians from the eastern two thirds of the island. While this struggle is cast as a war of liberation, not all Dominicans were supportive of the movement to free the country from Haitian rule. Many former slaves feared that independence would mean a return to slavery.

Dominican racial self-definitions grew out of this unique context and stand in opposition to the bifurcated system in the United States. In the U.S., following the infamous "one-drop" rule, anyone possessing any known African ancestry is legally classified as black. In the Dominican Republic, the rule almost operates in reverse, with any white ancestry, no matter how remote, excluding one from being classified as black. As anti-Haitian sentiment grew in the Dominican Republic, this appeal to remote white ancestors can be read as a defensive posture, an insistence that one is not black. As Dominican-American Nelsy Aldebot put it, "They bring out their heritage when it benefits them." Generally, race in Latin America follows phenotype: if one looks white, one is white. However, Dominicans have always defined themselves racially in opposition to the Haitians with whom they share their island. Dominican ideas about race have also been influenced by Americans, by how Dominicans were perceived and wanted to be perceived by their powerful neighbors to the north. In the 19 century, there was a movement in the United States to annex the Dominican Republic. American travel writers who favored annexation came to the island, and, in an effort to convince Congress to make the Dominican Republic part of the United States, endeavored to describe Dominicans as white in contrast to the Haitian other (Candelario 35-82).

Dominicans have a rich and nuanced lexicon for referring to skin color. Dominicans call themselves *indio, moreno, indio claro, indio oscuro, rubio, . . .* but never *negro*. The category "black" was reserved for Haitians. The use of the term "indio," still being hotly debated on the island today (DeLeon), emphasizes the native heritage which was eradicated shortly after Columbus's landing. Despite this, many Dominicans today still refer to themselves as "metizo." Trujillo, the dictator who came to power after the U.S. invasion in the early 20th century, sought to fortify the image of the Dominican Republic as a white nation. He imported Chinese and Jews fleeing Hitler and Spaniards fleeing Franco in hopes of whitening the race. He designated himself as "white" on his identity card and passport, and powdered his

face to appear whiter, although it was rumored that he had Haitian ancestry. Even after his assassination, this tradition was carried on by his successor, Joaquin Balaguer. Thus, Dominicans have been encouraged not to define themselves as black. To some degree, this has served them well. As Torres-Saillant points out, Dominicans have forged their own racial identity which has protected them from "state negro-phobia" and has allowed them "to step outside the sphere of their blackness" and thus "remain whole" (6), insulating themselves in this way from the full force of racism. By rejecting both whiteness and blackness, they step outside of destructive racial dynamics. This concept of being neither black nor white has positioned them well for the emerging idea of the multiple ethnic groups of Latin America forming a single "Hispanic" race.

After the signing of the Immigration Act of 1965 in the United States, the floodgates were opened for a massive Dominican migration. This act, known as the Hart-Celler Act, abolished the existing quota system, replacing it with one based on family relationships. This coincided with the end of the Trujillo dictatorship and a lifting of travel restrictions for Dominicans.

The Dominican U.S.-educated poet Chiqui Vicioso's classic quote, "Until I came to New York, I didn't know I was black" (quoted in Torres Saillant 9) is typical of the Dominican immigrant experience in the United States. Dominicans who come to the United States, if they have any contact at all with the mainstream American society, are forced to undergo what Frank Moya Pons has described as a "traumatic racial experience" (quoted in Duany 148). Their race is defined for them in unfamiliar and alien terms in direct contradiction to their Dominican upbringing. It is hard to overestimate just how disruptive this is to one's sense of self and identity. Suddenly, one is being defined by someone else's terms after identity has long been established. It is nothing less than a violent disruption of the self.

Interviews with three Dominican-American women representing three generations of migration to the United States reminded me how truly traumatic and painful this crisis of identity can be. Nelsy Aldebot recalls the second time she came to the United States, to New York City in 1967. She realized that there were different groups in her high school—whites (principally Jews), African-Americans, and Hispanics. The upper level classes were generally reserved for the whites, but she managed to get into them, a fact she now attributes to her lighter skin color. She said she did not become conscious of her own blackness until much later. When she went to describe how that happened, she looked away, finally saying only, "It [the process] was very hard."

Dominicans are forced to come to terms with American ideas about race when they immigrate to the United States, and this process is enacted upon their own bodies through the gaze of others. This traumatic reevaluation may be even stronger in the second generation. Erika Martinez, who was born in the U.S., but returned to the island as a baby, immigrated to New Jersey in 1979, when she was six years old. She lived in an area where there were many Hispanics, and didn't think much about race, except to be aware that her younger sister was considered more beautiful because she had green eyes, straight hair and lighter skin. Erika came to realize the way she was perceived in the United States when the family moved to Long Island and she began to attend predominantly white schools. She was thrown into an identity confusion, which she says she did not resolve until she was an adult working in a Latina women's theatre group in Chicago after college.

When I asked 13-year old Dalma Santos, who immigrated to Manchester, New Hampshire almost two years ago, how she would define herself racially, she was unable to answer. She became visibly uncomfortable, looking down at her hands which she twisted in her lap, a look of pain crossing her face. Despite their different generations and the different stages of the Dominican Diaspora these women represent, the common factor was their compulsory racial redefinition and the incredible hurt it produced.

Unlike earlier generations of immigrants, Dominicans in the United States are what José Duany terms "transnational:" maintaining strong ties to the island and often moving back and forth across geographical and cultural boundaries. This movement of Dominicans across borders causes Dominican and American ideas about race to directly collide in the bodies of those who make these journeys. Thus Nelsy Aldebot arrived in the first wave of Dominican immigrants, her father having been born in Puerto Rico and "asking for" the rest of his family to come to the United States. Erika Martinez's family formed part of the second and much larger wave of Dominican immigrants who arrived in the 1970s and 1980s, settling in the area around New York City. Dalma's family represents a new group of immigrants. Her grandfather arrived first, but instead of settling in the traditional Dominican enclaves of New York and New Jersey, he came to one of the newer settlements in Manchester, New Hampshire. By the time of the 1990 census, Dominicans were the fourth largest Hispanic group in the United States, after Mexicans, Puerto Ricans, and Cubans. In the 2010 census, they comprised 2.8% of the US population, an increase of almost 85% over 2000. Most Dominicans are concentrated in the Northeast, but no longer almost exclusively in New York City. In Rhode Island, they comprise the largest group of Hispanics (Ennis, Rios-Vargas, and Albert). As more and more Dominicans

enter the United States, the trends would predict an even greater increase over the next ten years.

Dominicans present a particular challenge to the American system of racial classification as they are the first Hispanic group with overwhelmingly African phenotypes. Simply put, they look black to Americans, yet they do not, as a group, tend to identify themselves as black. When they enter the United States, as soon as they have contact with American mainstream society, they are forced into racial redefinition as they must try to reconcile these new ideas with their own self-concepts. Americans respond to them as black people. African Americans expect solidarity with them, and whites treat them as black. No amount of insistence on their part that they are not black is likely to affect these reactions, leaving Dominican immigrants feeling trapped in someone else's definition of their own identity.

Dominicans have put up considerable resistance to this reclassification as black. Jensen et al. reports on the results of a survey conducted in Reading, Pennsylvania as to Dominican racial self identification. When immigrants were asked what race they considered themselves to be, 43.3% answered "Dominican" and a combined 46.7% used a panethnic label such as "Hispanic," "Latino," or "Spanish." None used the hyphenated "Dominican-American" and none identified themselves as black. Another survey conducted in Providence and New York by Itzigsohn, Giorguli, and Vazquez reported that the modal answer to an open-ended question about race was "Hispanic." The authors propose that Dominicans are trying to find an English equivalent to the term "indio" which has been used as a racial designation in the Dominican Republic. When informants were given a forced choice, however, more Dominicans identified themselves as white, but conceded that Americans did not see them that way. In a small study done in Washington Heights in 1991, Itzigsohn and Dore-Cabral found that almost two-thirds of their sample group identified themselves as "Hispanic" or "Latino," an identification which the authors believe represents an attempt to find an intermediate position within the American classification system. When given a limited choice between black, white or other, 50% chose "other." The US census form asks respondents to first designate whether or not they are Hispanic and then to designate a racial classification. In the 2010 census, 29.6% of Dominicans classify themselves as white, 12.9% as black, 1.4% Native American, 0.3% Asian, and 46% "other." An additional 9.7% classify themselves as "two or more races" (Ennis, Rios-Vargas, and Albert). The data tells an interesting story of resistance as the overwhelming majority of Dominicans would be identified as black by Americans. Dominicans, however, resist the black/white binary of the American racial classification system, and particularly resist identification as black.

Erika Martinez tells a story of when she was a teenager working in McDonald's and she needed to speak to a customer in Spanish. Her coworker exclaimed, "I didn't know you were Hispanic!" When Erika asked what the coworker had thought she was, the woman seemed embarrassed and refused to answer, unwilling to identify Erika as black, as if it were an insult. Through incidences like these, Dominicans become aware that identification as "Hispanic" may protect them to some degree from the lower status afforded to African-Americans.

Many Dominicans do experience discrimination as African Americans here in the United States. In a study completed by Oropesa and Jensen in Reading, Pennsylvania in 2009, 42% of respondents stated that they had experienced some kind of institutional discrimination, mainly from the police, and about half reported experiencing interpersonal discrimination (over one third, in the past month), usually consisting of poor service or being treated as someone not worthy of respect. The overwhelming majority attributed this to race or ethnicity, almost to the exclusion of other factors. The likelihood of being discriminated against was stronger for darker-skinned individuals, especially in dealings with the police. Contrary to what assimilation theory would predict, those more proficient in English or with more education and/or US citizenship reported more discrimination (Oropesa and Jensen). This may be because they have more contact with white residents or because they are better able to perceive discrimination when it occurs.

Dominicans also face discrimination from African Americans who perceive the Dominican stance toward race as a denial of their blackness. American blacks operate out of the same racial framework as their white compatriots, and interpret Dominicans' complex racial identity as a failure to accept who they are. In David Lamb's novel, *Do Plátanos Go Wit' Collard Greens?*, the African American protagonist meets the family of his Dominican girlfriend and has to contend with their prejudice towards him. He sets out to educate his girlfriend and her family about their blackness. As Torres Saillant notes, "Lamb's Freeman embodies the mindset of many African Americans who construe the reluctance of many Dominicans . . . to make blackness their primary form of identity as a form of alienation that requires urgent corrective treatment (9)." Nelsy Aldebot recalls that she thought she got along well with African Americans until one attacked her. She still is not sure why. It is revealing that even now she does not consider herself one of them. Erika Martinez recalls being ridiculed when, in sixth grade, she was doing a report about the Dominican Republic and quoted an encyclopedia article saying Dominicans were white and therefore, she herself was white. Even as a college student she did not consider trying out for a role in a production

of *For Colored Girls Who Have Considered Suicide When the Rainbow Is Enuf* because she didn't think the play was about people like her. In the film *Black in Latin America,* the African American scholar-narrator, Henry Louis Gates Jr., almost seems to mock his Dominican informant . In one scene of the film, Gates and his informant Juan Rodriguez, a Dominican anthropologist, are walking down El Conde, a street in the Colonial Zone in Santo Domingo. Gates asks Rodriguez when he first knew he was black, and Rodriguez replies, "When I came to New York." Gates interrupts him with laughter, saying, "That'll do it." Rodriguez seems apologetic about his previous lack of racial awareness, saying, "Unfortunately, not before that did I learn my roots were in Africa and not Spain." Gates laughs again, gesturing at the people passing in the street behind them, saying "In fact, all Dominicans are black."

Through experiences like these, many of them quite painful, Dominican immigrants are educated about American concepts of race. Their own identities are ignored or even mocked by Americans of all races, leaving them feeling as if the images reflected back to them in the eyes of others are distorted to the point of being unrecognizable.

Dominicans in the second generation do not have the luxury of insulating themselves from American racial categories. The children of immigrants attend schools with African Americans and other Hispanics, sometimes even, as both Nelsy and Erika did, with a preponderance of white classmates. They face judgments based on their African-American appearance. Nelsy attributes her position in higher tracked classes to her lighter skin color. Erika reports that every time the family moved she would start in the lowest track and have to work her way up, but that when she reached the highest tracks, she was surrounded by white students and came to see herself as white. Sometimes she would bring her much lighter skinned sister with her so that others would realize she was not black.

In a fascinating series of studies, Bailey observes and surveys Dominican high school students in Providence Rhode Island (Bailey, Dominican American and Bailey, Language and Negotiation). He discovers that these second generation Dominicans use the Spanish language as a way to set themselves apart from African Americans, while they also use African American Vernacular English to establish solidarity with them. Unlike their parents, they do acknowledge their African ancestry, and are frequently critical of their parents' overt racism. They use the labels Spanish, Latino, or Hispanic to separate themselves from the American racial hierarchy and to consciously resist it. They view the history of slavery as having relevance for Haitians, but not for themselves (Bailey, Dominican-American). Meszaros focuses on young Dominican-Americans who, like the young man I met in the bar, embrace African-American hip-hop culture, but also still resist the racial classifications of the dominant society by "performing Spanish" in certain situations to assert their "Dominican-ness." Thus they can embrace African American cultural forms while still resisting the racial classification system of the United States.

At the end of the latest census report on Hispanics in the U.S., the authors report, "Racial classification issues continue to persist among those who identify as Hispanic, resulting in a substantial proportion of that population being designated as 'some other race'" (Ennis, Rios-Vargas, and Albert). The authors of the census report seem to see this as a flaw in the system that Hispanics continue to resist the black/white binary system within which the US classifies race. The study also notes that surprisingly large numbers of Hispanics consider themselves to be white, which they report as if to cast doubt upon this assertion.

When I first moved to the Dominican Republic more than 20 years ago, I remember feeling an enormous sense of relief that I could interact with people of different racial phenotypes without the constant racial tension such interactions are likely to produce in the United States. It was as if a veil had been lifted and I was able to see people clearly without the film of racial mistrust between us. While racism did not disappear in the DR, the lack of rigid racial categories seemed to allow for more fluidity in interactions, enabling us to respond to each other as human beings first.

The enormous numbers of Dominicans who have immigrated to the United States since 1965 present a challenge to the existing racial classification system. Researchers agree that the US racial classification system has been destabilized by Dominican immigrants, but disagree on whether this is a good thing, or if Dominicans simply need to accept their blackness. The bifurcated system of racial classification, which has long held sway in the United States, has reinforced white hegemony and privilege. By creating strong and rigid dividing lines reserving whiteness for the racially "pure," the American system polices access to white privilege. If the borders become less defined and less absolute, we might be able to move towards a gradual weakening of racial boundaries and a dismantling of the systematic institutional racism present in this country.

At the same time, Dominicans who return to the island will do the nation "an inestimable favor" if they can rid it of the "white supremacist thought and negrophobic discourse" which has long dominated Dominican politics and culture (Torres Saillant 9). Dominicans in the United States will, as both Nelsy and Erika have, develop a consciousness of themselves as black. But both of these women have achieved this as transnational people, without losing their strong Domini-

can identities. They acknowledge that the road is hard and painful—it is a road that Dalma is only beginning to travel. No one chooses to be part of a Diaspora; circumstances less than ideal always render it so. However, as Torres Saillant puts it, "Whatever suffering Dominicans have learned on [the] foreign shores to which despair has driven them, they have come to see themselves more fully and fairly . . ." (9) When transnationals return to the island, as they do, they bring with them a new acceptance of their African heritage that has the potential to weaken Dominican racism.

There is an opportunity for transformation on this side as well. The continuous influx of people who resist racial classification can perhaps help their adopted country, the United States, to see itself more fully and fairly as well, and help us to begin to rid ourselves of the racism which has long defined—and divided—us. ◘

WORKS CITED

Aldebot, Nelsy. Personal interview. 19 Nov. 2011.

Bailey, Benjamin. "Dominican-American Ethnic/Racial Identities and United States Social Categories." *International Migration Review* 35.3 (2001): 677-708. Print.

Bailey, Benjamin. "Language and Negotiation of Ethnic/racial Identity among Dominican-Americans." *Language in Society* 29.4 (2000): 555-82. Print.

Black in Latin America. Dir. Henry L. Gates. Perf. Henry Louis Gates. PBS, 2010. *Video: Haiti and the Dominican Republic*. PBS, 12 Apr. 2011. Web. 12 Nov. 2011. <http://video.pbs.org/video/1877436791>.

Candelario, Ginetta E. B. *Black behind the Ears: Dominican Racial Identity from Museums to Beauty Shops*. Durham: Duke UP, 2007. Print.

De Leon, Viviano. "RD Será De Negros, Blancos Y Mulatos." *Listín Diario*. 11 Nov. 2011. Web. 20 Nov. 2011. <http://www.listindiario.com.do/la-republica/2011/11/11/210557/RD-sera-de-negros-blancos-y-mulatos-en-nueva-Ley-Electoral>.

Duany, José. "Reconstructing Racial Identity: Ethnicity, Color, and Class among Dominicans in the United States and Puerto Rico." *Latin American Perspectives* 25.3 (1998): 147-72. Print.

Ennis, Sharon, Merarys Rios-Vargas, and Nora C. Albert. "The Hispanic Population 2010." *2010 Census Briefs*. May 2011. Web. 31 Oct. 2011. <http://www.census.gov/prod/cen2010/briefs/c2010br-04.pdf>.

Itzigsohn, José, Silvia Giorguli, and Obed Vazquez. "Immigrant Incorporation and Racial Identity: Racial Self-identification among Dominican Immigrants." *Ethnic and Racial Studies* 28.1 (2005): 50-78. Print.

Itzigsohn, Jose, and Carlos Dore-Cabral. "Competing Identities? Race, Ethnicity and Panethnicity Among Dominicans in the United States." *Sociological Forum* 15.2 (2000): 225-47. Print.

Jensen, Leif, Jeffrey H. Cohen, Almeida Jacqueline Toribio, Gordon F. De Jong, and Leila Rodríguez. "Ethnic Identities, Language, and Economic Outcomes Among Dominicans in a New Destination." *Social Science Quarterly* 87.S1 (2006): 1088-099. Print.

Lamb, David. *Do Plátanos Go Wit' Collard Greens?* New York, NY: I Write What I Like, 1994. Print.

Martinez, Erika M. Personal interview. 19 Nov. 2011.

Meszaros, Julia. "The Dominican Second Generation Creation of a Subaltern Identity." Proc. of Multiculturalism: Conflict and Belonging, Mansfield College, Oxford. 28 Sept. 2009. Web. <http://www.inter-disciplinary.net/at-the-interface/diversity-recognition/multiculturalism-conflict-and-belonging/project-archives/3rd/session-5a-identity-constructions-1/>.

Oropesa, R.S., and Leif Jensen. "Dominican Immigrants and Discrimination in a New Destination: The Case of Reading, Pennsylvania." *City & Community* 9.3 (2010): 274-98. Print.

Santos, Dalma. Personal interview. 16 Nov. 2011.

Torres-Saillant, S. "The Tribulations of Blackness: Stages in Dominican Racial Identity." *Latin American Perspectives* 25.3 (1998): 126-46. Print.

NOO JORK
José Angel Figueroa

(cont'd *from pg. 72*)

it always fatigued him. I remember snow-skinned, shy Celia, hiding her smiles ever since a tooth ran out on her. And little sister Miriam was the best Puerto Rican thumb-sucker in the airport.

Speaking of sucking, I never ate my bubble gum drops that day: My brother Hector was the meanest vacuum cleaner from Rincón, and he took them from me. Ah, and Milagros: my Mama. Have you ever seen such a proud and passionate rose with indented cheekbones before? I will always see this miracle as a piece of wind, feeding my thoughts with the wonders of when and why tree leaves fall in a child's dream.

I dreamt of that day. When we reached the baggage terminal, Mama saw our luggage sprawled all over the cold city floor. Remembering that day feels like some knife stabbing my memory. It was the first time I had ever seen a proud and passionate rose, sighing while melting inside . . . SNOW.

"Your first *In-glish* lesson," said Mama, "is to learn how to say *hamburger* to make sure you do not starve when asked what you want to eat. Forget about yellow rice and beans with avocados. Think American. Our language and cultural spirit will not be welcomed nor accepted. Meanwhile, eat peanut butter and jelly sandwiches until you learn more difficult words." We learned a new word each day before school started. "But Mama," I asked, "what if we forget to

say *hamburger?* What then?" After smacking some sense into me, she replied, "Say *french fries!* And if you still forget your second lesson, say *ketchup!*" My brothers and sisters learned English by reading the eyes of strangers while remaining humble. This determined if they were friendly neighbors or cold-blooded assassins who smiled before crucifying you for daring to embrace the American Dream. Oftentimes, we didn't know if these strangers were smiling or simply grinding their teeth. But the message was clear: America was private property. Hands off! We had to grow up fast—and in perfect English.

1.

AS A TEN-YEAR-OLD WITH SILENT EYES—timid yet pensive—I was seen as a foreigner and called *perro-Rican* while laughed at by kids who invented bubble-gum racism. They were highly offended by my beautiful, deep accent, cinnamon skin, and very lively tropical clothing. It was a time of great prosperity, yet there was great public fear of the wave of newcomers. Perhaps if my face and color was depicted in Norman Rockwell's paintings of Americana, I would not have been a victim of educational oppression.

Instead, I was the funny-talker who the other kids loved to hate. Learning to speak *In-glish* while acting American became an undeclared tug-of-war. If I chose not to think and act like Dick and Jane, I was punished for speaking Spanish and sentenced to clean the blackboard. Jose, can you see? The U.S. invaded Puerto Rico in 1898 and branded me foreigner! It was pure murder.

Coming to school was a daily public execution with poison pouring from their eyes. Some actually aimed and cocked the mid-finger at me—shooting dead-center through my Spanish heart. But my dignity was bullet-proof. Shouts of *"Mira! Mira!"* were hard-nosed attempts to deface my self-esteem. It was a blatant conspiracy to make me feel insignificant while treated like some nonentity called *Other*. In short, I was an ego-alien projection. But why? asked my ten-year self. Why didn't they realize that I, like them, was *E Pluribus Unum*—one formed from many? Why must the English language be used to dominate my thinking rather than to cultivate my mind and creative potential? Why not English-plus! After all, the ABCs came hard, often intimidating me. I felt as if all the I.Q. and reading tests were outrageous attempts to invade my Boricua national identity, if not to color me invisible. When this did not work, I was straight-jacketed into some dull, characterless room that was disguised as a workshop for the "slow learner" who was "culturally deprived." Naturally, I was the minority who was also intellectually disadvantaged. Which came first: the label or the stigma?

As the months faded into years, I was less the newcomer than a prisoner of the New York City Board of Education, fighting to maintain my own integrity. I felt English was some gigantic nuisance or adversary on a mission to sabotage my Puerto Rican essence, blasting me with the Who, What, Where, When, Why and How! I was entangled in a web of assimilation and acculturation. It left a lasting impression on me: not being allowed to speak my own language. Instead, I was pulled back, red-penciled in, or pushed aside and railroaded into classes where learning was some dead-end dream. Frankly, the kind of education I received, I would never give to a rock. When I wasn't making colorful potholders in home economics classes, I was drawing perfectly beautiful square houses with sunshine gushing out the skies as the romantic palm trees stood paralyzed near the seashore. And if you were magnificent at mumbling, picking your nose, or losing your soul during some English exam, you were the class genius or clown.

2.

BEING LEFT-HANDED DIDN'T HELP either. I was often forced to write with my right hand, if not ostracized for being my natural self. But this alienation didn't succeed in breaking my spirit. I would not allow the stuffed shirts or "The System" to play football with my mind. I may have been "slow" with my ABCs at first, but I was definitely not some Juan Bobo! No one was going to belittle me. My pride was intolerable! Perhaps the fragrance, spice, and flavor of my Boricuaness was too deep-rooted. I simply refused to give up my romantic accent. I was not going to be deprived of my freedom of self.

While many like myself fought back against the hated system by joining street gangs like the *Purple Knights or Young Savages* (1961) with switchblade tempers flashing out of their back-pockets, I was reading the dictionary like bible study. Grandma Felipa and Mama had taught me well. And what happened when I stood defiant and spoke my native tongue? My teacher, Mrs. Schaefer, for whom I first experienced puppy-love, held my hand down as she scratched it with her outrageous fingernails, waiting for me to stop speaking Spanish when I did not understand her words. I was sent to the dean, a mild-mannered hypocrite who rolled his newspaper tightly and with his reliable nightstick on my head, he screamed "Speak English only! Spanish is bad for you! Repeat: Speak English only! Again! Spanish is bad for you!"

I was emotionally raped and left stranded in some corner of the world with a dunce cap on my head; later forced to remain after school to write on three huge blackboards: "Speak English. Spanish Is Bad For Me. I Will Not Speak It Again!" I came home with a bilingual headache. The next

morning, Mama was dragged into the dean's office with my teacher and school principal pouring nasty syllables out of their mouths. They lashed out and killed me with their eyebrows. Mama was confused and ashamed, as if I had set the school on fire. When I tried to explain myself to her, she slapped me hard across my face. I died crying inside. When I was ordered to return to class, the smirk on the faces of my classmates disheartened me. I drowned in my silence. And I could still remember Mama's slap across my face.

I knew then that the United States had declared war on my cultural heritage. But I was no longer resentful of the English language. I knew then it was a deliberate conspiracy to fear *In-glish* and as a result, succumb to invisibility. Instead, I chose to befriend English and to master its possibilities, but kept my Spanish close to the heart. Still, it was a damn pity that one could not be accepted nor admired for having the best of two worlds: two great languages and cultures. I was determined to survive the American Dream machine with its pressure to conform while you turned your back on your own identity.

The time came when I "graduated" from elementary school, but I was not sure if my five and dime ribbon was an A+ or a passport to excommunication. It taught me to be on guard and to develop crap-detecting antennas that gave me greater resilience and willpower to persist even when someone shook my hand while stabbing me in the back at the same time. I purposely chose not to return the hatred and racism so easily spit upon me. And I recognized how the intellectual and educational oppression with its grading and tracking system, also degraded me.

3.

I WAS DETERMINED TO LATER EMBRACE poetry as the greatest act of human liberation. And to listen much closer, not merely to what was said, but how. I learned to *read* eyes and peoples' expressions as if they were books of mirrors. Poetics saved my life. I grew to respect the beauty in the power of the spoken or written word. I slowly became The Searcher, learning that writing meant to seek and to envision, and to discover not what you know, but how you think.

When I became a high-school teenager, though still off-the-wall with my second hand clothes, leftover rice and bean sandwiches, and awkward rock n' roll rhythms, I remained married to the Spanish Language. At the same time, I often escaped into public libraries and met the master poets and writers—Blake, Papa Hemingway, Browning, Langston Hughes, Kerouac, Longfellow, and Willie Shake. I secretly met these great voices from eye-to-mind and introduced them to the indelible imaginations of my other grassroots *compadrazgos* (hommies), or *guaitiaos*: my "brothers of

blood"—Cervantes, Dario, Lorca, Vallejo, Neruda, de Hostos, Marti, Alonso, Llorens Torres and Pales Matos. I read, observed, and absorbed. Reading and writing became my second skin, an embodiment of words given life to create within me a fresh wind.

In the meantime, I continued to search for my own roots while living the anonymous hope of a poet of color who believed then and even now that someday the U.S. will still embrace me as part of its own national soul. During these transformational years, I also discovered that books written about Latinos were mostly looney tune caricatures of some Anglos' distorted vision of Puerto Ricans and other *colorful* people. I was more aggressive as the hunter of my national and cultural heritage, determined to create a spiritual and artistic balance in the present while getting a firm foot-hold on my future. Thus the poet within emerged and evolved.

Poetics became my vocation. *Mi Pana.* My confidence. My badge of honor. My solidarity. My weapon! The quest was not to determine what poetry *Is,* but rather, what it *Could Be:* a voice among many. As a Latino, I knew it was more important to define myself than to allow others to label me with negative stereotypes such as "Minority" when, in fact, I was (as poet Piri Thomas declared) "The majority of One." I was never an *Other.* Ironically, I am now a "hot" majority minority while the majority of Latinos are written off as illegal aliens of the new and improved social underclass.

4.

UNFORTUNATELY, THE GROWING CONTRIBUTIONS made by Latinos across the oceans—in education, commerce, government, in grassroots advocacy for health and human services, or in mass media, film and arts entertainment—to advance societal conditions for today's "Others," is often-times left ignored, unless some misguided soul with a black or brown face is criminalized or lynched in the headlines. Latinos are still depicted as migrant or immigrant sponges and rejects of the tainted American Dream, particularly by right-wing political maggots and false religious prophets who blame the downfall of the federal budget on women, the elderly, and misbegotten children who need this kind of tongue-lashing like they need domestic violence, HIV AIDS, child abuse, or other societal ills less important than global warming or President Bush's unlawful war in Iraq.

Yet, our Puerto Rican history and cultural heritage reflect incredible strength and veracity as one in our unanimity of being. We will not disappear. We have been both a part of and apart from the American impulse and browning of this great country before it became America in 1776. And afterwards when it invaded Borinquen as part of its Manifest Destiny in the name of prosperity,

democracy, and food-stamp colonialism as a perfumed colony in 1952.

Like other new arrivals before us, we have also played a major role in America's perpetual redefinition, dynamicism, and emerging talent. The nagging issue of "English Only" will not defeat Latinos who strongly believe in Spanish-Plus. America must understand that democratic principles do not solely exist in the English language, and that the Hispanic heritage is undeniably inseparable from our Puerto Rican roots. Above all, Latinos are more than bilingual voices. They are also just as multicultural as they are multinational by nature. And perhaps for these reasons and a millennium more, I chose a gateway to advocate for the freedom to learn while Puerto Ricanizing America. 🔲

SOURCE: "Noo Jork: From an Island To An Inner City," by Jose Angel Figueroa, NY: *Journal of Educational Facilitation (JEF)*, Volume 2, Number 1, Boricua College Press, January 1996.

HEY YOU, DR. PALOMA
Adriana Páramo

(cont'd from pg. 72)

But I had less than 32 hours. A flock of butterflies lifted my stomach all the way up to my throat.

"That's perfect," I said and she proceeded with a standard hiring interview that mercifully did not test my knowledge of humanities.

Two hours later—after collecting the textbook from the college library—I was at home flipping through the pages in disbelief. It became apparent that somewhere someone had made a mistake, and either I had applied for the wrong position or the position had been offered to me in error. I was a social scientist—that much was true—but I knew nothing about art history and shuddered at the sound of the names Achilles and Agamemnon.

I sat down at my desktop and typed every word I planned to say the following day—pages and pages. I memorized it all. At three in the morning, I was rehearsing my re-creation of the Socratic question-and-answer method in front of a mirror. *Whatever I see here is what my students will see in a few hours.* I put my hair in a bun and dusted off my geek glasses with black frames that made me look smart. I became painfully self-conscious about my accented English, and whenever I heard that boisterous roll of the tongue of my Colombian *R*'s, I forced myself to keep my tongue far away from my palate. *There, my name is Doctor Páramo, easy on the R, not Doctorr Párramo.* I needed to sound convincing, earn the students' respect, make them go *ooh* and *aah* until word of my excellence reached the dean's ears, so he or she would offer me a position with tenure for

the following semester. That was all I wanted: To be back in the classroom teaching higher education, a modest but certain check at the end of the month, a 401K plan, health benefits, the whole nine yards.

WHEN I WAS OFFERED THE ADJUNCT POSITION at the community college, I was living in Central Florida, far away from the Disney craze and the suntanned crowds. I lived on the outskirts of Kissimmee, in an immigrant community of seasonal citrus pickers, hotel janitors, cardboard recyclers, waitresses, truck drivers, and two Latina women who used to wash their beat-up cars in skimpy bikinis every Sunday morning. Their front yards, ornate with Puerto Rican flags and life-size statues of the Virgin Mary, bid me goodbye the following evening as I turned right on my way to the community college.

During the 50-minute drive, I passed abandoned phosphate mines filled with aquamarine water that gave the landscape a dreamlike appearance. For miles at a time, I saw nothing but orange groves, trailer parks, and sky. The farther I drove, the more rural the landscape turned. For a few minutes, I thought I was heading in the wrong direction. If the earth was flat, I had no doubt I was reaching the very edge of it. The railroad tracks, the abandoned fruit stands along the roads, the closed-down gas stations, all of it seemed an unbefitting setting for an educational institution. The last ten minutes of my trip were along Reynolds Road, a forgotten stretch of a country road flanked by rows of dilapidated trailers and flimsy structures. A monster truck passed me by. *Honk if you love rednecks,* read the bumper sticker. I was debating whether or not to turn around when I caught sight of the campus: small, immaculate, dignified. It stood sandwiched between a 250 square-acre citrus farm and a police station.

I arrived early at my classroom on the upper level of one of three identical two-story buildings. I wanted to be able to scan the students, get a quick feel of the class before the lecture started. A skinny cowboy was already sitting there. I sat behind him, his Wranglers, his snakeskin boots, his wide white hat, and his fringed blue jean jacket with *good ol' boy* embroidered in maroon letters on his back.

From my corner, I surveyed the students as they walked in. A petite middle-aged woman sat in the first row. She had an oversized dark black coat that read *Crime Scene Investigator* in bright yellow letters. She was followed by an older woman in a motorized wheel chair. I instinctively got up to help her through the door, but she dismissed me. "I've been crippled for 15 years, Hon. I don't need no help," she mumbled. She couldn't have known I was her professor.

Before 6:30 a couple of young black men walked in. Both were wearing black nylon do-rags, rapper's jeans

many sizes too big that merely covered their half exposed checkered boxers; they walked right by me, limping, dragging one foot more heavily than the other the way rappers do on MTV. They sat next to me; one of them was laughing at a professor who had just lectured on life, death, heaven, and hell. "An' he be sayin' if you good, you goin' t'heaven, that's bullshit, 'cause you ain't goin' to no heaven, 'cause it ain't no heaven. I mean, ye-eah, it ain't no hell either, 'cause this is hell right here, y'know. Three hours of paintings and shit? My big black ass."

By 6:35 the classroom was almost full and I was terrified. I dug my body further into the chair; a part of me wanted to get up and regurgitate everything I had so painstakingly memorized over the last 32 hours. The other part of me wanted to sprint for the door. With the exception of the two black rappers, I was almost certainly the youngest person in the classroom. I was flustered, panicky, and deafened by the sound of my heart pounding in my ears. I tried to button up my black jacket but missed two buttons because my hands were clammy and cold. With trembling fingers, I grabbed the holder of my leather briefcase and walked towards the front of the class. *Keep the tongue off the palate, don't roll your tongue, put your geek glasses on, don't hold any paper in your hand or your students will catch you shaking.*

"Good evening, I'm Doctor Páramo, and I'll be your humanities professor this semester." I got a "Good Evening" back and a roomful of smiles. A wave of warmth brought some life back into my frozen fingers.

"How do you say your name again?" the petite CSI woman asked.

"Pá-ra-mo," I said and wrote it down on the board for everyone to see.

After I gave a brief description of my academic credentials (anyone just out of graduate school can't miss the chance), they introduced themselves.

There was a firefighter, a construction worker in paint-stained overalls, a paramedic with a crackling two-way-radio fastened to his belt, a blonde who worked as a receptionist for an insurance company, a unit health coordinator at the same hospital where I'd been offered an environmental specialist job, the owner of a business called "We Buy Ugly Houses," a freckled bank teller, a chef at a local Italian restaurant, a black beautician, a slender secretary for a dental office, an overweight telemarketer, a carpenter, and two housewives who hadn't set foot in a classroom in sixteen years. They had all been up early in the morning, worked all day long, had fights, disagreements, were bosses or were bossed around, had had a bad or an OK day, and then drove to campus, ready or not, to sit through a three-hour long lecture. They didn't have to be there, but they had chosen

to. I was moved by their determination to better themselves.

I started my class with what I knew best: anthropology. I showed them a reproduction of the *Hall of Bulls,* the Paleolithic paint on limestone in the caves of Lascaux, France. I asked them to jot down the inferences they could make about the Paleolithic peoples based on their art legacy.

As they looked at the painting, some of them blank-eyed, trying not to fall asleep, I wondered if they could see through me. If they could see that I was a high school teacher with no experience in adult education, that I didn't know anything about art, that I was in debt, unemployed, and scared. I had just returned to the USA after a four-year-long high school teaching job abroad, ready to take America by storm. My strategy lay flat at the bottom of my suitcase in a brand new manila envelope: a bachelor's in petroleum engineering, a degree in anthropology, a doctorate in international relations and health services, and an assortment of resumes, cover letters, and recommendations, all typed in Times New Roman, font 12, on the best quality paper. I flaunted my academic credentials unreservedly. I felt entitled to. After all, I had battled my way to the highest level of education after 22 long years in more classrooms than I cared to remember. Under the skills section I wrote, *computer literate and bilingual,* in italics so that it would pop out, and when prompted to describe my job experience, I made a list of the fieldwork I had done in exotic places that my prospective employers probably hadn't even heard of. All of that, I thought, would make this young Colombian highly desirable in the corporate world of the land of opportunities. But life had different plans. After sending out more than 60 honest-to-God résumés, and getting no luck, I gave up on the corporate world.

TEN MINUTES AFTER I FINISHED my first lecture, I was getting into my Enterprise car, which I had rented that day for 20 bucks, so I could drive 100 miles and earn 75 bucks (25 an hour) at the college, when I was approached by one of my students. He went by Rocco; he was a car mechanic by day and a composer and poet by night.

"Hey Doctor Promo, is that how you say your name?" he asked. I was about to correct him, but he kept on going.

"I think I understood what you said about Plato's ideal world. What was it? Oh yeah, the idea of the thing is more real than the thing itself. Can I use marriage as an example for my homework? I mean, it's like that, right?" He removed the toothpick from his mouth, wiped it sideways on his chest, and put it carefully into his shirt pocket. "The idea of lovey-dovey love is more real than any real relationship. Something like that, right?"

We stayed in the parking lot discussing Plato until everybody else on campus had left. At around ten, I got into

my rental car, and Rocco into his brand-new 1500 Dodge Ram fully loaded pickup with leather interior. *Yes, Rocco, it's just like that.*

FOR WEEKS I LIVED IN A NIRVANA-LIKE STATE. I had finally found my niche. I was hooked. Although I had come to the community college expecting little more than a monthly paycheck, I found that teaching those classes was filling my life with a new purpose. Each Wednesday night I left campus with a renewed sense of self-worth; I was relevant again, as if being unemployed had turned me into a subhuman, an invisible life form unrecognizable by the naked eye. Now that I was a professor, I felt like a human being again. The system hadn't just given me a break; it had given me my life back, and my students, unknowingly, had become my respirator. The few who fell asleep in class, cursed me when I handed them back an F, or left the classroom feeling indignant because I asked them not to chew snuff during my lectures were as memorable as the straight A's. Life was beginning to make sense.

Admittedly, a community college had not been my first option. After giving up on the corporate world, I put my heart and soul into finding a social services job. More résumés went out. The few people who bothered to reply said they were flattered by my interest in their institutions, and in exchange, they flattered me back, telling me I was overqualified. *Do you mean overqualified as in "you're too good for us"? You've got to be kidding me.* Some even suggested that I modify my resume according to the job description. That, I learned, meant diluting my qualifications or "dumb-ing it down," as one of my friends put it. And so I went from a Ph.D. to a master's holder to someone fresh out of undergraduate school. When nothing seemed to work and my bills started to form a hideous pile on my secondhand desk, I stopped reading the job descriptions and applied to any position that sounded reasonable, including an "environmental specialist" job, which I foolishly mistook for an engineering-oriented position. It turned out that "environmental specialist" was the euphemism adopted by a hospital for its cleaning crew. *Thanks, but no thanks.*

Luckily, there was one realm reserved for misunderstood Ph.D.'s like me: the academic one. I launched an aggressive self-advertising campaign throughout the state of Florida. I reincorporated the fancy titles into my resume; colleges and universities would surely appreciate a bilingual professional loaded with credentials. But I had not foreseen the insurmountable mass of qualifications required in addition to the PhD: proven fund raising experience, ongoing researches, and a more than modest publication record, among others. I had none of them.

I called my doctoral dissertation director, an anthropology professor from Minnesota, who had wholeheartedly encouraged me to "shoot for the stars" before, during and after the defense of my thesis.

"What am I doing wrong?" I asked him. "I thought getting a job was going to be a breeze."

"Off the record," he said after listening to the details of my job hunting quest, "you ought to lower the bar, kiddo." The line crackled. I heard static and then his voice again.

"Imagine that you, an inexperienced graduate, are a tiny fish. Now imagine that a university is a big pond. Catch my drift?" he asked.

"I get that," I said. "What are my options then?"

"Easy. Turn it around. Try and be a big fish in a small pond, and by small pond, I mean something like a community college."

It was a brilliant plan. So simple, yet so wise. I wished I had called him earlier.

"One more thing—ahem—I'm only trying to help," my old professor said. He made a long, suspenseful pause during which his tone went from listen-and-learn to don't-take-me-wrong.

"Tell me this," he said. "After being turned down by just about everybody, doesn't the common denominator in your job applications jump out at you?" he asked.

"What do you mean?" I asked slightly confused. "*I am* the common denominator."

"Exactly," he said. "I mean, ahem, why don't you anglicize your name a bit so it doesn't sound so maracas and cha-cha?" he added.

A flash of heat made its way across my face. I heard my own breathing over the receiver.

"It's just a name," he said. "If they see Adriana, they may close the door right away, but if they see, let's say, Adrienne or even Adrian, they might call you for an interview."

I closed my eyes and bit my thumb.

"What happened to shooting for the stars?" I asked and hoped he could hear my indignation.

"Well, the stars are there for everyone," he said. "But you, by virtue of being Latina, might have to take the long route and pay tolls along the way."

I thought about a stream of colorful expletives in English as well as in Spanish. I wished I had the guts to show him the full extent of my bilingualism.

"And while we're on the subject if I were you, I'd omit my ethnic background. I mean—ahem—don't tick any race box when they ask if you are Latina, Hispanic, Indian or whatever. That's the game, kiddo."

This was the professor who had cheered me on for two years, who had given me consistent self-confidence

boosts, pep talks, and had repeatedly told me that Florida "loved educated Latinas." And while I never walked around wrapped in my Colombian flag, anglicizing my name and omitting my provenance seemed a pitiful act of betrayal to my identity. *Listen up all of you* hermanos *y* hermanas *going by Peter, Bob, Bill, Charlie, Mary and Rose. I know exactly who you are: Pedro, Roberto, Guillermo, Carlos, María y Rosa.*

Had this been the right place and the right time, I would have explained to my old professor a few things about me. I would've told him that my dad had abandoned us when I was a child and that my Mom was borderline illiterate. I was one of five women raised by a single Mom, the bravest woman I'd ever known, and that together we'd formed a clan of women warriors rooted in family tradition. Marriages had not altered our last names; Mom always carried her father's family name and the five of us, undeservedly, honored dad's last name, just because that's how it was done in my family. Also, I would have told him that Mom did not name me Adriana on a whim. It was a name she carefully chose after some chick named Adriana won a beauty pageant back in the sixties, and Mom decided that if she ever had another girl, she would name her Adriana after the beauty queen. In any case, what good would it do me to drop the last "a" in Adriana and become Adrian? The only Adriana I knew of to have become someone after anglicizing her name was Adriana Pennino, a pet shop owner who became Adrian Balboa after marrying Rocky Balboa during *Rocky II*. Then again, she wasn't a real woman but a character played by actress Talia Shire, the actress who, funny enough, dropped the Coppola, her very Italian family name, after marrying composer Shire.

"You go get them, kiddo," my professor said. "Give me a call when you reach the stars," he said and waited for me to say something. I remembered a line from Rocky: "*It ain't gonna be no rematch! Oh, come on! I had enough things in my face tonight! Adrian!*"

"Will do," I said defeated. "Thanks for your help." And with that, I hung up.

AT THE END OF THE SEMESTER I contacted the Arts and Letters secretary who'd interviewed me over the phone.

"It's been great, I'm having a good time teaching, but how can I put this to you?" I cleared my throat. "I'm having difficulty living on 75 bucks a week. Is there any chance of something more permanent?"

"No, Dr. Paramore," she said. Cordial and professional as always, she consoled me by telling me that usually you had to be an adjunct for ten years before the college offered a faculty position. This was definitely not the ideal time to correct her way of pronouncing my last name.

"I was about to call you, anyway," she said. "Would you be interested in designing an anthropology class? It's never been taught, but between you and I, if you manage to make it work, I'm sure that'll be your fulltime position here at the college."

It was perfect. That would give me six hours a week instead of three, allow me to put my experience as an anthropologist at work, and put me on the track to the stability I so desperately needed. I said yes, and the following semester, the community college had its first-ever anthropology class.

It was an early morning session, small and quaint, and had the appeal of being an elective, meaning that those who sat in class were genuinely interested in anthropology. Among the students, considerably younger than those in my evening class, was an ex-marine who had spent six months with the UN peacekeeping forces in violence-ridden Sierra Leone. At 20 he had already witnessed rapes, mutilations, lynchings, mass extermination, and been forced into complicity by inaction. Taking advantage of his accounts, I switched the order of my lectures. Chapter Eight: Genocide and Ethnic Cleansing became a floating topic that we discussed once a week for the duration of the semester. We discussed the Tutsi-Hutu conflict in Rwanda and the Arab-Dinka undeclared war in Sudan. We read about the plight of the Armenians and about Yugoslavia under Milosevic, the British invasion of Tasmania, the tragedy of the Kurds in Iraq, and the Sabra and Shatila massacre. I left the best-known genocide, the Nazi mass extermination of Jews, at the bottom of my list. I wanted the students to realize that we as human beings had been and continued to be our own very worst, most savage enemy across borders, cultures, and eras—and that our potential to senselessly destroy life would be unfairly belittled if, whenever we discussed genocides, we only remembered the systematic killing of Jews by the Nazis.

"I wouldn't go there if I were you," one of my students said. His name was John, a punk-looking guy in his late twenties who had introduced himself as an animal breeder at his family ranch. Tall, strong, rugged, and cocky, he always sat in the front row, from whence he hurled darts, arrows, and daggers at me with his piercing Floridian-sky-blue eyes. It wasn't dislike that I read in his eyes; it was something much more personal that I couldn't put my finger on. By the third class I began to notice that he always wore the same clothes: camouflage baggies tucked into army boots and a white t-shirt with the Confederate flag stamped back and front. Lettering under the Confederate flags read "Hendrix Lives" on one side and "White Powder" on the other. He played the electric guitar with a local heavy metal band in

some rowdy bars around Central Florida. This, I inferred, was his testimony of his passion for Hendrix and maybe even his allegiance to the mind-altering substance.

I asked John to clarify his comment.

"Didn't happen," he said after popping green bubble gum inside his mouth, an action that I imagined he considered much more masculine that blowing it out of the mouth.

"Sayin' that the Nazis killed six million Jews is like sayin' that six million people died with the submersion of the Atlantis. Ha, ha, ha." By the time John finished his sentence, I was really ticked off. I delivered an impassioned diatribe. "Think about this one for a second, John," I said in a very cordial tone but with enough sand in it for everyone to see my disagreement. "Imagine that we could rewrite every bit of history that we're ashamed of. We wouldn't be writing history, would we? We'd be writing a self-aggrandizing autobiography, a testament to our remorse. Now, what do you, John, suggest we do with the concentration camp survivors, the Gestapo files found that confirm the systematic annihilation of Jews, homosexuals, the handicapped and so on? What do we do with all the evidence?" I asked.

"I ain't that gullible, Dr. Paloma," he said. "You believe what you want to believe."

"It's not a matter of believing," I said. "History is not an act of faith, John." We held gazes for a few seconds. The rest of the class remained silent. "And incidentally, my name is Dr. Páramo. Right here," I said tapping the board where my name had been written since the first day of class.

"Never mind, prof, Promo, Paloma, Pom-pom, whatever. Don't mind me, go ahead with the class. Ha, ha, ha," he said bobbing his head and playing a riff in his air guitar.

I took a long, deep breath and wished him a catastrophic downpour of bad grades and a long, tortuous path to a very, very elusive graduation date.

From that day on, he expressed his disagreements during our discussions on racism, evolution, sex and culture, religion and magic, by playing a trill in his air guitar. He annoyed me immensely, but I chose not to object. We'd be out of each other's lives in a few weeks, not a big deal. He was now sitting by the door at the back of the classroom, giving me cold stares that said, "You're nothing to me," continuously shaking his head in disagreement, rolling his eyes, and smirking. I decided that for as long as he remained at the back of the class and his dismissive attitude remained of the silent persuasion, I'd refuse to be engaged in any type of verbal exchange with him.

Three weeks before the end of the semester, I collected the term papers. I had given the class a wide variety of topics to choose from. John had chosen Associations and Interest groups. He missed class that day but caught up with me in the parking lot. As I was getting into my car, I heard his voice.

"Hey you, Dr. Paloma."

I knew exactly whose voice that was, but I didn't turn around. I got into my car without looking back and put the car in reverse. I looked in the rearview mirror, and there he was, standing right behind my car, making it impossible for me to drive away. I rolled the passenger's window down.

"What is it, John?"

"My paper," he said slipping a folder through the window opening. "This is the real deal," he said pointing at the blue jacket now lying on the passenger's seat. I noticed the words "No Fear" tattooed along his right arm. "You'll be asking for a tuition refund from your graduate school after you read this."

"And if I get a refund," I played along, "can I take you shopping so you stop wearing your little soldier's costume?"

He gave me a curt wave and walked away from my car without looking back.

AT HOME, I READ HIS PAPER, which was not a research paper but a 25-page manifesto. His parents and grandparents had been active members of the Southern White Knights of Florida, a chapter of the Ku Klux Klan launched in 1949 by a plumbing contractor by the name of Bill Hendrix, a messiah, a prophet, a visionary, and a genius, according to John. I thought about his t-shirts, his Confederate flags, his "Hendrix Lives," and how he had convincingly diluted his "white power" slogan under the deceptive "white powder." I whispered under my breath *You little bastard! You yahoo!*

I don't know what angered me more: John's bigotry or the fact that when we talked about national identity and symbols, I had played Jimi Hendrix's guitar rendition of the national anthem which, I thought, my young students would relate to, especially John, a Hendrix music lover. John talked in his paper about something he called the golden period in Florida: the late forties and early fifties when 75% of the males in Orange County—where touristy Orlando is located—were Klan members. During this so-called golden period, his relatives had led and participated in anti-black, anti-immigrant, anti-Catholic, and anti-everything-different-from-their-own-version-of-white-Americans mass demonstrations. Jacksonville, Miami, and the citrus belt from Orlando to Tampa were the most powerful klaverns. The white power belt, he called it.

It was during this golden period that the Klan responded to a new 1951 anti-mask law with a surge of cross burnings and floggings from the Florida Panhandle to Miami. With delicious irony, Hendrix declared war on "hate groups," including the Catholic Church, and then nominated himself a candidate for governor. Under his baton, the Klan began trying to make history with sticks of 60 percent dynamite,

with so many bombings, or attempted bombings, that the period was dubbed "The Florida Terror."

Because John never came back to class, I was denied the pleasure of handing him back the F he had earned on his term paper and of challenging his ignorant statements during the subsequent oral presentation. I would have liked him to explain in front of the class, including Juanita, the Mexican-American, and Kamal, the black Muslim, why he thought, as he had written on his paper, that all non-white Americans should be mass deported to their homelands and how he'd carry out his brilliant scheme to cleanse America. I would have asked him if he seriously considered that white Americans will go on their knees to scrub public toilets, wash dishes, mow lawns, wait tables, and so on for three dollars an hour, without health insurance or benefits as poor immigrants did. I would have asked him if he knew that 40% of the physicians in our county were Indians (from India, not from the Seminole reservations) and that the citrus industry that was so important in Central Florida would collapse without the cheap, backbreaking labor of immigrants.

But more than anything, I would have liked him to tell me, a Colombian professional who had plastered the state of Florida with dozens of résumés, that immigrants were given undeserved privileges in the USA and that all an unskilled Hispanic had to do to be given preference over skilled white Americans was to state their minority status and the system would immediately bend over the barrel, cheeks spread wide.

The last day of class, after saying goodbye to my students, I pulled my calculator out of my briefcase as I thought about John. *In ten years from now, more than, let's see, one thousand students will have passed through this classroom. Their horizon and mine will be wider just because they and I will have learned something that we didn't know before our paths crossed. But you, John, my boy, you'll still be cleaning horseshit in ten years from now.*

THE FOLLOWING SEMESTER, one day after my anthropology class, now double in size, I was approached by a faculty member. He was from Boston and according to him, not very well-liked by his colleagues as they considered him a Yankee with a Boston accent that didn't gel with the good old redneck boys running the college.

"Welcome to the gang," he said, patting me in the back. It was unofficial, but he thought I'd like to know that soon I'd be offered a fulltime position for the fall semester. Something to do with an early retirement. "So, polish your Sociology," wink, wink, "that's where I saw your name," he hushed. "It's not official yet, but the powers that be have already decided. You're in, Adrienne. Is that how you say your name?"

I told him that it didn't matter; at this point in my life I went by anything. I joked and told him about John and how

he called me Dr. Paloma, Promo or anything but Páramo.

"Really?" he asked. "Gidadaheah, even a true blue Bostonian like me can say it. Pramo, right?"

THAT SUMMER I BUSIED MYSELF studying Sociology textbooks, designed a different curriculum that reflected our modern society rather than the 70's society that my predecessor had shaped hers by, and once more pulled my calculator out. For the last year I'd been making the minimum payments towards my credit card overdraft, but now with the new job, I could be debt-free after two semesters of serious belt strapping. No, I had a better idea, why wait one year and keep paying interest if the money was practically in the bank? I borrowed some money against the unofficial employment offer, paid my overdraft, and waited for the offer with open arms.

But the fall came, and no offer was made. It was a post 9-11 America. Some of my ex-students had put their dreams on hold and left for Iraq. There was talk of war, rising unemployment, low enrollments at the college, no need for adjuncts, no budget for new hires, and the sociology professor, rightfully frightened by the general sense of uncertainty, had decided to postpone her early retirement. The lights once more plainly and simply went out.

Three weeks into the semester, I was at home filling out more job applications, mentally commuting back and forth between becoming a stripper and slitting my wrists, when I got a phone call from the community college. The Sociology professor had a family emergency; her son was in trouble with the law. Would I be able to substitute for a few weeks? Holding the phone in my hand, I remembered a cartoon scene from Tom and Jerry: One of the characters sticks his hands through the telephone wire, reaches the person at the other end of the line, and punches him repeatedly. His neck jerks backwards, and his head bobs sideways with such force that his nose draws a horizontal line on the TV screen. I wished I could do that: reach out and beat the innocent secretary senseless—pow, punch, pow—in a harmless, cartoonish kind of way.

"I'm afraid I won't be able to, but thanks for the offer anyway," I said, feeling irritated, jaded, used.

I tore the telephone wire off the jack and let out a hungry, indebted, unemployed wail, which is the scariest of all human cries, *Shiiiiiiiit!* I felt tempted to say *Screw you, community college, screw the little pond that you are, and screw all your rednecks, and your wishy-washy sociology professors, and your bigots, and the kids you let go to get killed in Iraq.*

But I couldn't. That community college lingered in my mind with the warmth and comfort of a sweet promise. That

campus enveloped by orange trees and a citric stench had been, for the past two years, my life support, my antipyretic, and my walking aid. It touched the memories of my last few hundred days in my mind like a sore.

I invoked Jeremy, a student in my humanities class who nearly brought tears to my eyes during a synesthesia exercise with music. Every semester I heard Kenny G's languid clarinet; his music always smelled like cotton candy, like freshly cut grass, like roses in bloom. And Willy Nelson: his music smelled like tobacco wads, tasted like cheap whiskey, felt like burnt burlap. Black Sabbath's music was, well, black, tasted like blood, felt like needles, and looked like a group of hooded Inquisition monks.

Then Jeremy's turn came. His favorite piece of music was a prelude from Wagner's *Tristan and Isolde*. He apologized for not having been able to draw the music and asked instead to be allowed to orally describe his sensorial version of the prelude. "You have to really hear the strings to get into the story, there, you hear them? That's a green pasture, it undulates with the wind." Hmmm, Hmmm, he hummed quietly. "It starts out nice and easy, hear it? Close your eyes, Professor Páramo. Don't let the sight of your eyes overrun the sight of your soul."

Before I closed my eyes, I glanced at the class over Jeremy's shoulder. Some students were as stunned as I was by this Eminem-look-alike's unexpected passion for classical music. I closed my eyes and embarked into this magical journey with Jeremy. After two minutes, we were stalking game through some forest without name, hiding behind tree species not yet discovered, crackling twigs with each note, startling deer with each octave of the piano, with each variation of melody. I forgot to dismiss the class. When I opened my eyes, the classroom was nearly empty. There was only Jeremy sitting by my desk, mouth halfway open, tears streaming down his face.

"Sorry if I look like a fairy," he said and wiped his tears on his jeans. "That was awesome! What a trip! Woo man!"

He handed me his term paper before he left:

EUROPE WITHOUT GOD

And what Nietzsche's madman meant when he declared: God is Dead

I SAW JEREMY WALK TOWARD the classroom door pulling up his baggie jeans by the crotch. I wondered how many regal minds like his dwelt underneath white jerseys, unlaced Nikes, rappers' jeans; how many country hearts had the ability to transform a martial piece of music into a delightful fable.

"You'll never be a small fish, Jeremy," I said, still awestruck, as he grabbed hold of the doorknob.

"Hey, better a small fish than a bug. See ya'round, prof."

WITH THIS FLURRY OF MEMORIES I felt wiser as I looked at the unplugged telephone still on the carpet. *You're right Jeremy: Better a small fish than a bug.* I plugged the telephone back in the jack and dialed the community college.

"Hi, this is Doctor Páramo, you called me 45 minutes ago to ask me if I could substitute the sociology professor. Actually, I'll be able to," I said into the receiver.

Then, an ominous pause.

"Umm, hold on a second, Dr. what was that again?"

"Páramo," I said but what I thought was, *Promo, Paloma, Presto, Pringles, whatever the hell it sounds like to you.*

"Let's see, sociology, sociology," she said. I heard her flipping pages then striking the keyboard as if looking down a list.

"Oh no, I'm so sorry, we already found a substitute," she said.

I twirled the telephone cord around my index finger until it went white. *This can't possibly be happening to me, a highly educated Latina on her way to the very heavens, arms outstretched, groping hands reaching for the stars.* "But thanks for calling," she went on. "I'll keep your name in mind, in case anything comes up in the future, OK?"

I sat on the stained carpet, buried both elbows on my thighs, placed the whole weight of my heavy head on my open hands and exhaled into the receiver, "For future reference, my name is Adriana Páramo. Should I spell it out for you?"

UNA CUBANITA PASADA POR AGUA
Andrea O'Reilly Herrera

(cont'd from pg. 73)

Having been *made* in Havana [as my mother prefers me to say] and born in Philadelphia [the proverbial cradle of liberty] only a skip and a heartbeat after Fulgencio Batista fled a New Year's Eve party and my mother [who was carrying me at the time and had nearly reached full term] threw herself down upon a Victorian love seat [promptly causing the front right leg of the sofa to give out and, consequently, sending her to the floor in tears] upon learning that the cidra that my grandparents had brought with them from Cuba [and my father had saved for a special occasion] turned out to be as flat and bitter as vinegar . . . my earliest childhood experiences are inscribed by the Cuban Diaspora and the painful realities of exile. So immersed was I in these realities that I grew up identifying myself first as a Spaniard [my grandmother insisted upon aligning herself with her Galician ancestors, though she never actually traveled to Spain], and then as a Cuban [calling myself an American never entered

my mind]. After overhearing me tell a Puerto Rican shop-keeper, in Spanish, that I was Cuban, my mother affectionately began referring to me as una cubanita pasada por agua—a little Cuban girl "passed" through water. It wasn't until adulthood that I came to the realization that my social, historical, and cultural consciousness was displaced, for it had been shaped not nearly as much by the Civil Rights Movement, which I witnessed firsthand, as by the historical events in Cuba, which were discussed every Sunday at my grandparents' house [with variations] in counterpoint with the stories my relatives recounted about a place—a world—none of them would ever revisit, except in memory and imagination.

Despite the fact that my mother self-identifies as American, has no trace of an accent, and rarely spoke directly to us in Spanish, I—unlike most of my siblings and cousins—grew up longing for and dreaming about a physical place I have never seen, except in photographs, but somehow know. As a result, I am confronted with a sense of deep personal loss, which is at once ephemeral and haunting.

Over the years, I've tried to locate the source of my longing and discontent. Have I unconsciously acquired what Herbert Gans calls a "symbolic ethnic identity"? Would a day, or even an hour that happened to mark the passage from one year to another, have really made a difference? How do I begin to explain the fact that, even though my mother tongue is English and I was weaned on cheese steaks and scrapple, the soft singsongy rhythm of Spanish pulses within me like an inner cadence and I find a continuity between past and present in the ritual preparation of a "pie" de guayaba or an arroz con pollo. Perhaps, I tell myself, my emotions reflect some distant ancestral call or echo that manifests itself, as my poem suggests, in the three generations of Cuban women inhabiting my name and my person (Carmen for my grandmother, Andrea for my great-grandmother, and Teresa for my mother). At the same time, the competing and sometimes combative aspects of my ethnic roots reveal themselves in the curious juxtaposition of my Christian names with my surname, O'Reilly. Further complicating my life, as many Cuban friends and relatives have pointed out, is the fact that one of the main thoroughfares in Havana is O'Reilly Street. As a result, when I'm in Miami many of the people whom I meet assume that O'Reilly is my Cuban name, despite the fact that my Philadelphia twang and my physical appearance partially belie this association. Nevertheless, my Cuban colleagues and friends assure me that I am a Cubana. Where you are conceived, one Cuban friend assures me, is far more important than where you were born.

All I know is that the last time I was in Miami Beach sharing a pastrami sandwich with my tía-abuela, Ada, I felt as though I was in the presence of my grandmother once again. And when in Spain, I was certain that I saw my grandfather walking down a path in the Botanical Gardens across from the Prado [with his pants belted at chest level] leading my grandmother by the elbow. In both places, I was surrounded by tastes and sounds and smells and shadows that confirmed a way of being in the world, a past that is for me at once cherished and familiar.

Perhaps because I grew up in cultural isolation—in an extended Cuban "family" consisting of relatives and friends who collectively formed a kind of island unto themselves—the revelation that there were others who shared my nostalgic, vicarious longing for Cuba, coupled with the discovery that not all of us are called into this ambiguous and oftentimes troubling space, crystallized for me a lifetime of alienation and dislocation. In a word, it prompted in me a kind of creative and intellectual self-exploration regarding my own relationship not so much to the island itself, but rather to the idea of Cuba that my mother and my grandparents so lovingly nurtured in me and cultivated over all the years, as well as a world view that informed my unconscious life and has nourished my imagination since earliest childhood.

As I think back to the countless number of conversations I have had with others who have grown up in the margins of this diaspora, and those who, as Pablo Medina so aptly puts it, are *exiled by association,* I realize that despite the fact that this second-hand exile condition has been for some a source of creativity and possibility for others it is an endless journey, an unquenchable thirst. In spite of our differences, we all seem to be grieving the ability to recall firsthand or physically know a place that has been irrevocably altered. As a result, we are bound together in the search for a cultural home. We are all nomadic wanderers, undergoing a journey that has no final destination, for we are caught up in what Stuart Hall once called, "the enigma of an always postponed 'arrival'."(1) The journeying, I suppose, is the thing in itself. ▣

1 "The formation of a diasporic intellectual, An interview with Stuart Hall by Kuan-Hsing Chen"in Stuart Hall, *Critical Dialogues in Cultural Studies:* 490.

An earlier version of this testimonio as well as my poem "Inhabited Woman" appeared in my edited collection ReMembering Cuba: Idea of a Nation Displaced (Austin: University of Texas Press, 2001) pp. 317-319, 351

WHAT'S A SPIC?
Gizella Meneses

(cont'd from pg. 73)

Let me rewind to 1968, my great-aunt's arrival to the City of Big Shoulders. She landed in Chicago at sixty in a time when all the Ecuadorians in the town knew each other. Until the age of seventy-seven, she worked in East Roger's Park, only a few steps from the lake, at the Chicago Name Plate Factory. After the factory moved out to the "burbs," she grudgingly retired. She would have and could have worked at least ten more years, but who would hire a seventy-seven-year-old? She lived alone and cooked for herself until ninety-seven, when we hired someone to come in during the day to help with light cleaning and prepping Ecuadorian meals. Of course, in Leonor's view, if you're not Ecuadorian, then attempting to put together an Ecuadorian meal would be an utter outrage. This, needless to say, was a source of contention for my mother, the arbiter between her aunt's demands and the caretakers' grievances. Leonor's stubborn objections sent several Puerto Rican and Mexican women caretakers in a mad dash for the door. Still, my mom visits and brings her aunt food every Saturday, and, until this recent incident, Leonor has been on a surprisingly lucid quest to divest each caretaker of her last strand of patience.

So here we are back at the hospital filling out all the forms and questionnaires. There were the standard inquiries about health and health history, children, husband, alcohol, tobacco, prescription drugs and, of course, race. My mom checked off Hispanic, as she usually does for herself and for everyone in the family. I noticed later, though, that at the foot of Leonor's bed there was a chart swinging back and forth from a white, plastic chain . . . so I took a gander. There it was again, "Hispanic," in bold. I wondered why it so was important to have this information on her chart. At first I thought it had to do with some sort of hospital quantitative fact about the percentage of Latinos with heart disease. Well, this particular Latina was going to defy all statistics since she was just shy of a century. I finally concluded that this was how the information on heart disease and race was factored. After being parked in the emergency room for a good chunk of the day, we headed to the sixth floor, the heart ward.

Yes, the heart ward meant that the food was heart-friendly—that is, insipid and dull. And on Leonor's dinner menu Hispanic appeared yet again. The meal itself? Hard taco shells, a bean-like substance in the middle accompanied by an undetermined meat product and a few strands of puce-colored iceberg lettuce dangling from the side.

Obviously, they lumped her in as Mexican, and this was the pathetic attempt at Mexican "cuisine." Nonetheless, I guess this is what all Hispanics are fed on the sixth floor heart ward in a local Chicago hospital. Maybe all facilities were trying to accommodate the Latino population by serving Ortega taco shells. What if we had checked off white non-Hispanic? What were they feasting on in the hospital: Jello, lumpy, cold mashed potatoes and dry, shaved beef.

Well, it was simply inedible, and not just for a ninety-nine-year-old Ecuadorian woman who never tasted a hard taco shell in her life, or even a taco for that matter. But also for the four family members, crammed in the eight by nine room, which were equally repulsed by the sight and smell of the unsavory dish. In truth, my great-aunt could only palate home-cooked Ecuadorian meals or slight variations of them, and so began her fast.

Now I'm back to the fifth grade and the lunches my own mother would prepare for me to take to school: breaded chicken with muchines and fruit, yellow rice with vegetables and black beans, llapingachos in peanut sauce complemented by obsessively polished utensils. I begged her to pack a bologna or peanut butter and jelly sandwich to stop my classmates' winced-faced sniffing after I opened my lunch sac: the foreign scents assaulting the olfactory sensibilities of eleven-year-olds at St. Tim's grammar school in Chicago's West Roger's Park. It was the 1970s. Of course, it wasn't just the cuisine: speaking to my parents in another tongue, an unpronounceable first name, and forced farewell kisses on my parents' cheeks until eighth grade . . .

In fifth grade, one of our assignments in Mrs. Hartman's class was to draw our genealogical tree. We had to include our immediate family, first cousins, aunts and uncles. I had about forty names on my tree. Ryan Pearce glanced over at my assignment and started to read these bizarre bits of nomenclature: Carolina, Gabriela, Santiago, Francisco, Consuelo, Ramiro, Angelita, Alba, Víctor Hugo and Rafael. He then read "Rrrrrraaaaaffffaellll" several times out loud and inquired, "Are you a spic?" I said, "I don't know. What's a spic?" He replied, "Duh, someone who speaks Spanish." "Oh yeah," my skinny chest ballooning with pride, "I'm a spic."

That evening I went home and enthusiastically told my parents that we were spics. My mother had first heard the depreciatory epithet on the factory floor, and my dad's first encounter was after he was drafted in the U.S. army in the late 60s. They assured me that it was a *mala palabra* and that I shouldn't use it to identify myself. Well, I didn't utter it again, nor did I give it a second thought until years later when I heard it hurled in my direction at the cafeteria at my all-girls' Catholic high school on Chicago's North Side. By then, I knew its meaning.

It was the usual disorderly parade at Good Counsel of blue, green, grey and brown plaid skirts hovering over freshly dunked fries, faux-green peas, and perfectly proportioned circular pieces of meat. I gathered my grub and planted myself at the Latina table. After nine long years in grammar school of being the token "Spanish" person, I relished in my new *compañeras*. There were about seven or eight of us at the table chatting in Spanglish and contributing to the steady crescendo of the lunchroom raucous. Jacky Alvarez, the badass, freshman Mexicana of our group was a raconteur extraordinaire. As she unraveled her final denouement, we broke into table-slapping, feet-stomping, unabated laughter. The white girls' table launched the first hit: "SPICS!" Jacky's retort: "FUCK YOU, YOU PIECE OF WHITE SHIT." She stood up from our table, and we held her back. Then, five of the senior white girls stood on chairs and belted in unison, "Born in the USA, I was born in the USA, born in the USA, I was born in the USA." (I'm sure Springsteen's ironic intent was lost in their patriotic fervor). The *gringas* waved their hands up in the air and laughed. The leader of the group, Jenny, propelled her ice cream at Jacky. That was it—Jacky threw her chair aside, ran over to the table, and yanked Jenny down. We followed her lead—we had to—but only to restrain other girls who might engage in unfair fight tactics.

After about twenty seconds, brown, tan and white habits bobbed up and down the cafeteria isles. The nuns arrived five seconds before Jenny's demise. Jacky beat the *mierda* out of her. They were both suspended for three days: "Best three days I ever had," Jacky later proclaimed. The rumor travelled fast: Freshman Pummels Senior. I went back to the cafeteria to have lunch the following day, and not one of those *blancas* peeped. We were never pestered again. Admittedly, some of that badassness stuck with me. I walked the halls a little lighter, a little taller, a little more Jacky, and a little less me.

After four days in the hospital my great-aunt had already lost about five pounds. There was no update on her condition, and we figured the hospital was trying to milk Medicare. On the last day of her stay, my cousin, Ricardo, stopped by a Puerto Rican restaurant in Humboldt Park and smuggled some delightful delicacies into Leonor's room: arroz con gandules, amarillos, puerco frito, bacalaitos and empanadillas. If the stay at the hospital hadn't killed her by now, then certainly the deep-fried Borinquen cuisine wouldn't do her any harm. We fanned the smells out the window, and Leonor gleefully gobbled the food as quickly as her dentures would allow. No, it wasn't the Ecuadorian meal she had been craving, but it sufficed. She was released from the hospital shortly before dinner, just in time for us to head to Montrose Beach and order freshly made fritada con mote from the local vendors.

You owe it to yourself to visit
Queens Library's

Langston Hughes Community Library & Cultural Center

An oasis of knowledge and culture
Home of the

Black Heritage Reference Center of Queens County

(over 45,000 volumes of print and non-print
materials on the Black Experience)

Programs & Services

* **Children's Story Hours and Toddler Learning Center**
* **English Language Classes**
* **Adult Learning Classes**
* **Computer Classes**
* **Out-of-School-Time Homework Assistance Program**
* **Cultural Arts Program featuring artist exhibitions, author and poetry readings, creative writing workshops, film screenings, musical performances, two seasonal jazz brunches, annual Langston Hughes Celebration, Family Day and Kwanzaa Celebration**

**100-01 Northern Boulevard
Corona, New York 11368
(718) 651-1100 www.queenslibrary.org**

"Libraries will get you through times of no money
better than money will get you through times of no libraries."

Esmeralda Santiago ALWAYS A PUERTO RICAN

Talking candidly about feminism, cultural identity, class, and her family, Esmeralda Santiago admits that her literary success is attributed to her mother, the protagonist in her real life story that gave her the will and desire to succeed.

CONQUISTADORA IS AN HISTORICAL NOVEL that traces the life of a young Ana Larragoity Cubillas who, inspired by the adventures of her ancestors, travels from Spain to Puerto Rico. Ana confronts isolation, poverty, oppressive heat, disease and hard physical labor in Puerto Rico. As she faces each new challenge, Ana becomes stronger, and as she creates a place for herself on the island, she acquires a greater awareness and understanding of her true identity. Ana is a "conquistadora," a woman who overcomes obstacles in order to reach her goals, and like Ana, Esmeralda Santiago, who

(cont'd. pg. 94)

ESMERALDA SANTIAGO
Ida N. Torres

(cont'd from pg. 93)

immigrated from Puerto Rico to New York, from poverty to the ivory halls of Harvard, has found her place in American society and the literary world, creating a voice through characters that readers can believe in and ultimately see in themselves.

With the publication of her first book and memoir in 1993, *When I Was Puerto Rican*, Santiago's body of work chronicles her development into womanhood and the many challenges she faced and confronted in becoming the successful woman she is today.

She was born in Puerto Rico, the eldest of eleven children raised by a single mother. When Santiago was 13 years old, the family moved to Brooklyn, New York. Within two years, she learned enough English to be accepted into the prestigious Performing Arts High School. She spent eight years studying part-time at community colleges while working full-time until she was accepted as a transfer student to Harvard University with a full scholarship and received her Master's degree from Sarah Lawrence College. Upon graduating *magna cum laude* in 1976, she and Frank Cantor, her husband founded, CANTOMEDIA, a film and production company that has won numerous awards for excellence in documentary filmmaking.

Santiago's writing career evolved from her work as a writer of documentary and educational films. Class, gender, race, culture, poverty, education, family and the migratory experience are all factors that impacted her development and identity. In *When I was Puerto Rican*, Santiago narrates her childhood in the rural town of Macún in Toa Baja, Puerto Rico through her adolescent years in Brooklyn. In 1998, Santiago published her second memoir, *Almost A Woman*. Here, she depicts the loosening of family bonds as she travels from Brooklyn to Performing Arts High School in Manhattan where she trains to become an actress. *Almost a Woman* received numerous "Best of Year" mentions, in addition to an Alex Award from the American Library Association. It was adapted into a film for Exxon Mobil Masterpiece Theatre, which premiered nationally on PBS on September 14, 2002.

In her third memoir, *The Turkish Lover*, Santiago separates from her controlling mother and demanding family life to live with her lover, Ulvi Degan, who is 17 years her senior. Ulvi becomes increasingly controlling, and she begins to liberate herself from him when, at the age of 25, she applies to Harvard University and is accepted as a transfer student.

It was selected as a BookSense recommendation for September 2004 and appeared on several "Best of 2004" lists.

Besides her memoirs, Santiago has published two novels, *America's Dream* (1996) and *Conquistadora*. In *America's Dream,* the protagonist, América Gonzalez, is a housekeeper in a hotel in Puerto Rico when an opportunity arises to move to New York, and she leaves behind her alcoholic mother, abusive married lover and her rebellious teenage daughter. *America's Dream* was an Alternate Selection of the Literary Guild.

Santiago's recent book, *Conquistadora,* reads like an historical novel, where historical facts and the way of life in Puerto Rico during the 1800s become part of the story. Set mostly in Puerto Rico between 1844 and 1865, *Conquistadora,* the first of a planned trilogy, ends with Puerto Rico, Cuba and Brazil as the only colonies or countries yet to emancipate their slaves. In the novel, Ana, from an aristocratic Spanish family, is inspired by an ancestor, one of the earliest conquistadores, and inherits a struggling sugar plantation that relies on slave labor.

As in Santiago's memoirs, *Conquistadora* explores cultural identification, mother-daughter relationships and abusive relationships. Ana is a woman who makes unconventional decisions in order to reach her goals. She gives up her comfortable life in Spain to live and work in the underdeveloped countryside of Puerto Rico. The acquisition and development of the land takes precedence over her son whom she gives to his paternal grandparents after her husband dies.

Her essays and opinion pieces have appeared in national newspapers, including the *New York Times* and the *Boston Globe*, and in mass market magazines like *House & Garden, Metropolitan Home,* and *Good Housekeeping.* Santiago is also coeditor, with Joie Davidow, of the anthologies *Las Christmas: Favorite Latino Authors Share Their Holiday Memories* (1998); and *Las Mamis: Favorite Latino Authors Remember Their Mothers* (2001), both published by Knopf. She has done extensive work for victims of domestic violence, which includes the founding of a Youth Service Center and a shelter for battered women in Massachusetts. Santiago holds an Honorary Doctoral of Letters from Trinity College in Hartford Connecticut, Pace University in New York, and the University of Puerto Rico at Mayagüez. Currently, Santiago lives with her husband in the suburbs of Westchester County, 35 miles north of Manhattan. They summer in Maine ("my writing place," she says) and winter in Puerto Rico or "someplace warm." Their two grown children are professional musicians.

Santiago's stories, both personal and fictional, are about the struggles of women who move from one culture

to another and the many challenges they face in maintaining their identity and finding a path in life. The immigration experience, gender issues, race, education, family values, cultural values, and romantic relationships are all part of her stories. Esmeralda Santiago narrates the process of transformation and development of identity of her characters as strong women who struggle to live within the prescribed roles for women but whose actions often challenge traditional Puerto Rican cultural values.

℘ ℘ ℘

Amongst your literary work, you have three memoirs and two novels; your latest is an historical novel. Each one of these books is an exploration of your identity as a Puerto Rican and a woman. The theme of this issue of *phati'tude*, "¿What's in a Nombre? Writing Latin@ Identity in America," explores how Latinos or Hispanics see themselves and each other through literature and arts. The title of your first book, *When I Was Puerto Rican*, brings up the question, "What is a Puerto Rican?" What were you trying to convey about being Puerto Rican with this title?

Well, you cannot stop being who you are. The title actually is the single most frequently asked question about my work. Why is it past tense? It's really not about "being" but about what happens to us . . . not just Puerto Ricans but anybody who leaves home . . . the process of hybridization that takes place for someone who migrates from one culture and language group to another. So that is one of the reasons why it's in the past tense. I will never be as Puerto Rican as I was when I was living in Puerto Rico, a time when I didn't have any contact whatsoever with a foreign culture. But the minute you leave and another culture begins to enter yours, whether you travel to it or it travels to you, you begin to lose some of your cultural identity as you begin to adopt some of the culture that is coming into your world. That's part of the reason why the title is in the past tense.

The other reason is because of an experience I had that many migrants and immigrants experience, which is that after you leave, when you return, the people you left behind find you suspicious. For example, when I first returned to Puerto Rico, people would say things to me like, "You are no longer Puerto Rican," "You don't dress like a Puerto Rican," "You have a slight accent," and "Your Spanish is not as fluent," but when you look in the mirror, you look exactly the same to yourself. There is this other sense that you have changed even though you don't want to believe that you've changed. When these feelings come, you are shocked that you've become a different person in spite of every effort to remain exactly the same.

I think maybe it's our curse. When it comes to the culture, the people who never leave are very unhappy about the people who have left them behind. They will criticize you and make it very, very difficult for you. This not only happened to me in the mid-1970s, but it still happens to me today, and other immigrants as well. Let's say, a Dominican will tell me about going home after living in the United States for ten years, and when they return, their people are telling them they are no longer "Dominican." This process is continuous and invisible to you, but it's visible to the ones you've left behind.

> **"My mom . . . she passed on to all her daughters that we are equal in terms of our abilities, our intelligence, our ability to work, our visions, our imaginations, our dreams, our ambitions, all those things"**

Instead of making you a better person, this ordeal can make you into a different person in a negative way. Those kinds of issues, those kinds of questions, those kinds of scenarios, were part of my desire to begin a conversation about all of these things. So writing *When I Was Puerto Rican* was my attempt to get that discussion going. Naturally, at the time I didn't realize it was a global issue, I thought it was just a Puerto Rican issue but have since learned that this happens pretty much all over. If you leave your home, it's pretty hard to return as the person you "used to be."

Our identities are forged by our life experiences, the environment we encounter, and being Puerto Rican is complex because of the social, economic, and cultural factors that are complicated by the fact that Puerto Rico is a commonwealth of the United States. We are American citizens by law, but in some situations, we are not. When we come to the mainland and come in contact with mainstream American values, the conflicts get more complicated. When your mother brought you to New York when you were 13, which in of itself is a difficult age, what would you say were the biggest cultural and values conflicts you encountered?

I think for me the biggest issue was class. I was a *jíbaro*. We were a landless *jíbaro* family. I came from a rural part of Puerto Rico to the biggest city in the world, New York,

right smack in the middle of Brooklyn. For me, personally, learning the language was not as difficult as learning the culture, and learning how society is divided between the poor and rich, the whites and the blacks. What do you call yourself when you are a *jíbaro* in Brooklyn? That person doesn't exist here or does she? As a very curious, soul-searching kind of person, those were the kinds of things I was trying to figure out for myself.

I also felt the inequities between men and women. I was just entering adolescence and was beginning to understand these power issues. I lived with a woman who was both a mother and father to us, who worked just as hard as any man, who behaved with the freedoms that men had in the United States. Yet, she was also a woman who told her daughters to behave differently because she didn't want us to grow up to be like her. I found these ideas very challenging and found myself constantly going against

"Yes, definitely I think that writers whose ancestors are from Latin America have become a force in the publishing world."

the "status quo." I was trying to figure out and understand how I should behave, given those kind of rules that were running against my own ambitions. Yes, I was very ambitious and I was the kind of kid who had dreams for herself . . . in a sense, I was a visionary. I kept asking myself how do I fit in this new culture and these new friends, what is society telling me, and what am I learning at home? Those kinds of things I found emotionally exhausting, and it made things very challenging for me during my early and mid-adolescence years.

At the time you came to New York, the issue of class in Puerto Rico was more at the forefront than race. You came to New Your during the era of the Civil Rights and feminist movements, and when Mexicans and Puerto Ricans were struggling for access and equality in American society. You came to New York during a period of turmoil, especially around the issue of race. Did that make you more aware of your sense of identity in terms of color?

Yes, definitely I was very aware. If you look in the mirror, you have the awareness of who you are and what you look like outside of the mirror. Yes, I was very aware of that. I attended Performing Arts High School, and as I became

heavily involved in the arts, I found that race was not as challenging as class issues. For example, my very best friends were a Black Puerto Rican woman and an African American man. I accepted them for who they were, accepted them for their talent as musicians and artists. What I found challenging was gender and class issues . . . poverty. It was harder for me to be poor than to be dark-skinned because I didn't have access to the economic resources to do what I wanted to do in the arts. So, the concept of color was a little bit different, for me.

I think you are right. I arrived in New York at a time when these kinds of discussions were taking place, so I was extremely aware, and yes, while I suffered from prejudice and discrimination, for me it was more an issue of class, moving from being a *jíbaro* into something else. My desire to reach a certain economic level was not to get rich but to obtain the resources that I needed for art—that was always the focus for me. My mother never said to us, "because your skin is dark, colored, you are never going to be able to make it." She was more concerned about us doing our best, so we could obtain the resources we needed to succeed. This was the message I was getting. If you are born dark-skinned, you cannot become a white person—Michael Jackson tried that and failed tragically—but you shouldn't let your color get in the way. It doesn't matter if you are Indian, Asian, African or Latino *and* poor, you can still achieve certain things in life as long as you are willing and have the vision and desire to succeed.

Also, I have to add this: I don't think I'm a person who is easily offended when somebody says something that's humiliating. If someone says to me, "you stupid spic," well, I know I'm not stupid. You can call me stupid all you want but I'm not going to become "French" all of a sudden to make them happy because in the end, people have to deal with me the way I am. Let's just say I'm not easily offended by ignorant people, which is one of the reasons I've become the person I am today.

Your books would be considered feminist. The central characters are strong and resilient women. In your essay "First Born," found in *Las Mamis: Favorite Latino Authors Remember Their Mothers*, you also describe your mother in very vivid, colorful language. You describe her strengths and weaknesses and convey your mother's love for you. You refer to the strict disciplinarian measures she used, and you write, "I could not excuse it, but I forgave it. I forced myself to look beyond resentment to who she was when she and we were growing

up. And in looking at her life, I found lessons, chief among them: don't dwell in the past or you will drown in sorrow." (p.5) What other lessons did you learn from your mother?

It's really funny because I am living close to my mom again, and I get to see her often, and she still tells me what to do. One thing is certain, she is still a feminist thinker and believes that a woman can do anything a man is capable of. She passed on to all her daughters that we are equal in terms of our abilities, our intelligence, our ability to work, our visions, our imaginations, our dreams, our ambitions, all those things. When she was growing up, these were things that were allowed only to men. She told us, "You and your brothers are equal in my eyes, and all of you can become who you want to be, so long as you have ambition, vision and the willingness to work," something we have all shared and passed on to our children. This is why I believe there is absolutely no difference between men and women in terms of ambition and abilities.

Even today, my mother continues to talk to her grand-daughters and great granddaughters about relationships. "Don't stay in a bad relationship thinking that it's going to get better," she often says. And she should know, my mother had five husbands! Her thing was: If it didn't work out you just move on, the world is full of men. [Laughs] She said this to my daughter when she was thirteen, and my daughter went "Oh my God!" she couldn't believe her own grandmother was telling her this! My mother is always saying, "Live your life but don't get stuck in it. If you're stuck, get unstuck." If things were not working out in a particular way, my mother would try to change the situation, so she could have different outcomes. This advice has always been very, very helpful to me.

In *Almost a Woman*, you write: "Mami drilled into me that I had only one asset. I wasn't the prettiest of her six daughters, or the strongest of her children, but I was, she often said, intelligent. It was the power of the intelligence that I trusted" (p. 288). Intelligence was not a characteristic that was often attributed to girls; girls were more valued for their feminine assets and skills, a characteristic that many women do not recognize in themselves. How did being characterized as "intelligent" affect you?

That really was the biggest gift that my mother gave me, you know. Because the thing about being intelligent is that no one can take that away from you. They can call you names, they can torture you if they want to, they can do anything they want to you, but they cannot take away a quality or an ability of who you are because it is

innate. My mother was very clear about this. So as long as I used my intelligence, I could make it work for me. Things could happen for me regardless of what people might say or do. I think this is an amazing gift to give to your daughters. Instead of telling us how beautiful we are, because beauty often fades, my mother told her daughters they are intelligent, which is actually better. The older you get, the smarter you become, and then you get wise as an old woman. She gave me the biggest gift that I could ever receive.

In the *Turkish Lover* you describe a scene where you are walking on Harvard Square, and you say "I belong here." Your higher education experience can be considered nontraditional for a woman, especially a Puerto Rican woman from Brooklyn. You attended Manhattan Community College, transferred to Harvard at 25 years old, at a time when Harvard was just beginning to admit women. What made you so sure that you belonged in Harvard? What impact did the Harvard experience have on your life?

It changed my life. From the moment I arrived, I felt that I belonged there, I wanted to be there, and was happy that I did what I could to make it happen. I think it's a question of recognizing that very often we are stopped by our fears. I could have very easily remained in the same place and continued to be terrified by my surroundings, so terrified that I could have said "I am not even going to try." Even when I did get to Harvard, I could have easily given up and failed. But, when you have a sense of yourself, your ambitions, your desires and your abilities, this is what gets you through.

I have become very involved with women's issues and women's groups in New York, and one of the things I realized is that we defeat ourselves. That was one of the things I did not want to do. In a fair fight, if somebody else defeats me, I will accept defeat, but I will not defeat myself. I will not sabotage myself.

When I look back on my experiences at Harvard, I am so thrilled to have been there. When I read my journals from those times I find that I was upset a lot and cried often. I often faced a lot of humiliation, and there were moments when I just wanted to give up, but I didn't. At the time I thought, "I don't want to leave this place because it's someone else who wants me to leave." My attitude back then, as it is now, is they are going to have to deal with me. I always tried to use my own intelligence, rather than have other people use it. I think this attitude has helped me a lot.

As the oldest of eleven children, you were expected to be a role model, take care of them, and negotiate your place in the family with your siblings. Did this help or hinder your development?

I think it has both helped me and held me back. I can only describe it like dominoes that are lined up; if one falls, they all fall. That was the terror that my mother instilled in me. If you make a false step we all fail. It was really hard for me at times, and I was often afraid something bad would happen. I had to be really organized, have a plan "A," plan "B," and plan "C" on hand just in case, which helped me a

> ## "I don't introduce myself as 'Hi, I am Esmeralda. I'm a Puerto Rican / Black Latina / Black /woman writer.' I think these labels are imposed by other people, not by me."

lot. In terms of it having a negative impact, there was a lot of pressure on me from when I was a little kid. I was a very sensitive little girl, but I couldn't express it. I didn't cry easily. I wouldn't show my weaknesses because if I was weak everyone else would see I was weak. I was the kind of person that had to pull back her emotions because it allowed everyone else to have *los nervios*. To this day, everybody in my family can fall apart except "Negi." This is the attitude that is in our household. In my family, if I fall apart, they say we have to shore her up before we can get better. So that was the pressure, but strangely, it was also a comfort.

You have written three memoirs. How does your family feel about you telling their life story along with yours?

They have all been very supportive in every single way. Generous not only in their gratitude but in their celebration of the work I have done. This is especially true when I published my first book because there were things my family would have preferred I didn't write about. But to their credit, they let me do what I felt I had to do. They gave me the strength to continue to do it after the first one. Let me put it this way: If they had been negative after I published *When I Was Puerto Rican,* it's almost certain there wouldn't have been an *Almost A Woman,* and other memoirs, because I care about them and I wouldn't do anything to hurt them.

I am lucky. My family has been nothing but generous, welcoming, and celebratory. They have never said, "You shouldn't have done this," or "You said something that's

a lie." There might be some slight disagreement in the way a certain incident is perceived, but in terms of the big picture, they have been nothing but generous.

Your latest book, *Conquistadora,* is an historical novel. What inspired you to write this book?

I wanted to explore Puerto Rican history and my Puerto Rican ancestry. But I didn't want to do it like ancestry.com, listing a bunch of names and statistics. I was interested in how people lived and the history of their times. I wanted to learn more of what it might have been like for my great grandmother and great grandfather, or great aunts and uncles. That's really how this book began. I didn't set out to write an historical novel. I set out to find out more about the people I descended from and found a way to express it.

Would you say your books allow you to hold on to your sense of being Puerto Rican? Do the books keep on affirming your identity?

I don't have to hold on to who I am. I am Puerto Rican. I don't write for that reason. I write because I am a creative person, an imaginative person, and this is what I have chosen to do with my life. You could say that trying to learn more about my ancestors is a way of holding on to my Puerto Rican ancestors, but it's also the curiosity of someone who is at a certain stage in her life who knows that more of my life is behind me than ahead of me.

When you get to a certain age, you begin to look back beyond yourself. I did that with the memoirs, but it's much easier when you're writing a novel. When you write this kind of book, you're looking beyond your experiences into the experiences of the people who came before you and who made it possible for you to become the person that you are today. That includes, yes of course, Puerto Ricans, but it also includes Corsicans, Canarios, Asturianos, and in my case Catalanos, Bascos, Indios, and Africans. For me, my historical novel is my gift to my ancestors and to thank them for making it possible for me to become the person that I am today.

Would you consider yourself an American writer or a Latina writer?

I consider myself a Latina writer because I am a Latina. I am very specific that I am actually a Puerto Rican Latina. I don't introduce myself as "Hi, I am Esmeralda. I'm a Puerto Rican / Black Latina / Black / woman writer." I think these labels are imposed by other people, not by me. When someone asks me where I'm from, I say Puerto Rico. It's okay if people want to do it, but I'm not going to spend my emotional energy arguing about it because I made the

decision long ago it's not how I want to spend my creative time. You can call me whatever you want.

Today, the literary scene is very different from when you began publishing. Today, we have other Latinos: Mexicans, Dominicans, Cubans, and Central and South Americans, who are publishing. Do you think that Latino/Puerto Rican literature has found a place in the American literary tradition?

Yes, definitely I think that writers whose ancestors are from Latin America are becoming a force in the publishing world. Unfortunately, it's come at a time when publishing is changing very, very rapidly. So traditional publishers are completely baffled, and they are just as confused as everyone else with all this new technology, making it harder for anyone, regardless of culture, to find a spot in whatever is left of "traditional" publishing. But having said that, publishing has opened up for anyone that can blog, self-publish, use print-on-demand, and other kinds of possibilities we didn't have fifteen years ago. Even with all of this confusion, a good writer will always find an audience. It may be more difficult because there are more writers searching for an audience, but I think there are many more opportunities for us to express ourselves in the literary arts, and it's just a question of how we envision ourselves as writers. Do I call myself a writer because I'm a blogger that writes and publishes every single day, where people are reading my work and responding to it? I think the concept of being a "writer" has evolved dramatically and has become an individual and personal self-descriptor.

You recently had a health issue that affected your use of language. How has that affected you?

My stroke. It made me aware of how frail life is. We have to seize the day. Physically do what you need to do. Don't dream about something: just go out there and do it. I'm out there trying to write three books at once because you never know what may happen. It has made the time issue very present for me, and has made me very aware of my health. I've become healthier as a result of having had a stroke, and it has made me very aware of how I eat, and I exercise to keep my weight down. The people I see around me, my sisters and my mother, suffer from high blood pressure, diabetes, and other health problems that are related to life style, and so I have changed my life, so I can live longer and continue to write books, because I still have stories to tell and share with others. ▢

IDA N. TORRES has a B.S. degree from City University of New York and an Ed.D. from Teachers College, Columbia University. She is an educator that focuses on the adult learner.

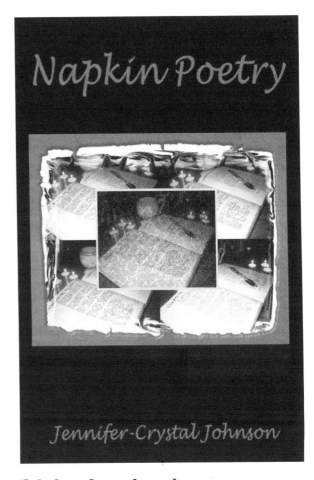

As the first Latino author to win the coveted Pulitzer Prize, with extraordinary insight and wit, Oscar Hijuelos engages in a frank conversation about the Cuban American experience, his books, and the unique challenges Latino writers face in America's publishing industry.

THE WAYS IN WHICH CUBAN AMERICANS have been able to keep a living memory of Cuba while developing and thriving in America are both intriguing and complicated. What's even more interesting is that Cuban American literature experienced a "boom" during the 1990s and, consequently, some of its writers have risen to national and even international prominence. Oscar Hijuelos, whose work has been noted for his rich, detailed descriptions of Cuban American life, is one of those writers.

(cont'd. pg. 102)

OSCAR HIJUELOS
Gabrielle David

(cont'd from pg. 100)

Hijuelos, whose parents emigrated to the United States during the 1940s, was born and raised in West Harlem, New York. As a young child, he suffered from acute nephritis after a vacation trip to Cuba with his mother and brother, that necessitated a year-long stay in St. Luke's Convalescent Hospital in Connecticut. This essentially took him from the language and the people he loved, an incident that would greatly impact his life and his books.

From a young age, music played a large role in Hijuelos' life. At about the age of 12, he began playing instruments, such as the guitar and even explored the violin and piano. However, his early music appreciation of classical music, jazz, and rock 'n' roll, did not include the Latin music genres that would later infuse his writing and make him famous.

Because he didn't have many books at his disposal, Hijuelos' reading came mostly from whatever he was given at school. This led to frequent trips to the library on 125th Street and many secondhand book shops, where he read anything he could get his hands on—from Huckleberry Finn to Tarzan.

After graduating from high school, Hijuelos eventually matriculated into City College of New York and studied writing under Donald Barthelme (who became a life-long mentor and friend), Susan Sontag, William S. Burroughs, Frederic Tuten, and others, receiving both his bachelor's and master's degrees. While in college, Hijuelos discovered a vast range of writers, and was especially taken with Mark Twain, Ernest Hemingway, Jorge Luis Borges, and Anton Chekov.

Hijuelos honed his craft while working full-time in an assortment of jobs, including advertising. By 1978, a short story he had published in *Persea* magazine, "Columbus Discovering America," received an outstanding writer citation from Pushcart Press. This exposure led to an Oscar Cintas fiction writing grant and, in 1980, a Breadloaf Writers Conference scholarship. Hijuelos also received grants from the Creative Artists Programs Service in 1982 and the Ingram Merrill Foundation in 1983. He published his first novel, *Our House in the Last World* (1983), which follows the life of a Cuban family in the United States during the 1940s. In the coming decade he went on to win several awards, including the American Academy of Arts and Letters' Rome Prize, a fellowship from the National Endowment for the Arts, and a Guggenheim Foundation grant in the category of fiction.

It was Hijuelos' second novel, *Mambo Kings Play Songs of Love* (1989), that put his name on the map. Set in the 1950s, *Mambo Kings* is a bittersweet exploration of the lives of two Cuban-born brothers and their journey from Havana to New York where they start a mambo orchestra. Described by critics as lyrical and exhilarating, Hijuelos won the Pulitzer Prize for fiction, becoming the first U.S. Latino author to do so. *Mambo Kings,* which was also nominated for a National Book Critics Circle Award in 1989, as well as the National Book Award, was made into a movie starring Antonio Banderas and Armand Assante. In 2005, Hijuelos adapted the novel for the stage. Unfortunately, while it played in San Francisco, it did not make it to Broadway.

The Fourteen Sisters of Emilio Montez O'Brien (1993), Hijuelos's third novel, focuses on a family dynamic that is dominated by femininity, where the maternal and sexual presence of femaleness overwhelms the household. *Mr. Ives' Christmas* (1995) has been referred to by critics as his most spiritual work. The title character was adopted as a young child and has few cultural roots, though Hijuelos implies that Ives is Hispanic, as he is drawn time and again to New York's Latino community. In 1999, Hijuelos struck a balance between his Cuban roots and his interest in American society in general with the novel *Empress of the Splendid Season*. For his sixth novel, Hijuelos brings music back to the fore in *A Simple Habana Melody: From When the World was Good* (2002). Like *Mambo Kings, A Simple Habana Melody* inhabits the fine-tuned world of working musicians with the story of Israel Levis, a Cuban composer whose 1928 Rumba composition, "Rosas Puras," or "Pretty Roses," takes Europe and America by storm.

Along the way, Hijuelos put out a CD and published a young adult novel. *Stranger Than Fiction* by Don't Quit Your Day Job Records, is a playful double-CD collection of 32 songs that features authors (such as such as Dave Barry, Matt Groening, Ken Follett, Molly Ivins, and Stephen King) playing and singing music. Recorded in 1998, Hijuelos performed lead vocal and guitar on the track named "I Want to Eat," with harmony vocal by Lori Marie Carlson and Ed Baker on keyboards. Proceeds from the CD are donated to the PEN Writers Special Fund and other charities chosen by the authors. Hijuelos took another detour and published *Dark Dude* (2008), a young adult novel that follows the adventures of Rico, a fair-skinned Cuban boy from New York City who never seems to fit in with his darker-skinned inner city peers.

In 2010, Hijuelos published *Beautiful María,* a retelling of the *Mambo Kings* story through the eyes of María García y Cifuentes, "the lady behind a famous song." After publishing eight novels, Hijuelos published his memoir, *Thoughts Without Cigarettes* (2011), which while introducing readers to the colorful circumstances of his upbringing, reveals his struggle to merge his Cuban and American identities. What's

interesting is that in each of his novels, Hijuelos has woven biographical events into some of his characters, so *Thoughts Without Cigarettes* seems like a natural progression that exposes readers to the "man behind the curtain."

Known and admired around the world, Hijuelos' works have been translated into 25 languages. He was honored at the Kennedy Center in Washington, D.C. in 2000 as part of the National Hispanic Heritage Awards, and in 2003 was the first recipient of the first Luis Leal Award for Distinction in Chicano/Latino Literature. In 2011, he was selected as a fellow at the American Academy of Arts and Sciences (AAAS), an independent research center that conducts multidisciplinary studies of complex and emerging problems. Hijuelos is currently teaching creative writing at Duke University in Durham, North Carolina, where his wife, writer, editor and translator, Lori Carlson-Hijuelos, also teaches.

One of the leading Cuban American writers working today, Oscar Hijuelos continues to depict the Latino experience in his work. The theme of separation and isolation, especially from family, saturates Hijuelos' novels. He has previously stated his disappointment about a U.S. literary establishment "that still typecasts Latino writers, still leaves us out of the discussion. I mean, I love Jonathan Franzen and Michael Chabon, too—but our books are as American as theirs." In this interview, with the delicious wit of Oscar Wilde, Hijuelos shares his thoughts on the Cuban American experience, U.S. Latino literature, and his place in the American literary scene.

∅ ∅ ∅

You've been classified as an immigrant writer, and it seems that most reviewers speak of you either as a Cuban American writer, a Latino writer, or a Hispanic writer. Since the theme of this issue is "¿What is a Nombre?" what's you____ on the whole Latino/ Hispanic label? Do you find these ethnic designations unfair or too narrow?

As far as I am concerned, Latino writers are definitely considered a sub-species, separate onto itself, as far as mainstream American Literature is concerned. Though we share many cultural attributes and linguistic similarities, we are by no means taken as seriously by the literary powers that be as are many of our peers of differing ethnic and social/economic backgrounds. We are to American literature as Samoa is to the mainland—we are defined as hyphen-American writers, whose work is considered (as I have seen over the years) quaint, exotic, colorful, vibrant, heartfelt, and-down-to-earth, but hardly ever "literary" in the good old Fitzgerald/Cheever/Vonnegut/Franzen sense; another term

usually applied to those of us who have written about our roots is that of "immigrant," which, while true, in most cases doesn't begin to convey the complexities of what I would call the REST OF THE STORY. . .

I know this first-hand. For example, my third novel, *The Fourteen Sisters of Emilio Montez O'Brien* (1992), was a pastoral and diverse portrait of three generations of Cubans, and though the notion is dated now (except among old school cinephiles), I structured its frame around a "Hollywood" movie of the late 1930s, *Sullivan's Travels*, a film about a coddled movie director, played by the actor Joel McCrea , who hits the road to find the real depression-era America. Intending to plant at least a few hints about this in the narrative—well, to hit people over the head—my main character, Emilio, looks almost exactly like Joel McCrea, to the point that when they actually meet at a party in "Hollywood," sometime in the 1950s, the real McCrea says to Emilio something like, "Hey, you could be my twin." The book is also filled other allusions to *Sullivan's Travels,* too many to relate (or remember) right now, but the upshot is that, while a number of European reviewers picked up on that allusion and saw that the book had many different sides to it, not a single stateside reviewer did, seeing the book only through the distortions of that catch-word lens or perception of us: "we-speaky-good-enough-English-writers" to write books about our number one (I mean *"numero uno"*) concern—our IMMIGRANT ROOTS, to the point that the REST OF THE STORY is ignored, overlooked, maybe not even absorbed at all.

Since you've pushed that button, and since I'm on the subject of *Fourteen Sisters,* I will tell you two more things about the way it was received here in the States that set off little bells in my head. I wrote most of that book, some six hundred printed pages long, while doing my best to utilize a female-oriented vocabulary (or what I considered as such), of words that sounded "feminine" and sentences that rippled with curvaceous language, soft vowels, delicate constructions and syntax, in the kind of literary sleight of hand and pastiche that I would not have the patience or ambition for today. Needless to say that aspect of the book was ignored, as was the fact that at its core is a narrative about an Irishman, a photographer, who travels to Cuba in the late 19th century and gets caught up in the Spanish-American war—a long section, one of the hearts of the book, that I did a lot of research for and which, nevertheless, was never mentioned by any of the reviewers. (On the other hand, around the same time, a much slimmer kind of portraiture about the same war, strung out over several hundred pages, with just little dabs of local Cuban color thrown in from time to time, by Elmore Leonard—not to pick on him, he is great at what he does—was greeted as an historical novel of the first

magnitude, or the second coming of Christ.) I have since supposed that my book might have been perceived differently were my name not "Hijuelos:": possibly, were I an Updike or, these days, a Franzen (among so many non-Latino others) that novel might have been perceived through the literary genius detecting microscope that is rarely pulled out when it comes to Latinos.

Well, since I'm starting to ramble, though I could, I won't go on—but you get the drift.

Your parents emigrated to the U.S. during the 1940s, making you a first generation Cuban American, well before Castro and the Revolution. Coupled with the fact that you lived in Harlem, I would imagine that you

> **"We are our history, and for a lot of Cuban Americans, the story of their life in this country seems always to have been told in the light of what was left behind/what could have been and, in fact, the truly beautiful sense of nature and culture that they will never know in its purest form."**

did not grow up with the expat attitudes that typically exist among Cuban Americans. In that regard, are you able to connect to the Cuban American community and its politics? And how does this relationship affect your writing?

First of all, I love just about every Cuban I've ever met, but I absolutely hate the question. It's far too complicated a subject to ask a writer to honestly address, particularly through this impersonal venue. But here, I will briefly try: Indeed, I grew up in New York City, during the 1960s, when every kind of anti-war, pro-civil-rights, down with the system, hurray for Che Guevara sentiment was in the air; at the same time, I was deeply aware that we had a lot of family down in Cuba suffering because of the revolution. So I grew up with two sets of ears, as it were—one attuned to the pro-Castro, the other to the anti-Castro sentiments that were quite polarizing in those days, possibly more so than today. But I've always tried to be fair-minded and balanced about those issues/polarities in my books, something that some Cubans haven't always appreciated. Or to put it differently, for super-leftists (usually non-Cuban armchair socialists),

I am never left-wing enough; while for the right-wingers, among the Miami community for example, my work has never been anti-Castro enough. Having seen/heard both sides, I have walked my own path: while I once turned down writing pamphlets for a very prominent anti-Castro organization in Miami, I have also turned down invitations to visit Cuba, years ago, from the government—I just didn't want to be used by either extreme; by any measure, I am a moderate, even a progressive, when it comes to Cuban politics. Just that alone would have made me quite unpopular in Miami were it not for the fact that, with Cubans—at least the ones I've gotten to know—their sense of pride over my accomplishments (for, to this day, I can still pack the house at Mitch Kaplan's Books & Books in Coral Gables) has made them forgive whatever faults and shortcomings they find in my way of thinking and politics. Or, as some nice old *abuela* once told me, "Don't worry, we know that you grew up in New York, but we still love you anyway, *paisano*."

One of the things that tires scholars of Cuban American letters is the fact that much of it is dominated by the metaphor of nostalgia (yes, the "nostalgia" word!). Do you believe this to be true and do you think there will ever be a time when being Cuban is looked at in a different light? Can Cuban American literature as a whole move beyond Castro and talk about other things?

Yes, that's true to a certain extent, there's even a joke about it that goes: "How many Cubans does it take to screw in a lightbulb?"—the answer being, "Six, one to screw it in, and five to talk about how the light used to be much nicer in Cuba." Yes, it's a problem, or has been a problem with a certain generation of Cuban American writers—but how could they/we/I help it? We are our history, and for a lot of Cuban Americans, the story of their life in this country seems always to have been told in the light of what was left behind/what could have been and, in fact, the truly beautiful sense of nature and culture that they will never know in its purest form. But, it doesn't particularly have to do with the revolution: my own father, who came to the states in the 1940s, missed the hell out of Cuba—a feeling that only intensified when it became politically/legally impossible for him or my mother ever to go back there; though I had visited Cuba in the 1950s, I didn't return until 2002—and what is true of my story is also the same with countless stateside Cubans of a certain generation. And while it may be a tired story to some (unlike the perennially told stories of dysfunctional upper income households) it was the story that many of us have been given: but to say that it is the only thing we can write about is pure rubbish, particularly given the new generation

of writers who have achieved a certain distance from that nostalgia thing, like the poet Adrian Castro out of Miami, who, while writing a hip-hoppy musically charged celebration of his Cuban roots, veers into contemplations about what it is like to be a young Latino/Cubano today.

No, all kinds of stuff is out there, and if it's not been out there it's because publishers have only wanted that from Cuban American writers—from my own experience I know that whenever I've attempted to write about new "non-Cuban" subjects, editors don't know what to make of it—or to put it differently, whenever "me no talkee *tan mucho* about *arroz con pollo*" in a certain work, I'm told that it doesn't sound like me: or to translate it into English: when it comes

Oscar Hijuelos teaching at Duke University in Durham, North Carolina. Photo: Megan Morr

to Cuban American (and I think Latino) writers in general, our work continues to exist in some literary colony, a sugar mill which is only occasionally checked on by the masters to make sure we're still breathing.

Still, I remain optimistic for the future. Hey, when the current vogues for the same kinds of stories by Asian/Eastern European/Indian writers has played out, a new generation of critics and scholars, bored with them, may well turn back to us.

To what do you attribute your passion for writing novels, and by the way, since you recorded an album, I think it's fair to ask if you have ever written or published any poetry, or are considering it? You seem like a guy who will try something at least once!

Oh yeah, I'll try anything at least once; the problem with being that sort of guy is that, when I first started to write, I became inexplicably (or "inner-spickily") enchanted with the notion of becoming good at something; it was like falling in love with a vision of a new me. The fact that I came from a

bookless household with, however, a rather poetic/creative mother, seems to have given me the mistakenly romantic notion that writing novels, which seems to have always been the form I've focused on, would be the stuff of dreams, rather than the fruit of much hard labor, particularly since I go out of my way to write correct sentences, avoid clichés, and plumb the depths of my soul, which, very few critics seems to notice. Having said that, I think literature, in its purest form—that is to say, the stuff that is somehow articulated from the heart and not written for the marketplace—is one of the last vestiges of a far more pensive, less noisy age. Think it was Paul Auster who said that writers are akin to 16th century Benedictine Monks, but that was 20 years ago before the current gadget in your face age—I can't imagine what he's thinking now.

As for an album? No, I only recorded one (I thought) half-witty tune that had nothing to do with my "Latino-ness," for a CD that was intended, or so I thought, to raise money for First Amendment rights.

And in a way, I have written poetry, if you count *Beautiful Maria of My Soul;* but you are right, perhaps that is something I should try one day.

Were you surprised about *Mambo Kings?* I remember that time . . . it seemed to explode into America's culture and consciousness, both the book and the movie. Did you anticipate or expect it, you know, did you have that writers' moment when you said to yourself this is a blockbuster and an award-winning book? Or did it come as a complete surprise? To what do you attribute to its success?

You have to remember that when I published *The Mambo Kings Play Songs of Love,* nobody, but nobody, in the New York mainstream press published homegrown Latino authors. As far as the American public was concerned, Latino writing had to do with the likes of Carlos Fuentes, [Gabriel] Garcia Márquez, Mario Vargas Llosa—the boom writers. We homegrown guys were largely overlooked, except by smaller regional presses. I'm talking about the likes of Rudy Anaya, for example, writers fighting the good fight but unknown to the greater American public. In my case, I had zero expectations for *Mambo Kings,* despite the fact that I knew it was a hell of a book, and quite original—and while my publisher, FSG—believed in it and were very kind to me, they, too, had no expectations. But, when the book came out, even in pre-pub-stage, enormous amounts of attention were heaped upon it, and even the *New York Times Sunday Review,* which rarely reviews Latino books now, gave it a front page rave. Of course, I was surprised, and while I can't begin to convey the complexity of that experience, I will say that to have authored

a book that seemed to have made a difference, in the way that publishers regarded Latino authors or opened doors to others, made me feel quite proud, as did the fact that it was published and well-received internationally.

Of course, its success was owed to its crossover atmosphere—its *I Love Lucy* meets the Cuban mambo—but it was also a sexy and interesting book in other ways, in terms of language. I have days when I pick it up and can't figure out how on earth I came up with parts of the novel—in other words, the fact that it had literary chops helped spread its popularity.

One thing I do know: it was the right book to come out at the right time, and while it had a real impact back then, I sometimes wonder if, given the plastic nature of current literature, it would have been published at all now.

What was it like to win the Pulitzer Prize? It was almost 20 years before another Latino took home the prize (Junot Diaz). Do you think this says something about the state of publishing? Or do you think Latino-themed books appeal to a much smaller audience, making it impossible for Latino literature to become fully mainstream?

My Pulitzer was a matter of luck: believe me, I know, given how rare it is for the prize committees to take Latino books seriously. I'm proud of my Pulitzer and happy for Junot, but it hasn't worked out when you figure in the percentages for Latino authors in general: we who speaketh in the lingo of the *barrio* or the *campo* and in the tongue of our immigrant mothers and fathers in the lit department; and we REMAIN objects of curiosity, And while I have always taken pride in my Pulitzer, I feel that all the progress that was made has been rescinded—poor Latino book sales are partly responsible—we just don't turn out for each other the way African American folks do for their authors (on the other hand, we are in so many sub-groups that solidarity is harder to achieve). Yet our work is also sluffed off to the side by the mainstream because of "socialogical" attitudes—another kind of ghetto; as if the issues that affect Latinos, personally and in terms of society, aren't really applicable to all Americans. Or to put it differently, "Yes Virginia, there is a subtle form of PREJUDICE at work, at almost every level of society." (I mean among the literary snobs of the establishment, as well as in the rest of the country: to wit, Arizona, where the Tuscon Public School system has banned a great number of books by Latino authors from their curriculum.)

But to reiterate: yes, we are viewed with a certain kind of caution and from a distance; we may have our own sections in bookstores (at least when they existed) under the heading of LATINO literature, but it's a rare thing to hear Latino authors included in any discussions of serious contemporary American literature. Twenty years ago, it was all about Mailer, Bellow, Updike, Cheever; now it's Franzen, Foer, Lethem; and while a bone is thrown our way occasionally—to wit Junot Diaz's success (and Pulitzer) and, to a lesser degree, with new lights like Justin Torres, whose main sense of identity has to do with his sexuality rather than his roots, most publishers haven't the slightest idea what to do with us. Part of that problem is ignorance—and the whole "sociology" cloud that hangs over Latino lit, as well as the fact that Latino writers are broken up into so

> **"My Pulitzer was a matter of luck: believe me, I know, given how rare it is for the prize committees to take Latino books seriously."**

many sub-groups—Puerto Rican, Dominican, Cuban, and Chicano (Mexican-American), etc.—so the audience is fragmented. Though a writer like Junot Diaz, whose books really appeals to young folks will, I think, continue to thrive, though I have once to hear him included in any discussions of American literature.

You've written eight novels thus far, but your latest book, *Thoughts Without Cigarettes,* is a memoir. Why the departure from novels and what would you say was your biggest challenge writing it?

Goodness, getting everything straight—or trying to remember, as best one can, how things seem to have happened—you do know that, after a certain point, unless you're the sort to keep meticulous journals, like say the late Reynolds Price, it's really difficult to get things right, particularly given the ever-widening amounts of time that have passed. In fact, if I had tried to write this memoir twenty years ago, I'm sure I would have made entirely different choices and had far more accurate memories—but I did the best that I could at the time.

As for my motivation? Oh, I've read once too often about some confused notions about my life: one of them had it that I had been raised in an upper middle class environment—it's even in a book—*From Bomba to Hip Hop*, by Juan Flores. What cracked me up is that the author seems to have confused me with some other Hijuelos whose father did not drop dead when he was seventeen, and who did not attend Brandeis High School and the CUNY system, and who did not come up without as much

as an inkling about how the world worked. (Wish the guy had bothered to actually talk to me instead of jumping to conclusions but, who knows, he probably got his info off the internet—like other folks who have written about me.) Having said this, I wanted to give a more accurate impression of my upbringing, though I could have approached the same sort of materials from many different perspectives—I just happened to chose one.

You also wrote *Dark Dude*, a book for teens. There were parts of *Dark Dude* that were clearly autobiographical, something one often finds in most of your books, that one character that's really Oscar. What was your intention, to appeal to Latino teens or raise awareness about Latino teens to a general audience? Any plans in the works to publish more teen books?

Uh, *Dark Dude* was sketchily autobiographical: but far more so in the outtakes, which the editor, the wonderful Caitlyn Dlouhy of Atheneum Books, found too "adult" in tone and language. In fact, the household and a few of the events in the books have parallels to what I went through, though the main character, the *Dark Dude*, Rico, is a far more pensive kid than I was at his age: but take the title—indeed I heard some blacks refer to me as a "dark dude" on account of my white skin—reverse thinking, yes?—and though that happened more than thirty years

> "So I agree that my writing provided me with the means—the mask, as it were—to approach and re-enter that side of my identity that is both language-driven and emotionally Cuban."

ago, it remained with me ever since; I also played down the race thing in my neighborhood, which was quite strong; that is, if someone got mugged on the street at night, or stabbed in the gut, chances were that it was predicated by race—I mean that although the civil rights thing had just happened, New York in the 1960s was still a city of neighborhoods—some rich, some middle class, but a lot of them filled with pissed-off-at-life kids of all races who found any perceived slight a reason to hassle you to death: all that was played down in the book.

As for your second question within a question: Not ever having been a typical Latino, I wrote this book for other kids,

both Latino and not, who might feel a bit different from their peers and friends. My point being that Latinos come in many shapes, shades, and backgrounds, though a lot of that direct messaging was also left on the cutting room floor. But, yes, I intended it for Latino teens, though I will tell you that it was a rough thing for me, bald, in my fifties, fair skinned and all, to be on tour and addressing a room of gangbangers from East L.A., to whom the Dark Dude's trauma's and scuffles with life seemed pithy in comparison to their own (much harder) experiences. But you do what you can do, *verdad?*

And yes, I'm thinking about another book as a YA—it's been on the boards for a while, I'm just trying to get something else going on the adult side.

You once said in the *New York Times* (1993) that you considered yourself a, "New York writer of Cuban parentage, with different influences," and that your, "background is an important element, the most important, but not the only one." Since then, your work continues to paint vivid portraits of Cuban American life in the U.S. What is "not the only one" you were referring to, perhaps a novel without Cuban American characters (if that is at all possible)? But even if one could entertain that notion, wouldn't this be difficult since writers generally write about what they know and the work comes from who they are?

My remark to the *New York Times*, which I do not particularly remember, probably came in response to the number of times I'd heard, "You sure don't seem Cuban," or, "You're not like any Cubans I know." My response about "different influences," then, must have been about my cosmopolitan upbringing in New York City, my interest in art and music, and that inward little world that somehow exists apart from one's roots. I love jazz, for example, and not just Afro-Cuban jazz, but everything from Jelly Roll Morton to Duke Ellington and Bill Evans: or to put it differently, the merengue is not always in my step, nor am I always ready to sing "Guantanamera" at a moment's notice. I have an interest in antiquity, in archeology, in aesthetics in general: I love music, both Bach and Chucho Valdés—so I guess what I meant to say is that yes, if you prick me I will bleed—yes, I am a human, with more than one side to him

I've read that you felt that you grew up linguistically and psychologically disconnected from your Latino heritage because you didn't speak fluent Spanish and that you are a "white" Cuban. What impact did this have on your growing up, and has writing

the type of stories you have written over the years helped you reconnect to your cultural roots?

Excuse me, but I think you should mention that I spent a year in a hospital, away from my family, as a four or five-year-old kid; that alone should have messed me up in terms of my sense of self, but to have the image/identity thing further complicated by the fact that I've never looked Latino—which really counts for something on both ends of the spectrum—I should have ended up in a loony bin instead of becoming the suave, infinitely self-composed

> " One of my mantras is that just because a book is successful commercially, or famous, or has won prizes, doesn't necessarily mean that it's good."

writer I am today. By the way, a lot of the Cubans I've known were also whiter than not, though I have cousins who are quite black—so it's always been a mix. Growing up I always felt like a spy, eavesdropping on what some "whiteys" feel about "spics" and, around Latinos I did not know, finding out what some very pissed off Latinos felt about "whiteys"—it was sobering to tell you the least. Yet, what it comes down to is not only skin, but the language thing—at least when I was growing up, my outsider-ness, as it were, was imposed on me. It was nothing that I asked for—surely not the year away from home—and yet, I have been lucky to have transformed those sad energies and circumstances into something compensational. So I agree that my writing provided me with the means—the mask, as it were—to approach and re-enter that side of my identity that is both language-driven and emotionally Cuban. As for my Spanish, I can get along with it, though I wish that as a child and teen I had been pushed, or had forced myself, to study it—even in school, something which never happened.

I found *The Fourteen Sisters of Emilio Montez O'Brien* particularly daring and brave because you wrote this book from a woman's perspective and, in fact, your narrative was once described as "male celebration of femininity." You have always had strong female characters in your books and, clearly, not only do they come from the heart, you are very mindful of them. How are you able to put your "machismo" aside to create these very real, poignant, yet powerful women? Where do these

characters come from? And as a result, do you think you've developed a special relationship with your women readers?

I mentioned something about *Fourteen Sisters* in one of my earlier response, but to answer your question, I wrote that book feeling a counter energy to *Mambo Kings,* and indeed, I did grow up around some very wonderful and powerful women. My relatives and my mother's coterie of friends, Cubans and Puerto Ricans and Dominicans, were ladies whom I rather adored because they were so kind to me. In addition, my father grew up on a farm in Cuba with eight sisters—on some level, I think just that knowledge empowered me to write about women, and I hope I did a good job. As for your query about building a fan base among my female readers—I really don't know. I do recall that readings for that book were mostly packed with women, but at readings for my subsequent books, it has always been a mix of men and women.

After being strictly a "professional writer" for years (after leaving advertising), what made you decide to teach? And being the consummate New Yorker, how did you land at Duke? How has it affected your life and your writing?

First of all, I left my private sector job, involving ads with subways, busses, trains, and airports, back in 1984. Not long after, I learned that my first novel, *Our House in the Last World,* had me in the running for a Rome Prize in literature—which I accepted, going off to live in Italy for almost two years—the beginning of a somewhat different (and far more fantastic) life than I had known. After that, from about 1986 until 2008, I had managed to survive off of my writing, though here and there were a few teaching stints—mainly Hofstra University for a year (1989) just before *Mambo Kings* won a Pulitzer, and other gigs that involved visits to cancer and suicide wards, and old age homes—even a six month stint teaching a night class up in Lake George. Aside from that, as of 1990 or so, I had been what I've always called "gainfully unemployed."

However, in 2007, I happened to be in New Orleans, at a post-Katrina Faulkner festival, participating on a panel with several other writers; it turned out that someone in Duke had been in the audience, and afterwards he approached me, asking if I would ever be interested in teaching at Duke. Whatever reservations I had at the time, I ended up making a visit down there, and, to my surprise (it's a much longer story), though they had been conducting a year-long search, they enthusiastically voted to hire me; and I've been there during the Spring semesters for the past five years.

Having said this, every time I go down there from New York, it takes me about a month to get readjusted to the different pace of life and quiet and also, as well, getting around in a car. On the positive side, I've come to really like the folks there, and I've enjoyed working with the students, most of whom are really bright. In general, I treat my time down here as a visit to an art colony, with the difference being that I set aside three days a week for my course work, and the rest for my own. Somehow I've managed to be productive enough, though by the time I leave, usually in early May, I'm dying to reconnect with the crazy city, whose energies I connect with, and feel nurtured by, in an entirely different way.

What do you teach and what do you convey to your students, in terms of the craft? What advice do you give to these upcoming writers?

I won't go into everything I do, but I try to make them "sentence" and "word" aware—and that there is a very great difference between just spilling your thoughts out on paper (or computer) and composing lines and narratives that have weight, swing, and integrity. Though most of my students are pre-med, pre-engineering, and pre-law (Duke being a professions-oriented university), I do my best to persuade them that writing well can be a great asset to their lives, no matter what field they go into. I also try to help them develop a discerning mind when it comes to books. One of my mantras is that just because a book is successful commercially, or famous, or has won prizes, doesn't necessarily mean that it's good. I will cite by name, for example, major prize-winning books that I have put into, "the-game-is-sometimes-rigged," category, something which seems to be happening with more frequency; that is, books that are written loosely, stupidly, without any sentence sense or nuance that are somehow raved about in certain important venues—the critics of which should be ashamed of themselves. I also point out that there is a difference between top tier writing and what is often passed off as such. In other words, I try to turn them into refined, discerning readers—the writing end of it works mainly to make them more aware of the craft involved.

Do you feel today's students have acquired an interest or an awareness about Latino literature and the writers? If so, why?

As far as I can see, today's students, unless they are lit majors, aren't all that interested in Latino literature. Or to put it differently, they aren't as aware or concerned about the history of Latinos in this country, this internet generation, whatever their ethnicity, have long since moved on to much cooler things like internet games and music and the diversions of YouTube, etc. While kids today are just as bright, maybe even brighter than students of my generation, they don't seem (for the most part) as sensitive to issues. It's a class thing, too. I've had Latino students, from fairly well-off backgrounds, who seemed oblivious to their roots, as if indeed their parents had encouraged them to move on and never look back. But literature is part of that looking back, of looking into the mirror, and if you are a Latino merrily dancing into a homogenized life as perpetuated by American-trans-world culture, THE ACT OF LOOKING INTO THE MIRROR OF LATINO LITERATURE, SAY A BOOK about hard issues and pity notions like prejudice and generational struggles, JUST WOULDN'T OCCUR TO YOU. Having said this, I've encountered Latino students (at Duke) who, in reading certain books that I recommend, are anxious for more. And in my travels, I have encountered many young Latinos who are absolutely determined to celebrate their cultures in whatever way possible—and, of course, they embrace that literature deeply, though I don't think Latino literature (always off in its own separate category) gets the audience among non-Latinos that it deserves. (There are exceptions of course. Junot Díaz with his "hip-hop-ghetto-speak" seems to really have a lot of cross over appeal, and, among readers, there are always discerning folks to be found, regardless of their roots.) Anyway, I'm boring myself to death with this prattle.

You were recently elected as a fellow into the American Academy of Arts and Sciences. What does this mean and what are your plans as a fellow?

It's the first academy I've been invited to join. I am pretty sure it happened because I got to know someone in that organization purely by chance—but I am grateful for the distinction, and at least they do seem to include Latinos in their membership, unlike the American Institute of Arts and Letters, for whom Latinos do not seem to exist. Last year, for example, among all the prizes given out, not a one went to a Latino: not in lit, architecture, music, the arts, drama, etc. The biggest irony, of course, is that their annual gala is held in a building that shares a plaza with the Hispanic Society of America located uptown in a predominantly Latino neighborhood, and this cracks me up.

What Cuban American writers should readers look out for?

Well, to shamelessly plug my wife's efforts, I would recommend an anthology of Cuban American poetry that she put together called *Burnt Sugar*. I also like Carlos Eire, Carlos Frias, Alfredo José Estrada, Miguel Estrada, Carolina Hospital, Roberto Fernández, Cristina Garcia, Ana Menéndez, Virgil Suarez, and Gustavo Pérez Firmat, among others, but this is to be a continued list. ☐

Nelly Rosario ONE THOUSAND AND ONE IDENTITIES

Dominican identity, developing and fleshing out characters, and their relationships with one another sets the cultural tone in Nelly Rosario's work, which is why *Song of the Water Saints* remains such a popular novel.

HE IMPORTANCE OF THE Dominican presence in America's literary scene has grown extensively in the past few years. As the ever-growing Dominican diaspora changes the cultural landscape of the U.S., it's Dominican-American authors such as Nelly Rosario who are redefining their "Dominicanness" from a contemporary diasporic perspective through literature.

Dominican-born and Brooklyn-raised, Rosario published her award-winning debut novel, *Song of the Water Saints,* in 2002. Sensual and emotionally honest, the novel explores the dreams and struggles of four generations of the women of one Dominican family as they move from the lush terrain of the Dominican Republic to the bustle of

(cont'd. pg. 112)

MARILYN KISS

NELLY ROSARIO
Marilyn Kiss

(cont'd from pg. 111)

(cont'd from pg. 111)

New York City. Like many of today's Dominican writers, who were born in the U.S. or immigrated as children with their families, Rosario utilizes elements of character, plot, setting, theme, and style in innovative ways that's poetic and on brutally frank terms. "I love writing and history," says Rosario. "When I started to write this novel, I did a lot of reading on world history and found myself asking how these facts trickled down to people's—women's—day-to-day. I wanted to examine my charters through the lens of the U.S.'s influence on the Dominican Republic and our subsequent immigration and integration into this country."

Rosario's path was unique: When she was in high school, she decided to become a writer but as a backup career, attended M.I.T. and graduated with an environmental engineering degree. She went on to Columbia University and received an M.F.A. in fiction, immersing herself in the literary arts.

She began publishing fiction, nonfiction, and poetry in anthologies and publications such as the *New York Times, Meridians,* and *Callaloo.* By the time Rosario published *Songs of the Water Saints* in 2002, she had made significant inroads in the literary community as a name to watch out for. In 2001, the *Village Voice Literary Supplement* named Rosario as one of seven people named "Writer on the Verge," and that same year, she won the Pen Open Book Award. *Songs of the Water Saints* was translated into Spanish and published under the title, *El canto del agua,* in 2003, bringing her work to an even wider audience. Having taught at Columbia University as an adjunct assistant professor, Rosario currently teaches fiction at the M.F.A. program at Texas State University and is at work on her second novel.

Throughout her career, Rosario has received numerous awards, including a 1999 Barbara Deming Memorial Fund Fellowship, the Bronx Writers' Center Van Lier Literary Fellowship in Fiction for 1999-2000, two National Arts Club Writing Fellowships, a 2006 recipient of the NALAC Fund for the Arts, an Urban Artists Initiatives Grant, a Kaye Artists in Residence at CCNY (2007), and was the recipient of the Sherwood Anderson Foundation Award for Fiction (2008).

It's been ten years since Rosario published *Song of the Water Saints,* yet she remains a popular writer because her stories spring from the diversity of other people's stories, and her female protagonists rebel against and conform to the ideas of womanhood set by the women before them. If contemporary Dominican literature is any indication of future trends, Rosario will continue to reframe, redefine, and rewrite what it means to be a member of the twentieth-first century Dominican diaspora community for generations to come.

℘ ℘ ℘

This issue of the magazine *phati'tude* deals with identity. When you are asked to choose a "category" on an official form, do you select "Hispanic," "Latina," "Dominican-American," "Caribbean-American," "Nuyodominican," or "Other"? What determines how you "self-identify"? Do you consider ethnicity, country of birth, or current passport?

First off, thank you for taking out the time to conduct this interview and for supporting the work of US Latin@ writers through your scholarship around literature.

I'm curious about the form that lists "Nuyodominican"— where in the world can I fill that one out?

About this naming game . . . The truth is, it bores me somewhat at this point in my life, in human history. I'm reminded of those box toys we quickly outgrow as toddlers, after we've figured out that square blocks go into square holes, etc. Watch kids play for a while, and you'll see that, soon enough, most start sticking everything but the blocks into those boxes.

Identity's too fluid and contextual for geometric language. So how I define myself depends on my GPS location, on the people I'm with, on the boxes provided in a multiple-choice test. I think back to grade-school math set theory when we'd draw colorful Venn diagrams, which better articulate the circles we move in and out of in relation to the world. Circles A, B and C only intersect here, but not here . . . in (T)exas, I now intersect (Y)ankee and (F)aculty . . . So, yes, I check "Hispanic," "Latina," "Dominican-American," "Caribbean-American," or "Other," given the choice.

I don't take for granted, either, that the power of definition is part of the definition of power. The relatively new separation of the racial ("Black") and ethnicity ("Hispanic") categories on some institutional and government forms signals an awareness about the limitations of past categories, an awareness that I imagine is the result of Black Latinos speaking out and attempting to define themselves as both. The reason I've never checked "Other" is because I want to, if anything, offer up two heads for the count. When we feel invisible, being counted counts. I love that story "Census" by Tomás Rivera, in which a little boy takes it upon himself to count all the people in his migrant-worker camp, has difficulties along the way, but in the end gives his community a stronger sense of empowerment when they learn that their populations is comparable to the town's.

Both the terms "Hispanic" and "Latina" have political overtones. How do you evaluate the national arguments regarding these labels?

I prefer "Latin@" because it: (1) is not a name given by the Nixon government, (2) localizes our identity and histories closer to Latin America than to Spain, (3) has political connotations, and (4) can be gender-specific (the more specific the better, right?). "Latin@" is to Hispanic" as "Chican@" is to "Mexican-American" on a smaller scale. Here in Texas, for instance, I've made the mistake of calling "Chicanos" those who consider themselves "Tejanos" and don't necessarily feel an allegiance to the political connotations in "Chicano." My naïve assumption was that ethnicity and a certain political consciousness are somewhat intertwined.

> **"Yeah, the historical, multi-generational novel has certainly become the clichéd genre of women and of immigrant writers of color—and, honestly, I don't care."**

It is fascinating to me that your own "identity" also includes a degree in engineering from MIT and an M.F.A. degree in fiction from Columbia University. This seems to suggest a marriage of sorts between "left brain/right brain" activities. You stated, when accepting the prestigious Sherwood Anderson Writer's Grant in 2008, that "I never left (engineering) for literature, as literature has always been with me." What made you change directions so radically in terms of formal education? Did you feel you were returning to a way of storytelling you had temporarily left behind? In what ways do your studies in the environmental engineering sciences inform and influence your current writing and teaching?

It's a common question, and it inspired a recent essay titled "This Bridge Called My Pen." To answer your question, here are some excerpts:

> "When asked how I went from civil engineering to creative writing, my impulse is to say, "I like bridges."

This answer, at once concrete and abstract, summarizes my approach to the classic divides that underpin the question posed: left brain versus right brain, science versus the humanities.

Over fifty years ago, British physicist and novelist C.P. Snow called the sciences and the hu-manities the "Two Cultures" (1993). Snow's protest against the gap between these discourses echoes what any child or adult with an intense curiosity about life intuitively understands: that in the real world, both disciplines operate as a pair of hands.

Literacy is the window through which we learn science; science expands our understanding of realms we encounter in literature.

Experience has taught me that when both sides of the brain are in conversation we're better able to acquire and retain knowledge. That the brain's left hemisphere is tuned to the quantitative ('linear/logical/analytical') and the right side to the qualitative ('non-linear/creative/intuitive') means little to a four year old who tests and re-tests the laws of gravity by throwing toys out the window of a third-story apartment, or who marvels at the schizoid chemistry her mother can 'magically' tease from cornstarch by merely adding water and heat.

My parents immigrated to New York City (2,027 bridges) from the Dominican Republic (two notable bridges). I came into existence across waterways, having been conceived in the United States (597,961 bridges as of 2009), born in Santo Domingo, and raised in New York's borough of Brooklyn (1,159 bridges).

I'm a Latina, an identity that, as corroborated by the fierce writings in the canonical feminist anthology *This Bridge Called My Back,* forces me to contend with severe lower-back pain and all other kinds of maladies felt by women of color living in a white-male-dominated society (Moraga & Anzaldúa, 2002).

I'm black, by lineage and by history, by consciousness and by a phenotype that includes a 'bridgeless' nose.

My first language is Spanish, whose word for 'bridge' is *puente.* My fluency in the language made me, already a middle child, the natural mediator between my parents and my three siblings, who preferred to speak English at home. Being bilingual also meant mediating between my parents and this country's bureaucracy . . .

I always struggle with voice. The writing in this essay itself feels like a patchwork of the engineering intern writing reports, the reader of romance books, the graduate student stuffing in too many clauses and adverbs and adjectives, the kid scribbling on lined paper, the annoying list maker. What is, after all, the literal meaning of the biblical writing

on the wall—*Mene, Mene, Tekel u-Pharsin*—but "numbered, weighed, divided"? I write precisely because my tongue and experiences are both so numbered, weighed, divided."

Language is inherent in personal and cultural identity. Since you moved to the U.S. at such a young age, do you consider yourself "English dominant"? In what situations do you still automatically use Spanish? You wrote *Song of the Water Saints* in English (2002) and then Patricia Antón did the Spanish translation, *El canto del agua* (2003). In what situations do you find yourself thinking and writing in Spanish? In your daily life, do you do a lot of code-switching?

I'm English-dominant because, at age five, I acquired both literacy and the language as a one-shot deal. Spanish is home, family, religion, rules, discipline, hard love, DR. I automatically use Spanish with family and code-switch with *amigas*. I code-switch with my siblings to tell a joke or two, but it's mostly English with them because it's like we'll feel the specter of our parents otherwise.

> **"As to a movie version of *Song*, I'm cautious. I'm afraid to think of how Hollywood would cherry pick some scenes and misrepresent the characters. If anything, I'd go independent, with a director like Julie Dash (*Daughters of the Dust*)."**

While writing *Song of the Water Saints,* I had a very difficult time writing dialogue in English for Dominican characters who are black, rural, illiterate, and who speak a Spanish specific to their experience. For a while, they didn't speak at all. During my MFA, a course in translation gave me the idea to use literal meaning as a way to communicate in English what my characters mean to say in Spanish. This I visually enhanced by superimposing over English the standards of punctuation used in Spanish. One rule I established in the text was to only use Spanish words in proper nouns. I wanted to bend and to infuse the English language with Spanish. The unexpected result was a narrative voice that some have told me reads as if originally written in Spanish.

The process of translating *Song of the Water Saints* to the Spanish forced me to think in reverse. How does one, for example, translate word play from the source language? My biggest issue with Pantón's translation for Emecé Planeta was that it was targeted to Spain's literary market. I argued that Spaniards go to DR and quickly learn to ask for *mangú*, that readers go out of their way to understand, say, terms used by the Russian writers in translation. I fought to make sure that my characters' dialogue did not include words like *tío* for *tipo* or *cacahuate* for *maní*. The Vintage Español edition, which is directly drawn from Pantón's translation, has much more of my changes.

As a columnist for *el diario/La Prensa* for the last four years or so, I've become even more intimate with the technical workings of the language as I try to find in it a unique literary voice. During the first year or so, I'd first write the column in English then plug it into Google Translate and make adjustments. Now that I've developed a more fluid sense of my literary voice in Spanish, I write the column straight, only using the translator to clarify some issues around vocabulary and usage. I seem to have a really hard time with prepositions in either language, which might speak to my difficulty in negotiating spatial relationships.

What differences, if any, do you notice among the Spanish-speaking populations of Brooklyn and the New York metropolitan region and Texas, where you now teach at Texas State University, San Marcos? Is there more of an emphasis on one language or the other or on bilingualism in the different parts of the country? What do you think of bilingual education, especially at the elementary school level?

There seems to be much more public comfort with Spanish in New York, where other nationalities also pick up the language for closer interactions in business, at school, at work. Here in Texas, it's like the Spanish gradient lightens to white the further north from the border you travel. In this central part of Texas, I find that openly speaking Spanish can mark you as a visitor (I'm near an outlet mall) or a recent immigrant from Mexico—the "nopal stain on the forehead" to some. And to Tejanos who don't speak the language, my apologies if I addressed you in Spanish—I didn't know there was so much baggage, wasn't trying to call you out, thought we could be friends in Espinach, too.

I think bilingual—trilingual, quadrilingual, infinitilingual—education at every level is important. Multilingualism grows the brain, the heart, and the spirit. It's the tongue's Swiss Army knife, opens up a world of values around how we relate to ourselves and to the rest of the planet.

Your novel, *Song of the Water Saints,* uses a generational structure that explores a family's relationship to historical events through strong

female characters. **Do you feel an affinity with such authors as Isabel Allende, Julia Alvarez, Cristina García, and Edwidge Danticat, among others, who also use this emphasis on the "personal as history" and the "historical as personal"? What writers have had the biggest influence on your development and in which texts in particular?**

Yeah, the historical, multi-generational novel has certainly become the clichéd genre of women and of immigrant writers of color—and, honestly, I don't care. In an a historical world so full of disconnection, I think the umbilical cord is more important than ever. So the writers you mention, along with the rest of the Latin@ and Latin-American canon, have definitely had a big influence on my development. Others, as in the case of—surprise—Toni Morrison and the rest of the African-American canon, played a major role in solidifying my racial consciousness. Beyond content, then are also the countless other literary canons that helped to redefine my understanding of form and the many technical possibilities of the craft. It's an encyclopedic list of texts, way too many to name.

What was the inspiration for the title of *Song of the Water Saints*? Did you discuss with your translator the differently nuanced Spanish version, *El canto del agua*?

I suck at titles. The ones I pitched for the book were ridiculous. My editor, Jenny Minton, gets the credit for coming up with the title *Song of the Water Saints*. I hated it at first for its religious connotations. Then it grew on me the more I said it out loud. It was long enough to offer a glimpse of the story but short and poetic enough to still keep a sense of mystery. This is why I like brevity and poetry of the truncated Spanish translation, *El canto del agua*.

For which one of the five women who form the backbone of *Song of the Water Saints* — Mai, Graciela, Mercedes, Amalfi, and Leila —do you feel the greatest affection? Why? In what ways are any of them "autobiographical" or about members of your own family? Do the experiences of Mercedes, Andrés, and Leila in the U.S. mirror the experiences of your own family upon leaving the Dominican Republic for "Nueba Yol"? Are Leila's "coming of age" experiences based upon your own adjustments to life in Brooklyn?

All of the characters have my DNA. As in dreams, they all represent aspects of me. The stories are emotionally autobiographical, not factual. In my fiction, I try to avoid directly transcribing other people's stories, not only out of respect for their privacy but also in favor of exploring the wider canvas of imagination.

My own family had slightly different emigration and immigration experiences from those of the characters mentioned. For one, my parents came to the U.S. as teens, during the 1960s, nearly 20 years earlier than the wave of Dominicans that came during the 1980s. As to Leila, I had to step away from my own personal experiences when writing her. Aside from getting good grades, she dares to do almost everything I didn't think of doing at that age, given how strict my parents were.

Your prize-winning debut novel covers a century of uneasy relations between your own two countries, the Dominican Republic of your birth and the United States where you now live. From 1916-1999, as a backdrop to the generations of this fictional family, there looms the imperial power of the U.S. with its invading army and concomitant rapes and heartbreak, and then with its support of Trujillo's dictatorship, and finally with its economic influence. How have you reconciled your own relationship to these two political entities? How do you see the future of U.S.-Caribbean relations? How did your summers in the Dominican Republic help shape your own political viewpoint?

As with identity markers, I question the politicized notion of countries, even in understanding that self-definition is important. Maybe fact that I was grew up in a global empire makes me downplay the importance of nationhood, but to be honest, flag-waving makes me cringe. While patriotism can be empowering, especially to an oppressed people, I can't help but see in it the seeds of xenophobia, an us/them mentality.

The way I reconcile my relationship to the two political entities of DR and U.S. is to accept and honor that I'm a product of historical and economic currents: My parents came to the US from the DR after Trujillo's dictatorship for a better life. Summers in the DR kept me from forgetting that though the leaves and the fruits of that life thrive in the US, its roots thrive in DR soil.

My vision of the future of U.S.-Caribbean relations is less rooted in the political, economic, and militaristic history of the past, but more in the fruitful exchange of solutions. I think of how the Civil Rights Movement in the U.S. influenced the same across the Caribbean. I think of how, given the economic crisis, the U.S. is now looking to Cuba for ideas about how to implement sustainable infrastructures.

How do you view Haitian/Dominican relationships currently since there has been such historical tension between the two countries? How did the

Dominican Republic respond to the disastrous earthquake in Haiti?

The key to improved Haitian/Dominican relations might lie in the two countries' emigrant communities, who, on being lumped together as underdogs elsewhere, find common ground. A beautiful example of intersecting circles is the *New York Times* op-ed piece, "The Dominican Republic's war on Haitian workers," co-authored by Edwidge Danticat and Junot Díaz in 1999. And there are more of these kinds of honest conversations happening in the U.S.—among friends, writers, scholars in the community. I hope that the same is also happening in both the DR and Haiti.

One opportunity for translating these conversations into positive action was DR's overall strong response to the earthquake in Haiti. Of course, it's heartbreaking and deeply embarrassing that, on top of the injury of such a terrible event, I heard the typical barbs coming out of Santo Domingo: "Those poor people are people, too" and "They're human first, then Haitian." But there was also the swift and critical response towards the first rescue/relief efforts by the Dominican Republic and the generous contributions by the Dominican community abroad. These are the stories we need to keep hearing, believing in, remembering, and actively creating. "We must refuse the old stories that tell us to interpret social disasters as natural disasters," says Díaz in his unflinching essay, "Apocalypse: What Disasters Reveal."

Ours is no ordinary border-nation beef with Haiti. When Díaz says that "the world has done its part in demolishing Haiti," he's also reminding us that we all have a responsibility towards loving our neighbors. In the end, fault lines run throughout the our entire planet.

Food —in its scarcity or abundance, its preparation, its centrality to feasts and festivals, and in the memories of individual families — seems to serve as a cultural marker in so many novels, including *Song of the Water Saints*. What is your own relationship to cooking and eating in both the US and the Dominican Republic? How is your personal narrative tied to food? What is the meal you long for the most?

As a kid, I hated to eat. I loved and still love to cook with my mother. Cooking is chemistry, connection, culture. It's among the best aspects of my relationships with my mother and with my own daughter. Food and cooking is also deeply tied to a woman's identity in my family—whether *fulana* cooks with too much salt or to little, too greasy or too dry, too spicy or too tasteless—so I had to develop my chops early on. My mother was always conscious of "not eating from cans," of serving foods as close to their natural state as possible, going as far as getting our meats from live-poultry shops. At the risk of sounding campo-nostalgic, I especially enjoyed watching (operative word, here) how my family in DR made cheese, raised cattle, grew their own food, and the daily trips they made down to the beach for fresh water from a sinkhole. This makes me value the enormous amount of energy it takes to produce food. Here in San Marcos, I find myself constantly challenging students who denigrate their farm town origins. Farmers and agricultural workers the world over get a bad rap when they're really the hands that feed us. For me, it's exhausting just to keep a garden going on Texan soil.

We essentially migrate to where we can find food with greater facility and eat it in peace. It's in part why a Dominican New Yorker finds herself in Texas, and on a mission to find a place that sells *plátanos* and *yucca*.

So, yes, food is a big part of my personal narrative. An essay like "Feasting on Sancocho Before Night Falls" is an example of how food can serve as a great point of departure for discussions of all sorts—there it is, the meal I crave most.

It strikes me that hair plays such an important role for the women in literature across cultures and it is prominent in the lives of your principal characters. Please elaborate on this theme, especially as it relates to Leila and her adolescence in the U.S.

It goes without saying that, as with cooking, hair plays a strong part in female identity in Dominican culture—also, in racial identification. Adolescence is a time of defining identity and, in the case of Leila, womanhood. Hair was a good way of doing some exposition around how Leila negotiates her sense of self in a world with muddled messages around sex and around culture.

Just curious, but the relationship between Mercedes and Mustafá reminded me a bit of the one between Eva Luna and Riad Halabí in Allende's novel. Was that in any way an intertextual homage or just a coincidence?

I read *Eva Luna* as a teenager, so I don't quite remember the Eva-Riad relationship. The Mercedes-Mustafá relationship is just coincidence—or, who knows, maybe an homage stored by my subconscious.

I find Casimiro a fascinating personage. What or who was your inspiration for this wonderful stepfather figure?

Casimiro was my comic relief. He serves as counterpoint to the paternalism in which that world is steeped. He reminds me of all the good men in my family and in our culture, the men who end up finishing last. Though he's

not exactly based on my paternal grandfather, Casimiro does exude his trickster spirit, his calm, and he inherited Abuelo's six digits.

While Mercedes certainly turned to religion for solace and sought a sojourn in the convent, Catholicism does not seem to dominate the women's lives in *Songs of the Water Saints*. What role does organized religion play in your own life?

I'm quick to say, "Spiritual but not religious." The long answer is that organized religion has played a huge role in my development. Not only did it tell me my first stories and serves as a rich font of cultural imagery, but it also politicized me early on. I grew up in a church community that took a strong and controversial stance against the wars in Central America during the 1980s. Transfiguration Church went as far as housing refugees and was often scolded by the Brooklyn Diocese for doing so. The late Msgr. Father Karvelis preached liberation theology, speaking out against "neo-paganism" and "modern-day Pharisees," warning against the abyss of addictions that many immigrants fall prey to: alcoholism, materialism, dreams of a big house "back home," workaholism at the expense of a balanced family life. I remember our youth group shouting anti-Contra slogans at a protest in Washington.

Today, I still interpret the teachings of Christ in my life at their most basic and most complex: to love thy neighbor. Even stripped of all the religious fixin's, this isn't easy. Many a time, I've had to turn away neighbors who invite me to Bible studies or to other religions. The Buddha (whose teachings I also consider) at my doorstep sometimes does the trick.

In *Song*, I do draw from these fixin's with Catholic imagery like that of the *Virgen de la Altagracia*. They incarnate both the messy and touching ways we relate to faith—but I also want to be careful with imagery that comes so pre-loaded and does the work I should be doing as a writer.

Also curious about the interesting pairing of Mercedes and Andrés. Where did that spring from since most women seek partners who are as tall if not taller than they are? Was it the green eyes? Or was it because, as you intimated, he took her seriously and *listened*?

I see "mismatched" couples all the time. Yes, Andrés' green eyes, his listening to and taking Mercedes seriously definitely trumps his lack of height in her view. I love those love stories.

Your first novel received many accolades as well as several awards. What are you currently working on and are you close to finishing this project? Does teaching writing enhance your own desire to write? What advice do you give to the students in your writing program?

The second novel's an exploration of sight, a search for light against the kind of despairing narratives we often find ourselves telling. So I'm being literal, using the eye, the organ that detects light, as point of departure. At the narrative's center is a home-schooled ophthalmologist who gets in trouble for performing an illegal procedure. Of course, there's a happy ending, though I'm nowhere close to it.

My advice to M.F.A. students is to allow process and not product to define them as writers. Find your voices. What do you want to say, ultimately? If you have little to say, don't hold the mic. Publish when the work is ready. Be patient. Put in the work. Set aside the time to learn the craft. Don't as for piggy-back rides. Read everything and everyone.

How often do you get back to the Dominican Republic? Where else do you travel? What are your future plans, especially regarding your interest in film? (I read in a 2004 article in *phati'tude* that you were a member of a women's film collective.) Will there be a movie version of *Song of the Water Saints*?

I visit DR about every two or three years to see family. Writing-related travel is two birds in that it mixes business and pleasure. My most recent trip abroad was to Ethiopia, which counts among the most intense travel experiences I've ever had.

As to a movie version of *Song*, I'm cautious. I'm afraid to think of how Hollywood would cherry-pick some scenes and misrepresent the characters. If anything, I'd go independent, with a director like Julie Dash (*Daughters of the Dust*).

You were named "Writer on the Verge" by the *Village Voice*, mentioned as "one to watch" by *Publisher's Weekly* and called a "Caribbean Scheherazade" by Julia Alvarez. Which of the many sobriquets attached to you after the publication of *Song of the Water Saints* has become a part of the way you see yourself, as your intimate identity?

To be called "Writer on the Verge" at the time was nice, but a decade later, the name starts to sound like Pedro Almodovar's "Women on the Verge . . ."

I'm really flattered by "Caribbean Scheherazade," since *One Thousand and One Nights* is one of my favorite works of literature for its fractal nature and for its depiction of what a woman can do when she wields the power of storytelling. ◪

MARILYN KISS is Associate Professor of Spanish and Department Chair of the Modern Languages Department at Wagner College.

Gary Soto A CONVERSATION WITH THE FRESNO POET

In a dialogue filled with engaging anecdotal memories and candor, Gary Soto describes the role of family history, the meaning of labor, and the lasting impression of childhood as it features in his poetry.

ARY SOTO IS THE KIND OF WRITER who comes along once in a lifetime. There is humor, the wryness of wit combined with charm, but also a seriousness of intent in the works of Soto. He is at heart always a storyteller. Having published thirty-five books, including young adult fiction, fiction for adult readers, memoirs, essays, plays, and most notably poetry, Soto's work offers readers poignant, impressive glimpses into the everyday lives of working-class Chicanos.

Most notable among Soto's fiction are the works *Buried Onions* (2003), *The After-life* (2005), and *Accidental Love* (2006). Laudable among his works for children are

(cont'd.)

P A U L A H A Y E S

GARY SOTO
Paula Hayes

(cont'd from pg. 119)

Too Many Tamales (1996) and *Chato Goes Cruisin'* (2008). His accomplishments as a poet stretch far and wide and are almost too numerous to name, beginning with *The Elements of San Joaquin* (1977) and continuing with *The Tale of Sunlight* (1978), *Where Sparrows Work Hard (1981)*, *Black Hair* (1985), *Who Will Know Us?* (1990), *Home Course in Religion* (1991), *Neighborhood Odes* (1992), *Canto Familiar* (1994), *One Kind of Faith (2003)*, *New and selected poems* (1995), *A Simple Plan* (2007), *Partly Cloudy: Poems of love and longing* (2009), and *Human Nature* (2010).

Likewise, his awards are almost too many to count, but they include the Literature Award from the Hispanic Heritage Foundation, PEN Center West Book Award, and the Author-Illustrated Civil Rights Award (awarded by the National Education Association), a finalist for a National Book Award (for *New and selected poems)* and also a finalist for the *Los Angeles Times* Book Award. If this were not enough to prove that he is indeed a living legend, he has been given his own museum, The Gary Soto Literary Museum; it is part of Fresno City College.

It should not be overlooked that he is a concerned activist for literacy and a Young People Ambassador for the United Farm Workers of America. His books *Jessie de la Cruz: A Profile of a United Farm Worker* (2002) and *César Chávez: A Hero for Everyone* (2003) are each written in the spirit of informing young readers of the Chicano experience of labor history in Fresno, California.

Born in 1952 in Fresno, Soto grew up knowing that economic survival could be an unforgiving but ever-present reality for his family and for others. Survival equated to working in any of the large, industrial owned agricultural industries or in the factories of Fresno; it might also mean picking up odd-jobs and any form of work that one could find. When he writes in *The Elements of San Joaquin* that, "The skin of my belly will tighten like a belt / And there will be no reason for pockets," he is describing the plight of the migrant worker, the field laborer. Today, those lines, which were published three decades ago, might be said to ring true for the middle-class worker. His concern has often been for those who must define, at least parts of their lives, by labor. In the poem "Summer," he gives a portraiture of agricultural labor, writing, "What about the farm worker? / He had no bedroom. He had a warehouse / Of heat, a swamp cooler / That turned no faster than a

raffle cage." The land of Fresno is of importance as well; he describes in the same poem the relationship of the farm worker to the farms, "And the farms? / There were groves of fig trees that went unpicked. / The fruit wrinkled and flattened / Like the elbows of an old woman." Soto's writing as a whole is filled with childhood memories of Fresno—the land, the people, his family's residence there, and the indelible impression it all left upon his mind. Recalling what it was like as a child to live in an industrial neighborhood on Braly Street, Soto writes in an autobiographical essay, "The Childhood Worries, Or Why I Became a Writer" (1995), how awakening to a new day, "You could hear the siren blast of the Sun-Maid Raisin plant and answer that blast with your own chirp-like cry." Life on Braly Street could be hard, but it was filled with drifting, imaginative play.

Soto continues to wrench meaning from those childhood experiences in Fresno, as even his recent collection of poems, *Human Nature* (2010), attests. If you haven't picked up a copy of *Human Nature* yet, I highly recommend it. It is chocked-full of the raw emotions of a poet recalling the levity, splendor, but also the natural apprehensions that accompany the various phases of life — childhood, burgeoning adolescence, the youthful energy of early adulthood. In *Human Nature,* Soto returns to Braly Street but with the advantage of the wisdom gained during middle-age. Walking once more among the mulberries and the orange groves, feeling again the stains of cherry tomatoes thrown at him in make-believe war by his brother, finding the chickens that were chased by neighborhood kids and gathering them again, fingering the bruises and scars of falling down in a fallen world, Soto makes real in *Human Nature* the great proclamation of Wordsworth that the "Child is the father of the man." But Soto also ventures beyond the borders of youth, exploring the satiety of marriage, friendship, and those familial unions that bind together the human experience. In the poem that rounds out *Human Nature,* "The Fountain Pen," Soto writes about the literary influence of Pablo Neruda. He says, "When Neruda dotted the end of a sentence, / When he stood up at his desk / And capped his gold-tipped nib, / Others quickly dipped their own pens / Into the still dark but eternally wet ink." Reading Soto we know that here too the ink never dries and that there is something eternal to be had. The meaning of the images he hands us resonates for readers time and time again.

℘ ℘ ℘

You are such an accomplished writer that finding a point of entrance into your writing can be daunting,

but I would like to focus primarily on your poetry. I would like if we could go back in time for a moment to your first collection, *The Elements of San Joaquin* published in 1976 by the University of Pittsburg Press in the well-known Pitt Poetry Series. I am selecting *The Elements of San Joaquin* as the starting point for understanding your legacy as a poet, not just because it was your first collection of poems, but more so because of the centrality of the immigrant experience in it, and also the importance of labor. Is it fair to say that you began your career as a poet by writing about and trying to capture what was under the radar for many Americans — the humanity of immigrant experiences? Or, would you offer a different starting point to help readers understand you as a poet?

I have never used the word "immigrant" in any form of my writing, poetry or prose, for children or adults. By immigrant we're speaking of first-generation, new arrivals, and I'm third generation Mexican American — or Chicano. True,

"We're not sociologists. We're storytellers; we're poets."

I do write about labor in *The Elements of San Joaquin,* in particular farm and warehouse work, two recurring tasks my family knew firsthand and which put food on our table. My grandparents worked at the Sun-Maid Raisin factory within view of our house on Braly Street. They knew work. They stooped in the fields in California, Michigan, and Texas — they measured earth with a hoe. My grandmother also worked in a tortilla factory and sold *helados* — ice cream — from a paleta cart. Moreover, labor was part of our neighborhood, which was industrial by nature. We lived next to a junk yard, for instance, and down the street was a broom factory and not too far from us several soda bottling companies.

How would you characterize the shifts in representation of Chicano communities and immigrant experience in poetry since the 1970s? In what ways has your own representations evolved since the 1970s?

I'm not certain if I can speak about the shifts of interest since the 1970s. This is a lovely question, one that an assistant professor who can get away from brain-killing committee meetings might find engaging. I will say, however, that in the late 1960s much of the newly found

Chicano literature was loud and rhetorical and functioned as a way to inspire youth into political action. Much of it, I'm afraid, was just bad but necessary. With the arrival of *The Elements of San Joaquin* there was a shift from the loud to an introspective poetry. The older Chicano poets couldn't grasp what I was doing — I once jokingly said that I was the first Chicano to write in complete sentences. And as far as my own evolvement, I would say that the poems became less angrily dense to a lighter form encompassing our human silliness.

Do you think current political debates over immigration are impacting how Chicanos are portrayed in literature today?

No, I don't believe this political climate affects portrayal. We Chicano writers (Luis J. Rodriguez, Sandra Cisneros, Dagoberto Gilb and the younger ones such as David Dominguez, and Mike Medrano) never think of how we're portrayed in literature, in part because we're the ones responsible for providing these images in this literature. I don't quibble with others — let Rodriguez write his testimony about gang life, let Gilb sing his song of failed love in El Paso, let Sandra color Chicago brown on a school map . . . I'm not certain if there is any Chicano writer putting immigrant issues down on paper, except, of course, a few poems here, an essay there, etc. Each of us is engaged in what we feel at heart. We're not sociologists; we're storytellers, we're poets. We bring a political climate to the page in different ways. For me, I've been pretty much engaged in the oddities of childhood.

Since this edition of *phati'tude* is looking at the question, "¿What is in a Nombre," can you explain to me what "Chicano" means to you personally in terms of your self-identity? How important is it that writers are free to express their self-identities through ethnic and communal representations?

"Chicano" is a Mexican American person with a political mind-set. Chicano is a person who, when possible, separates himself from the use of "Hispanic." When I was asked, "What's the difference between Chicano and Hispanic?" I answered in the glare of a television camera, "A Chicano votes Democrat and Hispanic Republican." The camera light went off immediately.

You return to the topic of labor in *Human Nature,* which was published in 2010 in the Tupelo Masters Series. In referencing *Human Nature,* I am thinking specifically of the poem, "Some History about Raisins." The poem alludes to labor in the San

Joaquin agricultural industry, as well as describing the death of your uncle. Why did you decide to recount this personal memory in *Human Nature?* Has anything changed in terms of how you approach the topic of labor in your current poetry as compared to your early poetry?

I revisited "Some History about Raisins." It's a glib yet haunting poem which explores naivety — notice how, at age

"I'm closer to earth than ever before."

five, I'm "afraid of the garden hose / tired in three places with rags— / was it injured?" This simple observation says so much about me as a really young boy, one who was full of wonder at the world I was living in. Moreover, the poem speaks about the connection of raisins and the mole on my uncle's back. This mole, in reality, became cancerous. It would claim my uncle's life — how could that be? How could something so small, such as a raisin-sized mole, cause death? To answer your question directly: I can think of only a few poems that deal with immigrant issues. My poems have to do with the self.

Am I correct that as a young man you worked in the agricultural industry of San Joaquin? How did working in the fields of San Joaquin shape your vision of the world at that point in your life?

I was the fastest boy with a hoe in the fields! This is not true. I did my share of field work — beets and cotton with a hoe, a knife to castrate clumps of grapes from the vine — but I would not consider myself a true former farm worker, not, say, like my wife who grew up on a small farm and did manual labor from age eight to eighteen. But what shaped me, internally, was Cesar Chavez, labor leader who brought both large and simple changes to the fields. I can say from experience that field work is really hard work, possibly the hardest, and the absence of labor laws (or the enforcement of those laws) crippled people, literally. For a picture of labor, I suggest readers get a copy of *Beasts of the Fields* by Richard Steven Street. That this book, published five years ago, didn't receive a deeper appreciation is traitorous to readable scholarship.

In *Human Nature,* several of the poems, "Waiting at the Gate," "At the Stationary Store," "Some Ideas about Jesus," and "Being Difficult on 'Voice

of America,'" recall your childhood memories of Catholicism. Why did you decide to include religion as one of your topics in the collection?**

I'm not Catholic these days, or for the past twenty years. I did have formal training in the shape of four years in Catholic school, which supplied me with plenty in the sense of unworthiness. A funny story: I flunked third grade and when I returned to the third grade and found a chair by the window (I had every intention of looking out this window for the rest of the year), a nun came into the room, saw that there were more students than chairs, and asked, "Who flunked third grade." A few idiots boys, myself included, raised our hands. She clicked her clicker and said, "You're in fourth grade now. Get your lunch pails and go upstairs. How is it possible that I'm not going to use this material, plus my confusion about the meaning of God, Jesus, and Apostles bleeding from their palms? I have a book called *Home Course in Religion,* long out of print. My Catholic years twisted me just enough to make my observations quirky and resonate with others who made it through their Catholic educations.

There are, indeed, Catholic overtones in *Human Nature,* especially in the poems you point out. One of the Ten Commandments says to honor your father and mother. I don't adhere to this — blasphemous me! I won't dwell on this matter, but will say that it affects me and affects them — or at least the one who is still living. Guilt is present in my life over this separation, but only a mild guilt.

Does writing about autobiographical experiences and memories make a poet more vulnerable, in some way? Perhaps, more vulnerable to critics or even to readers?

Vulnerable? No, I do have a readership among children and young adults, whole classrooms from the east to the west, and a tiny readership among adults — my adult novel, Amnesia in a Republican County, sold so poorly that the only people aware of this book are me and the publisher. Those adult readers provide me with plenty of slack — that I have written about panties here and there doesn't raise eyebrows. Adult readers of poetry don't really care; they're worldly and better read. We're aware that we poets are good and bad, generous and stingy, loud and quiet, spiritual and pagan. Very little surprises the adult readers because we don't venture to the page to be outraged. We don't visit literature for the perfect world.

You have written several memoirs. What is the relationship of writing memoirs to that of writing poems that also draw on autobiographical

experiences? Is there more autobiographical 'truth' in your memoirs than in your poetry or fiction?

I have written three autobiographical books — *Living Up the Street, A Summer Life* and *The Effects of Knut Hamsun on a Fresno Boy.* Each of these books dwells on childhood, among other themes, and several of the narratives carry over into my poetry. It's not unusual for a poet to take what has been done in one genre and rework it in another, say poetry into prose. It's always an experiment, always slightly different, each tale rewoven into a brighter cloth.

Can you explain a little of the creative process of how autobiographical 'truth,' memories and experiences, get distilled into poems?

My autobiographical poem, "Oranges," is known in all middle grade and high school textbooks. I believe it has been reprinted some 28 million times, legally, too. Does this make it the best known poem by any contemporary ever? Unless someone else comes up with another figure, I will answer yes. But let's get off the math and think how this autobiographical poem departs from how things happened. In the poem, I've invited a girl, age thirteen, on a walk around the block and then lead her downtown where, lacking the necessary funds, I purchase her a dime candy bar for a nickel — "purchase" it with a nickel and an orange because the sales lady behind the counter realizes that love is blooming, flower-like, right before her eyes. She feels tender, she feels it her duty to let me slide. Did this happen? I won't answer this directly but will say that the frame of reference in the poem is true. Now who said, "You don't owe anything to reality"? Bend, like a paperclip, one kind of truth for another kind.

Following along on this line of thought, describe for me a few aspects of your own personal creative process of writing a poem. Do you revise the poems you write? Do you ever feel that some poems are more complete than others? Do you ever feel that some poems are never quite complete?

My poetry editor is first my wife of thirty-six years — poor darling must read my sloppy script and offer advice while her vision recovers from close readings. Then my poems will head off Pony Express to Chris Buckley, who will edit them using a slash-and-burn technique. He's very demanding. I'm lucky to have him on my side.

I want to turn to some of the collections of poems you have written through the decades and ask if you consider these to be 'confessional' works. For

example, would you consider *The Tale of Sunlight* (1978), *Where Sparrows Work Hard* (1981), and B*lack Hair* (1985) as confessional poetry? It seems at times that many of the poems in these collections are written with a degree of personal catharsis in mind.

All poets are confessional. We speak in whispers, we shout. I want to be heard by a few, not legions, and these few will be not unlike me, middle-aged. My new manuscript of poems is called *Sudden Loss of Dignity,* which has everything to do with the breakdown of the body — the face slumps, the hearing goes, and even snarling fangs chip off. Poetry by nature is confessional. Like a carton of milk, my due date is just about up. The word confessional, of course, was coined around the time of Anne Sexton, possibly earlier with Robert Lowell. But if you consider their work, you see how timid they were compared to the poets that followed, poets who really hang out dirty laundry, myself included, I suppose.

How important is it that Chicano youth find positive representations of cultural identity in literature today? I can think of the example, your collection of poems, *Neighborhood Odes* (2005), which is geared toward younger readers, as a positive representation of Chicano neighborhoods and communities. Do you approach writing a poem differently when it is written for a younger audience as compared to when you write poems for an adult audience?

I began writing for youth in 1990—no, I take that back. I began to write for them in the late 1980s, and when I say youth I'm speaking of young Mexican Americans—Chicanitos. At the time, we were absent from any textbooks, any advertising, movies, songs, all the popular messages that would say that being brown is OK. When Isabel Allende's book *House of Spirits* was made, not one of the lead actors was Latino — Jeremy Irons a Latino? Isn't he from England? The movie is not memorable film work, but why couldn't the director cast Latinos? After all, the movie is set in Chile . . . I have gotten off the point. My little book *Neighborhood Odes,* as you ask, is light. It's positive, is sweet, is well-written, I believe. It speaks of neighborhood because for a lot of kids this is all they have—neighbors to the left, right, and in front. They are not well traveled. They are not worldly. The dust of adventure they kick up is right around home.

I would characterize you as a tireless warrior, and not just an activist, in the efforts of increasing literacy in Chicano communities. Why has this been a cause that you have never relinquished?

I have the honor of walking into any school in California and the teachers and students will beam at me—and I'll beam back. They will stop what they are doing. They won't

know—or care—about the poet laureate. No, Gary's in the house! I have visited over a hundred schools and most of these schools are Latino, brown as me. I'm probably the closest thing to a Mr. Rogers—or Señor Rogelio. I recall visiting a school in Texas and the entire school was dressed up with images of my twenty-five plus books for younger readers. I had four hundred kids sing me a song, each of them like a little bird! I spoke to them in assemblies and was later led out to meet even the three-year olds in day care. I had to carry each of them for a few seconds, all the while I was wondering, "Is this in my contract?" I recall a teacher, by the name of Patricia, chiming, "See, they love you!" Drool was all over my arm.

You must be very proud of the Gary Soto Museum. Tell me about this. How is the museum a reflection of the legacy you are leaving to the next generation of readers and future writers?

A museum and I'm still above ground, not underground in an unkempt plot nobody visits? I'm speaking of The Gary Soto Literary Museum. It's located at Fresno City College where I got my start in 1972. But why a museum? Does my ego have no bounds? Actually it's a tidy museum of 700-square feet but holds all the hardware of a writer's life, from writing table to typewriters to first computer, all now resembling the goods of Fred Flintstone. To argue support for literacy I'll say this: we poets and writers must think collectively, and we must think of innovative ways to bring literature to the public — thus, this museum of mine, which is visited by children, college students and the occasional wanderer. Readership is shrinking, both for poets and fiction writers. Let's not be a boutique enterprise. Let's think how we can make poetry and fiction, other genres, a part of the world. Moreover, I have a large readership. People are curious about me.

Fresno, California, as a place, has had a large impact on your development as a writer. Describe for me the importance of region and geography for you as a poet.

All poets and writers see a value in region — Robert Frost claims New Hampshire as his own back yard, Mark Twain paddles down the Mississippi, William Faulkner smokes a pipe in the very deep south, Sherwood Anderson sweats in ramshackle towns where the only breezes are the yawns of the very bored. There's nothing complicated here, really. For me, Fresno is the place where I've set quite a few poems, stories, essays, and novels. Let's add plays, too.

In accounting for both your fiction and your poetry, you often describe failures (as depicted through memory, family experiences, personal experiences, and fictionalizations). Why is it important in powerful literature to depict the failures of people as well as their successes?

Who was the smart ass who said that happy literature has no history? Failure — human foibles, I would say — is so much the makeup of serious literature, from the unsatisfying marriage of Ana Karenina to a middle-brow doctor to the mediocre boxers of Leonard Gardener's Fat City, boxers who possess some talent but not enough to be contenders. I have been recently laughing at myself and what I will call my sudden loss of dignity, how at one time — ten years, twenty years ago? — I was viewed as a contender in literature and then Well, we know the story: a poet hustles to national recognition only to be overtaken by others.

If you had to select just one poem that you have written throughout your career, that you consider to be representative of you as a poet, which poem would you select?

My choice would be "Bean Plants" from A Simple Plan, published to no notice and no readership. I'm really one of the beans in this poem. I'm a simple seed tossed in the ground, given just water to pop from the earth, and then, with my leaves like arms up in and a semblance of praise to the sun and god. It's a poem about recognizing metaphors in the world at an early age. I'm eating M&Ms at the window and then stop when I notice that the plants rising from the earth are the pinto beans that a week before had been my army men. The lack of toys in our household taught me to use my imagination. A quote from the poem is called for:

> Then night came, bed with its strangled sheets,
> and insomnia . . .
> You put your brown M & M into your mouth, let it melt,
> And scooted its sweetness over your molars.
> You made out in the yard the arms of your bean plants
> Throwing themselves up to get more light,
> Even if the light was from the porch. You went back
> To bed and placed your hands over your head:
> How sorry you were for the bean plants eating dirt,
> With their skinny arms always raised and so tired.

That's it, a world of workers with arms outstretched, a world of people who just pop out of the ground, forced to turn as they grow, then wilt and become a part of the earth again. My own arms have come down. I'm closer to earth than ever before. ▢

PAULA HAYES is poet, scholar, and educator. She holds a Ph.D. in Textual Studies / English from the University of Memphis and teaches in Memphis, Tennessee.

Junot Díaz ENGAGES THE WORLD

In a wide ranging discussion, Junot Díaz waxes poetically about the abandonment of Haiti, U.S. immigration policy, the benefits of a strong work ethic, school days, the overarching theme of his works, the 99%, Tyler the Creator's new album, and his disdain for *that* question.

DROWN CAPTURED MY ATTENTION the moment I saw it, sometime in the late 1990s. A black and white photo of a nighttime rundown city street placed atop a sparse white cover with the simple gritty typeface words: "DROWN – Junot Díaz." The stories of DROWN were a revelation, offering a fresh vibrant take on a tired genre: the short story. Moreover, the young author was from New Jersey, and he spoke my language. Well, maybe not my language but a grainy, realistic, musical Spanglish: an alchemical amalgamation. The critics noticed as well, "Graceful and raw and painful and smart ... His prose is sensible poetry that moves like an interesting

(cont'd. pg. 128)

JUNOT DÍAZ
Danny Shot

(cont'd from pg. 126)

conversation *(The Boston Globe)*, and "Díaz transfigures disorder and disorientation with a rigorous sense of form" *(New York Times Book Review)*. More importantly, my students noticed. I convinced the librarian at the school where I taught, Samuel Gompers Vocational and Technical High School in the South Bronx, to purchase a couple of copies of *Drown*, which soon joined Piri Thomas' *Down These Mean Streets* as the library's most stolen book. That's no small praise.

I kept up with Junot Díaz's writing over the next decade catching the occasional story in *The New Yorker* or *The Paris Review*. In 2007, we saw the publication of Díaz's magnum opus *The Brief and Wondrous Life of Oscar Wao*. Wow! Here was our 21st century *Moby Dick* and *Invisible Man* rolled into one: a singing, soaring, wildly funny, tragic story of immigration, alienation, and obsession. And, it was set in New Brunswick, New Jersey of all places, and I could walk the streets of my old college town with the rotund ghetto nerd protagonist Oscar. Díaz also took us to the post-Trujillo Dominican Republic where the ghosts are real and lurking around every corner. But aside from the setting, truly original characters, and inspired footnotes, it is sparkling sentence after sentence that deems this novel a post-modern masterpiece. The critics once again recognized Díaz's genius awarding *Oscar Wao* numerous publications' *Best of 2007 lists, The National Book Critics Award,* as well as the *2008 Pulitzer Prize.*

A collection of short stories entitled *This Is How You Lose Her* (Riverhead Books) is forthcoming in September 2012. He is currently working on a science fiction novel that he says, "has something to do with Dominicans and the end of the world." Writer, activist, teacher, realist, sci-fi enthusiast, and sociologist, Díaz is more than the sum of his parts, firmly believing that the writer must be engaged with the world around him or her. During the course of our interview, I found Junot Díaz to be friendly, thoughtful, and thoroughly grounded. It felt more like a conversation with a friend than an interview with a famous author. And that's a good thing.

℘ ℘ ℘

This issue of *phati'tude* is based on the idea of Latino identity and you often identify yourself as a Dominican writer, and at times you refer to yourself as a Caribbean writer. In your mind, is there a difference?

We're talking about overlapping identities, about simultaneous ones. I for one am a Dominican, a Latino and also Caribbean. There's a lot of overlap, but depending on how one is thinking about your identity matrix or how you're interacting or building solidarity, there's a different stress. There are plenty of groups in the Caribbean who are not Latino, yet as a Caribbean myself, I'm linked to them very intimately, very palpably both on a cultural and historical level. It's the way most identity tends to work: It's extremely complex, but also it's something that functions easily and elegantly for many, many people. In this case, I don't have as much problems negotiating between these poles, but it helps to imagine identity as something that draws upon powers of simultaneity.

Obviously the Dominican Republic shares an island with Haiti, and you've been active in raising funds for Haiti. You've also mentioned or been critical of the treatment of Haitians by the Dominican government. Julia Alvarez deals with Dominican-Haitian relations in her novels, and I know you read her stuff. What do you see as the main issue standing in the way of these two peoples who share the same island yet have had a problematic relationship for years?

This is one of those issues that's extremely complicated and yet rather prosaic. There's nothing unsurprising about groups taking advantage of each other, groups being in conflict with each other, and groups feeling that another group is invading them or there's too many of them, or that immigration of these so-called undesirables should be resisted by every mean possible. We see that this is the default setting of America's vision of Mexico and its other southern neighbors. So it's not surprising that a county like the Dominican Republic might have the same kind of attitudes, politics and reflexes towards Haiti.

Yeah I understand that.

If we're asking what the hell is really going at a larger level, we couldn't do justice to it in this Q and A. As we well know, Haiti has been utterly abandoned, has been completely taken advantage of by the larger Western capitalist, has been ravaged and been victimized by basically most of the global powers, the U.S. and France leading the pack. We in the States have been the chief culprits to abetting in Haiti's evisceration; there is responsibility enough to go around. These 'attacks' have made Haiti impossibly vulnerable, impossibly poor. Then of course you have the internal situation in Haiti—political leaders and factions who through their opportunism and cruelties, have compounded Haiti's misery. And then there's the Dominican Republic's

anti-Haitianism, a brutal racist ideology that has old roots in Dominican political culture, an ideology that the elites within the Dominican Republic love to fan, love to provoke, in order to mobilize people away from examining what the hell the elites are doing—which is usually stealing and fucking up the country. We need to talk about what's going on with the Dominican Republic and Haiti, but I suspect this is a way for other nations and groups to evade their own responsibilities, their own hand in Haiti's catastrophic actualized. The DR's anti-Haiti madness must be talked about but so too must we expose always the world's anti-Haiti madness. We can't have one without the other. Otherwise, Haiti becomes all about local brutalities and not the larger global brutalities that have made a Haiti possible. On multiple levels, the Dominican Republic has added immensely to Haiti's miseries but so has the U.S. and France. Even if Dominicans were the most gentle, wonderful neighbors, you would still have Haitians dying and suffering in ways that are unimaginable, absolutely unimaginable, so I guess whom do we blame—or better said how do we talk about a situation like this? First by talking about it and second by making sure you round up all the suspects. Otherwise, the problem will continue.

You mentioned the Haitian-Dominican community. In New York is there such a thing? Do Haitians and Dominicans interact?

Well, I was speaking mostly of Haitian Dominicans living in the Dominican Republic.

Oh, okay, I wasn't clear.

Haitian-Dominicans like African-American.

Right, got it.

Now I am no expert.

(Laughs) I'm not holding you to that.

I'm no expert as far as how many interactions Haitian and Dominicans in the States have. I do a lot of work and have a lot of friendships in the U.S.-Haitian community, so if you ask me are there a lot of connections, I'm going to say yes. If you ask someone like my crazy uncle who I don't think has spoken to a Haitian since he arrived to the U.S. ,he would be, like, absolutely not.

So let's go back then to the Dominican Republic. Because in *Oscar Wao*, Trujillo is everywhere, and you know I've taught Alvarez's *In the Time of the Butterflies* to my students. But to you, what does the persona of Trujillo represent, because he was gone before you were born?

When we speak about Trujillo, we're speaking also about the Trujillato, about the deformative effect of a 31-year fascistic coercive cult-like regime, a regime of a charismatic egomaniacal leader. What happens when one single perverse personality inflicts itself on a fragmented, isolated, already traumatized from colonialism community like the Dominican Republic? After all, we're not talking about a country like Cuba, which historically has had diverse wells of intellectual, artistic, cultural, historical waters to drawn upon in the face of its tyrannies. For a time, Cuba was the heart of the former Spanish empire in the Americas, and certainly Cuba was at the crossroads of the Old World and the New World. The Dominican Republic while sharing some of these strands, some of

> **" . . . if I think about what's my great American theme, I always say Dominican masculinity."**

these contacts, was far more isolated; its communities far more atomized, which made it highly vulnerable to the kind of sequestration Trujillo inflicted up on it. "Sequestration"—I'm thinking in Spanish.

"Sequestration" sounds like an English word.

Yeah—like being held hostage and this isolation made it very vulnerable to being imprinted by a leader like Trujillo. For many Dominicans, Trujillo and the Trujillato often represented their first contact with what we call modernity, with the nation. Just imagine the damage one personality could do on a nation that's cut off and isolated. One of the reasons we have such ferocious anti-Haitianism in the DR is because one of Trujillo's most notorious moves was to further isolate the Dominican Republic by carving a bloody ditch between it and Haiti. The genocide of 1937 was as much about brutalizing Haitians and Dominicans as it was about securing Trujillo's control of the Dominican borders. A control that allowed him to keep the Dominican people more isolated, more vulnerable, cut off from traditional competing solidarities to the West. When we're talking about the Trujillato, we're not just talking about Trujillo; we're talking about the immense vulnerability, the immense isolation of many sectors of the Dominican community that Trujillo seized control of and began to shape— shape would be too nice of a word, began to pound and form in very terrible ways. This shaping, this deformation, continues to be present in what can be called the Dominican character. It might be semi-invisible, but its power is no less significant.

Okay. Good, thank you. You were talking about your uncle before, and much of your writing revolves around family dynamics whether it be *Drown* or *Oscar Wao*. What did you learn about yourself and the world around you watching your parents' relationship? I mean I have some ideas from *Drown*, but just from watching your parents as a boy growing up, what did you learn about the world from observing them?

One of the things that I discovered very quickly was that adults spend a lot of time hiding shit and that this idea of secrets and this idea of putting a very positive face on whatever the hell is happening struck me very deeply. Where I grew up your house could be on fire, and my mom would be like, "Oh gee that fire sure does provide a lot of warmth." Not because she wanted to put a positive spin on things but because she wanted to obscure what was really happening.

Yeah, I know I'm like that. I have two kids.

I had a rather tumultuous childhood with parents who—you must understand I care very deeply about my mother—but I certainly wouldn't wish my childhood on anyone. I guess some people with shittier lives would prefer it to theirs—we weren't on the complete bottom of the horrorscale by any stretch of the imagination—but if I had my way I'd keep healthy kids away from that sort of upbringing. Growing up in my family I learned very quickly that I had to be independent. For all the support that I could get from my folks, there was an enormous amount that wasn't being covered, wasn't being given; it was very clear to my child's mind if I didn't step up there would be a lot of problems. In my family, if you waited for your folks to resolve anything, you were going to be waiting a long time. I'm not always sure I had much of a childhood in the way my friend's children are having childhoods right now. Another thing I learned from my parents, on a positive note, was a tremendous work ethic, an enormously valuable skill set. My parents they gave us the work ethic, and that is not something you can buy. Let me tell you I love my younger family members; I love the new generation of kids but if there ever was a work competition between my 16 year old self and my 16 year old cousins, I would crush all of them combined. That may sound like boasting, but if you grew up immigrant the way I did, that's just the way shit was. I feel that anything I've done that's been useful and productive comes out of the fact that my parents took the time and the energy to press upon me the value of work, the value of being disciplined. That has been the motor, the fuel that has driven me everywhere I've gone.

And I imagine that's what got you through high school and into college, away from other friends or influences.

I'm telling you it's like having a super power. That shit is useful always. A work ethic.

I agree. So let me ask you another question. In *Drown* and *Oscar Wao*, you present really strong female characters, and you raise questions about how to define masculinity. How important are notions of masculinity and femininity to you as a writer and as a person, Junot Díaz?

Certainly masculinity has been a singular preoccupation of mine for many years. It seems that from the moment I entered college and began to become exposed to feminism and to the various critiques of masculinity and patriarchy and to lot of the writings, a lot of the political activism produced by feminism that I began to feel as I'd finally found the other side of my artistic calling, my great topic, my great scheme. I had Santo Domingo as my artistic focus but I needed something else. I could feel that in my

". . . the Dominican Republic is the New Jersey of the New World."

bones, and the feminists at Douglass College of Rutgers University gave it to me. Some people are obsessed with Napoleon, some with WW2, my freak became how masculinity and patriarchy work in a very specific narrow New Jersey Dominican community. It just absolutely took hold of me, partially because I was the son of someone who considered himself, and was considered by the community at large, as fantastically masculine. My father was considered in many ways a tribune of Caribbean masculinity and living under such a person, with this kind father who was attempting to bootstrap all his sons up to that same level of manliness, provided me with a real scary insider's view of some of these processes. An explicit view of how this kind of very specific Dominican masculinity attempts to transmit itself across generations and how it's acquired, how it required training, rigorous repetition, many brutalities, and what is its great toxicity. This stuff gave me as a writer and as an artist lots of fucking energy, lot of inspiration. I wanted to explode these patriarchal scripts, to draw maps to their silences, to inform against myself. My dad's attempt to make me into a hyper-masculine subject fucked me up for life and so I figured the one thing I could do with the damage was expose. To misquote Caliban: Father, you taught me your language, and my profit on it is to curse it.

Would you consider this one of the legacies of Trujillo? Didn't he embody that?

Trujillo rode—sort of like a surfer on a wave—Trujillo rode into already functioning patterns. Trujillo in many ways just rode the wave of a very American, very new world, very Spanish patriarchal design. Trujillo tweaked it, but the Trujillo masculine regime would certainly be recognizable to someone in the 1800's in the Dominican Republican and certainly be recognizable to someone in the 1800s, in let's say, the territory of Nevada. It's a very new world thing, very new world pattern, a very new world dysfunction if we can call it that, one that's had a great amount of reach and that had at its heart the foundational experience of the plantation. And if I think about what's my great American theme, I always say Dominican masculinity.

So let me ask you this: When you went to Rutgers, you went as a freshman?

I did. I transferred in as a freshman from Kean College to Rutgers.

Okay, were you in some state of culture shock with this view of yourself and then going to Rutgers with all these kind of people?

It was a brilliant, important experience; it was like the best awakening any young person could have. To have the opportunity to realize how delusional the person I was when I came to Rutgers. There was a realization sometime in my freshman year about how backwards ass crazy I was. The fucked up ideas and simplification and biases and ideologies that I clung to. So exciting to be given a chance to work on myself, to change those things—those early years in college that's a time when you're open to be educated, to be transformed, and in terms of a lot of my fucked-up ideas from my youth. At Rutgers I was transformed towards a more progressive, activist world-view.

That's impressive.

I don't know if it's impressive.

No, it is because I went through the same things.

To wake up and discover that you can change direction and realize that you really are interested in being educated, which means being transformed, that's just, you know . . .

Yeah, I went through the same thing. I just shudder to think how I presented myself as a freshman. I didn't realize it as quickly. For me it was an ongoing process. I grew up pretty poor and I wasn't expected to go to college, and I just came in there, and I don't know what the fuck I was thinking, and it was a culture shock for me as well.

It was certainly an ongoing process. Let me say I was just less moronic as the years went on. There was never an end point to the de-moronicizing.

I understand that. I'm with you there. Since we've gotten to Rutgers let's talk about New Brunswick for a minute. I recommend *The Brief Wondrous Life of Oscar Wao* to everybody. But what stands out to me is the sense of place. I'm from New Jersey, and I went to Rutgers—and with Oscar I walk the streets. I had friends in Demarest Hall—we used to always hang out there. And Greasy Tony's is there, and I get a certain feeling of place with Perth Amboy and *Drown*. How has growing up in New Jersey impacted your writing, and how you see the world?

It's been fundamental, absolutely fundamental. I joke around, and I say the Dominican Republic is the New Jersey of the New World. New Jersey is the Dominican Republic of the United States.

I can't say that, but I do understand totally.

I certainly see it like that because in one way New Jersey is one of the most misunderstood and maligned states that lives in intimate proximity to the most stupendous metropolis in our cultural moment. Not to put too fine a point on it (after all there are many, many differences) but the Dominican Republic is also very misunderstood and maligned, and it lays within 60 miles of the U.S. and yet in terms of its marginalization, it might as well be on another planet far far away. I always say this, but I do believe the artist Robert Smithson's ideas of somewhere and elsewhere is very useful here, where New York is a somewhere and New Jersey is an elsewhere. If New York is the ultimate somewhere, then New Jersey is the ultimate elsewhere only a mile away. If the U.S. is the ultimate somewhere, then the Dominican Republic, which lays within viewing distance, the colonial egg from which the American imperial eagle sprang, is another elsewhere, very marginalized and yet such close historical proximity. That relationship between marginality and being so close to the heart of the powers of the world, *that* in many ways provided me with the grammar, my sort of artistic and literary grammar, my critical grammar and my ethos, if you will.

That makes sense to me. We're going to switch for a minute and move to politics. As you know there's a presidential election coming up, and I've got to admit I've been enjoying these Republican moments

the past few weeks. Do you think that immigration will be an issue, or not? What reforms or changes would you like to see in U.S. immigration policy?

I watch these debates and I wonder: Can we, as a country ever take the racist white supremacy fear-mongering off the table? That could help us have a clear debate and a clear plan of action in regards to immigration. That would be utopian. When you look at immigration policy going back to the Reagan period, it was nowhere near as fucked up as it is now. Immigration was not this enormous bugbear by which politicians drove fearful whites into the voting booth, but it has become that. These political parties, Republicans specifically, and the Democrats aren't far behind, are jumping on these well-worn wedge issues, but what they do when they hit us with wedge issues to try to rally their troops, what they do is make it impossible for there to be a discussion that would help our nation move logically and progressively towards resolving a real problem or issue. You're using this harsh racist rhetoric to get votes for your parties, but what you do is inflict enormous amounts of damage on your actual community, on your country but also on the people who are being victimized by many of the laws through which this stuff sets off. All this fear mongering, the amount of suffering, the indifference people have towards this. It's astonishing that as a nation we've abandoned the kind of ethical center around immigrants.

Yeah, it seems like the 1920's to me.

It is unimaginable. Unimaginable. It's one of the most ridiculous things. This is the way the country is wired now. You can't really have an honest discussion about immigration now. You can't say to Americans, "You, my dear Americans, are fucking addicted to immigrants the way you're addicted to your cocaine, to your weed, to your cheap fucking shit produced in other countries." America wants to have it both ways. It wants to smoke its crack, but it wants to drop bombs on the people who make the crack. We want to live a very wonderful life provided to us by immigrant bodies and immigrant suffering. At the same time, we want to stick knives straight in the backs of those immigrant bodies because that makes us feel better while we're enjoying, while we're benefiting from all their work.

So let me ask you this: In a few sentences you went from utopian to unimaginable. What other political issues would you like to see addressed in this presidential election?

Well I want to ask fucking Obama why did you fucking deport more Latinos than any president in modern history.

Is that true?

Close enough to the truth. We know straight up what the fuck is devouring this country and none of those issue are going to be talked about because our political leadership is so deranged and absolutely disconnected from reality, and is so intent on guaranteeing that no one sees this reality and for this reason, we're not going have any of the conversations we need to have. Obama has not been interested (until now that it's time to be re-elected) in inequality, disparities on economic equality, in the rapine of the rich against the poor. He hasn't. So now he has to talk about it because he needs a stump to get reelected. Okay, fine, knock yourself out. Better late than never. But the reality is that we have a totally rotten to the core national imagination—corpora-

Richard Oppel, Pulitzer Board co-chair (left), presents the 2008 Pulitzer Prize in Fiction to Junot Díaz, for *The Brief Wondrous Life of Oscar Wao* (Riverhead Books).

tions are considered human beings, we have no interest in economic justice, in educational reform, in understanding why our country is so incredibly sick on so many different fronts—we have no interest in that — and no one is going to talk about it. We're just going to go along and say that a 50 percent dropout rate for high school students is a great idea, the fact that income disparities increase every single year over the last decade, that's fine, and the fact that more people are under pharmaceutical regimes, whether it's being a drug addict or being under some kind of medication, that's fine too. The fact that we've lost, unlike Japan, we've lost the ability to have high-end technological manufacturing jobs that Japan and Germany have been able to maintain, oh that's absolutely fine. No problem. Gay marriage, Mexicans, black people and abortion, that's the real problem bringing American down. Abortion matters have been quiet of late but these candidates will get to it, believe me.

Let me ask you the next question, you sort of half answered it already. The Occupy Wall Street

WHAT'S IN A NOMBRE?

WRITING LATIN@ IDENTITY IN AMERICA

movement has managed to get a lot of attention. The mainstream media has often cited the lack of focus or clear goals in the movement, and for me it was pretty damn clear. Have you followed the OWS movement at all?

Well, deeply, of course. I am a member of the 99 percent. And as an old activist, I'm thrilled to see so many people fired up and through their activism changing the national discourse. Mitt Romney on the defensive because he's a predatory zillionaire? Who would have thought it! One other note: It is the absolute essence of journalistic hypocrisy that the deranged nonsense of our political leadership goes unquestioned, but the very clear directives and objectives of a youth movement organizing around the abuses of Wall Street are persistently questioned as being unclear and somehow vague. I mean it was unbelievable. The OWS is vague, but what comes out of Newt Gingrich's mouth and Mitt Romney's mouth, that's okay, that passed?

So do you think the movement will have an effect?

These kinds of predictions always make you look stupid. But I'll give it a shot anyway: You can draw a direct line between how disaffected, how completely marginalized this growing demographic of young people across the world are, you can draw a direct line between the OWS and the revolution that threw Mubarak out. As many have pointed out what we may be seeing are the first tremors of a seismic upheaval, that it may take years to fully come into being, but I do believe that eventually there's going to be the same kind of reckoning that occurred in Egypt in the U.S. You can draw a direct line from Obama being elected to the OWS movement; it was basically a youth movement that got Obama elected. Of course, as soon as he was elected, Obama abandoned the youth movement completely; he has absolutely no interest in their issues and keeping them engaged and keeping them politically active. The youth section did not go away. It appears stronger, and it appears in the OWS movement. Even if the OWS movement seems to have retreated, the youth that fueled it, their disaffection, their desire for a better world, is not going to go away. The numbers are going to increase and eventually people are going have to deal with it. This election right now is an attempt by both political parties to pretend that there's no such thing as this new young demographic. It's a bunch of old white men and one old black dude farting at each other and running the same old toxic lines against each other, and truly none of them are addressing the new generation of active young people—the people who powered the OWS —and eventually that blindness, that stubborn disregard is going to cost these self-assured political assholes.

Yeah, I see it as already having an effect. I don't think it's so far been monumental, but I do see that the conversation is changing.

I agree with you. We wouldn't be having this conversation about Mitt Romney's taxes if it weren't for OWS. OWS has made it more difficult on a very simple level for Romney to run.

It's almost an embarrassment, his running, even for the Republicans. Might be because he's a Mormon, I'm not sure. Let's switch gears. Let's talk about teaching because I've been teaching forever. How do you like teaching?

Without question I love my students. For me teaching is a wonderful experience. I love my job. It's part of my civic engagement. There's no better way at giving back to a community than to help educate its youth. It's fantastic but it's terrible for my writing.

Tell me about it.

It's probably the worst thing. What takes away most time from my writing is certainly teaching.

It almost comes from the same place to be a really good teacher, to be a creative teacher. It almost comes from the same place, and it's a shame.

Yes. Absolutely.

What I like about teaching, being that I've been doing this for 27 years now, I'm always learning things from my students, and the world is constantly changing. Do you learn stuff from your students?

Yes, endlessly. We are in a classroom every day. Imagine a football player that never gets old —or at least gets old more slowly. Imagine if you could stay in the game 30 or 40 years. The amount of shit you would learn at the end of that. Brother, I'm like you—my students—every time I'm in there I'm like goddamn, what a privilege I'm having to be in this constant learning place. Sometimes you feel like your class is at its best, you feel like you're playing football with an all-star team, and you're learning a lot of shit in the process. But let's also be honest, when your class is at its worst, you feel like you're carrying 40,000 pound bags of salt. But hey, it's the world – the world is that way. And the salt is a small price for all the learning, for being around young people nonstop.

Let me ask you about music. I just finished reading *Invisible Man* by Ralph Ellison with my students, and there are times in *Invisible Man*, each chapter almost, when he just goes off, and the prose sings. You have

VOL. 3
NO. 4

133

moments like that also, I notice, when you just sort of go off. What rhythms are going on in the background when you're writing in your mind?

To talk about musicality after you mention Ralph Ellison—he thought very deeply on music. He was one of those guys who just had it going on. I have not thought on music in any way that is . . .

But it's in there. There is a musicality in your writing, especially in *Oscar Wao*. Even my students who read it over the summer talked about that.

No, of course, listen, I come from a community that truly lives and dies on its music. It's an Afro-Caribbean nation. We've forgotten more about music than many countries have ever known. In the family and the community, music was as important an element as ambition, as important an element as education, and of course, it's going to leak into your work. It's going to form a strata, an armature, a baseline. I'm certainly conscious of wanting to make language do something musical; I want to make the language play *rada*. It helps that I was one of those kids who danced; I was one of those kids who they exposed to music very very early and that helped at each part of this writing process.

So what do you listen to know?

God, I'm a typical very old man.

Ha-ha. What are you, 40?

Yeah, 43. What ends up happening is that you don't have the time to follow music like I did when I was young. So of course I've been listening to the new Romeo CD. That's the *Aventura* lead singer who went off and did his solo thing. I've been listening to a lot of reggaeton mixes that my crazy friends put together. Of course, I love *Calle 13*.

That's one of the best things about having children. When I was 50 my kids were 19 and 16. I didn't have a chance to be the tired old man. They were bringing new stuff in always, which I'm so thankful for.

Yeah, right now I have Romeo on and I've been listening to *Calle 13* like crazy. I love *Omega,* who is my absolute motherfucking man. Just one of those things that makes you go, "Oh shit." I love that guy *Tyler the Creator,* his album *Goblin*—That shit is nuts!

I just see his name, and I laugh every time that that's his name: *Tyler the Creator.* So let me get to the next question. You've cited Julia Alvarez, Salman Rushdie, and Edwidge Danticat as influences, or as at least fellow travelers. Are there any writers you've read over the past few years that just knocked your socks off?

Wow, I really loved Yoko Ogawa—I've been obsessed with Yoko Ogawa, in translation, she's a Japanese writer whose had a couple of books out in the U.S. She had *The Diving Pool*, *Hotel Iris*, *The Housekeeper*, and *The Professor*. Ogawa just blew me the fuck away. For me she really had it. You could feel the world in her books and the human heart at struggle with itself.

I'll look for her work; I'm not familiar with her.

Of course I really love that novel that won the National Book Award, Jesmyn Ward's *Salvage the Bones*. She's another one. Then, of course, there's a young writer whose first book was incredible. Her name is Chloe Aridjis—*Book of Clouds*—and she's amazing because she's like part fucking Mexican and part Dutch and has talent to spare. Her novel is really awesome: great, moody, impressionistic. Loved it. Fucking loved it. You know who else is really cool for both music and writing? Do you know the Dominican writer-singer Rita Indiana? I really love her work.

Really? What does she write? Does she write novels?

Yeah, she wrote these small novellas. There's one called *Papi*, which is really fantastic and her music is all over. You'll love her.

Do you ever feel pressure or responsibility, and sorry for putting you in this position, almost to speak as a voice of Dominican Americans or immigrants, do you ever feel pressure to speak for a whole group of people?

Oh *that* question. People of color are *always* supposed to stand in for their group. You're never going to ask Rick Moody does he feel pressure for speaking for white people. That's the question that reveals our society's racially insane logic. If you're a person of color you're naturally thought to be representative of a collective—shit you *are* a collective —but we don't conceive of white people that way. White people are allowed to be individuals, to exist beyond their whiteness, but I will never be allowed to exist beyond my colored cultural otherness. No way. These types of questions reinforce and reify that perverse white supremacist logic. Me, I tend to drive the white writers crazy; I will ask them that question in the middle of a panel. How much of a burden is your whiteness?

How do people respond? Do they usually laugh?

No, no, because I'm a person who knows how to drive it in. Listen: I am always asked to stand in for a collective because that's sort of the racial logic of the U.S. But I'll tell

you that I am absolutely an artist by my nature, and if you're going to make large claims about Dominicanness, about the African diaspora, about New Jersey-ness from my very individualistic point of view you're in for a really long night.

It's been four years since *Oscar Wao*. What are you working on now?

Well, I've got a collection of stories, another book of stories coming out in September, and I'm working on a novel.

Want to give us any hints about the novel?

I'm hoping it's going to be Dominican Science fiction. Not much more to say about it. Hopefully it entails the end of the world.

It is 2012, you know. Better write it quick. Okay, last question: What advice would you give to young writers just starting out who have been influenced by your talent and by your success?

I mean I'm not so sure there are many that have been influenced . . .

No, no, no, stop. There's been a lot.

What I was going to say was that I meet so many young writers that don't read at all. They don't read at all, and if they read, they read little. And I always ask my young writers when they ask me, when they say, "Professor Díaz," or "Junot," "What can we do to be better writers"? I say, "Hey, don't write for three years and read three-hundred books. Those of you who do that will be better off than those of you who spend three years writing, I promise you that." One of the things that has happened is that we've increased the pressure on all kids to be more professional. We want kids not to be artists anymore; we want them to approach creative writing in the way you approach being a dentist. And you can't do that. So many young people I meet want to go from undergrad to grad school and then be a writer like it's a career in dentistry they're pursuing. The problem with that pace is that it denies you time in the real world. You're an artist because of your engagement with the world; you're not an artist because you've pursued your professional degree with avidity and without any questionable gaps in your resume. It's the gaps in the resume that make you valuable as an artist, not the efficiency with which you rack up your degrees. So in some ways I always argue with my students. I'm like (a) you need to read—I don't care about your writing, reading will take care of that, (b) if you want to be a real writer, then you have to be an artist and (c) to be an artist you need to have an engagement with the world. If you're pursuing your art like a professional degree—hey I respect you and I'm sure your books will be great—but for real, those are never the writers I've been interested in at all. So if you're saying there are people out there who were inspired by me, they might be less inspired if they knew the way I conceive of myself as an artist, as someone who comes out of reading and engagement with the world, and not pursuing writing as if I was a dentist. And so many of my kids are in a rush to be famous and to be published—it's all about the dentistry input that's seeped in and infected the arts.

That's also about being 19.

Well, no. You talk to people of different generations and one thing stands out: Kids these days are under incredible pressure to show profit. They can't even conceive of a world where they can be artists and engage in the world for 5, 6, 7, 8 years without showing any profit, without any resumé timeline or corporate logic. I do believe the pace of life has become more machine, and less art orientated. I can't imagine a harder time to cultivate an artistic ethos—but I can't imagine a time more in need of artists. So that's the grumpy me. My advice is to read and to imagine yourself as an artist. Your work will last a lot longer than if you imagine yourself as a dentist who writes because this is your way of handling the corporate capitalist exigencies of our contemporary moment.

Well, let's go back to the wide-eyed bushy tailed you. When you were 19 . . .

I knew I wanted to be an artist.

And you knew it was going to take some time?

I just knew it was going to come out of my engagement with the world. There's no question about that. The reason I write the way I do is because as an artist I was connected to the world. Listen, I will probably prove this for the rest of my short life. If a book takes 11 years, it takes 11 years, but if you're a dentist writer 11 years writing a book is unimaginable. You would never do that because you got to show profit. You'll write two or three inferior things rather than what your heart really needed to write. But again, self-serving. This is a description and a narrative and a set of poetics that is deeply self-serving, but I mean where else can you speak from than from what you experience.

Yeah of course, that's what I've asked. I want to thank you so much for giving me your time.

No, for real, thank you guys for this. ◻

DANNY SHOT was the head of Long Shot productions for over 20 years, which included *Long Shot* literary and arts magazine and Long Shot Books. He has appeared throughout the country and his work has been widely anthologized in books and literary magazines.

ARTWORK: Manuel Adolfo Villalobos
"Concrete N' Urban Roses," acrylic and spray paint on ply wood (5.5X 3 ft.) Copyright © 2010

NESTOR BARRETO

preámbulo 3

juzgamos estas realidades auto
evidentes: que tod@s somos diferentes
desde antes de nacer, que somos dotad@s
y privad@s de cosas y aptitudes de
propensidades y excusas de buenos malos
y peores equipos de azares y albures
incontables, que entre estos se hallan la salud,
el acceso y la iniciativa del un@ que define
[la] [el] sujet@ de la definición que no hay
derechos sólo privilegios y oportunidades
que se configuran como estados naciones
para imitar una voluntad que se llamará
común como aspiración y para asegurar
estos privilegios, entre las personas se siguen
los patrones del servicio, y que derivan sus
poderes legítimos de las urdimbres de los
pudientes. y que esta forma se da y se fatiga e
hipertrofia pues concentramos masivamente
para después quejarnos y no se quedæ
ahí y que podamos tumbarl@ y hacerl@ a
nuestra imagen [y semblanza] frustrando
así toda mínima posibilidad de felicidad. de
hecho siempre habrá una excusa para no
moverse [hasta que dejæ de haberla] incluso
en la dehesa de un mundo completamente
original donde todavía no se sabrá la hora
que es y los más listos se ocuparán del resto
y los ajustes cosméticos proliferarán por una
idea axiomática de la conveniencia quien no
entienda esto no soportará el despotismo y
buscará su libertad en el borde mismo de la
media unidad que es la naturaleza sin terminar
desde el principio

we hold these truths to be self-
evident: that we all are different
since before birth, that we all are endowed
with and deprived of things and abilities of
propensities and excuses of good bad
and worse teams of chances and risks
innumerable, that among these are health,
access and the initiative of the one that defines
the subject of the definition
that there are no rights only privileges and opportunities
that autoconfigure as nation-states
to imitate a volition that will be called
common as aspiration and to warrant
these privileges, the patterns of ser[vice][fdom] are followed
by the people, who derive their
legitimate powers from immeshing with the
upscale and that this form [occurs][is given][happens] and
[eventually] becomes fatigued or
hypertrophies because we concentrate on it massively
to afterwards complain [and][but] [it] do[es]n't stop
there, [and] we could overthrow it and [re]make it in
our image [and semblance] thereby
ruining the slightest possibility of happiness. in
fact there will always be an excuse not to
move [until there isn't] even
in the pasturelands of a completely original
world where what time it is
will not be yet known and the brightest will take care of the rest
and the cosmetic adjustments will proliferate through
an axiomatic idea of convenience whoever doesn't
understand this will not bear [the ensuing] despotism and
will look for their freedom on the very fringes of the
mediumnity that nature is unfinished
from the [start][get go][beginning][onset][outset]

Translated by Nestor Barreto and Adam Wier..

CARLOS CESAR VALLE

Making Roll Ups

Mi rostro
Que nunca sonríe

Mi rostro estrecho
Y alargado

Mi rostro celeste
Y oscuro

Muchas veces rosa

Muchas veces rojo

Siempre azul

Mi rostro
Del que todos desconfían
Y se asustan

Mi rostro agestado
Triste

Mi rostro rápido y atípico
Mi rostro de diamante

Nunca dice nada
Nunca dice hola

Aunque siempre se despida
De todos ustedes
Infinitamente agradecido

(at Diageo, 7 de Octubre del 2008)

My face
That never smiles

My thin and elongated
Face

My dark and celestial
Face

Many times rose

Many times red

Always blue

My face
That no one trusts
And everybody´s scared of

My suggestive and sad
Face

My quick and atypical
Face

My diamond face

It never says anything
It never says hi

Although it always says goodbye
To all of you
Infinitely thankful

(at Diageo, October 7th, 2008)

Translated by David Fernandez Patiño, Jose Tavarez and
Joanna Morales.

Empiezo a envejecer

Empiezo a envejecer
y no me reconozco ante el espejo
soy objeto y sujeto de un pasado que me miente
aguijoneada de amapolas en mi cuello
lloro risas
aspavientos
recuerdo los bambúes que a la una y catorce
despojaban mi otro yo dejándome despierta
Una interrogante que se vuelven miles en mi boca
no llego a pronunciar
hora y locura gritan en mis sienes
la mirada a tientas muerde rostros
las pestañas son el muro
los silencios
las audacias de quien no quiere asumirse como amante
perdón pido a la noche que me trae el retroceso
los temores / el sí / el no
y a Descartes con su duda
la agonía de un beso que se pierde entre lengua y dientes
una nariz congelada por el susto
una boca que no se abre porque ignora su futuro
Empiezo a envejecer
envuelta entre rubores
malabarista de momentos nunca olvidados
el agua sobre el zinc
mis pies en el lodo
truenos como muerte vomitando sorpresas
Me miré vuelta niña jugando a las escondidas
toqué las acacias
los perejiles
las santomas
olí la yerbabuena
los lirios
Empiezo a envejecer
y veo a los niños (ya no tan niños)
repitiendo mis dias
Empiezo a envejecer
Empiezo a envejecer
Empiezo a envejecer.

I start to age (Tr.)

I start to age
and I do not recognize myself before a mirror
I am an object of and subject to a past that lies to me
pricked on the neck by poppies
I cry laughter
exaggerated movements
I remember the bamboos that at one-fourteen
stripped the other I leaving me awake
One query that becomes thousands in my mouth
I do not get to say
hour and madness scream in my temples
the groping sight bites faces
the eyelashes are the wall
the silences
the audacities of one who does not want to assume themselves a lover
I ask forgiveness of the night that brings the setback
the fears / the yes / the no
and Descartes with his doubt
the agony of a kiss lost amidst tongue and teeth
a nose frozen by fright
a mouth that does not open for fear of its future
I start to age
wrapped among blushes
juggler of moments never forgotten
water above zinc
my feet in the mud
thunder like death vomiting surprises
I saw myself a girl again playing hide and seek
I touched the acacias
the parsley
the santomas
I smelled the mint
the lilies
I start to age
and see the children (no longer children)
repeating my days
I start to age
I start to age
I start to age

Translated by Joanna Morales.

MAIRYM CRUZ-BERNAL

Poema de las manos cortadas

Le cortaron las manos a las hijas del mar Ámbar Past

Si te cortaran las manos?

Después que una ha muerto
cómo quieres que responda a esta pregunta?

Mis manos cortadas jamás dejarán de escribir
sin mí, escribirán mejor
vueltas alas, no necesitarán mis pies para andar
vueltas palomas, no necesitarán de mis ojos para elevarse
vueltas corazón, no necesitarán de los dedos para la caricia

Podrán cortarme las manos
pero mi lengua seguirá cantando

Podrán arrancarme la raíz de la tierra
pero mis manos cortadas
dibujarán en tu pelvis
los contornos de un nuevo país

Brindo con mis manos cortadas
la copa de luz de tu mirada

Vuelta risa
mis manos saltarán a carcajadas
emitiendo el eco a través de las líneas finísimas
de un universo holográfico
hasta llegar al Valle del Elqui
donde espera el hombre que amo

Voy a cantar hasta rajar el cielo con mi canto

No existen ejércitos humanos
ni fuerzas militares
ni gobiernos de turno
que puedan tapar el canto de mis manos

Desde Safo, Cleopatra, María de Magdala
mujeres de manos y vientres
hijas del mar

Tengo por herencia
manos inquebrantables
manos adúlteras
dadas a la caricia de toda piel

Manos manchadas de esta tinta menstruante

Manos que no claudican la batalla
la batalla dulce de tu cuerpo con el mío

Manos que le nacen dedos
dedos que le nacen hijos
hijos que le nacen ríos
ríos que inventan puentes
manos que echan raíces y son ramas
y le crecen árboles
árboles que dan nido a los pájaros
pájaros que enredados en mi melena azul
se vuelven alas
alas que no necesitan de mis manos

Ah mis manos cortadas
sobrevivirán mi nombre

Tal vez si fuera hombre
sabría cómo contestar a esta pregunta

Pero mis manos son mujer
y hace ya mucho
se han desprendido de mi cuerpo

Translated by Amy E. Savage.

Poem of the severed hands (Tr.)

They cut off the hands of the daughters of the sea . . . Ámbar Past

If they cut off your hands?

After one has died
How do you want her to respond to this question?

My severed hands will never stop writing
without me, they will write better
becoming wings, they won't need my feet to walk
becoming doves, they won't need my eyes to fly
becoming a heart, they won't need fingers for affection

They might cut off my hands
but my tongue will continue singing

They might tear my root from the earth
but my severed hands
will draw on your pelvis
the contours of a new country

I toast with my severed hands
the cup of light in your gaze

Becoming laughter
my hands will laugh uproariously
emitting the echo of a holographic universe
through very fine lines
until the Valley of Elqui
where waits the man that I love

I will sing until the sky cracks with my singing

Human armies do not exist
nor military forces
nor Governments of the Day
that can crush my hands' singing

From Sappho, Cleopatra, Mary Magdalene
women of hands and bellies
daughters of the sea

I have inherited
unbreakable hands
adulterous hands
given to caressing all skins

Hands stained by this menstrual ink
the sweet battle of your body with mine

Hands that sprout fingers
fingers that bear children
children that bear rivers
rivers that invent bridges
hands that take root and are branches
and grow trees
trees that give nests to birds
birds, which entangled in my blue mane
become wings
wings that have no need for my hands

Ah, my severed hands
they will survive my name

Maybe if I were a man
I would know how to answer this question

But my hands are female
and it has been a long while
since they have been removed from my body

Translated by Amy E. Savage.

CARLOS AGUASACO

Bajo esta piel mestiza duerme un enano

Usa mi epidermis como una manta de vagabundo
La enrolla alrededor de su cuello
Y, con una taza de café en la mano, pide limosna

Me molesta su olor a acróbata de circo
Sus ínfulas de domador de trenes
Sus deseos de saltar de una plataforma a la otra
En la estación del metro

En ocasiones, juego a dejarlo descubierto en mitad de la calle
Halo mi piel y echo a correr por Lexington Avenue
Lo abandono allí, en la esquina de la sesenta y ocho,
Con su cuerpo de yuca y su taza de café
Corre tras de mí, iracundo
Mi piel ondea como una bandera agarrada a mi puño

Bajo esta piel mestiza duerme un bufón
Arlequín neoyorquino que bromea en otra lengua
Una lengua gruesa como mi piel,
Una lengua-manta que cubre a quienes tienen frío.

Beneath this mestizo skin sleeps a midget (Tr.)

He uses my epidermis like a homeless' blanket
He wraps it around his neck
and, with a cup of coffee in his hand, he begs for money

His circus-acrobat smell bothers me
the airs he puts on of being a train-tamer
his desire to jump from one platform to the other
in the subway station

Occasionally, I play at leaving him uncovered in the middle of the street
I pull off my skin and start to run along Lexington Avenue
I abandon him there, on the corner of sixty-eighth,
with his body of cassava and his cup of coffee
he runs after me, irate
my skin ripples in the air like a flag clinging to my fist

Beneath this mestizo skin sleeps a buffoon
a New York harlequin who jokes in another language
a language as thick as my skin,
a mantle like language that covers those who are cold.

Translated by Carlos Aguasaco and Joanna Morales.

ETNAIRIS RIVERA

La mascarita de tiempo

Ando en el cuerpo con la mascarita de tiempo estrujadísima en la mano.
Mi cara es un antifaz contra todas mis caras. Conozco la mano que me aparta,
el hilo que circunda un espacio de pronto reducido. Allí permaneció el despierto
transcurrir, el pájaro, todos aquellos matutinos homenajes. La noche avanza
trenzada al cuerpo, la veloz noche, lo rojizo del segundo, esa bandada que pasa,
despide al sol y me lleva consigo. Conozco el antiguo talismán de la espina y la rosa
cuando la luna es una boca que huye y en la puerta de casa, la piel aguarda su turno.

From: *Ariadna del Agua (Ariadne of the Water)* 2011

The mask of time (Tr.)

I walk in my body with the mask of time squished up small in my hand. My face is a domino mask against all
my other faces. I know the hand that separates me, the thread surrounding a suddenly dwindling space. There
remains the waking passage of time, birds, all those old morning homages. The night advances, interlaced with
the body, the swift night, the erubescence in a second, that flock passing by, taking their leave of the sun and
me with them. I know the old talisman of the rose and its thorn when the moon is a mouth that flees and at the
door of the house, the skin awaits its turn.

Translated by Adam Wier.

The deep blues

Coming of age while I'm still young, feeling the blue note of the deep blues,
brings my leaves to fall too soon, sometimes so early that I can feel
solitude has moved into my space ahead of time.

Deep as well I find myself lifting the flowers of survival and deeply hoping
for the thought of the first rain of spring to come and swiftly change the feeling.

YSABEL Y. GONZALEZ

Azabache

Martyred mother pin me close to la figa, an Azabache fist full of a peeking thumb.

How the amuleto came to be is this: Tia Zola did not only make sancocho. In Puerto Rico she
had a room on the side where a memory will be placed in my mind that
runs a backward timed line. I see her pressed palms now, pushing back
against cracked concepts. A cigar smoked spell seeped from her lips into Mami's
nostrils as the translation was made. I believe. I believed.

My next bath was filled with red and white carnation petals perched upon
oil spilled waters. My first mistake was I did not dip my head under,
fearing it would wipe my English clean. My second was that once dressed, I
refused to wear Santa Barbara's sword hidden in my breast, lest a white boy find it.

I changed. As granules slip past chutes, my americana praise played like a smoky lens streaming
summer's sun. I clung close to a melting mirror, something off a Dali canvas, watching my face
dribble then meld as if it was for God's play.

I change back. To my origin. Metamorphosis into smooth jet fossil, healing hailing like cosmic
showers, power soaked Azabache. Cloaked in forbidden faith, scolding scepter in my Borinquen
grasp, I will last.

PHOTO: Pablo Delano
"Mr. Russell Foster portraying an Authentic Indian at Traditional Carnival Character Competition,
Victoria Square" 16 x 20 inches, photograph, silver gelatin print, Copyright ©2008

EMANUEL XAVIER

A Reading From The Book Of Xavier

And Emanuel said, "Heaven is for homosexuals! I mean, who the hell do you think designs all those beautiful white dresses the angels be wearing? And have you ever seen a messenger of God with fucked up hair? Hello! They don't be visiting no corduroy skirt wearing Bible-thumpers looking like they just came all the way down from the clouds with wrinkled fabric and frizzed out locks.

And who do you think keeps Jesus looking like a really hot modern day hipster? Of course, he only hung out with gay men that had styling skills! The House of Jesus, otherwise known as The Twelve Apostles, were legendary. Seriously, he was made over from a rag-wearing blotchy skinned carpenter with a kinky 'do to an ivory white God with perfectly partitioned long straight hair, trimmed goatee, and only the best of robes. Even on that cross with his six pack he set the tone for all future underwear models. Frankly, his entire icon status is due largely to gifted gays who reimagined and immortalized his image through paintings and art.

And don't even get me started on that God! Like how old is he, really? Do you honestly think that silver fox keeps himself in great shape and maintains that lovely white hair brushed all on his own without some sound advice from Chelsea Queen gym bunnies and fabulous hairdressing angels? Somebody call 9-1-1 because homophobes are gonna get burnt in that lake and I don't think fire and brimstone is good for any kind of hair. So learn it and learn it well because when your time comes and 'We're Here! We're Queer!' is heard up on those clouds, you better get used to it! And don't think Ms. Satan, that hell-bent diva, is gonna be pitiful on your soul either. So, if you don't open up those small minds, come heaven or hell, you're gonna be doomed, bitches! You will gag!

Never mind an 'Amen', can I get a finger snap?"

Just Like Jesus

Just like Jesus, I want nativity and childhood to be simple introductions
Summarized to make way
for the mythology of adulthood
Evading early suffering and teen angst
to grant the world peace
Not only celebrated with mass spending during my supposed birth
but always

I want to encourage and motivate
just like Jesus-
An uneducated peasant
with spoken word skills
few academic literates could ever conquer
Simply by having faith in what I say
I want to arouse revolution

I want to comfort just like Jesus-
make you believe there is a God above
watching over us
Without need for proof
or scientific explanation

Just like Jesus, I want to cast out
your demons and disease
Cleanse your feet with mother's tears;
the scented hair of prostitutes
Liberate your oppressed soul
from the possession of others
Bring back lost friends from their tombs

Just like Jesus, I want to create my own family
and break with tradition
Host gatherings and feast
with sinners and whores
Be a shameless pervert and deviant
while indulging in the subservient role
of feeding the hungry

Instead of miracles,
I want to document my own history
Derail power hungry men
from the possibility of integrating
sexism and paternalism
to burden society with guilt and sin

I want to build my own cross
with carpenter hands
Carry it down the streets
where I will be found bleeding
Pierced with wounds not self-inflicted

Just like Jesus,
I want to hear the voice of my father
Sacrifice myself in his name—
arms stretched out
Bask in the brightness of stars
with lifeless eyes
Aware this preposterous death
is not an end but a beginning
Offering this body to be devoured by scavenger dogs and birds of prey
a sepia toned symbol of martyrdom
I want my image captured to snatch the breath
out of the oppressor's mouth
Leave them powerless to recreate my looks

to frame the minds of ignorance
launch crusades, sponsor slave ships
and stage brutal wars
while blindly following the utterance
of selfish leaders

Just like Jesus, I want to be nestled
half naked against your chest
Sanctified, even after my time spent
with over a dozen lovers
Claiming your spirit when I come
Baptize you with the promise of salvation

Just like Jesus,
I simply want to live before I die

MARIANELA MEDRANO

De Cómo Aprendimos El Juego Al Escondite

Yo porque nos tuviesen mucha amistad, porque conocí que era gente que se convertiría a nuestra Santa Fé con amor que no por fuerza les di a algunos de ellos unos bonetes colorados y unas cuentas de vidrio y otras cosas muchas de poco valor.

—Cristóbal Colón, *Diario de Navegación*

En la mentira de bonetes colorados
simula esconderse el sedoso azabache
más tarde sale a tomar aire en el milagro de la
textura hirsuta del consuelo africano
Ochùn nos inhala con fuerza divina

En la fragmentación del vidrio parecemos abatirnos
hasta descubrir el milagroso colorido de los vitrales
filtrando los rayos calientes del Gran Sol
En el espacioso vórtice de las catedrales volamos
rezamos el padrenuestro para cantarle a Yocahù
Detrás del avemaría vibra la figura
incorpórea fluida de Atabey

La isla misma de vez en cuando
parece enroscarse en la tristeza
su cuerpo de río ensangrentado empapa al Gran Sol
-por eso son tan hermosos nuestros atardeceres-

En las raíces de la yuca
las diosas y los dioses continúan haciendo milagros
Caguama nos resguarda en su carapacho indomable
aún en estos días de playas colonizadas por turistas
Gente retozona y calmada
jugamos bajo las pieles descoloridas de los santos
para proteger nuestra epidermis dorada.

On How We Learned To Play Hide And Seek (Tr.)

So they would trust us, and because I knew they were people who would convert to our faith with love and not by force, I gave them some red berets and some glass stones and many other worthless things.

— Christopher Columbus, *Diary of Navigation*

The silky black pretends to disappear
in the lie of red berets
Later it comes up for air in the miraculous
kinky texture of the African consolation
Ochùn inhales us with divine force

We seem to succumb in the fragmentation of glass
until we discover the stained magic
filtering the hot rays of the Grand Sun
In the spacious vortex of cathedrals we fly
pray the Holy Father in order to sing to Yocahù
In the background of the Hail Mary
vibrates Atabey's ethereal and fluid figure

From time to time the island herself
seems to coil up in the sadness
Her body a bloody river moistens the Grand Sun
–that is why our dusks are so beautiful–

In the roots of the yucca
the goddesses and the gods continue making miracles
Caguama protects us in her untamable conch
even now with beaches colonized by tourists
Playful and calm people
we play under the discolored skins of the saints
to protect our golden epidermis.

Translated by Marianela Medrano and Reggie Marra

MARIANELA MEDRANO: "De Cómo Aprendimos El Juego Al Escondite" reprinted from DIOSAS DE LA YUCA by Marianela Medrano Copyright © 2011, with permission from the Author. Ediciones Torremozas S.L., Paseo de la Castellana, 190, 28046 Madrid España, http://www.torremozas.com/

Cara Sucia

Nació de pie como un augurio
Presta a la batalla nació
El cordón tres veces anudado al cuello
Arrancó de cuajo las raíces a su madre
Dos azabaches brillantes
desafiantes como el Diablo los ojos
Caimito morado
A plena luz del día hizo sombras
Piernas abajo con un grito de sirena se lanzó

De pie como un augurio creció
Con la tinta de la mala suerte
La abuela no quería una niña morena
De pelo crespo burlando la raza
Otra marca incrustada en la estirpe
Otro pelo sediento de vaselina
El discurso bajo el ala

En lugar del pan trajo desgracia

El mundo no quería otra niña morena
Otra piel cantando salves en los montes del Cibao
A la junta vinieron todos
A mirar la afrentosa criatura
La que nació de pie
Con la piel morada azul marino
envejecida por las horas
Anudado al cuello el cordón invisible
El diagnostico insalvable
Mil veces maldecida criatura
La que nació de pie
Dicen que antes de desprenderse
mordió el vientre de la madre
Desapercibida jamás ha de pasar
Escandalosa presencia
Escandalosa piel
Escandaloso el pelo
Se pasea por las calles

Fuerza no hay para detener
a la que nació de pie
con la piel oscura
con los ojos brillantes
el discurso bajo el ala
Ángel negro voz cantante.

Dirty Face (Tr.)

She was born standing up like a bad omen
Ready to battle she was born
The cord tied three times around her neck
Yanked out her mother's roots
Two brilliant azabaches
Defiant like the Devil her eyes
Caimito Purple Star apple
In the daylight she made a shadow
Legs down with her siren voice she went

Standing like a bad omen she grew up
With the ink of disgrace
La abuela did not want another brown girl
with kinky hair betraying the race
The grandmother did not want another morena girl
Another trace embedded in the lineage
Not another hair thirsty for Vaseline
The discourse under the wing

Instead of bread she brought disgrace

The world did not want another brown girl
Another skin
singing salves in the forest in El Cibao
To the junta they all came
to meet the weird creature
The one who was born standing up
with purple navy blue skin
Tied to the neck an invisible cord
—insurmountable diagnosis—
A creature cursed a thousand times
The one who was born standing up

They say before she detached
She bit her mother's womb
She would never go unnoticed
Scandalous presence
Flagrant skin brazen hair
She paces the streets
No force will stop her
The one who was born standing up
With dark skin with bright eyes
Discourse under her wings
Black angel singing voice.

Translated by Marianela Medrano and Reggie Marra.

MARITHELMA COSTA

Neither Latino Nor Hispanic Just a wish
Litany for the Millennium

Christ of Bethlehem, son of Mary,
God and man, who came from Palestine into the Americas
 CHORUS: PROTECT US FROM OURSELVES

God the Father, God the Holy Spirit,
unsolved mystery of the Christians
 PROTECT US FROM OURSELVES

Yahvé, also known as Elohim, also known as Adonai,
pushed into the lagers of the Nazis,
sometimes managed to escape into the Americas
 PROTECT US FROM OURSELVES

Allah, God of the sword and of the book,
From Africa into India, your voyage
also ended in America
 PROTECT US FROM OURSELVES

Buda, Confucius, Tao
 PROTECT US FROM OURSELVES

God of the Rastafarians
 PROTECT US FROM OURSELVES

Olorum, owner of the Yoruba heaven
 PROTECT US FROM OURSELVES

Obatalá, river god who flowed from
The Niger into the Americas
 PROTECT US FROM OURSELVES

Yemayá, mother of all waters in Ifé,
Mother of all Orishas in America
 PROTECT US FROM OURSELVES

Coatlicue, Ixchel, Buffalo Woman,
Mother of the Americas
 PROTECT US FROM OURSELVES

Protect us from ourseles,
from the confusion of names
that pigeonhole us
save the Earth from our folly
and lead us through the third Millenium
AMEN

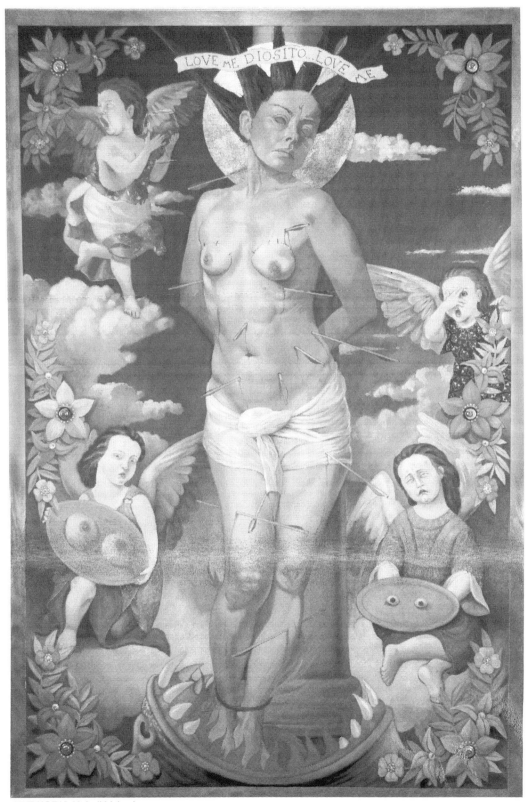

ARTWORK: Kukuli Velarde
"Love Me, Diosito, Love Me " Oil painting on Aluminum plate (46" x 72"), Copyright © 2008

YOLANDA ARROYO PIZARRO

The master walks around us, Jwaabi

here we are, Jwaabi
two slaves
two similar with distant color skin
with different *lenguas*
do not know why he called me Teresa, Jwaabi
do not know why he called you Juana, Jwaabi
my mother use to sing my name
me Tshanwe
yo
esa soy
as it was the *tambora*
as it was the rain over my head
while my continent is screaming
rainsticks open their mouths
kalimba drums dancing
marimba ankle shaker
as there is no kingdom warrior after us
to capture me and my sisters
my brothers
my little ladies to play with
djembe doum doum
bougarabou hand percussion
while looking for giraffes and turtles
my little lionesses
my pets

my weak ones
those who cry even if they are strong
even if they are tall
my dark muscles
like mangrove monsters

the master walks around us, Jwaabi
yo soy Teresa
or Therese
tú eres Juana
or Jane
he *desenfunda* his penis
it's my time to wait
until he finished with you

you're not crying this time
brave *guerrera*
the sound of my voice is no *maraca*
no flute
there is no sound, actually
ngoma moropa balapho power
nada de voz
and you look my eyes
I look yours

PHOTO: miguelÁngel
"Juan Boza" bw photograph (11 x14 in.)

The Littlest Warrior

Many moments of my days are spent contemplating your face
I remember your beaming eyes and precious nose
Your strong little body, which at an early age had the semblance of strength
You had a gaiety in your soul,
That led me to believe that warrior genes are happy ones.
I remember your first step,
Your first words of defiance:
"No Mama" you proclaimed.

Early on you had a softness about you that I shared when you caressed me, seeking
comfort in my arms and at times just comforting me.

Yes you have comforted me although I never asked because we have been intertwined
with each other since the first moment of your existence.

And now you have reached the age of reason,
But I know not what you look like or where you are.

I envision you with curled locks of dark mahogany—with a halo of red sparks!
Hands, strong, capable of holding a gun.
Limber, ready to move
Joyful, because you possess a spirit of triumph and victory
(it is difficult to write of you because when I begin to express that which I hold inside,
emotionally I am over whelmed)

I wonder if you know our names
That of your true parents
You have come from an act of Love—totally conscious of your birth, You were chosen to
be born—contrary to all the obstacles in the way
You arrived, "Triumphantly"
You were embraced by our comrades
Our friends. You Are Our Little Warrior
Before you is a challenge, my Son,
a responsibility to yourself and our people.
Right now this may not be clear to you,
In due time as you continue to grow,
you too will see the necessity for change.

Even though I have not glanced in your eyes
Or held you in my arms
Or cared for you in times of fear or hurt,

I have done so in my mind
because I feel your spirit in me.

You are a fortunate child,
because many love you.
Some have crossed your path,
Others extend their love for you
by their commitment to struggle.

Oh little Warrior of My heart
I embrace you from a distance
Hold you in my heart,
Awaiting the time when we will meet again,
eye to eye, spirit to spirit.

I will know you at first glance,
At any given moment;
Because I have seen you
In the children of the world of struggle
Happy Birthday Hijo Querido

February 28, 1986

Why did you name me Javier, Dad?

Why did you name me Javier, Dad?
my son Javier asked me this question
as we were driving home from his T-Ball game
after we stopped off to grab a single scoop ice cream cone.

"Can I change my name when I get older?"

Each one of my other three children
had asked me the same question
when they were about five or six years old.

My oldest son, Diego asked me one night
when I was reading him a go to bed book.
why was I named Diego Jesus Marjil Barbosa-Mireles?
I informed him, as my first child, in which my wife let me pick the name,
that he was named
after the Mexican Muralist, Diego Rivera
and found out later,
that my Diego was born almost on the same day as his namesake,
100 years, minus one day.
he was named Jesus, after my older brother
whom I never thought would have children
and named Marjil, after my grandfather.

But he was not impressed,
he still thought I should have probably named him
Bill, or Tom or another name that doesn't take too much space.
and no one would notice the first day of school

Sergio Andres, my second oldest son,
asked me the same question, when I was trying to get him out of the bathtub
he said that the kids had a hard time saying his name and
came up with words like Surgery and Sergio Valente
and words we can't say in a family style poem
he finally said "Didn't you know any English names Dad?"
I told him his mother and I purposely
picked names that could not be easily changed to English ones
like Carlos to Chuck, Juan to John and José to Joe.

But when my daughter Lorena Pilar
asked me right before we read a book
why we named her Lorena.
I told her that it was the most beautiful name
I could ever think of

and why would she want to be
one of the thousands of Jessica's or Amber's or Tiffany's
she was very hurt and thought I was punishing her
or something

which gets us back to my youngest son Javier,
who was initially named Oscar Javier
but after less than 24 hours of repeatedly hearing "little Oscar"
in the nursery room of the Hospital
my wife and I agreed that we would not subject him to 20 years of that
so we switched his name to Javier Oscar

and I was ready to give my personal cultural pride speech
to my six year old and was about to open my mouth wide with advice
when suddenly I got this inspiration
to say nothing and to keep quiet
and listen to what my son had to say

"you know . . . Dad,
I want to change my name when I get older
to Oscar . . .
so I can be more like you . . ."

The Bullfight

Beer bottles hang in bare brown tumbleweeds,
rock-cement fences crumble and maquiladora
workers buried in shallow graves along the border;

Indian mothers smudged with asphalt beg for dimes
near the Tigua reservation where drums rumble
to a statue of a Spaniard long dead and the voices

of rage, and history cannot be redone like a poem.
It's something we carry, something we can never carry.
I am so far gone from the memory of myself, even Chicanas

Ask me who I am. *What is your name they say.*
What is in a name? Names are like languages; they come,
they go. I am counting seashells from a trip to the bayou.

My thigh cut on an oyster shell there, green trees sang
with crickets all night as this flesh bled into the water.
Salty sea meets freshwater marshes, and animals slither

through grass. Alligators thin in their numbers,
hidden within themselves. Creole women singing.
The Rio Bravo slow with a muddy past. The river

that divides me, crosses me daily like the forgotten
history of my grandmother. The way her abuelita snuck
pennies beneath her pillowcase. "She was the only one

who cared," she sighs. The way children fight
among themselves. How an egg is divided
among eight crying mouths.

My legs went limp in the cold Mississippi. Lifting
my chin up to the boat again and again, I sank.
I was all desert, brown sand and cacti blooming

Small red flowers. Want grew through my veins
like weeds. The Spanish I half knew fell from my lips
as water onto sand. Even the people I longed for,

La raza, forgot my face. The same one I tried to forget

always reflected in endless mirrors, the doughy hosts
of an endless penitence for the shame at my border birth.

Never Mestiza enough, never English enough.
A face always following me, demanding homage
For its vast desert. I left the barren place where men flee

Shanties and maquilas and the darting murky traffic.
Ran from my stepfather's fear of my mother's language,
from my mother's half-Jewish history. Her own lost

Heritage buried in a cemetery plot. I ran hard,
fast, for so long that when I returned, I was exiled,
yet forever needing the place.

Perhaps I'm fighting an imaginary bull: its single eye
blinking against the sun as it slowly dies
and its dark blood seeps into the desert sand.

My blood, of necessity, will eventually seep
into the desert; it is the way of my people;
it is the way of all people: crossing borders,

learning of caliche and wind, building monuments
from mud, finding something of themselves,
losing something of themselves.

SANDRA MARIA ESTEVES

castles in the sand

they say my name comes from alexander, as in
great warrior destined to conquer life's battles,
but i say my name comes from the sea,
sun-lit crystals born of ocean pounding rock,
filtered blue and aqua light, salty sailing wind
conjuring shades of soft sky, translucent stone, distant mountains
this house i live in, as fragile as undulating waves.

when spoken correctly my name can be music,
toning, dancing in the sunrise, singing operettas to the moon.
my name means faithful lover and caring mother,
freedom bird from a latina rainbow,
a tumbling merengue,
wildflowers in the green garden, the flight of a wing.

sometimes my name means
peaceful calm in the hurricane's eye,
a hermit withdrawn from the one-thousand things,
the zen of quiet wondering,
the azo of yellow, the alizarin of crimson,
a giant heart filled with the imprint of many names,
the lush rain forest,
the rushing river through this mysterious earth.

my name is nothing like the sounds of battles,
guns blasting or bombs bursting in air.
not a warrior who chooses the fight,
but a healer with magic hands and juju words
that ring deep in your inner ear, picking up pieces
to make us whole with the wealth of ourselves.

there are no ghettos here
hustling fast-talking illusions for sale,
no dark uniforms strapped aside the threat of bullets

my name is the dark forest where doves roost,
and tree frogs sing lullabies at dusk.
it is gentle and precious like a newborn,
a glass of water,
a small speck of life ever changing form,

a chameleon you almost don't see
unless you are ready to embrace the image of love
reflected in the mirror.

How They Get You
for Mariposa

It begins on the day you are born,
before that first breath when you arrived
the descendant of former slaves.
Already you have been stolen from your land,
your legacy, your heritage and your name.
Already there are things you will not be told,
precious information about your past, your history.
Already you will be kept in the dark.

They will replace this knowledge of your true being
and fill your mind with trivial things from oversized electronics
by plastic teachers only concerned about their future pensions.
They will make you fight inhuman wars against each other.
You will be forced to eat bad food and fast food
that are poison to your health and your true wealth,
that will be agriculturally manipulated, nutritionally depleted
and manufactured in laboratories.
The water you drink will be contaminated and infiltrated
with strange unnatural chemicals, approved for consumption
by greedy entrepreneurs who want to control your sacred spirit.

They will convince you to buy a thousand useless items
that you don't need, but must have,
and then a thousand more, just because;
the new model, the next version, the latest style.
None of which will make you happy, whole, complete or wise,
because there is never enough when there is too much
that means nothing in a material existence of little value,
except to own you, day by day, moment by moment.
A slave to your job, they will own your next check before you get it.
They will make you do things you never wanted,
and become who you didn't plan,
and go where no one should ever be,
and live in ways you never imagined,
until you have shut down to the song in your soul,
and become deaf to the dance of life,

living in a box like a tomb before your time.

They will dangle glittering carrots before your eyes
to entice you, to razzle dazzle you.
They will get you caught up in so many clever schemes
they invented and invested,
marketed and infested with grotesque expectations,
leaving you frazzled,
until you won't even know you've been got

Confronted and confused, they will hold you hostage,
confined in a gilded cage,
until you are mentally enslaved,
emotionally starved and spiritually depraved.
They will get you in a hundred million ways
while you are unaware and asleep,
until you fall into your grave.

Or . . .
until the day you decide
that you are not going to get got,
that a slave you are not,
that you were born for a purpose,
who you are meant to be.

And you begin to read books
to learn and see and reach
from deep within that hole they buried you in,
and push the rising of your heart, mind and soul
onto higher ground and greater treasure,
the dream of the you within you are meant to discover,
to uncover, like no other, unique,
choosing to hold on
to the One you always wanted to be
by yourself, on your terms,
wide awake with your wild and beautiful spirit free.

http://www.sandraesteves.com/poetrybookslinks/
poetrybooks.html/

NOEL SHAFI

Taino

You are the sons and daughters of the Arawak peoples
who emerged from the hidden caves of antiquity
from South America to the Antilles and Bahamas
overcoming the violent tides of your ancestors

you filled stomachs and souls with yuca, maize, and guava
becoming one with the earth; lovers of your land and waters
worshipping the ancient spirits of crops, winds and rain
with stories carved into wood; engraved into stone; molded into clay
your throats and lungs meditated to the smoke of tobacco
breathing life into the village, while singing songs of nature

> tongues praying

hearts beating

> arms waving

legs dancing

> hips shaking

lips moving

indigenous voices in the fire—speaking to the gods

brown skin

> yellow flames

white sand

> purple sky

you made the air shiver from the whistling of your spears
and the silver clouds taste the poison from your arrows
moving waves by the shore with your cries to the heavens
while tickling the ground with the language of your feet

. . . are you now sleeping somewhere high up in the mountains?
awaiting the storms to cleanse the island of guns, germs and steel?
for you may one day place your hands into the soil that was once yours
and find the roots of Yúcahu, living in cassava—humming underground.

CARMEN BARDEGUEZ-BROWN

Rican Issues

Say **W**hat?
Could you please, Pleaseeeeeeeeeee repeat
Did you said:" Molleta?
Prieta?
Morena?
Ohh African!
Hmmm Soy **P**uertoriquena
Yes, **P**uertorican

That I don't look **W**hat ?
Oh , I guess I don't look cafe con leche
mancha de platano
Mulata,
high yellow
grifa
By the way
I did not know that there was a puertorican look.
And what exactly is that?
That I just look more what?
Well, Y Tu abuela donde Esta?
I should said abuela, tio, Tia, y to el barrio
Let me tell you something
FOR YOUR INFORMATION
Most ricans are a mixed of Africans,Spaniards and Native Americans called Tainos
By the way noone has seen a taino in the last 500 years.
Sooooo exactly . . . You know what that means

My **E**nglish is covered with spices

Spices from the Caribbean

Spices that you might find **S**trange
Because you were born in this cold fast food mall of a country
Where **S**panish is a foreign word
That you are ashamed to learn
And when you try
Is not there
Only mumbles of a murmur
Susurando el olvido
A reganadientes
Pretendiendo
Escondiendo la verguenza

You remember Puerto Rico on the 2nd Sunday of every June
When everybody is suddenly proud to be Puerto Rican

No the word is **B**oricua

Boricua Here, **B**oricua THERE, **B**oricuas everywhere
And everyone waves the flags
The flags that they don't even understand
And no one knows why they are here
Yes HERE **N**ow
Do you Know ?
why your parents or grandparents vinieron aqui?
De que Pueblo?
Cuando te banaste en las aguas calientes del Caribe?
Better yet
Do you really know that . . . ?

We all came from the **Motherland**
Yeap Africa

Even the Spanish people that came with **Colon, Columbus**
However you want to say it
Lived 700 hundred years under the **Moors**
You heard that right
The moors as in Arabs as in black Arabs
SO . . . in other words
Not only I

But **we**
Have over 500 years of African mestizaje
The so called "white people that everyone is so proud of"
As in "my grand parents are from Spain
Well if they are . . .
They
Too have **negrITOs** in them
Remember the **Gitanos**
But that is another story . . .
Getting back to the **Boricua's issue**
What history do you know?

Ever heard of
Agüeybaná
Albizu Campos
Palés Matos
Rafael Betances
Arturo Schomburg
Francisco Oller
Julia De Burgos
Rafael Hernández

Segundo Ruiz Belvis
Enrique Laguerre
Mariana Bracetti
Pedro Pietri

Still havING problems figuring me out?
Or is it that you just don't know
Who you are?

Chapter 3: Peinate el pelo
El que no tiene Dinga tiene Mandinga

"Carmelita ven a peinarte el pelo"
"Ya voy mami"
Hmmm . . .How I hated when mami used to comb my hair.
I have black curly hair, what some people will call: "pelo malo."
Mom will always use aceite to comb my hair. She will use any oil. Sometimes
even mayonaisse and avocado to "condition my hair." I had to wash it so hard
to make sure that little pieces of the aguacate will not stay in my curls. The
mayonesa made me feel that I was carrying a "sanwich" in my head. It bother
me a lot.

I felt like my hair was a cocina. And believe me, I was reminded of that in many occasions. Can you imagine be-
ing the new kid in class and have your hair smell like rice and beans!
There was a girl in my class that used to called me exactly that: " Carmelita rice and beans." Yeap! She was my
first fight.

Mami said, that I have
"Un pelo malo pero manejable" . She also said, that I was lucky I didn't have Dad's kinky hair. I wonder what
he would say about that?
I always thought that I had a beautiful lioness mane.
There are only two kinds of hair in Puerto Rico:
"pelo malo" or black hair and pelo "bueno" or "white, people's hair."
Which I don't understand because in here we are all the same.
But then again, what kind of hair is bad?
Black,brown,yellows. What is the difference?

It is not like the hair has done anything to you.
In Puerto Rico everyone wants to have "white people's hair" or "pelo bueno" Even if their mother is black or in
my case my father.
Well, in here we are all Ricans or Nuyoricans which is kind of a different version of black.

As I was saying, in Guayama you will see everyone going to the beauty salon to get their hair straighten. But
then everybody denies it. Mom already had planned for me to get a "mild relaxer" but then we move here.
Well, that has been one of the few advantages of moving here because for some strange rcason I have been
able to convince mom to let me have my long curly, kinky hair, tranquilo.

Poet Victor Hernández Cruz Explores the Nexus of Islamic Artistic Influences in Spain, Puerto Rico & North Africa

O N A LAZY SUNDAY AFTERNOON in New York City, you can easily take the subway, bus or cab to Margaret Troupe's Harlem Arts Salon. Your "lazy Sunday afternoon" will quickly transform into an intellectually and visually stimulating time. You'll meet and greet literary icons and visual artists, and the drinks and savory food will entrance and prepare you for an exhilarating artistic experience.

On one such Sunday afternoon, November 13, 2011, the acclaimed poet, Victor Hernández Cruz, was on hand to present his latest book of poems; *In the Shadow of Al-Andalus,* a work that examines Arab influences on Puerto Rican culture. We were in for a special treat as Quincy Troupe, author of noted biographical works; *Miles Davis* and of *Miles and Me,* conversed with and interviewed Cruz.

Elected to the Board of Chancellors of the Academy of American poets in 2008, Cruz was a finalist for the Lenore Marshall and Griffin Poetry Prizes. He won the World Heavyweight Championship in Poetry twice and was featured on Bill Moyers' Peabody Award-winning series, Language of Life. He is also a Louis Reyes Rivera Lifetime Achievement Award recipient.

(cont'd. pg. 176)

(cont'd from pg. 174)

The poetic narrative of Cruz's work has consistently earned him high praise and is a sensorial journey centered in his immigrant family experiences, his intense exploration of different lands and cultures and how they are inter-connected. Among his body of work are these earlier volumes of include *Red Beans, Maraca, The Mountain in the Sea, Bi-Lingual Wholes,* and *Mainland.* Cruz divides his time between Morocco, his native Puerto Rico, and the United States.

And so, amidst the high ceilings, oriental rugs, antique wooded furniture, shelves stocked with books and postmodern paintings, in Margaret's cozy living room, we gathered with drink in hand and listened to Victor Hernández Cruz discuss, read and share his latest collection of poetry, *In the Shadow of Al-Andalus.*

℘ ℘ ℘

I WAS BORN IN PUERTO RICO, which is a Caribbean island and I also come from the Spanish who were there. Who were these people though? Because there was no such thing as Spain in 1492, Spain was something that was forming. They had just acquired their territory back from the Muslim occupation and so those who came to Puerto Rico were probably a *mestizaje;* a group mixed in blood and culture and we have a lot of that influence in Puerto Rico. If you look at the Puerto Ricans, the Dominicans, the Cubans and most Latinos, we have a very striking Arabic resemblance because we have their blood. People always say, my mother *patria es España*, but my *mother patria* is *también el Norte de Africa* and just ask where the guitar comes from? It slides out of the Laud culture; India, through Angar, through Persia, and comes out towards the Arabs in the form of the Laud and the Laud gives birth to the *guitarra*.

So our culture is full of camouflaged Arabic words that were already in the language when the Spaniards came to Puerto Rico. Part of the meters of the poetic forms, if you take *La Decima* is possibly a descendent of the Arab Mushu Lak . *La Ronda* and *La Decima* are poetic forms and they are also a singing style. In Puerto Rico it's cultivated by *oradores* (orators), who sing in this format which has 8 syllables across and a writing pattern where every 3 lines have to rhyme; very complex and very difficult to write. And, don't ever try to write them in English I've tried and it would drive me crazy! When Puerto Ricans sing, *ay lo le lo lai,* and they always sing that, why do they sing that? Well it's the same thing that the Moorish Arabic Muslims sang in Andalucia when they started to sing so that's a direct link with the Arab culture. The Spanish language has something like 4000 Arabic words. The Amohas and Amoriri peoples were the Berber people in Spain. So, we also have Berber blood. Berber words are also found in the Spanish language. That element is also Moroccan. The Moroccans (*los Moros),* were in Spain 800 years. It's been an exciting learning experience for me with my Moroccan wife and son.

You talked a little bit about it – I want you to expand a little about what you said in the introduction "I am in the same shadow" the shadow, talk a little bit about that with us, the shadow.

Well Morocco is below Spain and we're in the shadow of Spain because of the proximity. We are in the same shadow in Puerto Rico through language and culture because the language was left in Puerto Rico by the Spanish and the social culture of the Muslims, who were in Spain. Puerto Rico is under the same shadow of culture, spirituality and even music. To understand modernity, you have to understand what I have seen in Andalucia, in the great city of Cordoba, which was the greatest city in Europe. It's an anomaly. It's a strange thing what happened with Spain. It was invaded by Muslims whose spirituality was from the Middle East. They entered Spain, definitely something that was strange because this did not happen to other European countries. Thus, our language, as well as our spirituality, is full of Arabic laws and even our spirituality is. We are Christians (practice Christianity), the way the Moroccans were Muslims; the woman wear veils. The elderly Catholic women in Puerto Rico, Mexico, and all of Latin America wear veils when they go to church. They do that from the cultural influence of Muslim women and their practice. No other Catholics do that. I don't think the Swedish or British do. It's something the Latin-American culture holds on to; that tradition of putting veils or handkerchiefs, kerchiefs on for Mass or church services.

When I first met you 35 years ago, I saw in your work that it was this mixing of Spanish, and Spanglish, and English. Now you've moved on. Now you're living between not Puerto Rico and the United States but between Puerto Rico and Morocco. So, now that brew, that stew, has included Moroccan Arabic. Can you talk about that a little and how it's changed your work, how it's expanded it or what it has done to your rhythms; the language that you use, like metaphors and images?

It's kept the language flowing you know. I used to do Spanglish of course and I've been meaning to switch with

Arabic words that I learned in the Moroccan dialectic like *Helu* and *Dulce*. For me, hearing the language of course, and mixing it with the concepts and sense I have of history, knowing also that the Muslims were in Spain, it's all one big flow. It's like when you think of the Blues, you think of the *Bolero*. *El bolero también le decían la canción de tragedia*; the song of tragedy. It was a song of mishap, things were wrong. It was the Blues, the *Bolero*. The Portuguese *Favo* was also the Blues; the Blues here, the Blues in Portugal, and the Blues in the Caribbean. The *Bolero* is from the Caribbean, it has its roots in Cuba so it's like a slow *Rumba*. Just like the Tango is an African form. According to Jorge Luis Borges it's a *habanera*. The cadence of the *habanera* has its roots in the *Rumba*. It just slows down. I like seeing those things you know, giving them energy and life.

J. Wright is a great poet but where'd he get this thing about me weaving history? I'm not weaving anything, everything is already woven, already weaved. I'm undoing the weave! Other poets like Machado and Lorca in Spain, were also throwing light on the Gypsy and the Arabic influences in Spain. Almost like an anthropological poetry, a cultural mix that's at my hand, in my fingers, on my tongue, in my cuisine, in everything. I'm just throwing light on what's already been done, what history is, what we are made up of, this historical thing. So poems are wings, *alas* for flight you know.

Victor Hernández Cruz at the Harlem Arts Salon.

So talk about where you see your work going for you. This book, this new book where do you think it's going for you?

I'm writing more and more stories. I'm writing more prose, and prose for me is like slow, slow, slow. I write like 2 pages or 3 pages a day. If I write 3 that's a lot. I write as if it was a job around the clock. *Vivo en el campo* so I have the mountains around and I try to get up at about 7:30 a.m. and start where I left off. Prose is this thing where we gotta look back and look forward. We gotta anticipate things and I don't do that so much in poetry. Poetry is now, *ahora*. Poetry is the present, now and it's also connected to my nerves and probably to my high blood pressure as well. It's *ahora*, now.

Do you think of the shadow in the way you think about being, belonging, and identity, from being involved with the Umbra poets of the Lower East Side in New York City, to your movement across culture and space and your work with language, where you explore really beautifully weird aspects of being a Puerto Rican? Do you see a kind of continuity between the shadow bond of what's right and the beautifully shadowy unpredictable identity that has underscored your work so far? Also, did you get slack from people because you weren't being militant enough or political enough in your work? You've created your own turf by now; we're all familiar with the world you've created.

I'm always making bridges you know. I'm always making bridges. I grew up as a Nuyorican if that's a term—from the Lower East Side to East Harlem—it was like an invasion in east Harlem. I went to high school up there and so I was walking those streets when I was into *Snaps*. Many in high school were African-American and Puerto Rican. It was that kind of school at that time and that's how I grew up. So my belt was full of Rhythm and Blues and Jazz and what my African-American friends said and, it was my culture. It was the culture of the New York City streets in the 1960s and it was what it was. Then I went downtown to the Lower East Side. When I was downtown there was a group of white writers and a group of African American writers called Umbra that I became involved with. It could be the imagination also, which is what I filtered through all the time, through what I live—you know, identity.

We should be Muslims then! What are we doing being Catholics or Christians; the religions of Spain? There was no such thing as "Spain" in 1492! Spain was a series of kingdoms: Leon, Navajo, Castilla. Those three kingdoms were the ones that started to organize themselves to gain back territories of Spain; the peninsula. The real culture, the real spirit, the real social life that was there, was the Muslim Arab culture mixed with the so called Spanish culture. Spain became Spain later on in the 1600s, what is known as Spain today.

People today are formed by people who were forming and dis-forming going from one religion to another, changing from one language to another. People change and people stay the same.

Thank you for the presentation and poetry. ▱

RICHARD VARGAS

the road taken

they had seen this before
the name-calling
the pointing of fingers
the feverish waving of
the flag and signs
telling them to
go home

so they did
where they watched
us look for new reasons
to blame for the fall
of our empire while
the roads crumbled
the bridges sagged and
collapsed as weeds
pushed through
the many cracks
in the pavement

they heard us cry
while our crops rotted
in the fields because we
had become too lazy
and soft to pick our
own lettuce and grapes
strawberries and onions

they shook their heads
when we started fighting
amongst ourselves
the clouds of acrid smoke
and the sound of gunfire
floated over the barb-wired
wall and that invisible line
in the dirt we once
patrolled diligently
with flying drones and
neo-nazi patriots

then the walls of inclusion
became the great walls
of exclusion as all
the brown people
were kicked out
black people were next
soon followed by anyone
deemed to be not white-
enough to stay behind
last but not least were
God's chosen people
befuddled and confused
because they thought they
had finally passed over
to the right side of the
color line

then all that remained
in the United States
of America besides
the angry the old
and the white
were a bunch of dried up
golf courses and an
abundance of vacant
Walmarts

it was then that they
decided it was safe to return
with their lawnmowers
paint brushes
bags of cement
mops and buckets

the country was a bigger mess
than before and once again
there was plenty of work
for everyone

ARTWORK: Elvis Irizarry
"San Miguel," Mixed-Media on board (9 x 12 in.) Painting, Copyright © 2011

JAIME "SHAGGY" FLORES

Negritude

For Pedro Pietri, Tato Laviera, Jesus Papoleto Melendez and Trinidad Sanchez Jr.

We be those Negroes
Born to Slave Hands
Resurrecting forgotten African Gods
When Transplanted to New Lands
Mixing Ebonics
With Splanglish Slang
We be those Negroes
Children of Yoruba y Ibo
Bilingual and Indio
Afro-Caribes
Masters of plantation work
Race mixing
And Orisha Spirit raising

We be those Negroes
Creating Jazz with cats
Named Bird, Dizzy, Duke, and Armstrong
Cubop Bugalu Sal-Soul Searching Journey men
Mongo-Santamaria/Chano Pozo Drum Gods
And Celia Cruz
AZUCAS!
Legends leaving our cultural footprints
On the muddy minds
of the mentally dead

We be those Negroes
Creating Schomburg museums
of Black Studies
In Nuyorican Harlem streets
Where we once dance
during zoot suits riots
to Conga
Maraca
Bata
Break beats
and Palladium Massacres

We be those Negroes
Drawn as Sambos and Jigaboos
By political cartoonist

Who couldn't erase
The taste of
Africa
From Antillean Culinary
Magicians
Creating miracles
with Curries call SoFritos

We be those Negroes
Younglords
Island Nationalist
Black Panthers
Vieques Activist
Santeros
And Guerreros
Brothers of Garvey
Children of Malcolm
Black Spades
Savage Skulls
Chingalings
And Latin Kings

We be those Negroes
Like Harvard Educated Lawyer
Don Pedro Albizu Campos
Stationed
In all Black regiments
Learning the reality
Of Jim Crow Society
And their gringolandia
Government Race public policies
Calling Bilingual Niggers
Spics

We be those Negroes
Before Sosa
Before Clemente
Before Jackie
Giving Negro league
Baseball legends

A place
Under the sun
to call home
When no one else
Would have them

We be those Negroes
Dancing
Moving
Breaking
Egyptian
Electric Boogalooing
Locking
On concrete jungles
To Cool Herc
Jamaican
Sound Boy Systems
And aerosol
symphony backgrounds

We be those Negroes
Charlie Chasing
Rock Steadying
A dream called Hip-Hop
In Bronx Backyard Boulevards
Between
Casitas and Tenements
With Roaches for Landlords

We be those Negroes
Writing Epics
Like Willie Perdomo testaments
Called "Nigger-Recan Blues"
And Victor Hernandez Cruz
Odes to "African Things"
Hiding our dark skinned
Literary Abuelitas
With Bembas Colora
In places where the Whiteness police
could never find them

We be those Negroes
Denied access to Black Nationalist run
Karenga Kwanza Poetry readings
Because we remind the ignorant
Of the complexity that is their culture
Neither Here nor There
Not quite Brown

Not quite White
We navigate uncharted
Waters
Of Black Identity Boxes

We be those Negroes
Mulatto
We be those Negroes
Criollo
We be those Negroes
Moreno
We be those Negroes
Trigueños
We be those Negroes
Octoroons and Quadroons
We be those Negroes
Cimarrones and Nanny of the Maroons
We be those Negroes
Cienfuegos y Fidel
We be those Negroes
Luis Pales Matos and Aime Cesaire
We be those Negroes
Puentes,
Mirandas,
Riveras,
Colons,
Felicianos,
Lavoes and
Palmieris
We be those Negroes
Judios
Y a veces
Jodios
We be those Negroes
Dominicanos y Cubanos
We be those Negroes
Jaimiquinos y Haitianos
We be those Negroes
Panameños y Borinqueños

We be those Negroes
Seeking freedom from
Irrationality
In an age of Nuclear
Goya Families
And Television
Carbon Copy Clone

Univision/BET/MTV
Slave Children

We be those Negroes
Known by many names
And many deeds
Spoken of in Secret
By African-American
Scholars
In envy during their nightly
Salsa
Dance classes
As they try
To pick up White Girls

We be those Negroes
Caribbean
Negritude
Heroes
Sometimes negating our destiny
But always finding
Peace
In the Darkness
Of Sleep

We be those Negroes
Negroes
We
Be.

PHOTO: George Malave
Occupy Wall Street, Lady with Flag, NYC, Copyright © 2011.

ARTWORK: Marcos Dimas
"Cortijo y su Combo " mixed media collage (42"x46") Copyright © 2006

SUSANA CABANAS

My Story: I'm white but not really; that's just the color of my skin.

I'm white but not really because inside of me I'm really Puerto Rican. I'm white but not really because I do not talk, walk, think, act like they do although I was taught how, and could get by if I played the part. I'm white but not really because inside of me I'm pink and yellow and black and red and brown. People of the rainbow is from where I am, at least the half of me that came from my mother's womb. My father I do not know who he was although I carry his name which I don't use except when I have to like for passports and government things. I'm white but not really because as soon as I say from where I was born they say, oh, but you're different as if that were supposed to be some kind of complement to be told that you should be proud to be different from your people, your own kind. I'm white but not really not being wanted neither here nor there because my people don't accept me either, speaking to me in English although I address them in Spanish as if to say I know how to speak your tongue also white woman and also staring in disbelief but where were you born and even after I present my credentials still the stare through half-closed, serpent staring eyes, skeptical and disbelieving, half on guard as if to say we'll see; let's see how long it takes you to slip up and give yourself away. I'm white but not really, not in my heart. I don't want to be part of a world where you don't celebrate differences; only your white, pale colorless sameness; static, cruel, hard, like the white ice of the iceberg frozen by the hatred you carry as your heart, heartless, bloodless, cold, frozen heart. I'm white but not really nor neither am I Puerto Rican; an outsider is what I am. Been classified a Nuyorican even though I was born there. Can not claim membership in any group, in any clan because nobody wants me although I've longed all my life to be a part of the gang and at times I'll admit that the need was so strong to belong, to be loved, that I made the mistake of thinking that I could belong but sooner or later it was the white man this or the black man that or the yellow or the red or the brown, always something cruel to say about the people on the other side of the gang and sooner than later I would open my mouth because I couldn't close my heart and ultimately got thrown out of the group or the clan or the gang or else have to leave understanding that it would do my spirit harm were I to stay and suffer and try to repair all of the heartlessness all over the land. I am white but not really. I guess most of all I'm just lonesome and sad, very sad because of all the cruelty I see day to day. Been speaking all my life against injustice. Gotten beaten up many times; in school, by men, lost jobs, lost homes, lost lovers, lost friends, although when everything is said and done, I'm glad I'm not white, really.

(May 17, 1997)

Songs of My Childhood 5 — Colors of the Rainbow

I learned about poverty, in Cuba. My aunt's husband's mother was black and poor. Vivían en un solar. My father, when they went to visit my aunt's husband's father who was a poet, would not let me go with them. I could not understand what there was that he did not want me to see. It was the poverty. Now I see, now I see. I remember when my mother and father had a fight and my mother decided to go to his mother's house in Cuba to see if she could save the marriage. On our way down to Florida to take the ferry from Key West, when the bus hit Washington, after that things changed. By then I knew about prejudice.

When we were looking for an apartment one time in Brooklyn—I was about 12—we had gone to a really pretty neighborhood and had seen this apartment; my mother, my father, my sister and me. A really nice looking family all dressed up in their Sunday finest. A really nice looking family the landlady said. She asked us where we were from with a name like San Antonio. Were we Italian? My mother said that my father was Cuban and she, Puerto Rican. The lady looked at us in amazement and said but you look like such a nice family. Oh, I'm so sorry but I can't rent to you. My neighbors would not like that. They would be very upset at me if they knew that I rented to a Puerto Rican family. I'm sorry but I can't.

After Washington, at first the change was subtle; just a feeling of uneasiness settled in on the bus. I was day-dreaming most of the way. I had agreed to go with my mother and not stay to finish high school. I had one semester to go. It was January when we left. I would have graduated in June but not really because I had messed up; gotten into men and courtship ways. No time for my studies, no time for me; was pulled here, there, everywhere by everybody but me.

When we pulled into a bus station around dusk I glanced out the window in a half-curious way. Up and down the platform I looked. I don't know what I saw first; if it was the water fountain or the men's room but all of a sudden my eyes stopped on COLORED. Frozen in time, in space. It took me back all the way to my ancestors. What am I? I said. Am I white, am I colored? What will they think? What will they say? What would they do if they knew that I was colored? Not black entirely, not white entirely but colored, just like the sign says.

STEVEN ALVAREZ

& NOW niños

that Great Amurkan Prophet / Patriot
w/ colors that ain't ever gonna run
bleedin stripes & stars
barbacoa'd redmeat eatin
freedom starlovin
pickup truck drivin
prophecies transnationally:
O Sr Citizen Henry w/ Borders
— Operator Gatekeeper himself —
our gendered Amurkan Citizen
from güey on Right
not waiting one Minute(man)
for questions abt all them "beaners"
makin babies & fillin
classrooms w/ their primitive
landgwedge & spickin of that
bringing in lice & vermin / & venereal diseases
from that land o' tortillas
& to grease OUR lovely Amurka
w/ fatty carnitas & slimey cornhusked meatcakes . . .
invading our pie-loven Amurka
them goddamned animals
livin in trailers w/ 65-70 aliens after all
& thus takin 'pon himself O Sr Citizen Henry
(pos w/ additional Patriots like himself)
always always always urged them brownie drones
on back yonder to their Queen Shakira
or whoever
back into that dysfunctional haven of narcos
& death they have always ran from

& O Sr Citizen Henry of impeccable
personified smoothness
& slender veiny whiteglove
encased hands
& enormous —nay—vast—cultural geometry
complex & awkwardly dignified
behind his paleface / one vast distinctly Amurkan
face between here & his historic formerly
reading to school kids
at Francisco Kino Elementary

in Tombstone / AZtlán turns
that next page in his newest picturebook
Down from Amurka / Back to Castizalandia
young reader version of his equally as childish
adult study ¿Who Are They? The Greasing of Amurka's National Identity
invited by his teacher wife to read to these
chamacos / mostly brown in shape & texture
but Amurkan in location / & lookin
at him all settin there all brown & bigeyed
lookin up at Sr Citizen / I tell ye / ye'da
split yr Levi's & dropped bears
if ye'da seen it —

 lo que pasa es . . .

he held up that selfpublished picturebook
& ¡O racista Henry!() read:

"& one day some beaner son of a shameless squah —

[image of moustachioed Tío Taco]

"decides to try his
"luck against il reeyo bravo
"but first prays to his 'santo'
"some masked loochadoor wrassler named San Avabiche
"& after a-lightin four candles
"walks close
"on his dry Meskin land & he aint been
"away from this same spot for but two weeks
"& as he's wading w/ his black plastic sack
"containing his clothes & his cacahuates
"tortillas & energy drink some 'greengo' hero out
"of nowehere pops up in front of him"

[image of Uncy Sam w/ thick cristalino frontier pointed finger]

"'CHINGAO' sez that paylado con grasa

"& Sammy our Sammy that Amurkan hero
"who of course that Beaner wdn't know
"sez 'hey there Meester Moehaydo
"'hello aint seen you for a spell
"'¿where you been?'

"well this pepperbelly sez something in Messikin
"& Tío Sam sez somehow knowing
"that wet nodding yonder

"right / up on that theah dry land / tierra firma
"back on over the madreland"

[image: ¿now where's that? / dark wasteland contrasted with green lushness]

"'say compadray: ¿ain't it wet up there
"'on that dry land you descend from ameego?
"'¿zit coo & refreshin there?
"'¿duz it have waves & ripples?
"'¿cain't ye sur-vive in it?'
"& just then his gabacho retired professor friend pops
"up too / some sunbird from up near Twin Cities
"his RV plugged in over under yonder mexquite
"reality court television shows talking justice
"& this fast-talkin gabacho / dedicating thirty days
"to defend Amurka like a true [sic->] pitriot
"sacrificing his own time to defend Amurka's desert
"wasteland border & this Dr Birote —"

[image: yanqui blowhard blofero sportin tweed blazer w/ elbowpatches]

"PhD sez:
"'this dry land ye descend from's imaginary Paco Taco / one completely non-existent
"'imaginary thing / nothing real at all' sez thisun
"'Makesicko makes this nation retch so swim on back
"'less ye want this leather Amurkan size 10 straight up yr coolo —'"
[image: size ten school-of-the-Amurka's-issued-red/white/blue combat boot]
er . . . ¿chingao? ¿quien es este güey?
one buki in the back calling the ghost of Cortez / Gregorio Cortez plees plees come plees . . .
"'ahem' in unison kids"
"'so sorey seniores' as that cookaratcha crawls
"back to that shitpile he came from . . .
"here / let me hold this illustration high so y'all can see
"real nice what Messico looks like—"
[image: brown babies w/ bulging hunger bellies / & shacks walled w/ newspaper]
"¿now where was I? . . . ah —
"'that's right' sez Prof Birote to Uncy Sam
"'our duty our Amurkan duty
"'our neverendin battle to secure Amurka's borders
"'& to reveal to all the 3rd world Paco Takos those real aspects
"'of their putrid nations' inferiorities relative to Amurkan
"'wealth / sweetness / goodness / in our kind eyes shining so clear
"'& how dare ye challenge our national sovereignty
"'& rule of law/ brownies'"

[image: WALLS & WALLS & still more WALLS conrete WALLS & razorwire]

"& our Uncy Sam smugly & w/ outstretched hand
"shakes Prof Birote's extended ringed fingers & sez —
"lissen closely niños—he sez:
"'well They sey eternal vigilance is the price of liberty . . .
"'They sey that / & they sey this Amurka's Being in Time
"'this Amurkan chonotope's suffering from invasive
"'dirty beaners from down on southward luggin northward
"'babies / they try to anchor to this land spickin backward slangwedge /
"'& bringin over that plain ol inferior Indian blood . . . brown bastards /
"'kaysadilla-eatin / greasy-headed / filthy drugsmugglin
"'mules / got-damn . . . gotdamned freehelayros . . . '"

[image: la Sra Guadalupe w/ five soiled Chueys at her unsandaled feet]

"now lemme ask ye one question kiddies / & be honest
"lemme axe ye : ¿ how can an Amurka of 300,000,000
"absorb 100,000,000 poor / uneducated / Esthpanich
"spickin wets & still be Amurka? answer & axe yr padres
"that & see what they sey / got that smartypants —
"yeah / I'm talking to you in the back there w/ those
"Amurkan subsidized glasses there in the back / yeah TÚ
"quit cryin . . ."
y los niños: "."
"I argue in my controversial ¿Who Are They? that yr arrival
"in Amurka from 1970-2000 threatens our Amurkan
"core of identitas & culture / bc ye don't SPIC ENGLISH
"ye spic to yr enclaves of like-spiccin spics
"quit crying / ye don't wanna assimilate
"ye wanna make babies / ye want me
"to remake my life into some Amurkano Dream —
"¡bullshit! THERE'S ONLY ONE AMURKAN DREAM
"CREATED BY WASPs / BEANERS CAN SHARE
"THAT DREAM ONLY IF THEY LEARN ENGLISH"
" . . . "
 sniff sniff / sniff
"¿nuthin to sey? tha's wha' I thot / thanky for yr time
"& heart yr freedom or get yr ass out
¿& how 'bout some applause for our special guest class?

(1) ¡O Henry! pues suck this tamale / cabrón / for YOU have greased all of US as one nation w/ yr tamalefear / ¡grasa a tu madre! /
& soft Henry's soul appears suddenly & clears its throat / clinking chains / ahem / ahem / & offers that poetic Amurkan sensibility & that
Carolina propriety: "shut yr mouth greaser / spic / taco choker / bean guzzler / wet / peon / spiggoty spic / dirtcaked paylado" yeah:
not bad / good ghost guest & host & zás: gone / always w/ that last word / chingao

LYDIA CORTÉS

I Remember

I remember kindergarten

I remember having to say good-bye to Mami, crying

I remember not understanding the teacher

The English lessons with pretty Miss Powell
who made the boxy words fit just right in my mouth with no pain
I remember the teachers who said, "You don't look Puerto Rican"
expecting to hear me say thank you very much
I remember overhearing some saying Puerto Ricans
don't care about their children, Puerto Ricans aren't clean

I remember the heat of shame rising in my face
praying no one had heard what the teachers said, or
see my hurt red as a broken heart

I remember Mr. Seidman in the 4th grade and how he chose
me for a big part in the school play
I remember feeling important
memorizing my lines and Mami helping me
both Mr. Seidman and Mami smiling, proud,
the night of the performance. Looking at me!
I remember the audience laughing and . . . the applause

I remember moving to Flatbush from Fort Greene
going from a 5th floor tenement walk-up to
our very own private house on a quiet tree-lined street
I thought we had moved to the country
I remember going from Girls' High to Erasmus Hall
and how I went from smart to borderline in one day
the bio teacher, Miss Nash, called me stupid
because I didn't know how to use a microscope

I remember Mr. and Mrs. Hamburger—hamburger?
how I laughed hearing their name, that I was getting
one for political science and the other for economics
I remember being amazed when learning became
a wonder-filled adventure
the faith each of them had in me
I worked hard for them both
I remember the A's I got in their classes

I remember being Puerto Rican in Erasmus Hall High School
I was the only one—until my sister followed next year — on the academic track
I remember the guidance counselor advising me to become
a bilingual secretary since I certainly was not college material

I remember Papi, with his third grade education, saying,
"Lidin, tu puedes hacer lo que quieres. Yo te apoyo en todo. Siempre."

JOHN RIOFRIO

Why Do I Teach Latin@ Studies?
A Spoken Word about the Pedagogy of Latin@ Studies

The conversation goes something like this:

— "So what do you do?"
— "I'm a professor at William and Mary."
— "Wow! Great!

. . . and here I can see them in their minds going through the possibilities of what I might teach. Is it something important like Business or Finance? Economics or Government? Then again maybe not since I don't know that I'm even capable of looking or sounding like a professor of Finance.

And finally the inevitable question:

— "So, what do you teach?"
— "Latin@ Studies," I say, revealing as much enthusiasm as I can without scaring people.

Or maybe I try to say it in a smart way: "Latino Studies."
Or maybe I try to say it in a cool way: "Latino Studies."

No matter, the result is always the same: crickets. *grillos*. loooong pause. *silencio*.

And then it becomes difficult to know what they're thinking: Do they wonder why there are professors of Latin@ Studies? Do they assume that I'm another flaming liberal [I am] that thinks that immigrants are people [they are] and that thinks it's good that you can hear Spanish everywhere now (pues, así es).

Or maybe they ponder the fact that there are people [like me] who actually devote their whole lives to teaching "about Latin@s?" What does that mean for this nation? Just more PC nonsense: let's all adopt a person of color and call them "African American" or "Asian American" or "Hispanic" (No, not "Hispanic?" Latino? . . . whatever).

To be honest, although I've spent precious lines here trying to imagine what you think, the truth is, me vale huevo. Me importa un pito. I, Scarlet my dear, don't give a coño, a carajo, a damn. Your silence gives me time to ponder my own decisions, my own commitments and confirms to me the work that I, you, we, have ahead of us.

Why do I teach Latin@ Studies?
I teach Latin@ Studies because Latin@ Studies isn't about Latin@s. "¿Qué no?!"
No hermano, It's about people. People and Society, Society and People.
It's about Cumbia and Country; it's about a society that's given us Jennifer and George Lopez but also Juan González and Elián González.

But Latin@ Studies is also about Taylor Swift and Taylor Reveley, Glenn Beck and Barack Obama; it's about a system that populates our prisons with men of color and our government with a lack of color.

Al final de las cuentas Latin@ Studies is about the sad rift—la triste discrepancia—entre who we say we are, who we want to be and who we really are.

And yet, amigo míos, the question really isn't "why," it's "who." "For whom," says the English professor in my head, "do I teach Latin@ studies?" I teach for us. I teach for those of us that believe that if we set our minds right, change is possible. Because if my mind is right. If I'm smarter and more prepared then you. If, over and over again, I counter your "immigrants are sucking the system dry" with "immigrants are the basis of an economy which fuels your dinner table, your lexus, and your fragile sense of moral superiority." If I can face the hard facts about my own privilege and help you do the same then maybe we can, together, begin to see our way out of this mess.

And so, ultimately, I teach for those of us who believe in our abilities to resist oppression. I teach for those of us who believe that Latin@s can come in different sizes and shapes and colors. They can come from the barrio or the hood, but they can also come from NoVa and from Bolivia, Batabanó and Kalamazoo. They can be fathers and fighters, criminals and educators, victims and revolutionaries.

I teach for Isabela, mi hija linda, so that she can grow up tall and strong like her sisters, una Latina que conoce su historia. And for mi'jo Juan Lorenzo, so that he can grow up a man who speaks languages and uses his tongue not to seduce the "Latino" way but to decry the oppression which turns Latino men into caricatures of their own potential.

But most of all, I teach for *you*.
Because "you've got questions?" Well I got more questions."
You feel a truth that hovers just outside of reach, that coalesces and dissipates in incoherent ways, and I have knowledge pana, humble knowledge: books and books and books of knowledge. And music and poetry and gente, mucha gente—cada uno con su historia.

And so I teach so that you can learn, and I can learn and someday, algún día, we'll weave a revolution out of the modest threads of what we know and what we don't know, what we think we know and what we hope to know.

I Learned All My Spanish in School

I never tried to pass for White
but I have been passed
because it's good to be White in America
and Mother knows best
to give a not-quite-White baby
White names that don't explain
such dark eyes and such tight curls
My name never stopped mean girls hissing
gringa cola prieta and guera and taco
brown on the inside
and not-quite-White on the outside
You would not believe how White people talk
about Other people when they think you're White
How it's more polite to say Spanish
instead of Mexican
and the subtle shift in tone
when your Mexican is discovered
your tortillas uncovered
I never tried to pass for White
but I have been passed
because White people who like me
want to give me the benefit of the doubt
and let me tell you, sister
There's nothing like White Privilege
and my mother knew it
So when people would ask
"Are you Italian or Greek?"
she would laugh and say
"Good guess!"
It is so disappointing
such dark eyes and such tight curls
 fail to fit in
not White, not Mexican
I have been passed
I identify as White Trash
My mother is Mexican
but her family doesn't mind
porque no hay indios en la familia
And since I learned all my Spanish in school
it was years before I understood
It's good to be White in America

FLOYD SALAS

Wedo

When I was 15 I was a pachuco
which is a Mexican zoot-suiter
& very dark
& very curly-haired
& tough
& can whip sailors & Okies by himself
or with his gang

But I was small for my age
& Spanish
& so white for my Mexican buddies
they nicknamed me Wedo
which means white
& didn't have curly hair
& would never be 6 feet tall
& wasn't very tough

But I was brave
& had a Hollywood haircut
that was wavy on top
& fell onto my forehead
like Frank Sinatra's
& combed into such a smooth duck's ass in back
that everybody admired it
in fact
it had so much pomade on it
to keep it stiff & in tight place
as a helmet
that I could dive into a forest stream
from a high rock in Mendocino County
& go way down
& coast way up
& get out
all dripping & wet
without even putting a dent in it

SHEILA MALDONADO

Clashing in Coney Island

In the 1984-85 picture of Class 5B
at P.S. 90 in Coney Island,
Brooklyn, New York
I'm wearing gray Lees and
a big white, gray, and pink sweater,
a style half-ghetto, half-Guido

Me and the other Lee wearers
would walk to school and home
with our hands planted
on our back right waistbands
so no one would snatch our
Lee patches, the sport of the day

I got the sweater at Ceasar's Bay,
which used to be Korvettes, which later
became K-mart, but then was haven
for high-haired Bensonhurst Guidettes
and Ma, who got a flavor for chiclet jeans,
which made you snap your hips like gum

Makea is next to me in the picture and
lived in my building, along with her
cousin Tecia, whose house was a
cool, gray cave in the summer where we
watched Whoopi Goldberg on early cable
play with her "long, luxurious" blond hair

I flinched the first time I saw Tecia's mom
put a metal comb over the stove fire
and then to Tecia's head but had
no problem playing Double Dutch with
her and Makea's telephone cable rope,
that whipped us if we didn't jump right

Stacy is below me in the picture and
was my best friend the next year,
going out to lunch with me,
the sixth grade privilege,
and encouraging me to buy more
big sweaters, half-Italian that she was

Out in the drugstore one day with her
during lunch, I was decked in
Ceasar's Bay regalia and when an old man
spoke to me in Spanish I had
the nerve to be surprised but he told me
Try as you might, you can't hide

honduras of despair

I've known depths
of mountain valleys
of flood waters

my family comes
from the Depths
depths of scarcity

they clawed
their way out
into another abyss

honestly I've only
known their depths
on vacation

I'm from fortress projects
on an island at the edge
of a city far north
of the ancestral deep

I've been integrated into schools
incorporated into office buildings
institutions all with walls so high
they could house armies jail masses

you could scream and no one would hear you

my depths are depressions grooves in the soul eroded
hieroglyphic etchings can barely make out definitions infinite
how far I am from my blood how low I can sink how ugly I get
how little I can handle how few I can save how I can't save myself

KEVIN TOBAR PESANTEZ

Ecuador Para Mí

Para mí
 El Ecuador significa
 algo que se me ha quitado.
 Significa palabras mal-formadas,
 oraciones tartamudeadas
 y un cielo ebrio que no se despeja.

El viento otoñal de Quito enfría mis pensamientos
 y la identidad se queda atónita
 en las bocas de transeúntes momificados.

 ¡Ya no hay desnudez jubilosa!
 Ha sido reemplazada y reiterada
 por esta condición moderna:
 Cuerpos cubiertos
 en verdades sintéticas,
 ponchos sin color
 y el reo enclaustrado
 en una botella de plástico.

Eso es el Ecuador para mí.

 A veces alucino el despejar de mi ser,
 un ciclo sempiterno en donde pueda vivir.
Pero
 de las cloacas de esta existencia
 siempre emergen nubes grisáceas
 que cubren la llanura infinita
 y me dejan con una visión cegada por cataratas.

Ese ojo infectado
 es el Ecuador.

Ecuador For Me (Tr.)

For me
 Ecuador means
 something that has been taken away.
 It means misshapen words,
 stuttered sentences,
 and a drunken sky which does not clear up.

The autumnal wind of Quito chills my thoughts
 and identity is astonished
 in the mouths of mummified passersby.

 There is no longer joyous nudity!
 It has been replaced and reiterated
 by this modern condition:
 Bodies covered
 in synthetic truths,
 discolored ponchos,
 and the accused cloistered
 in a plastic bottle.
This is Ecuador for me

 Sometimes I hallucinate about the clearing up of my self,
 an everlasting cycle in which I could live.
But
 from the sewers of this existence
 greyish clouds always emerge
 which cover the infinite plains
 and leave me with vision blinded by cataracts.

That infected eye
 is Ecuador.

Translated by Kevin Tobar Pesántez and Amanda Cunniff.

MÁS ALLÁ DE MÍ MISMA
Further Away From Myself

HE ESCRITO NUMEROSOS ENSAYOS en los que reflexiono sobre las razones por las que salí de Cuba y mi revaluación del proceso revolucionario desde la emigración. Algunos de estos trabajos se han publicado, otros permanecen inéditos. Una vez más me siento a escribir sobre el tema, esta vez motivada por la expresión de la cara de Silvia Gil, quien sentada en el público el pasado mes de enero, durante una presentación que hice en Casa de las Américas sobre la situación de la cultura de los latinos en Nueva York, mencioné el hecho de que con frecuencia cubanas y cubanos que emigran a los Estados Unidos, a su llegada dan explicaciones de índole personal para haberse ido, explicaciones que van desde haberse enamorado de alguien que vive allá hasta que el día a día era muy difícil, en términos materiales. Estas

(cont'd. pg. 202)

I HAVE WRITTEN NUMEROUS ESSAYS in which I reflect over the reasons why I left Cuba and my reevaluation of the revolutionary process since the emigration. Some of these works have been published, others remain unpublished. Once more I feel like writing about this theme, this time motivated by the expression on Silvia Gil's face, who sat in protest during a presentation I made in the House of the Americas about the situation of the Latino culture in New York, where I mentioned the fact that often times upon their arrival, Cubans who emigrate to the United States give explanations of a personal nature as to why they left, explanations that go from having loved

(cont'd. pg. 204)

Translated by Amanda A. Cunniff.

S O N I A R I V E R A V A L D É S

MÁS ALLÁ DE MÍ MISMA
Sonia Rivera Valdés

(cont'd from pg. 201)

son razones comunes entre los inmigrantes latinoamericanos y caribeños, pero según va pasando el tiempo un gran número de los cubanos va poniendo el peso de su decisión en el irredimible proceso revolucionario, del que cada día se expresan con mayor animadversión, y no es raro que este creciente resentimiento vaya acompañado de una, también creciente, nostalgia por la música, la comida y el paisaje cubano. Y Silvia Gil me preguntó a qué yo atribuía esta transformación. Pueden darse numerosas explicaciones, pero de verdad, no lo entiendo, contesté entonces, y digo ahora, sobre todo porque gran parte de las historias que conozco directamente proclaman como proveniente de su memoria lo que proviene de su imaginación. Pero si no puedo entender cómo piensan los otros, sí decidí hace muchos años tratar de entender mis verdaderos motivos para haber dejado Cuba y mi proceso de revaluación de la salida y de la Revolución.

Además de los ensayos que he escrito cuyo tema central es este proceso, el mismo aparece de manera implícita en un gran número de mis relatos, el primero de ellos un cuento titulado *El beso de la patria,* que escribí al regresar a Nueva York después de mi primer viaje a Cuba. El cuento habla de cómo a una niña de diez años, con el expediente académico más alto de la escuela a que asiste, en la playa de Santa Fe, no le permiten llevar el estandarte del plantel en la parada del 28 de enero por no tener zapatos negros. Se desarrolla en el año 1947. Esta historia, muy divulgada en los Estados Unidos y muy enseñada en universidades y escuelas secundarias nadie la ha estudiado en su aspecto socio-político, nadie le ha prestado atención al momento histórico en que se desarrolla, pero mi propósito fue denunciar una situación terriblemente injusta, típica de la época en que se desarrolla la trama, y lo escribí como una respuesta a las alabanzas que escuchaba, con demasiada frecuencia, a la vida en Cuba antes de 1959.

Escribí el primer ensayo sobre Cuba entre 1984 y 1985. Se publicó en *Esta puente mi espalda,* editado por Cherríe Moraga y Ana Castillo, en 1988. A fines de 1992, los editores de *Bridges to Cuba/Puentes a Cuba* me pidieron un trabajo en el que actualizara la opinión que expresé en el que había publicado en 1988. El principio de la década de los noventa, como todos sabemos, fue un período extremadamente difícil para la sociedad cubana. Lo escribí y titulé "Veintisiete años después de

la partida." No lo aceptaron y en su lugar publicaron un relato que había enviado como algo secundario, "La noche de la abuela." Este relato ha sido analizado como un alegato contra la ruptura de la familia, provocada por la Revolución, algo lejos de mis intenciones al escribirlo. Lo que digo ahí hubiera podido decirlo una emigrante de cualquier país, incluso mi propia abuela, sobre su abuela, que está enterrada en Islas Canarias. El texto que están leyendo ahora es una especie de collage, compuesto de fragmentos de ensayos anteriores unidos a reflexiones actuales.

Llegué a los Estados Unidos el 27 de abril de 1966. Tenía veintiocho años, iba a cumplir veintinueve en agosto. Iba dispuesta a comenzar una nueva vida para mí y para mi familia. Quería olvidarme de la política, educar a mis hijos en un ambiente en el que no tuvieran que hacer trabajo voluntario los domingos. Tenía la esperanza de que mi marido sería menos celoso en aquel país y de que yo conseguiría un trabajo que me gustara. Quería estudiar, aprender inglés, aprender a manejar y tener mi propio carro. Quería tener una casa cómoda donde no sintiera el miedo constante de que en cualquier momento podría ser bombardeada, como me sucedía en Cuba desde 1959, sobre todo durante los días de la crisis de octubre en que me sentí metida en la piel del personaje de *Memorias del Subdesarrollo,* preguntándome, pegada al radio día y noche ¿Por qué hemos tenido que meternos en esto? Quería vivir tranquila, realizarme como ser humano. Sentía la necesidad de hacer algo diferente de lo que había hecho hasta aquel momento. No sabía bien qué hacer ni cómo hacerlo, pero ya se me ocurriría allí donde, con todo lo malo que se dijera en Cuba, había tantas oportunidades. En aquellos primeros años era fácil responder a por qué te fuiste de Cuba. "Fidel y el comunismo," males absolutos cuya sola mención explicaba todo, motivos del exilio de todos los cubanos. Razón justificadora de unos privilegios de los que carecían el resto de los inmigrantes latinoamericanos y caribeños.

Muy pronto muchas de las ilusiones con que llegué fueron desvaneciéndose, una a una. La primera fue la que, probablemente, con mayor vehemencia había ambicionado antes de ir: olvidarme de la política y de los problemas sociales. Tuve que enfrentarme con la realidad de que no era solamente en los titulares de primera página de los periódicos cubanos en los que aparecía a diario la Guerra de Viet Nam, y de que la violencia que tenían la discriminación y el racismo en los Estados Unidos no era una mera invención creada como propaganda antiimperialista.

En Nueva York fuimos a vivir a Astoria, a un apartamento que pagó en los primeros meses una asociación

de ayuda a los refugiados cubanos, en un barrio de Queens habitado por quienes yo pensaba eran italianos, y en realidad eran griegos. En uno de los apartamentos de aquel enorme complejo de edificios conocimos a otra familia cubana, mulata, recién llegada también, cuyo niño, Robertico, tenía la edad de mis hijos y era su único amigo y ellos los únicos amigos de él, entre otras razones, por el idioma. Debo haberlos conocido porque la tía del niño y yo trabajábamos en la misma fábrica. En aquellas fábricas en que trabajé durante los diez meses que permanecimos en Nueva York nació el cuento "Los ojos lindos de Adela," que aparece en *Las historias prohibidas de Marta Veneranda*, pero para el tiempo en que pasaba cada mañana, de lunes a viernes, por el apartamento de la tía de Robertico, para recogerla e ir juntas a trabajar, hubiera sonreído irónicamente ante la sugerencia de que aquellos días se convertirían en literatura al pasar los años.

Una mañana de invierno, pocos meses después de llegar, al llegar frente a su puerta, pintada de verde oscuro, como todas las del complejo, la encontré decorada, incluyendo el marco, con letreros puestos con un cuño gomígrafo blanco, que decían, "White Power." Atónita, leí los letreros, uno a uno aunque todos decían lo mismo y me dije: pues resulta que es verdad, no era propaganda comunista, y no me atrevía a tocar a la puerta por la pena que me daba cómo iba a sentirse mi amiga y su familia, y Robertico, que tenía ocho años, ante aquello. Tan fuerte fue el impacto que hoy, después de cuarenta y cinco años estoy contándolo.

De cualquier forma, pensé cuando me repuse, en este sistema hay más cosas positivas que negativas. Hay muchas oportunidades y, si se trabaja fuerte, se consigue lo que se quiere. Me propuse proteger a mis hijos, eso sí. Por lo demás, trataría de criarlos de manera que al llegar a hombres fueran buenos y trabajadores. Aquella tarea era más que suficiente para sentir que estaba cumpliendo mi deber con la sociedad; yo no podía arreglar el mundo.

Mi estrategia de entonces, para sobrevivir psicológicamente, fue tratar de aplicar a las situaciones que me entristecían o me indignaban uno de los primeros refranes que aprendí en mi nueva vida: "Si la vida te da limones, haz limonada," por lo menos allá era fácil conseguir azúcar, pero después de un tiempo de hacer constantes limonadas me convencí de que por más azúcar que pusiera el sabor era siempre ácido. Había demasiadas cosas que no funcionaban ni para los negros norteamericanos ni para los latinos ni para muchos otros, incluyendo a las mujeres. Aprendí que tener un buen trabajo y vivir decentemente no era tan fácil. Aprendí que la alienación formaba parte esencial de la vida de aquel país. No era

posible, como pensaba antes de ir, tener el televisor a colores y el carro y, a la vez, tiempo para compartir con los hijos y los amigos.

Nos mudamos a Puerto Rico. Llegamos el sábado 4 de febrero de 1967, unas horas antes de que Violeta Parra se suicidara en Chile, y desde que lo supe incorporé el luto a la grata memoria de mi llegada a Puerto Rico. Así son los recuerdos.

Pasó el tiempo, mis hijos fueron creciendo y yo hice mucho de lo que había planeado hacer al emigrar: trabajé, estudié, hasta saqué la licencia de manejar. Pero nunca imagine, cuando estaba en Cuba, que aquella isla vecina en la que no pensaba con frecuencia aunque los famosos versos que recitaba en los actos cívicos de la escuela dijeran que era la otra ala del pájaro, iba a enseñarme lo que quiere decir la palabra colonialismo. Fue impactante que, el primer año que mis hijos fueron a la escuela allí, al regresar de clases el 23 de septiembre les pregunté qué habían escrito en la composición por ser ese día el aniversario del Grito de Lares y me respondieron que no habían escrito nada, la maestra no lo había mencionado.

Después de diez años regresé a los Estados Unidos. Fui directamente a la Universidad de Kent, Ohio, donde me solidaricé con los estudiantes que trataban de mantener viva la memoria de lo sucedido el 4 de mayo de 1970. Estábamos en 1976. Para esa época ya me había dado cuenta de que mi gente, aquella con la que me identificaba y de la que me sentía parte era la llamada "gente de color." En Cuba, mi familia decía que era blanca, pero allí era con las minorías con quienes compartía la discriminación, los abusos y los atropellos. La idea de ser feliz sin tener que luchar para que los demás también lo fueran se había desvanecido. Mi tranquilidad y la de los míos estaba indisolublemente unida, quisiera o no, a la de los demás. Y un día me di cuenta de que, sin poder evitarlo, el dolor de Conchita, mi amiga de San Juan a cuyo hijo de diecisiete años habían asesinado por un problema de drogas, me dolía casi como si hubiera sido hijo mío. Ya en este punto entendí que la única forma de vivir contenta conmigo era manteniendo la esperanza de que el mundo sería mejor en el futuro, más justo o por lo menos, que yo estaba contribuyendo en algo para tratar de que lo fuera. Y en junio de 1980 regresé a Cuba, con una visión del mundo distinta de la que tenía al irme. Entre otras cosas había aprendido que durante los años sesenta la mayoría de la humanidad pasaba más hambre que nosotros cuando comíamos carne rusa y frijolitos chinos. En los sesenta, cuando muchos productos alimenticios escaseaban, podía conseguirse con relativa facilidad, al menos donde yo vivía, unas latas de carne importadas de

Europa del Este. No estoy segura si eran de Rusia pero así era conocida. Los frijoles a que me refiero son los rojos, pequeños y redondos que se distribuyeron en los mismos años que la carne enlatada y que el pueblo, ajeno a que su nombre era adzuki, y muy altos en proteínas, conocía como *frijolitos chinos*. La primera vez que los vi en el Barrio Chino de Nueva York me detuve frente al saco que los contenía, y los mire, hipnotizada, era un déjà vu. Averigüé, y pensé qué ignorancia la mía cuando criticaba acerbamente los frijolitos.

Al regresar de aquel viaje hice un balance de la experiencia. Puse de un lado de la balanza los aspectos negativos, del otro los positivos. Ya conocía condiciones sociales, fuera de los límites geográficos de esta isla, tan inhumanas, que encontré las de Cuba incomparablemente mejores, aunque lejos de ser perfectas. Me gustó que hubiera tantas mujeres, muchas de ellas negras, doctoras en medicina. Eso casi no podía creerlo, recordando la situación de antes del 59. Hubo quien me enseñó parques y me señaló que allí se reunían más de doscientos muchachos todas las noches y ahora no quedaban ni veinte. Se habían ido por el Mariel, pero yo no veía niños comiendo de los latones de basura. Se lo dije a una concuña mía, hipercrítica de la sociedad cubana, y me contestó: "Ah no, eso ha cambiado del cielo a la tierra". Ella acaba de cumplir noventa años y ahora vive en los Estados Unidos. El peso que tenía y que tiene la educación gratuita y que todo el mundo tuviera acceso a tratamiento médico, pesó sobre lo demás. Sé que hay gente que hace chistes y dice que uno no está siempre enfermo ni estudiando. Lo dicen mientras están saludables y ya han sido educados. La vida es condición sine qua non para luchar por lo que se quiere. Si un niño muere antes de los cinco años de edad por mala nutrición o enfermedades evitables, como sucede en tantas regiones del planeta, le dije a más de una persona que me preguntaba cómo podía apoyar el proceso revolucionario cubano con la política homofóbica que sostenía, se le ha negado para siempre la oportunidad de luchar por sus preferencias sexuales, y este es uno de los aspectos en que la sociedad cubana ha mejorado sustancialmente. En todas mis consideraciones fue fundamental el hecho de que Cuba había estado asediada desde el principio. Nunca sabremos cómo hubiera marchado la revolución sin el bloqueo.

Hace treinta y un años de ese primer viaje. Los he pasado hablando, escribiendo, caminando, viajando, llevando en el abrigo botones por diferentes causas, y lazos rojos por el SIDA, participando en eventos y organizaciones dondequiera que se alzaba una voz tratando de conseguir un mundo mejor. No ha sido solo por Cuba, y el haber emigrado también ha aportado aspectos muy positivos a mi existencia y me ha enriquecido como ser humano. Creo . . . creo que al final la manera cómo evalúas el proceso revolucionario si emigras depende de si tu proyecto de vida está centrado en lo inmediato que te rodea, o sea un proyecto de vida totalmente personal o si sientes que tu vida está imbricada con la del resto de la humanidad. Dicen que una muerte es una tragedia, un millón de muertes es una estadística. Si tú sientes, si llegas a sentir que cada persona de ese millón nació con una cara que la diferenciaba de todos los otros seres humanos, con sus propias huellas dactilares, y tenía manos y pies, ilusiones y gente que quería y la quería, y eres capaz de imaginarte cuánto le dolió morir, si sientes, si llegas a sentir eso, no te queda más remedio que tratar de que esa tragedia no se dé de nuevo. Voy a terminar con una cita. Las cubanas y los cubanos somos muy aficionados a citar. Esta es de Rabindranath Tagore:

> "Cuando una persona comienza a tener una visión que va más allá de su verdad personal, cuando se da cuenta que todo va mucho más allá de lo que parecía, comienza a tener conciencia de su estatura moral. Su perspectiva de la vida necesariamente cambia, y su voluntad ocupa el lugar de sus deseos. Ahí viene el conflicto entre su yo inferior y su yo superior, entre sus deseos y su voluntad, entre su avidez por objetos que apelan a sus sentidos y el propósito que viene desde el fondo de su corazón." ▯

FURTHER AWAY FROM MYSELF (Tr.)
Sonia Rivera Valdés

(cont'd from pg. 201)

someone who lives there to the day to day was very difficult, in material terms. These are common reasons amongst Latin American and Caribbean immigrants, but as time passes a large number of Cubans put the burden of their decision on the unredeemable revolutionary process — which they express with great hostility — and it is not strange that this growing resentment would be accompanied with a (also growing) nostalgia for Cuban music, food, and countryside. Silvia Gil asked me to what I attributed this transformation. There are many reasons that could be given, but as I said to her, the truth is that I don't know, and now I say that above all it is because a large part of these stories I know directly proclaim how foreign that which originates in their imagination is to their memory. But if I cannot understand how the others think, I decided after many years to try to understand my own true motives for having left Cuba and my process of reevaluation of the departure and of the revolution.

Apart from the essays I have written whose central theme is this process, the same theme appears implicitly in a large number of my stories, the first of them a short-story titled *The Kiss of My Homeland,* which I wrote upon my return to New York after my first trip to Cuba. The story talks about how a ten-year-old girl from the beach of Santa Fe, despite having the best student record of her school, was not permitted to carry the school banner in the parade of the twenty-eight of January because she did not have black shoes. It takes place in 1947. This story, though widespread in the U.S. and often taught in universities and secondary schools, has yet to be studied for its socio-political aspect, nobody has paid attention to the historical moment in which it developed, but my purpose was to denounce a terribly unjust situation, typical of the epoch in which the plot developed, and I wrote it as a response to the all-too-frequent praises I heard about life in Cuba before 1959.

I wrote the first essay about Cuba between 1984 and 1985. It was published in *This Bridge My Back,* edited by Cherrie Moraga and Ana Castillo in 1988. Towards the end of 1992, the editors of *Bridges to Cuba/Puentes a Cuba* asked me for a work in which the opinion I expressed in my 1988 publication would be brought up to date. The beginning of the nineties, as we know, was an extremely difficult time for Cuban society. I wrote it and named it "Twenty-seven years after the departure." They did not accept it and in its place published a story that had been sent as a backup, "The Night of the Grandmother." This story had been analyzed as a statement against the rupture of the family, provoked by the revolution, something far from my intentions upon writing it. What I say there could have been told by any immigrant from any country, even my own grandmother, about her grandmother, who is buried in the Canary Islands. The text that is being read now is a species of collage, composed of fragments of previous essays united with current reflections.

I arrived in the United States on the twenty-seventh of April 1966. I was twenty-eight, about to turn twenty-nine in August. I was ready to start a new life for my family and me. I wanted to forget the politics, to educate my children in an environment where they didn't have to voluntarily work on Sundays. I had the hope that my husband would be less jealous in that country and that I would get a job I would like. I wanted to study, to learn English, to learn to drive and to have my own car. I wanted to have a comfort-able house where I wouldn't feel the constant fear that in any moment I could be bombed, as I felt in Cuba since 1959. But above all, during those days of the crisis of Oc-tober in which I felt mixed up in the skin of the character of *Memories of Underdevelopment,* I asked myself glued to the radio night and day, why did we have to have put ourselves in this? I wanted to live calm, to fulfill myself as a human. I felt the need to do something different from what I had been doing up until this moment. I didn't really know what to do or how to do it, but there it would occur to me that, with all the evil that was said in Cuba, there were many opportunities. In those first years it was easy to say why I left Cuba. "Fidel and communism," absolute evils whose only mention explained everything, motives of exile of all the Cubans. It was a justifiable reason that all the other Latin American and Caribbean immigrants lacked.

Very soon many of the illusions I arrived with were van-ishing, one by one. The first was probably the one to which I had most vehemently aspired before leaving: to forget the politics and the social issues. I had to face the reality that the Vietnam War appeared not only on the headlines of the front pages of the Cuban newspapers, and that the violence, discrimination and racism in the U.S. was not a mere invention created as anti-imperialist propaganda.

I was left to live in Astoria, New York, in an apartment paid for in the first months by a relief association for Cuban refugees, in a neighborhood of Queens inhabited by those who I thought were Italians, and in reality were Greeks. In one of the apartments of that enormous building complex we met another Cuban family, mulattos, also recently ar-rived, whose son little Robert had the same age as my kids and was their only friend and they were his only friend, amongst other reasons, because of the language. I knew them because the boy's aunt and I worked together in the same factory. Those factories where I worked during the ten months we remained in New York inspired the short story "The beautiful eyes of Adela," which appears in *The Forbidden Tales of Marta Veneranda*, but for the time in which each week passed from Monday to Friday, on my way to the apartment of little Robert's aunt to pick her up and go together to work, I would smile ironically at the suggestion that those days would convert into literature after all those years.

One morning in winter, a few months after we arrived, at the front of their door, painted in dark green like the rest of the complex, I found it decorated, including the doorframe, with letters made by a rubber stamp. It said: "White Power." Astonished, I read the letters, one by one although all of them said the same and I told myself: this result is the truth, this was not communist propaganda, and I didn't dare touch the door due to the shame it gave me as it would my friend and her family, and little Robert, who was eight years old before that. So strong was the impact that today, after forty-five years, I'm still telling the story.

Anyway, I thought when I recovered, in this system there are more positive things than negative ones. There are many opportunities and, if one works hard, one will receive what one wants. Therefore, I decided to protect my children. Otherwise, I would try to raise them in such a way that they would become men who are good and hard working. That task was more than enough to feel like I was fulfilling my duties to society; after all, I couldn't fix the world.

Therefore, my strategy to survive psychologically was to try to apply one of the first sayings I learned in my new life to the situations that made me sad or angry: "If life gives you lemons, make lemonade." At least that way it would be easy to get sugar, but after some time of constantly making lemonade I convinced myself that no matter how much sugar I put, the taste was always acidic. There have always been too many things that didn't work for neither black North Americans nor Latinos, nor for many others including women. I learned that to have a good job and to live decently was not easy. I learned that alienation formed an essential part of that country. It wasn't possible, as I thought before, to have a color television and a car, and at the same time, time enough to share with the children and friends.

We moved to Puerto Rico. We arrived Saturday the fourth of February 1967, hours before Violeta Parra killed herself in Chile, and from there I knew that I would incorporate the mourning with the pleasant memory of my arrival in Puerto Rico. Memories are like that.

Time passed, my children were growing and I did much of what I had originally planned to do: I worked and I studied, until I got my driver's license. But I never imagined when I was in Cuba, that neighboring island which I rarely thought of (although the famous verses recited in the school assemblies said that it was the other wing of the bird) would teach me what the word "colonialism" really means. It was shocking that, the first year that my children were in school there, when they returned to class on the twenty-third of September I asked them what did they write because it was the anniversary of Grito de Lares and they responded that they hadn't written anything, the teacher did not mention it.

After ten years I returned to the U.S. I went directly to the University of Kent, Ohio where I found solidarity with the students who tried to maintain the memory of what happened the fourth of May 1970. It was 1976. For that epoch I already had noticed that my people, those with whom I identified and with whom I felt a part were known as "people of color." In Cuba, my family was called white, but there, with the minorities, we shared the discrimination, the abuses and the outrages. The idea of being happy

without also having to fight for the others faded. My peace of mind and that of my family was inextricably linked, like it or not, to the others. And one day I noticed that, without the power to avoid it, the pain of Conchita, my friend from San Juan whose boy of seventeen years bad been killed due to a drug problem, hurt me almost as much as if he were my own son. Already by this point I learned that the only way to live content was by maintaining the hope that the world would be better in the future, or at least more just—that I was contributing to what it could be. And in June of 1980 I returned to Cuba, with a different vision of the world from when I left. Amongst other things I had learned that during the seventies the majority of humanity was hungrier than we were when we ate Russian meats and Chinese beans. In the seventies, when many food products were running low, one could get cans of meat imported from Eastern Europe relatively easily, at least where I lived. I'm not sure if they were Russian but they were known that way. The beans to which I refer are red, little and round and were distributed in the same years as the canned meat. They were called adzuki, very high in protein, but were known in the town as little Chinese beans. The first time I saw them in New York's Chinatown I stopped myself and looked at the sack that contained them, hypnotized—it was déjà vu. I ascertained, and thought of my ignorance when I bitterly criticized the beans.

Upon returning from that trip I took stock of the experience. On one side of the scale I put the negative aspects, on the other the positives. The social conditions of Cuba, like the geographical boundaries of this island—so inhuman—I found to be incomparably better—although far from perfect. I liked that there were so many women, many of them black, doctors of medicine. That I could almost not believe, remembering the situation from before '59. Someone showed me parks and pointed out that there, more than two hundred boys would get together every night and now there remained not twenty. They were gone because of Mariel, but I did not see children eating from garbage cans. I told this to a sister-in-law of mine, hypercritical of Cuban society, and she responded: "Ah, so it has become heaven on earth." She just turned ninety and now lives in the U.S. The value that free education had and has, and that everyone has access to medical treatment, weighed more than the rest. I know that there are people who make jokes and say that one is neither always sick nor studying. They say this because they are healthy and have been educated. Life is a condition of sine qua non to fight for that which one desires. If a child dies before the age of five due to malnutrition or avoidable maladies, as in many parts of the world, I've asked more than one person how can they support the Cuban revolutionary process with

the homophobic policies they sustain, forever denied the opportunity to fight for their sexual preferences, and this is one aspect of Cuban society that has substantially improved. In all of my considerations the fact that Cuba has been besieged has been fundamental from the start. Never would we know how the revolution would have worked without the blockade.

It has been thirty-one years since that first trip. I have spent them speaking, writing, walking, traveling, carrying in my coat buttons for different causes, and red ribbons for AIDS, participating in events and organizations that raise a voice trying to obtain a better world. It has not only been because of Cuba, having emigrated has also provided positive aspects to my life and has enriched me as a person. I believe that in the end the manner in which you evaluate the revolutionary process if you emigrate depends if your life plan is centered on what immediately surrounds you, or rather a life plan totally personal, or if you feel that your life is interwoven with the rest of humanity. They say a death is a tragedy; one million deaths are a statistic. If you come to feel each person of that million born with a face that differentiated him or her from all of the other humans, with their own finger prints, and had hands and feet, illusions and people who loved and wanted, and are capable of imagining how much it hurt to die, if you feel, if you come to feel that, you have no other remedy than to try to prevent this tragedy from happening again. I will finish with a quote. We Cubans are fond of quoting. This is Rabindranath Tagore:

> "When a person begins to have a vision that goes beyond their personal truth, when they take note that everything goes beyond what it appeared to be, they begin to be conscious of their moral height. Their perspective of life necessarily changes, and their will takes the place of their desires. There in lies the conflict between their me inferior and their me superior, between their desires and their will, between their eagerness for objects that appeal to their senses and the purpose that comes from the bottom of their heart."

SONIA RIVERA VALDÉS is a writer, literary and film critic and professor of Literature, Spanish Language and Puerto Rican Studies at York College, City University of New York. In the fall of 2009, this institution granted her the Presidential Outstanding Scholarship for her literary work.

AMANDA CUNNIFF is a junior at New York University, studying History and Romances, with a focus on Spanish and French. She is currently translating oral histories regarding the US/Mexico border wars from Spanish to English.

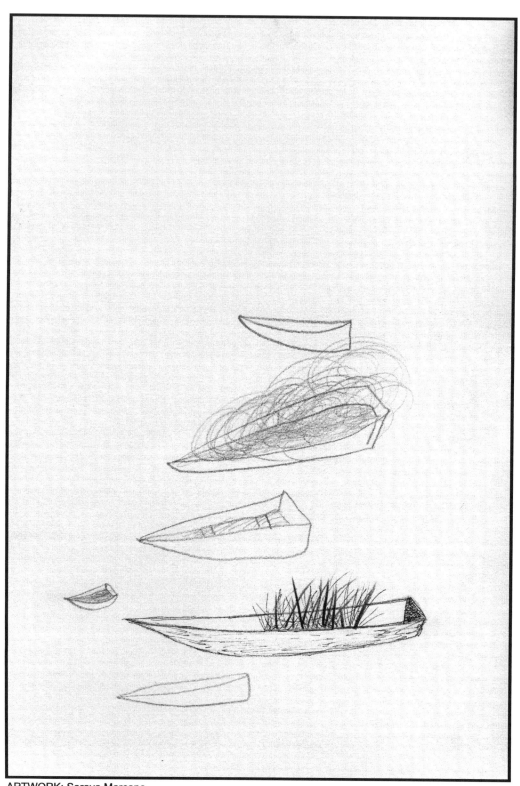

ARTWORK: Soraya Marcano
"Boats" Pencil Drawing on paper (11" x 6") Copyright © 2011

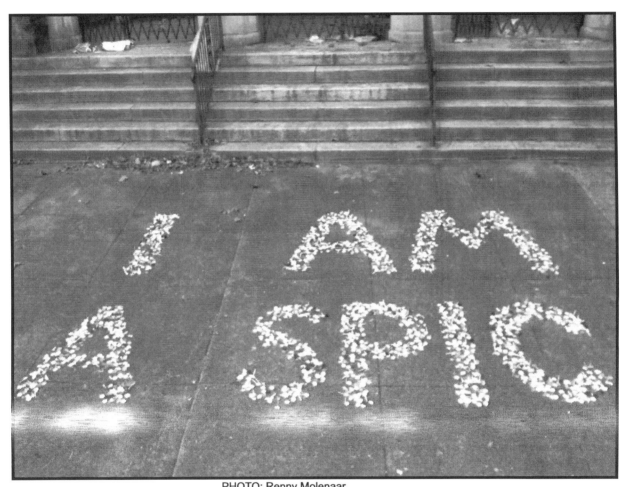

PHOTO: Renny Molenaar
""I am a spic," plastic hair barrettes on sidewalk, photograph, Copyright © 2012

HENRY I. PADRON-MORALES

Dos worlds/Two mundos

Cuántos tendrán que
pasar
until we realize
lo que está pasando
people moving
to and fro
todos siempre
llamándonos bro-sista
qué pasa
raza
Qué pasa
con mi raza?
lots of party
lots of laughter
Always somthin
Hapnin
Porqué será
que nuestro future
ya preparado está
without us having
a say
on what affects
us from day to day
Quizas you don't
understand lo que
está pasando
¿porqué es que nuestra
lengua
is slowly disappearing?
Sera la programación
Que le han dado
A nuestra nación
Nuestra juventud
En tremendo lio
están
they don't know
from where they vienen
y no saben to where they van
aunque muchos
listos y muy
bien preparados

están
Trying to understand
this system
mejor dicho cistern
can cause you
mucho pain
puede causar un tremendo
stain en tu brain
Compañeros-Compañeras
yo he llegado a una
realizacián
Que what we need
es una revolución
Don't jump to conclusions
if the total scope
you don"t understand
porque eso pasa
mucho throughout
the land
Gente hablando
sin saber de lo que
hablan
Nosotros somos
una raza divided
divididos por una
mentalidad que
ideologicamnete
está oppressing
a nuestra gente
Es imposible
tratar de entender
something we
didn't create
Halgo que no
fue hecho con
nosotros en
mente
This land tis the
home of the free
and the brave
Porqué es que fue

built by slaves
who today wear
no cadenas
physically
pero are still
chained to it
mentally
Eso es progreso? . . .
Pueblo del future
despertais
open up your
weary eyes
empiezen to see
para que el future
no
les sea
how it's been for
you and me
Aprendan from our
mistakes
Aprendan a distiguir
Entre los que son
for real y los que
son nada mas que
fakes
Si tu no has
podido entendeder
la ironia de
esta poesia
te lo trataré
de explicar
sin dolor de
cabeza darte
ha habido una fusión
la cual ha afectado
a nuestra nación
la cual nos ha
dejado casi sin
ton ni son
Hemos tenido
que adaptarnos
y tener que aprender
las fuciones
y los mecanismos
del Americanismo
Maldito sea
el precio que hemos
tenido que pagar

jamas sera impuesto
a nuestros hijos e
hijas porque, basta ya
Basta ya que las
drogas nos matan
Basta ya que nos
maltratan
Basta ya que nos
matan en guerras
Basta ya que
Basta ya que
Basta ya que
Children se
levanten con hambre
every morning
Basta ya que
you want to go to
college but can't
porque no hay chavo
Basta ya que
Nuestros trabajos siempre
Estan en jeopardy
No matter who the
Hell you may be
Porque todo depende
De fondos y hondos
From here there everywhere but
Ourselves
Basta ya que
Statistics-logistics-complistics-molistics
fuckistics-youristics
yoistics be so
important
si lo que vale es
el pueblo no ceros a la derecha
Basta ya que
los jovenes
no se llevan con sus
padres y que the
parents tampoco estan
too interested en sus
hijos e hijas
can't you see
that is the problem
constant confusion
dilusion, pollution
contusion
fusion

They are trying to
numb our minds
mientras que nos
comen el coco
who they think
they foolin
Nuestras mentes
no están trancadas
aunque las cadenas
estén apretadas
de vicio estos
elementos no nos
tumbaran
Porque somos
Puerto Rican
la mezcla divina
de hombre y mujer
el arcoiris
siendo el color de
nuestra piel
La profundidad de
el mar
no se puede
comparer
con lo que siento
por ti
Yet, here in cold
brick, asphalt,
iron, neon-lighted
streets
We find ourselves
still having to exist
Puertorican
Nuyorican
Buffalorican
Syracuserican
Chicagorican
Pennsylvaniarican
Massachusettsrican
Los Angelesrican
Hawaiirican
Europeanrican
wherever you may
be rican
we are a movimiento
un movimiento mundial
somos una clase
una clase universal.

Dos worlds/Two mundos (Tr.)

(English)

How many must
pass
until we realize
what is going on?
people moving
to and fro
always
calling each other bro-sista
what's up
race
What's up
with my race?
lots of party
lots of laughter
Always somthin
Hapnin
could it be
that our future
is already fixed
without us having
a say
on what affects
us from day to day
Maybe you don't
understand what
is happening
why is it that our
language
is slowly disappearing?
could it be the programming
That they have given
To our nation
Our youth
In a tremendous mess
they are
they don't know
from where they come
and they don't know to where they go
even though many
bright and very
well educated
are
Trying to understand
this system
or better yet, cistern

can cause you
a lot of pain
it can cause a tremendous
stain in your brain
Brothers-Sisters
I have come to a
realization
That what we need
is a revolution
Don't jump to conclusions
if the total scope
you don't understand
because that happens
a lot throughout
the land
People talking
without knowing what they're
talking about
We are
a race divided
divided by a
mentality that
ideologically
is oppressing
our people
It's impossible
to try to understand
something we
didn't create
Something that
wasn't made with
us in
mind
This land tis the
home of the free
and the brave
Then why is it that it was
built by slaves
who today wear
no chains
physically
but are still
chained to it
mentally
This is progress? . . .

Village of the future
arise
open up your
weary eyes
begin to see
so that the future
isn't
for them
how it's been for
you and me
Learn from our
mistakes
Learn to distinguish
Between those that are
for real and those that
are nothing more than
fakes
If you haven't
been able to understand
the irony
of this poem
I will try to
explain it for you
without giving you
headaches
there has been a fusion,
which has affected
our nation,
which has left
us almost without
rhyme or reason
We have had
to adjust
and had to learn
the functions
and the mechanisms
of Americanism
Damn
the price we have
had to pay
never will it be imposed
on our sons and
daughters because enough is enough
Enough already of the
drugs that kill us
Enough already of
them mistreating us
Enough already of

them killing us in wars
Enough already of
the children getting out of bed hungry
every morning
Enough already of
you wanting to go to
college but can't
because there's no cash
Enough already of
Our jobs always
Being in jeopardy
No matter who the
Hell you may be
Because everything depends
On funds and sums
From here there everywhere but
Ourselves
Enough already of
Statistics-logistics-complistics-molistics
fuckistics-youristics
me-istics being so
important
if what matters are
the people not zeros to the right
Enough already of
the youth
not getting along with their
parents and that the
parents aren't too
interested in their
sons and daughters
either
can't you see
that is the problem
constant confusion
delusion, pollution
contusion
fusion
They are trying to
numb our minds
while the boogeyman
eats us up
who they think
they foolin
Our minds
aren't locked up
even though the chains
are tightened

by vices these
factors will not
bring us down
Because we are
Puerto Rican
the divine mix
of man and woman
the rainbow
being the color of
our skin
The depth of
the sea
can't be compared
with what I feel
for you
Yet, here in cold
brick, asphalt,
iron, neon-lighted
streets
We find ourselves
still having to exist
Puertorican
Nuyorican
Buffalorican
Syracuserican
Chicagorican
Pennsylvaniarican
Masschusettsrican
Los Angelesrican
Hawaiiarican
Europeanrican
wherever you may
be rican
we are a movement
a world-wide movement
we are a class
a universal class.

Translated by Henry Ignacio Padrón-Morales and Adam Wier.

URAYOAN NOEL

Voice Creaks / Voz Quebrada

talk poem (smartphone voice notes),
Cripple Creek, Tallahassee, 2009

the swamp doesn't scare me neither does the bestiary it's all about the surrounding noise
even though there's no wind what county are we in? we've been sentenced to which coordi-
nates?

 el pantano no me espanta el bestiario tampoco se trata del ruido del ambiente si bien
sin viento en qué condado estamos? a qué coordenada se nos ha condenado?

between fall and spring there is a silence hardly reciprocal the voice I owe to you is doubt-
ful here here the voice is fitful and dodging potholes because you see there are gators here
it's written like "gat" but with an "or" at the end I don't count oars all I count on is that
voice that won't be heard echo perhaps you see?

 entre otoño e invierno hay un silencio poco recíproco la voz a ti debida aquí dubi-
tativa aquí voz como equívoco esquivando baches y es que en el sur hay caimanes
se escribe como imanes pero sin la K o la K de aká tú cuentas 47 yo cuento con la
voz que no se deja oír eco tal vez ves?

they talked of tourism but I'm far from the island isolated if you will this south is not my south
nor my north really lawnmowers wake of cloud wake of voice a pier made of wood just
like so many others yet unrecognizable in this topography

 como decían del turismo pero estoy lejos de la isla aislado si se quiere este sur no es
el mío ni mi norte tampoco cortagramas estela de nube estela de voz un muelle
de madera a la manera de tantos otros pero irreconocible en esta topografía

at last there's a breeze unexpected voice breeze body breeze text breeze the breeze in the
debris of meaning that the machinery just won't pick up the presence today turning to penance
because it's connected to territories that are or aren't incorporated or are about to be so

 hay brisa por fin inesperada voz brisa cuerpo brisa texto brisa en la brisa está la
brasa del sentido la maquinaria no deja que se capte la presencia hoy se hace peni-
tencia por estar conectado en territorios con o sin incorporar o por estarlo

now is the stateless hum of hemisphere no status updates no statute the ducks swim in
the marsh is this a creek? lagoon? it's not a river it doesn't move although it contains
movement that looks like a pair of eyes in the distance under the water I'd say a gator but
I'd be pushing it let's say they're eyes detached from the voice that frame a true or false rela-
tion with the environment

ahora es el zumbido de hemisferio sin estado no status updates sin estatuto los patos nadan en el pantano será esto quebrada? laguna? río no es no se mueve aunque contiene el movimiento eso parece un par de ojos a la distancia debajo del agua diría que caimán pero sería apresurado digamos que ojos desprendidos de la voz que marcan una relación real o falsa con el ambiente

now I'm moving towards the pier there is a rusty chair on the pier no doubt the locals escape six-pack in hand and tan themselves and sleep and the more outgoing ones say to their neighbors hey, y'all (no tally-ho, see?)

me voy moviendo en dirección al muelle hay una silla mohosa en el muelle sin duda los locales se escapan six-pack en mano se broncean se duermen los más audaces saludan al vecino qué tal! ajá?! sí?!

I don't say Hi instead I greet my gadget a gadget ritual that's what I offer breeze without cool I recite and I melt but now that I said that it's cooling and it's just that you can't read the weather here days as illegible as cries days of confusion and pragmatism days of another rhythm unfinished hard to repeat referring back to another instant another babble in the fake breeze another illusion of expression that which I hold onto

yo no saludo o más bien solo al aparato rito de aparato eso es lo que ofrezco brisa sin fresco recito y me derrito ahora que dije eso está enfriando y es que este clima no se deja leer días ilegibles como gritos días de confusión y pragmatismo días de otro ritmo inconcluso difícil de repetir que se remite a otro instante otro balbuceo en la falsa brisa otra ilusión de expresión de la que me agarro

soon the pier is going to capsize but for now this tale goes on and on towards the territories of voice mine and the bird bird voice slurred voice the voice of false haves the one I'm left with I'm 15 minutes from Georgia and light years away from nowhere I'm sentimental I know my only antidote against the monumental

pronto el muelle se irá a pique pero por lo pronto la crónica pica y se extiende en los territorios de la voz mía y del ave ave voz voz averiada la del falso haber la que me queda estoy a 15 minutos de Georgia y a años luz de ninguna parte sentimental lo sé único antídoto a lo monumental

this accident of voice this surrounding unmarked except for the mark I carry with me I recharge it the gadget defines my song but no battery in the world can power the promise of this brown orange green of this hazelnut pine hazy water

este accidente de voz este ambiente sin marcas salvo la que me toca cargar y recargar el aparato define mi canto pero no hay batería que valga para encender la promesa de este marrón naranja verde de este pino avellana agua llana

island fruits don't grow here much less BlackBerrys but growing are the flows of people of thoughts making room for voyages dislocations diasporas all is displaced even in this swamp that makes invisible my gadget's screen the voice is scared away the battery dies

no plug no exit spittle falling into the water returning again to the moment of saying re-
turning to the voice

aquí no crecen frutos de isla mucho menos BlackBerrys pero crecerán flujos de po-
blación de pensamiento donde sea caben destinos dislocaciones diásporas todo
se desplaza hasta en este pantano que hace invisible la pantalla de mi aparato se
espanta ya la voz se acaba la batería sin enchufe sin salida saliva caída al agua
vuelta de nuevo al momento de decirse de vuelta a la voz

Translated by Urayoan Noel.

On Writing, Quimera & Other Fears

1.

FOR AFAR, YOU LIE IN WAIT, A DISTANT POINT ON THE HORIZON, where the dark night sky falls into chaparral and salt marshes of Tamapulipas, or perhaps an old Tamarisk tree which you've hidden behind, the strong winds of the Sonora Desert whistling through patches of bristly *cholla*. Perhaps you are waiting for a *panga* on a Gulf coast beach to steal you across.

And as you draw closer, I see the bent, thinned-out body, the diaphanous haze of sleeplessness and worry, a face like warped wood and twisted with determination. You were never out for war, which you are walking into, even before you cross over from Matamoros, Rey Nosa, Nuevo Laredo, the swipes of your nimble feet running across the river's edge and vast deserts where *coyotes* have stolen you across the border.

(cont'd. pg. 220)

ON WRITING QUIMERA AND OTHER FEARS
Rosebud Ben-Oni

(cont'd from pg. 219)

Most likely, this is not your first trip.

Most likely, this is at least the second time you've handed over several years' worth of savings to a *coyote* who promises to smuggle you into *Gringolandia*, all the while knowing he might betray you and dump you in the river, which you then brave in the dead of night only to have *la migra* shine a flashlight in your face, herd you into a mass roundup, police truck, fingerprints, mug shot, waiting room especially for you, roundup, police truck, deportation, dumped by the river and then work yourself to death to try again, you knit buoyant islands from brushwood and brand-name auto parts and brand-name dresses and brand-name by-products from chemical plants so you can cross that river again, because you believe there is still time to supplant the sky with scrap-metal dreams, that you will hot-wire the sun to burn up the border that keeps you from leaving a mark upon the world you are about to reach, when you cannot even leave a trail behind from where you came

As you can see, the talk about you, which is not about *you*, never stops.

And I imagine a woman who made it to *Gringolandia*, who has listened to that talk for over 20 years. You've given two decades of your life to a ranch in the Texas Hill Country owned by a Mexican-American, which has been in his family since the 1830s, which you come to know better than him. And yet you cannot claim it as your own, not even one speck of dirt, although you are the first to see that the land has become exhausted and depleted and unable to give anymore, and therefore loses its value and the ranch goes into foreclosure.

That is when an Anglo (as my mother calls white men) from the North, who'd originally came for a taste of cowboy churches, silos, and the storefronts on Main Street, buys the ranch and ends up on the porch swing, still in loafers, listening to the tarnished metal chains creaking until the sun goes down, as pretty little somethings (but not you) wait at his feet until he decides to cut his losses and sell the land to developers to turn into a golf course. He turns the other workers loose with nothing except their wits and their grit, in the middle of a storm that's rolled in all the way from the Gulf coast. But not you— you will not leave just like that and, what's more, you're taking the land with you, you will raze it to the ground so it will be new again and belong to no one, so women like yourself don't have to go on the run from *la migra,* from those who want to send you back to a place that you no longer call home.

And just before lighting the match in your deft, weathered hands, you find the storm tries to stop you, to drown out your voice and anger and opposition, and that is where I will leave you, riding below the winds that come before the rain, riding until the fire catches, until it surges high and higher, flinging you further from all that the land as barren and unloved and consumed as you, burning up only you, burning up the tomorrow that you, in truth, never had anyway.

Querida, my mother says when I call to tell her of my idea. *That is the stupidest thing you could do.*

Stupid? (I'm just as taken aback by response). It's not stupid—it's beautiful. And it's better than what she'd get in the end if it really happened.

What she'd . . . "get?" My mother sounds even more upset. *Look, you might as well be writing propaganda for the Tea Party: "see this play, see how the illegals will burn your house down." You can't be poetic with this; it will be taken from you and used against you— and you won't even be the one to feel the effects.*

But I'm not being stupid, I retort. I'm trying to show the impossibility of her dream— that's the *tragedy.* What is done to these people—they work and slave with no—

'*Querida,* she cuts me off, *you're too far away in New York to understand this. You don't know what's become of the border—and I don't just mean what's going with the drug cartels. You've been gone too long. You're out of touch. . . .*

As you can see, the talk about you, which is not about *you*, never stops.

But all too soon (I realize later), I've stopped listening. It's not me but my mother who is out of touch with the new generation. Where she sees *quemadura,* a burning and destruction, I see the possibility of *quimera:* a woman living outside the law who still takes action.

I will call you *Quimera.* Chimera. In Greek mythology, an indomitable creature exhaling fire and waging wars against those who seek to go against the unsympathetic lawlessness of the natural world because the imposition of law leads to mass extinctions. You are also, by this definition, a desire and hunger which cannot be fulfilled because it is impossible, and in the end, one must settle for the beauty to be found in the attempt itself, however futile.

II.

THAT SUMMER I BEGIN WRITING YOU, I return with my mother to my aunt's home in Harlingen, a small, neglected Texas town about 15 minutes away from the U.S.-Mexican border. Outside a half-abandoned strip mall, we see your image peddled and misplaced on a ceramic plate by a Mid-western artist who came to paint the local color. He *has* left you barefoot. Every other part of you is hidden in the folds

of a ratty *rebozo*. You look like something that someone else had discarded. I imagine this middle-aged Anglo imagining you smelling like old newspaper left out in the rain. I imagine him greasing rouge over your wounds and then tearing you down again, until you are born with clothes ripped in the right places so that he can cover you and make you properly, politely, *native* again, back into a *peso* who had thought herself a penny.

While my mother smiles politely and shakes her head as he explains the local color to her, as he explains the jagged, thin line on which she grew up, I shut him up by forking over the ten bucks that he was asking for his local color. Only out of earshot does my mother tell this is more distasteful than the plate itself.

It's like you're collecting certain artifacts, she says, *because they are not authentic. To protect yourself.*

When I protest and tell her with a straight face that I've found you, Quimera, she cuts me off: *don't try to be cute. Don't talk irony. And don't think you can make the distance your own.*

And don't think you own it all either, I snap back, forgetting myself.

But she isn't angry; she's disappointed.

It's like nothing is sacred anymore. I see the Mexican Nationalists with money coming over wearing t-shirts that say "NACO." You know how offensive that is? First they call the poor of their country that, and they won't even let them have the word. They have to turn it into a joke.

It's not that it's a joke, I explain. It's more of an image thing, a soft-core rebellion without having to live the real life. It's suburban kids listening to gangster rap. It's like the hipsters in Williamsburg in New York pretending they are slumming it with their unwashed hair and torn clothes when they are really living in million dollars lofts.

It's all a bunch of BS, she says, and I start to agree when she says: *and it's one thing for that Anglo to believe his own BS, but it's another for you to encourage it, whether or not you were laughing at him inside.*

After a while, she adds: *BS is contagious, you know.*

That night, she says little to me as she prepares dinner with my aunts. I sit with my male cousins and uncles—I can't cook to save my life—my feet skimming the ground on the porch swing as we simmer along with the *barbacoa* and drank warm Lonestar beer. The men pass around the plate and have a round of laughs, especially when I smother you in meatless tamales and ate off your ratty-*rebozo* body. When I finish, your image has bald spots and I realize I have ingested some of the local color. My mother is silent, but her eyes look worried and vaguely disappointed. I avoid them for the rest of the night.

Perhaps due to paint toxicity, that night I dream of women who work in *maquiladoras* (depending on one's translation, either "factory" or "duty-free-enslavement") across the border. Instead of gluing together the soles of athletic shoes or dipping their bare hands in solvents, they are stitching up the border with simple thread. They are speaking to an unseen presence, perhaps my own: *What if we said 'shall?' What if we experience linguistic momentum to earn Webster worth? How long will it take, in what edition, will you allow our tongue to manipulate pronunciations, to carry over the remnants to our own mother tongue, to create from the fragments of our memories of what we've left behind? What if we leave our mark through words you cannot track, arrest, and send back?*

I am not there, but I am all around them, hovering as close as I can get, when suddenly, windfall men without saddles dust down from Southwest plains and try to stop these women. But their skilled fingers are too quick. Like a long-festered wound, the Rio Grande disappears, its seams nearly invisible. The air became very thin. Birds fell from the sky like spent stones.

I awake quickly and throw up, unable to keep down what I have done.

For it was my doing. I cannot possibly know what you have left behind, Quimera.

Decorative plates, after all, are not meant to be used.

III.

IN A NAUSEOUS HAZE THE NEXT DAY, I wake up worried that all I can do is write you as a costume and not even know how to wear you. I realize I've done it before. Once in high school I decided I wanted to be a *pachuco* for Halloween. A Jewish Mexican of mixed race dressing up as a kind of Mexican-American rebel/criminal (depending on your version of history). The zoot suit belonged to my mother's uncle who lent it to me only when he realized I wouldn't shut up about it.

In his collection of essays *The Labyrinth of Solitude,* Octavio Paz inferred that the kind of *pachuco* he met in Los Angeles "seeks and attracts persecution and scandal . . . his dangerousness lies in his singularity"(16). But from my mother's memories, I don't think that's what my uncle and his friends were after. Persecution wasn't the goal, nor was it the image of a social menace. They were after something larger: an aggressive (though not necessarily threatening) aspiration to claim a space both physical and linguistic.

When my mother first saw her uncle in his zoot suit, she thought he was . . . well, *muy padre.* Cool. She wanted to wear one, too, but since she was a *ruca* (Pachuco for "girl"), it wasn't allowed. And she was too young, a mere child who hadn't lost all her baby teeth and was still somewhat new

to language in general. Still, she was old enough to envy the *pachucos* for having their own Spanish and fathers who couldn't understand most of what they said, much less their need to rebel. *La raza unida nunca sera vencida,* my mother recited, recalling an old motto that sounded like a call-to-arms. It means "United, the people will never be defeated."

We used to believe that, my mother had told me, before I'd ventured into the bathroom to figure out the suit, beginning with the wide-legged but tight-cuffed pants and a matching coat with padded shoulders. *The whole family,* she had gone on, *whether they said it or not, believed it because he believed it. Even the women who worried that they were walking bulls-eyes for the police. Because we still believed that that my uncle was onto something. Something new and promising that would last. That our place here would finally be carved very clearly. With definitive lines, understand? A dangerous but necessary dream that was going to happen regardless of how the rest of us felt about it.*

But now, how many decades later, who speaks *Pachuco* anymore? It was just slang, a fad that faded away along with the fashion of the dress. It wouldn't be a new language for Mexican-Americans, or a new way of living. Who today says *Viva La Raza* when there's all this talk about putting the National Guard on the border to hunt down people like they're mosquitoes swarming the Rio Grande, *people* — my mother had lamented, her voice hoarse and quiet so my uncle who's hidden himself in the kitchen wouldn't hear — *people* who are closer to us in blood and breathing than those who told my mother as a child to leave small-nowhere-border-towns like Harlingen to get somewhere better? It got them nowhere. Her uncle became old and bitter and used-up by the time he was twenty-five.

Still struggling with the suit, I was thinking of what she said when there was a knock on the door. When I opened it, I saw it was said uncle, who indeed had heard everything she had said earlier, who took one look at me, snorted in amusement, and announced that he should've just kept the damn thing hidden in back of the closet, out of my covetous reach.

(Years later, that summer when I ingested the poison of an Anglo's take on the local color, I realize the insult of playing dress-up in his discarded dreams on Halloween. Of invading a space where a lot of men his age hid a whole generation's failures. After all, where did it get them? He and his friends never went through any riots. They didn't have the kind of stories that made national headlines. They weren't out there defending East L.A. from bigoted sailors who were burning zoot suits right out in the streets.)

And yet I remember there was something subversive about putting on a pair of *tramas,* attaching a long-chained watch that had stopped working long ago, and draping a *carlango* around my shoulders. In that moment, I even thought it would make my mother proud, reclaiming something she was denied as a young girl. I didn't notice how the lapel was twisted back, or how crumpled and threadbare the feather on the hat was after years of regret and shame and neglect.

When I brought the vision over to my mother, her mouth dropped open.

I was a gangly teenager who was a third of his size.

Take it off, she said, trying to save me further embarrassment before anyone else saw. *Querida, you look really dumb.*

VI.

THE QUESTIONS AND FEARS AND DOUBT, I suppose, will remain. The look of suspicion and then disappointment from theater-goers, as well as my family, that I gave you the name *Quimera*.

But in the end, am I pretending to be part of something that I am now too far away and removed to understand, even if I carry it in my blood? At what point does your story become nothing more than a sounding board for border politics, or worse, a foolish portrayal of woman whom I've ironically locked into a stereotype in order to seem authentic? Can I really tell the reality from the illusions of borders, laws, and the facelessness that come along with being *Quimera*? What does it really mean to be a Mexican woman in South Texas without papers or rights, but with the will to speak of things other than these that come from my mouth, which I'm shoving into yours? What is really the story of a woman without choices who nonetheless takes action? Am I doomed to paint the same fantastic yet recognizable image on the plate? Costumes and the local color: an image that captures you, though not in the way I mean. . . .

And who am I to think I can free you from that plate?

It must be believable, my mother advises. *Don't put her in a costume, but don't make her too grand, either. There should be some quiet, some solitude.*

Nothing too grand. You are not a prophet for the world, Quimera. If I put you in a loin-cloth, you'd wear it with self-loathing purpose. As I write you, I anguish how many lives you have had, only to tear you down again, tear off the ratty *rebozo.* And perhaps I, too, grease rouge over your wounds, and now it seems you were born with clothes ripped in the right places and I know I have failed once more, I —

Have yet to let you finish a sentence, Quimera . . .

That summer I visited Harlingen, I met some of my great uncle's friends, the surviving *pachucos,* and they had grown old and fat and half-deaf and molded into their porch rocking chairs. My uncle long since has passed away, and I don't know what's happened to the zoot suit. One of his grandsons was in the process of selling the house so he could move up north to San Antonio, Houston, Austin, anywhere but here.

During the entire visit, my mother insists we do not stay too long. We drift into old, small houses, visit family, the ones who didn't leave Harlingen for one reason or another. In the last days, when it is so hot and humid that the sun seems to set twice, I stick to her like glue. She is my guide, my way in and in which I see and understand what she has left behind. I want to be in synch with her as I fall into the back-and-forth on the porch swings of those houses, the lethargy and idleness I taste in their warm beer until I, too, am enveloped in the heat and half-hearted intoxication and only then become somewhat resistant to local color's suspicion of me.

But my mother does not give in so easily; she does not drink and reminds certain members of her family several times. And it is then, in the haze, that I see how her relatives cast sideways glances as she wipes down the swing before she sits down next to me, as she answers their questions about how life is up in San Antonio with reserve and a great amount of conservation, as if she's storing up energy for some impending attack which never comes fully but hangs in the air, creating a very palpable screen of smoke and steam between them and us, between how they see me through her and who she's become. When the silence finally hits, when the beer and *barbacoa* and questions have been exhausted and it seems like talking would do some real damage I can't even fathom, I turn to her and recognize that look in her eye, the distance she, too, carries as someone who got away from the border town snare.

The entire time I am in Harlingen, I hardly write one word.

And certainly not of you, Quimera.

The talk continues about you, and yet it is still not about *you.*

On the last night, the hottest during our entire visit, the thin, cotton sheet sticks to me in my aunt's un-air-conditioned house where I lay on a hard couch in the living room. I feel exposed from the lack of privacy without a door that I can shut. I worry that my thoughts of you will become visible and someone will see you. I put my hands just beneath my ribs as if this will protect my ideas of you, but all I hear is the buzzing of the many Harlingen

mosquitoes. My cousins joked that I'm always an easy mark for them, the appeal of the fresh blood of drifters. I am no longer drifting through family, stories, inheritance that doesn't fit. I become very still. I have never been this still, Quimera. In the darkness, I try to move my lips to the sound of your name, but can't even open my eyes. The buzzing in my ears continues, and I fall into it, continue falling though I am completely still, surrendering, not even daring to squash the infinite blood-suckers roaming the bare walls, that during the day disappear into the back of closets where nothing can be un-hidden, much less found, just waiting for drifters like me to fall asleep. ▣

Author's Note: As a child, I sensed rather than understood, the complex relations between Mexican-Americans and undocumented Mexican workers living on either side of the U.S.-Mexican border. Later, I came to realize why: there is a paradoxical dependence that bordering U.S. States have on undocumented workers. The recent immigration "reform" in Arizona is not merely a matter of general xenophobia or discrimination; the possible unwarranted detainment by police of those suspected as "illegal" stands in direct opposition to the fact that Mexican immigrants have had a significant impact on historical development of the border states (and arguably beyond, stretching throughout the United States). Yet, they have been denied a rightful recognition in claiming their space in that history of the border in particular. Female undocumented Mexican workers in South Texas occupy a distinctly unsettled space in this development, as they've faced exploitation, misogyny, and other indignities from both sides of the border.

As a female Hispanic playwright of mixed race, I have tried to capture the unsteady, uncomfortable relationship between these women and the work they do within the United States. In my play *Quimera on the Storm*, I intended to portray a "realistic" representation of such a woman who, after living in the U.S. for over two decades, comes to know the land better than anyone and reclaims a space from which her Mexican-American boss himself has been evicted. Shortly after conceiving the story, I had concerns: How would she *speak*? I wanted to write an innovative, sharp-witted woman who'd not only learned English but used it better than the native speakers around her. But what would it mean if I wanted her to sound lyrical? I knew I did not want to transform her into an "Aztec Earth Mother," or turn her into a political soap box. Lastly, the stage itself already gives way to a sense of "unreality," which provided both freedoms and obstacles in telling this story, which was imagined but not *imaginary*. What followed in writing the actual play was a meditation on her character and my anxieties on how I should portray her particular experience.

WORKS CITED

Paz, Octavio. *The Labyrinth of Solitude and other Writings.* Translated by Lysander Kemp, Yara Milos and Rachel Phillips Belash. Grove Press: New York, 1985.

Quimera on the Storm. By Rosebud Ben-Oni. Dir. Melody Brooks. New Perspectives Theater Company. New York, New York. 20-26 Sept 2010.

ARTWORK: Rafael Colón Morales
"Huidobro," Acrylic on masonite (15 x 30 in.) Painting, Copyright © 1979
Collection of Félix Toledo

TAMMY MELODY GOMEZ

Home Away from Home

(a land proclamation in 5 parts)

I.

My great-grandmother Rafaelita was born here, in the
Gonzales, Texas area. Before that, we're not so sure
who it was that went to bed Mexican and woke up
Mexican-American. Overnight. In the same bed, la
misma tierra. Imagine that. It would be like keeping
your same room, with the same panadería calendar on
the wall and your favorite huaraches by the bed, but
everything else completely different, even the food,
even the landlords. Crazy, huh? Now they're still
making crazy lines on the map, separating our gente,
deleting or diluting our collective potential by
splitting us apart, again and again, como piñatas with
voting rights, con esos damn líneas redistricting us,
restricting us. But they have no idea. One night, they'll
go to sleep after Conan O'Brien and wake up to Concha
O' Suna. On the tv and radio and newspapers and books
and movies and billboards, will be our faces, our cultura.
This will put us back together again and set us firmly on
the national map, where we know we've always belonged.

II.

I went to Oaxaca and Chiapas by myself for a month,
back in 1991, to let the Mayas reclaim me. In San
Cristóbal de las Casas-my favorite pueblito-a young
family stared at me through the windows of their shiny
vw bug. They laughed and shook their heads and the
car, as it sat parked curbside. We recognized each
other in some wave of vague familiarity, and I wanted
to believe that they were my blood relatives,
direct line to Mayan ancestry. I tried to talk to
them, ask them, "Que créen? Somos família?" but they
kept the windows closed and continued giggling at me until
I gave up and went away to be adopted by more willing
Chiapanecos. At the zócalo, the vendors from the
outlying villages were more willing to hear my
questions. But when I asked if I was one of them—a
Mayan from Zinacántan, Chamulan or a Tzeltal, speaking
Tzotzil—they said no. I asked if I looked Azteca, or
even Raramuri to them. They just nodded and said

"Sí, pareces una india." "De Mexico?" I urged. "No, de los Estados Unidos." Native American Indian.

III.

The southwestern division of the National Archives, a
government storehouse of statistical data, is located
two blocks from my childhood home in Fort Worth,
Texas. In some drab government-issue file
cabinet, official documents and census reports might
possibly confirm my family's tenure on this continent,
in Tejas, as original residents. But we have better
things to do than get eyestrain reading files on microfiche,
and besides, we already live with an innate sense of our rightful
place here as native folks in a nation-state over which have
flown many flags. Those flags, flapping and flapping, like
the mouths of statesmen who have served to alienate and other us.
But we persist, as "minorities," our family blood never diluted,
our brown feet stoically rooted.

IV.

It was a tradition for my parents to take me and my
sister, every summer, to Six Flags Over Texas, the
sprawling amusement park in the Fort Worth-Dallas
metroplex. I reveled in the fast rides that swirled
and confused me round and round, not realizing that
the Six Flags, los seis banderas, reflected layers of
siege that have served to smother First People ways
of speaking, working, and honoring this, our
homeland. As a kid, I could only register how
sluggish the gigantic sombrero ride was, spinning like
a lard-laden oversized UFO, up and down and barely
around. We would hurry through this and the other lame
rides in the Mexico section in order to get to the
more thrilling and engaging areas ruled by the French,
Spanish, and American flags. Now, as an adult who is
easily queased by fast-talking government heads and
dutiful spin doctors making travesty of our nation, I
would prefer the slower, languorous pace of that
turquoise blue sombrero, treading a familiar
revolution of a flavor so long I have missed.

V.

"Dejenlas quitar mis modos gringos y esconderme para
siempre en la selva Maya."
Mexican culture abides in me even as I live north of the Rio Grande.
But I have to admit that I am and have been gringo-ized.
Sometimes I feel like it would be great to go back in
time and place to a simpler way, close to the mountains,

deeper in my ancestors' culture. I could click my
shiny red shoes and chant my desire, over and over,
como la Dorothy incanting, "No hay lugar como home,
no hay lugar como home." Yet I always come back to the fact
that I have been schooled, seasoned, and whitewashed in the
culture of the U.S. and I am a different sort of Mexican now.
This American life has adopted me and Mexico only gets visitation rights.
It catches up to me as I speak its Spanish, honor its heritage, and
celebrate its culture. Como me hace triste, como me hace feliz.
Por allá no me puedes mandar, desde allá no me puedes sacar.

In memory of abuelita, Aurora Sanchez.

CHRISTOPHER CARMONA

Mexicans Without Means

They say April is the cruelest month
well it certainly was for one white boy
on a Spring Break trip in the last year of 1980
found in a ditch on a Matamoros ranch
his name splashed across newspapers and television screens for years
but this poem is not about that boy
this poem is about the 14 other Mexicans in that shallow grave
whose eyelids have been eaten away by the grub worms
revealing nothing but mud and the bottom of boots
tongues long ago cut off and sacrificed to the gods of popular media
their names only worth the space of a number: 14.
They were Mexicanos sin nombre.

Or maybe August is the cruelest month
when 26 migrants were found locked in a railroad car
broiled to death in a desert land where even the air burns
but not before they paid Coyote everything for a chance
to work 12 hrs a day stealing jobs that Americans forget ever existed
They work in order to feed families left behind
certainly not before their towns were decimated by mass production
and the lowest price cost analysis
They were Mexicans sin dinero.

Or maybe the cruelest month is October
where a visiting Colorado man was "killed by Mexican pirates"
while his wife watched in horror
his body never recovered
Her shock was heard round the world from early morning news program to early morning news program
Mexican pirates are worse than Caribbean pirates
No Johnny Depp here looking like a gay Keith Richards on acid.
This man was just another innocent casualty in the Mexican Drug Wars
A war Heartland America has nothing to do with
Just vacationing in its waters while the river washes away 50,000 dead
no names
no space for memory
no thoughts more than a passing pity
no voices one tongue speaks for them
nothing but laser fences and shaking heads.
They are just Mexicans sin causa.

But lets not forget about January
where a vanished woman lost her hand and her life
she launched her voice and her body
into the war for equality
no soldiers funeral for her
no folded flag
no 21 gun salute
she fought a war of insurmountable odds with her ideas and her tongue
she stood at the frontlines of every woman's right
shoulder's straight fists clenched
conviction in her eyes.
She slung poems at the abyss marked her words with blood
She gave her soul to the wind hoped that she would be felt
Yet, there she lies in a dumpster filled with yesterday's rage
her left hand taken a warning to all
No national Susana Chavez holiday
No patriotic swelling of eyes for this soldier of change
who helped shape this world for the better
Just a few words from a few papers
Mexican woman risked it all so that a girl could walk the streets
without fear of being taken violated left like yesterday's facebook post.
She was just a Mexican sin luz.

Or maybe it was May when little Brisena Flores was swallowed whole
leaving a mother wondering why bullet have you feasted on such young flesh
but the bullet knew it is not the physics of combustible powders
the spark of metal on metal
it is the force of a finger pulling hatred and righteousness
because Mexican flowers can't bloom in Arizona
they simply don't have the means.
Little Brisena did not die without her name
she was buried on the tenth page of the paper of record
no Today Show special for a mother left without husband daughter
no 24 hour news cycle repeating the tragedy of a little girl's death
nothing for Mexicans without means.

JOE MONTOYA, JR

I am Chicano

I am proud of my heritage happy to have been
San Diego born, Balboa Hospital, border captain
Family concept, hopeful in a middle class war
A real life baby boomer rich in subject futures
Into the fray of loyalty respective of two fights
Born 100 years after Mexico became California
1957, Zoot Suit Riots 14 years since removed
Dad fought in Korea mine-sweeper first class
Neglect, G. I. Bill, living in poverty-collections
Mexicans died facing a Sino war/ hate machine
Dependable in a new country of recent arrivals
Liberating ourselves from lost stories of history
For democracy beyond forgotten southwest maps
Farm workers respect education people-whole, us
Long since forgotten Villa and Zapata led battles
Men and women beaten and destroyed, deported
Racism and hatred bracero program, work and jail
We suffered behind movements toward equality
People seeking ownership families and an answer
Liberation from a long forgotten sense of existence
My grandmother was born in Fresno same as mom
What is our country for my kids and grandchildren
Five generations born in California illegal at best

Shamed by a government sought by minutemen
Slandered by perspectives diminished of worth
Third World without End-amen, disunited faces
Possession of our future enemies in a sacred home
Silenced by brutality ancestors of Aztec and art
Provoked by Europeans children of Mayan slaves
Once resplendent in gold property of past wealth
Conquered before the Pilgrim rulers in our wake
Sabotage-murder profit in hand distant citations
I am Chicano call me what you will we are strong
This continent worth the struggle beyond dreams
Mexican and American labels not withstanding
Spirit of our roots prepared to stand on our own
Following a hard work mentality freedom's face
Our past is our future hatred makes us stronger
Liberated by accomplishment educations door
Working class people responsible and common
Providers in agriculture and tolerance of pride
I am Chicano brother of our sisterhood Chicana
Late of indigenous values with aspirations keen
Never to be forgotten or overlooked here to stay
Reticent within the family, aware of duties hand.

MÓNICA GONZÁLEZ VELÁZQUEZ

Manifiesto migrante

Declaro ante la gente de buenas costumbres
(aunque después hablen mal de mí)
que soy de los que manifiestan su amor en las letrinas
(para ello me sobran las frases y el sentimiento)
que pronuncio mal algunas palabras
que apenas estudié la primaria
que mi padre, tampoco tuvo un mejor futuro
que mis hijos, probablemente tampoco lo tendrán
que viajo en tercera clase
que sudo a mares y de sol a sol
que soy la sal de la tierra
cuando ejerzo mis labores
y sé muy bien que a la pizca* nadie de ustedes le entra.

From *Le mystère de la vulgaire mondes o mejor dicho: El misterio de los mundos vulgares*, Mónica González Velázquez (Unedited, 2008)

Migrant Manifesto (Tr.)

I declare before well-mannered people
(even though they make speak ill of me after)
that I am one of those that show their love in the latrines
(about which I have more than enough words and feelings)
that I pronounce some words poorly
that I hardly went to primary school
that my father also did not have a better future
that my children probably will not either
that I travel in third class
that I sweat buckets from dawn till dusk
that I am the salt of the earth
 when I perform my labors
and I know very well that none of you will begin the harvest.

* Cosecha

Translated by Adam Wier.

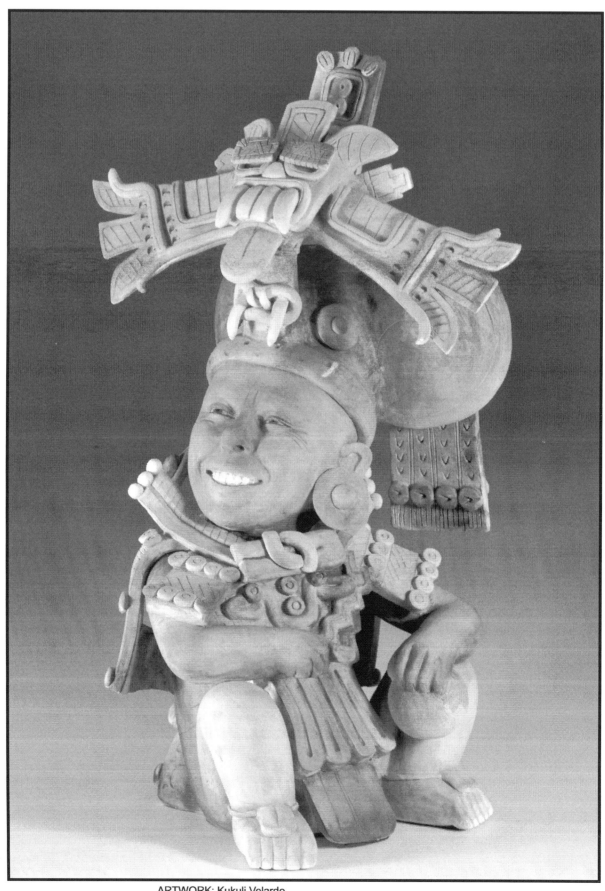

ARTWORK: Kukuli Velarde
"Jodida Indeja De que se rie? Gotta be trained... what the f...!," Zapoteca, Mexico ad 300/700"
ceramic piece mocha clay mixed media, (30"h x 19 1/2"d x 17"w), Copyright © 2010

MARIA APONTE

The Clothesline of the Rosas

Rosa looks out the window that faces the back yard of the tenement building on the corner of 117th Street and Second Avenue. She watches her *Italiana* neighbor with the funny last name, wave as she pulls the clothesline across to her side to take in the laundry. The clothesline creaks like a rusty hinge on an old door. It is their only form of communication, this clothesline. They share it twice a week, the rope strung from window to window.

Rosa does her wash. Then her neighbor does hers. Back and forth, forth and back the rope goes, each woman lost in her own culture, her own tradition, her own language. Although both Spanish and Italian have the same roots, it will take awhile before the two women know that, and find understanding in words that sound the same.

But they do have these things in common: they are women with families, they are immigrants, and they share a clothesline.

And they are both named Rosa.

Rosa from Puerto Rico and Rosa from Italy, each coming from pueblos/towns they left for better tomorrows.

Rosa from Puerto Rico still remembers the smells of *Coamo*, her hometown. Sometimes she has to close her eyes and wrinkle her brow in concentration so she won't forget. It's easy to get distracted in the big city where no speaks to you because you do not look like them or speak like them. Gray tenement buildings streaked with city dirt, dish towels, wet mops with pails hanging out of windows. Definitely not *Coamo*. There, her backyard had *gandule* patches, the dirt black with herbs ready for the picking, the eggs warm, straight from the coop.

The creaking of the clothesline brings her back to the land of concrete and metal. Taking a deep breath, she looks at the other Rosa and wonders if she misses her home too. Naples, she once said.

Rosa from *Coamo* waves to Rosa from Naples. In a wavering voice, she calls out, "Halo, Señora Santaniello!"

Rosa from Naples smiles and says "Halo" in her own thick accent.

Rosa from *Coamo* smiles back. And with that, she starts to hang her wash.

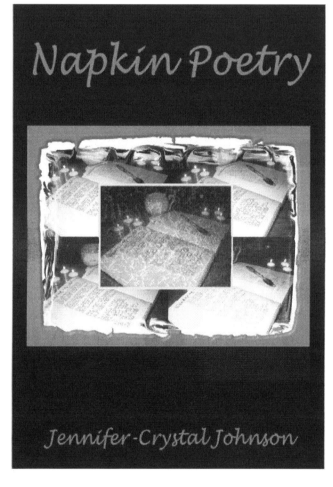

SANDRA C. BARRERAS DEL RIO

Honor et Fidelitas
Para Wanda Delgado

Invierno 2011

1.
Las Cruces de Malta
florecen.
La suave brisa
de diciembre
la hace sonreir
al buscar el carro.
No más huracanes.
En sus manos
la manta caliente y suave.
Él se quejó de frío anoche.
Quisiera aliviar
la incomodidad del viejo
en quién su padre se ha convertido.
Sabe bien
que todo intento de sanar
su cuerpo será en vano
si él no siente
el honor que
se le debe a un ser humano.
Sube al carro
que la llevará
a San Juan.
a estar allí, con él,
a probarle su fidelidad.

2.
Abre sus ojos alarmado
Honor et Fidelitas.
Sólo el lema.
No escucha granadas
pasar sibilantes a su lado
y explotar.
Ve la mujer,
en quién se ha convertido su hija,
cubriéndolo
con una manta.
Ella sonríe y él también.

Poco a poco
se calienta y
las memorias de Korea
se disipan.

Un hospital,
y sus venas penetradas,
abiertas por el suero,
Quiere ir a su casa
en Hatillo.
Llevame a casa,"
le pide deprimido.
La hija suspira
y le da un masaje
los pies.

3.
28 de octubre de 1952.
Hill 391
Korea
Mi fin se acerca.
Truena sin cesar,
la artillería China provoca
una iluminación fantasmal
del cielo
en esta helada
noche de Manchuria.
El ruido perfora mis oídos.
Las vibraciones constantes
de sonido y de luz
penetran
mi sucia y cansada carne.
La incómoda sensación de estar
bajo observación enemiga
ha cesado.
No queda nada
que amerite ser observado.
Sólo,
sin amigos,
ni compañeros.

Nada queda en pie.
Me caigo en la tierra fría,
agarro una pala
y me tapo la cara.
Ruedo por la cuesta.
La compañía G,
no existe.
Sólo,
rezo:
"Mamita, sálvame."
Invoco a la madre
que no conocí,
murió en mi parto.
Mi corazón que aún late
golpea el congelado suelo.
Y entonces,
silencio.

4.
Invierno, 2011
Llegaron;
la mujer abre
la puerta del carro
su padre

se apoya en el cristal
de su ventana. .
Necesita ayuda.
Le arregla la frisa
y espera.
Su mamá y hermano
vienen a recibir al padre
que regresa .
a casa,
en Hatillo,
en su territorio.
El árbol de Navidad
refresca el aire con su olor.

El padre pide
que acerquen
su sillón de ruedas
al pino verde.
Estación de regocijo.

Honor et Fidelitas (Tr.)
For Wanda Delgado

Winter, 2011

1.

The Cruces de Malta are in bloom.
A mild December breeze
makes her smile
as she moves towards the car.
Hurricane season is over.
In her hands,
a blanket, warm and soft.
He complained last night
about the cold in his room.
She would like to lessen
the discomfort
of the old man
that her father has become.
She well knows
all the efforts
to heal his body
would be in vain,

if he does not feel
the honor
due to a human being.
She gets in her car,
which will take her
to San Juan;
to the hospital,
to be there with him,
to prove her fidelity.

2.
He opens his eyes alarmed
Honor et Fidelitas.
Just the motto.
No grenades whistling by,
exploding.
He sees the woman

his daughter has become
cover his body with a soft blanket.
She smiles, and so does he.
As he warms up,
memories of Korea fade away.

A hospital,
his veins punctured
exposed to the serum.
He wants to go home,
to Hatillo.
"Take me home," he says.
The daughter sighs
and massages his feet.

3.
October 28, 1952
Hill 391
Korea

My end is near.
Relentless thundering,
the Chinese artillery provokes
a spectral illumination in the sky
on this frigid Manchurian night.
The noise perforates my eardrums.
Constant vibrations of light and sound
penetrate my dirty, tired flesh.
The uncomfortable sensation
of being observed by
the enemy is gone.
There is nothing left
worth observing.
On my own,
no friends,
no companions,
no-thing standing.
I fall to the cold earth,
grabbing a shovel to cover my face.
I roll downhill.
The G company's gone.
On my own,
I pray.
"Mamita, save me,"
invoking a mother
I never met,
who died giving me life.
My heart, still beating,
hit the freezing soil.

And then,
silence.

4.
Winter 2011

They have arrived.
The woman opens the door
of the car; her father
leans against the glass of his.
She fixes his blanket
and waits.
Her mother and brother come
to greet the father,
now returning home,
to Hatillo,
to his territory.
The Christmas tree's scent
refreshes the air.

The father asks
his wheelchair be moved
near the pine.
Season to rejoice.

Translation by Sandra C. Barreras del Río and Adam Wier.

LOURDES VAZQUEZ

Elegy

Con este corazón . . .
Los Van-Van

Who died? My mother, on the other side of the ocean, gives me the details. The great-aunts have died. One died one day, and the next day, the other died. As if one were dragging the other behind her. One flew through space and touched the other on the shoulder. That was enough for the second to understand that it was time to leave, and they left. They abandoned their photos, their souvenirs, their memories, their caring, their laughter; and in their will indicated that their ashes should be scattered in Central Park.

The aunts contracted marriage with men from Jamaica and Trinidad, and were the owners of an imperial forest of cannabis plants, which grew as tall as human beings. They lived with the conviction that tea made from the leaves of that plant cured any ill. On holidays, they added pieces of the magic plant to bizcochos and appetizers. People felt happy. Children's laughter was transformed into birds' feathers that caressed my skin. Loving food and good music, their flesh grew until they were twin replicas of some singing Buddha.

One day they decided to move to New York and opened a Laundromat in the middle of Manhattan. They adored islands, and so they decided to live on this island, rotten with plagues. In their Laundromat, they cleaned up immigrants' calamities and bitterness.

"I'm not myself without you," one whispered in the other's ear. "I'm not myself, I'm someone else; someone imperfect and incomplete. I don't want to be condemned to the limbo that awaits me. Without you, I am fated to travel this highway with no exit, in the midst of other souls' senile dementia. I invoke you by this heart of yours, a heart pierced with moldy ironwork; I insist: we must leave." And they left.

One unremarkable autumn afternoon, I went to the park. I went in search of the ashes that were scattered across the grass, the mud, the branches, the statues, the squirrels, the fish, and the seals. Each has a cannabis flower sprouting out of its skin. Grass with a cannabis flower is understandable; what's difficult to understand is the great number of statues, fish, and seals covered with flowers.

Translated by Bethany M. Korp-Edwards

ARTWORK: Diana G. Hernandez
"Amor to the Power of Love," Charcoal Drawing (44 x 36 in.) Line Drawing, Copyright © 2010

TATO LAVIERA

I am a wise Latina

I am a wise Latina
Nuyorican daughter of Boricuas
I am a Judge
Interpreting legal decisions
From their purest constitutional framework
Amended by congressional laws
Adopted with state clauses.

I am a wise Latina
Circuiting words in statutes
Reviewing precedence
Strictly defining issues at hand
Thank you for my nomination President Barack Obama
Thank you for the privilege and trust.

I am a wise Latina
Nuyorican daughter of Boricuas
Emerging from Bronx projects/caseríos
Puro orgullo/pride inside modest poverty
Rich in familia, community and identity
Emerging from los de abajo/the downtrodden.

I am a wise Latina
Endowed with intelligent maneuvers
Educated from Catholic Spellman High
 to twice Ivy Leaguer.

I am a wise Latina
Serious pensadora/thinker
Be prepared to defend your legal argument.

I am a wise Latina
Nuyorican daughter of Boricuas
At my US Senate confirmation hearings
Me atacaron
They accused me of short-sightedness
Of being enraged and angry
Me atacaron
They intimidated me with a row of firemen
Accusing me of negating their civil tights.

I am a wise Latina
I contested with discipline and truth, wise Latina
I contested with intelligence and candor, wise Latina
I contested with reverence and love of my constitu-
tion, wise Latina
I contested by not tipping favoritism to any issue.

I am a wise Latina
With my family at hand
A supportive force on my behaff
I'm now confirmed with the
Highest historical Puerto Rican achievement.

I am a wise Latina
Nuyorican daughter of Boricuas
Sentenced to lifetime serving,
Judge Sonia Sotomayor,
United States Supreme Court.

"... memorable lines that will remain with you long after you have put the book down."
—Jan Carew
author of *The Guyanese Wanderer*

ISBN: 978-0-88378-330-4
$18.95 (Paperback)

Tony Medina's latest collection of poetry, *An Onion of Wars*, is satirical and surprising commentary on contemporary issues facing young and old alike. His mastery of language, imagery, conversation and voice permeates each and every selection within this 146-page volume. The Caribbean writer and novelist, Jan Carew shares the following: "The poetry . . . is complex. It strips the street to its simplest common denominator of survival and tears off layer upon layer of stark realism." We are pleased to offer this work along with *Committed to Breathing, Role Call* and other Third World Press titles.

Available at Third World Press

773-651-0700 or www.twpbooks.com

and other online outlets

Orphans and Hoodlums
Judith Mercado

by the barracks-style senior citizens building and looked around uneasily. Across the street, railroad tracks bordered a rusting factory which iron-eating locusts must have just left. Down the block, faded asphalt shingle houses seemed to huddle together against the bully wind. The occasional tree groaned under the weight of dirty ice.

How long would they let him stay in this No Parking zone? All he wanted was to go in and check the roster of residents. If he found María Cristina Leyva, he'd park the car legally and come back.

Carlos glanced at the package beside him. The royal blue box looked almost tropical in this setting. Had he known how stark a place this was, he might have bought something in crimson instead of the black cashmere shawl now inside the box. After all, he was celebrating meeting his grandmother for the first time, even if first he had to tell her that her daughter died two months ago. He had imagined softening the blow by draping the silky wool shawl over her shoulders and whispering, "Abuela, I bought you cashmere because the winters here are brutal."

Órale, but that was one sorry excuse. The fact is he blew his schoolteacher budget buying cashmere because he had no idea how to make a grandmother think he was special.

Nah, face it. That wasn't the real reason, either. He had splurged on cashmere hoping she was his grandmother because that would mean he still had a relative left. Mom, no matter how much he pressed her, never mentioned a single cousin, aunt, or uncle, much less a grandmother. As for his father? Domingo Reyna died before Carlos was born.

Somos tú y yo, Mom would say. You and me. She described them that way often enough that Youandme could have been their last name instead of Reyna.

Down the block, a bundled-up guy crossed the street with movie-still jerkiness. When had the city last sent out a snow plow? A police siren wailed in the distance.

Okay, better get moving.

He entered the vestibule of the multi-story building. In the tiled lobby beyond the inner glass door, about two dozen old people sat on cheap, white, molded plastic chairs. Mostly black and brown, hardly a white face among them, they all lacked color somehow. One man watched Carlos intently, his chin propped on ash-brown fingers, grasping what looked like a homemade cane.

Carlos quickly scanned the list of names. No María Cristina Leyva appeared. His shoulders sagged. His grandmother wasn't here after all.

The inner door banged open. Carlos looked up.

"That your car?" barked the burly security guard.

"Yes. I—"

"You gotta move it. Didn't you see the sign?" The guard snapped his head sideways as if to adjust a crick in his neck. "Move out the back if you want to park."

"I was just looking to see if someone lived here."

"Did you find him?"

"Her. No, I didn't. Do you know if María Cristina Leyva lives here?"

A tall Hispanic woman suddenly jumped up and rushed to the lobby elevator. She kept glancing at him over her shoulder, her eyes frightened. You have to be kidding. She was afraid of him? He glanced at his down jacket, khaki chinos, and Timberland boots.

"Check with the building manager," the guard said, "but first you gotta move that damned car! I mean it."

Carlos knew better than to talk back. This crazy town might not know the difference between a hoodlum and an orphan.

Behind the building, he found the parking lot. More than one car lay buried under snow. Guest parking was so far away, he wondered if they made a point of not encouraging guests.

Once parked, he remained inside his car, scanning nervously the area he had to cross to get back to the building. Nobody had ever accused Carlos of being a coward—he had been a take-no-prisoners defensive back in high school—but he kept rechecking the parking lot, remembering what that newspaper article had said about this town.

"In Calumet, every few weeks, somebody dies from yet another misspent bullet. In between killings, rampant drug trafficking and gang banging warp the lives of good people who cower behind curtained windows, afraid of hoodlums who excel at creating orphans."

Carlos had emailed the reporter to let him know how ironic it was, in light of his article, that in Mexican slang, the word for hoodlum, güache, was almost identical to the one for orphan, güacho.

(cont'd. pg. 244)

ARTWORK: Lorraine Miller Nuzzo

ORPHANS & HOODLUMS
Judith Mercado

(cont'd from pg. 243)

The reporter replied by warning him not to show up with his out-of-state Illinois plates.

Carlos stepped onto the filthy snow. Cringing at the crunching noise his shoes made, he kept glancing at the bordering two-story, asphalt-shingle buildings. Did any güaches lurk in the dark recesses?

When he rounded the senior citizens building, railroad crossing gates suddenly started clanging. Startled, he slipped on ice, but caught himself in time. Once inside the vestibule, he pressed the Office button. The guard pacing the lobby kept checking him out.

"Yeah!" shouted an impatient female voice.

Inside the lobby, the elevator whisked open. A tiny, brown-skinned woman shuffled out, her lips contorting over probable dentures. Her oversized red-checked dress looked thrown on. She wore thick socks on feet inserted into battered terry cloth slippers.

"I'm Carlos Reyna," he shouted, not sure if the intercom required it. "I'm looking for my grandmother, María Cristina Leyva."

"Who?"

"María Cristina Leyva."

"No one here by that name."

The tiny old lady gawked at Carlos, her jaw slack. Then she approached the man with the humble cane. She was so short she hardly needed to bend over to whisper in his ear.

"Could you possibly check your old records?"

"Are you kidding? She doesn't live here is all I can say."

Carlos sighed. The train roared past outside, making everything rattle. The security guard kept an eagle eye on him. Carlos knew he had to leave. Instead, he watched as the tiny lady shuffled toward the vestibule door, her lips moving constantly. Those teeth must hurt, Carlos thought.

The old man lifted his cane high and pounded the tile floor. Then he did it again. The guard whirled toward the noise. The man kept pounding the floor. The guard rushed toward him. The tiny lady reached the vestibule door and unlocked it. Come in, she indicated with a wave of her hand. Surprised, Carlos lurched toward her and pushed the door open. She grabbed his hand—her skin soft—and pulled him in with surprising strength.

Perhaps alerted by the twittering of the other residents, the security guard looked around. "Hey, what you doing in here?"

The old lady pulled on Carlos's arm to keep him from talking. "He's my nephew," she said in a voice apparently used to having its way.

Carlos gave her a swift look. Her nephew? Really? She was probably closer to 90 than to 50, the likely age of any aunt he might have. He looked at her closely, but felt no shred of recognition. She was just a withered old woman, of the right color, maybe, but with foreign features. Not that he had any idea what his extended family looked like. His mother's papers had only included pictures of him and her and a name, María Cristina Leyva, with Calumet, IN scrawled below it.

"Mrs. Vargas, you sure you know what you're doing?" the security guard said.

Carlos sure hoped so. He was counting on Mrs. Vargas having recognized the name María Cristina Leyva.

"Mind your own business. He's my nephew, and I'm taking him upstairs." She yanked Carlos toward the elevator. She really did have astonishing strength.

The guard stepped aside. Mrs. Vargas punched the elevator button with an arthritic knuckle and kept adjusting those ill-fitting teeth with her lips, all while holding fast to Carlos's hand. He stood mutely beside her, acutely aware of how she barely reached the middle of his chest.

The elevator door opened. She pulled him in and then snapped, "You're not Carlos Reyna."

"What?"

"You're not Carlos Reyna." She punched the third floor button.

Carlos stared at her. What had he just gotten himself into? But he didn't dare pull his hand away now. She might scream. The guard already figured him for a hoodlum. No need to confirm it.

All the way up to the third floor, Carlos kept smelling the mustiness coming from her. When had she last taken a bath?

When the elevator door opened, she stepped out and pulled him down a gloomy hallway with gray concrete block walls and black metal doors. Near the end of the hallway, she stood in front of a door and searched in her pocket without releasing his hand. Then she inserted a key in the door.

"Push it open."

Carlos pushed the door open into a narrow room packed so tightly with odd pieces of furniture there hardly seemed room to walk. Now he understood, though, the source of the musty odor. Everything here must have come from a thrift store.

"¡Ándale! ¡Ándale!" The old woman shouted as if he was hard of hearing.

Carlos walked into the crowded room. When he reached the sitting area, he noticed the old woman remained standing just inside the now closed door, watching him.

"Mrs. Vargas," he said when the extended silence became uncomfortable.

She waved him on. "¡Siéntate!"

He half stumbled to the vinyl-covered sofa and sat down. The vinyl felt so stiffly old, he was surprised it didn't crack under his weight.

Mrs. Vargas opened a cabinet drawer and fumbled through its contents. Eventually, she pulled out a faux-tapestry album. Tucking it under her arm, she shuffled to a lumpy upholstered chair across from him. The album reached her chin when she placed it upright on her lap. Her intensely dark eyes bulged as she stared at him.

"You're not Carlos Reyna."

That again? Man, what a waste of his time. "Mrs. Vargas, I appreciate you helping me downstairs, but I don't know why you keep saying that. I'm definitely Carlos Reyna."

Her lips seemed to curl. "Oh yeah? Who're your parents?"

"Domingo and Sonia Reyna."

She laughed. It was almost a cackle. "Domingo was my son. I should know."

What? This was his grandmother? "Wait a minute. You can't be his mother. My father was an orphan."

Her eyes narrowed. "An orphan! That's what she told you, hah?"

He leaned back. The vinyl squeaked. Could this be his grandmother, really? Had Mrs. Vargas once been Mrs. Reyna?

No. Come on. Couldn't be.

"Your papá and his parents died in a car accident," Mom had said.

Still, Carlos looked around to find pictures of someone resembling his father, the stocky twenty-year-old, brown-skinned Domingo Reyna appearing in the only picture Carlos had of him.

He found no pictures on the walls or on any surfaces.

Mrs. Vargas opened the album and clumsily started turning pages.

He looked around him at the rummage-sale-like living room. His compulsively neat mother would have blown in like a whirlwind to clean all this up. Mom used to vacuum their townhouse daily to eliminate dirt he could never see. He repeatedly offered to do it for her—the woman already worked two jobs, which she wouldn't quit even after he started working—but she never allowed him to touch her yellow Kenmore canister vacuum cleaner.

Mrs. Vargas turned the album pages so roughly that pictures sprang onto her lap and on the floor.

Mrs. Vargas suddenly stopped turning pages and glared at the page in front of her. Then she thrust the open album toward him.

He bent over to look.

No way!

He grabbed the album. He knew this picture. It was of his mother in her cap-and-gown high school graduation picture.

He lowered the album to his lap and looked up. "Why do you have this picture?"

She smiled crookedly, more a sneer than a smile. "That's your mother, isn't it?"

He nodded, barely breathing. Dare he hope?

Her facial wrinkles hardened. "She was the town whore."

He jumped up, the album clattering to the floor. "Don't you dare speak that way about my mother!"

She grunted. "You're looking for María Cristina Leyva, right?"

Though sorely tempted not to respond, he nodded.

She pointed to the album on the floor. "That's María Cristina Leyva."

He gave her an incredulous look. That wasn't María Cristina Leyva. That was his mother Sonia Reyna.

"If you don't believe me, look at the back."

He fell to his knees and tore the picture from its fastenings. On the back was written, "To mama, from your daughter, Cristina."

"Where did you get this picture?" he said hoarsely.

"My estúpido son stole it from her mother when that puta left town."

"Her mother?" he said weakly. "You knew her mother?"

Her laugh exploded from deep inside her belly. "Oh, yeah, I knew that cagada Puerto Rican. She was my cuñada, my husband's sister-in-law. Psst! We weren't related by blood. I'm Mexican. Anyways, she died, I don't know, sixteen years ago."

He couldn't believe it. His mother's mother, for whom he had bought a cashmere shawl, had still been alive for eight years after he was born. It made him ache to think what it would have been like to meet her.

Órale, a real grandmother and Mom kept her away. Why? Mom was the kindest person he ever knew. Why would she do something like that?

He remembered the first time his mother visited his classroom after he started teaching. Her mouth hung open as she stroked the student chairs and peered at the Mexico and Puerto Rico travel posters taped to the walls. You don't

have to work in a factory, she kept whispering. Well, yeah, Carlos had said, I did go to college, Mom.

Now he swallowed hard. What had it cost Mom to ensure that he become a teacher? Because a healthy, non-smoking, 135 lb. woman didn't just up and die at 42 from a heart attack, unless her heart had been broken sometime back.

"Why do you hate my mother so much?" he said after a while, wishing he could just run away from the oppressive thrift store smell of the room.

The old woman's dark skin flushed. "That puta couldn't be satisfied with my husband, que en paz descanse. She had to go after my son, too."

Wow.

He forced himself to say, "Tell me your son's full name again."

"Domingo Vargas!"

"Then he couldn't be my father. My last name is Reyna."

"Ha! If he isn't, it's because all the town's güaches took their turn with her."

Stay cool, dude. Stay cool. This woman's crazy. Just see if you can get something useful out of her and then move on.

"Mrs. Vargas. With all due respect, I have a birth certificate with Domingo Reyna listed as my father."

"Made up."

"I don't think so. It's authentic, with a water seal from the city of Chicago."

"Made up, I tell you. Made up!" The last came out in a screech. "Your mother was a whore!"

He grabbed her bony shoulder and shook it. Her fragile bones under his fingers brought him to his senses. He let her go.

She fell back in the chair and glared at him.

He should leave now.

But what if she really did know something?

He sat down. "So where's your son now?"

Her eyes flooded, but she brusquely brushed away the tears with her arthritic fingers. Then she thrust her jaw out; the jawbone so sharp, it seemed capable of piercing her age-thinned skin. "None of your business."

"Well, my mother is my business, Mrs. Vargas." He picked up the cap-and-gown picture by its corner. "How did you get this?"

She leaned forward and snatched the photograph. Before he could stop her, she tore it to pieces and threw them in the air. He grabbed her arm and twisted it down to the chair.

"¡Ay!" she screamed.

This evil woman had turned him into a güache after all.

He ran to the door and yanked it open. Then he looked back. The woman was ripping pictures from the album and throwing them on the floor.

He fled down the hallway. Bypassing the elevator, he entered the stairwell and bounded down the three flights of stairs.

The first thing he saw when entering his car was the royal blue box. He locked the doors and sat back, thinking about the absolutely crazy woman back there, not a single rational cell left in her body.

But that picture! How had she gotten it? Was Mom really from here? Is that why that tattered note was in her papers? If she had known she was going to die prematurely, would she have thrown it out before he could find it? It was so unlike her to hold on to any scrap of paper.

For years, Mom had paid for his parochial schools out of minimum-wage jobs. How she did it, he didn't know, but he should have guessed by how anxiously she reviewed his report cards that she feared he might revert to the ruin she had fled. Should he have hugged her more often, massaged away the tiredness in her shoulders? Maybe he should have said and meant it, Ándale pues, mamá, you don't have to worry about me.

He reached blindly to his side and pried open the box wide enough so he could finger the black cashmere shawl inside. Was that what this black cashmere shawl was about, a belated offer of atonement for his insensitivity?

He had spent a fortune on that shawl. Now there was no grandmother or even a girlfriend to give it to. A good girl, not loose, his mother kept urging him to find. Long story, but the good girls he found never lasted.

Did any of that have to do with who María Cristina Leyva had been?

. . . the town whore . . . all the town's güaches took their turn with her

All around him, the backside of tired buildings stared back at him. The bone-cracking cold blustered in. This actually tore him up worse than when Mom had died. Because now he would always wonder about her. That shriveled old woman back there might be crazy, but if there was one sliver of truth in anything she said, the Sonia Reyna he'd known as his mother never really existed.

He fingered the cashmere stole and thought about how Mom would have stroked the soft black wool against her cinnamon-colored face, smiling with eyes so full of gratitude that it might dislodge the sadness usually there. Neighbors had found her sprawled on the sidewalk in front of their townhouse. Upon impact, her grocery bag had split open and the pan dulce she liked serving him for breakfast

dotted the pavement with confectioner's sugar. Now, two months later, in this desolate parking lot, he felt as if he had accidentally intercepted the stone of sadness Mom tried so hard all his life to fling away from him.

He kept hearing in his head the echoing cackle of that surely demented witch back there. Why did she bother to seek him out in the lobby? Was it possible that crazy old bat just needed a grandson as much as he needed a grandmother? And he just happened to show up? He laughed. Lucky, lucky him.

But that picture! What was she doing with that picture?

He couldn't just walk away from here. If he did, he'd be wondering about that picture all his life.

He got out of the car. At the front of the senior citizens building, he lingered outside, looking at the now empty railroad tracks across the street. A long time ago, had his mother, maybe already pregnant with him, gazed at these same tracks? Had she dreamt about a better life and decided to change her name as well as her identity?

What *had* happened in this sorry town? Mrs. Vargas hated his mother. That much was clear, but why? Could Mrs. Vargas' son, who might also be Mom's cousin, be Carlos' father? Or was Mom's uncle, Mrs. Vargas' husband, really Carlos's father?

What if Carlos' father hadn't been Mrs. Vargas' son or husband, but one of the town's *guache* hoodlums? How convenient for Mom to say then that his father had died before Carlos was born.

Come on, Man. How can you buy into anything that crazy old woman said?

That picture with his mother's familiar handwriting on the back, that's why. He had to find out how Mrs. Vargas got a hold of that picture.

He entered the building, scanned the roster, and found Vargas at the very bottom.

M. C. Vargas, it said. He stared at those initials, stunned that he hadn't noticed them before.

M. C. Did that stand for Maria Cristina? Was this the Maria Cristina Leyva of his mother's note? Had Mrs. Vargas remarried and changed her last name?

Was he really not a total orphan then?

Carlos looked into the lobby. The man with the homemade cane still sat there. The security guard was nowhere to be seen. Carlos turned to the listings and watched himself punch the button for M. C. Vargas.

After a while, the intercom sputtered. "Who is it?" the raspy, grating voice said.

He pressed the royal blue box against his chest.

"It's me, Carlos. I have a gift for you. May I bring it up?"

PHOTO: Wanda Benvenutti
"Love", (24 x 36 in.) black and white giclée photographic print, Copyright © 2002
(The image was created in Philadelphia, PA near the intersection of Fifth & Lehigh, a
predominately Puerto Rican neighborhood in North Philadelphia.)

AMINA MUNOZ-ALI

Grandpa

My 74-year-old grandfather, God bless him, does three things: (1) He sleeps, (2) He wakes up, usually shouting, "Wha hoppen?" and (3) He makes pasteles. He lives in a beige recliner in front of the television. The TV is usually tuned to the History Channel, the Discovery Channel, or the Learning Channel.

Sometimes on Sunday he will put on one of the Spanish channels to watch an old Carlos Gardel movie or mariachi music. The only time he relinquishes control of the TV is weeknights at seven for Grandma's novelas.

Grandpa will not miss a Hitler special on one of those educational channels. Sometimes they'll have a whole day dedicated to World War II. Those are great days for Grandpa. You'd think he fought in the war himself, all by himself. He is a big fan of General Patton and General MacArthur. But Patton is the Man because Patton was "tough" the way "you have to be." Forget about it, if it hadn't been for Patton, the whole world today would be "Heil Hitler." He'll tell you the whole story about Hitler. Another favorite dictator is Trujillo of the Dominican Republic. He waits until the whole family—and when I'm talking about my family I'm talking about a small town—and extended family, which means a few recruits and volunteers —are all there, and then he will tell us his Trujillo stories. All the people he killed and cut up and tortured. It makes you glad to be an American. I guess with the Dominican Republic being so close to Puerto Rico, the story traveled.

Grandpa came to New York City from Yauco, Puerto Rico in 1948. He went to work on the Brooklyn docks and got married and lived in the Red Hook section of Brooklyn. His first English teachers were Italian longshoremen, which is why he speaks English with an Italian accent and knows how to say very bad things about people in Italian.

One afternoon in November I was sitting in my grandmother's kitchen. Grandma has about twenty five coffee mugs and pot holders hanging on the wall. She contends that, "You have to give people something to look at." She also has various calendars, clocks, figurines and family picture, which are joined by souvenirs from California, Florida, Pennsylvania, Puerto Rico, and everywhere else her five children have ever lived, visited, or set foot upon. There are so many pictures in magnetic frames on the refrigerator, I would not be surprised if one day I found pictures inside the refrigerator.

The living room is worse. Grandpa made shelves three deep for the living room walls to hold the various little statuettes and Disney character figurines, not to mention pictures of five children, seven grandchildren, and four great-grandchildren at various ages. In every room of the house, with the exception of the bathroom, one can find various depictions of Jesus Christ and the Virgin Mary, honorary members of every Puerto Rican Catholic family. Grandma has a huge statue of the Virgin Mary on the coffee table in the living room, with a rosary wrapped around her hands. This always confuses me because that means she is praying to herself.

That particular week Grandpa had made pasteles and I was eating one that Grandma had heated up for me. It tasted like the pasteles I had always eaten, mildly tasting of root vegetables, bits of meat, and an olive or chickpea or two, until I came to one particular bite. My tongue started burning. "Grandma! What did Grandpa put in these pasteles?" Grandma pointed to the spice rack. "Everything went into the pasteles," she said, showing me the empty red pepper jar.

Grandma gave me a second pastel to take home with me. As I headed toward the door, I passed Grandpa, who was sleeping in his recliner. I said, "Goodbye Grandpa, and thanks for the Mexican pasteles." He opened his eyes and shouted, "PUERTO RICAN PASTELES!" Then he went back to sleep.

Ode to the Dominican Restaurant
Near the 36th Street Subway Station

In the morning
your café con leche aroma
follows me down
the snowy subway steps
as I make my way
to the planet of Manhattan.

I wear your smell like a scapular —
an invisible Barrio souvenir
from a bohio made
of glass and steel.

When darkness arrives
an Island greets me at your tile doorstep.
Every night is a rice and beans honeymoon
on Fourth Avenue
as the jukebox pours
a hot layer of bachata
against the industrial sky.

You are the Church of the Holy Sancocho.
Your icons, larger than life photos
of platanos, chuletas, avocado
and bacalao.
I want to dip my finger into
the steam dripping down your window glass,
make the sign of the cross,
and pray to each one:
"Ay Dios mio!
Deliver me from this frio!
Amen."

Esas Cosas
by Angie Cruz

WE WERE CRUISING IN LA CIUDAD

Colonial, in downtown Santo Domingo, when I spotted the poster.

"Look, Mami, they're showing the *Vagina Monologues*."

"What's that?" Mi Tia asked.

My cousin tried to change the subject, "Did anyone see the novela last night?" She steered the car to the right, honking her horn aggressively to the other cars on the road. My cousin was a Dominicanyork who was transplanted to D.R. when she was eight, and now, at the age of thirty, she thinks that she'll never marry and die a spinster. When I tried to convince her otherwise she accused me of being muy moderna mainly because I admitted to things like having sex before marriage, because I liked living alone, and didn't feel any rush to marry or have children.

"How do you say vagina in Spanish?" I asked my cousin again, marveling at the fact that I didn't actually know how to say or pronounce it, which is revealing in itself, being that my Spanish is pretty muc limited to what has been shared orally.

My mother answered for her, "I think it's the same as vagina but instead of a 'g' sound it has an 'h' sound."

I said the word aloud over and over again like they do in the play. "It's about the Va-hi-na." I said it slowly right into my cousin's ear.

(Cont'd. pg. 252)

¿Qué son esas cosas?

ESAS COSAS
Angie Cruz

(cont'd from pg. 251)

Mi Tia looked confused and with reason because saying that a show is about the vagina didn't tell her anything about the plot. It could be porn. It could be scientific. It could be about love. It could be about vaginas that needed repair. She had just finished telling me about a woman who's cosas down there had fallen out because she hadn't used it, because of gravity, because that's what aging is all about. "With time, everything heads south," she said regrettably.

I tugged at my cousin's shirt, trying to get some kind of reaction. I knew deep down she wanted to be more moderna. I knew she watched *Sex in the City* like a religion, that she secretly wanted to be the kind of woman who admitted to enjoying sex and that she would happily move out of her parent's house if only los vecinos wouldn't find it in such poor taste.

As a Dominicanyorker, a person who had a foot outside the country and inside of it as well, she could've gone a number of ways as far as the kind of woman she wanted to become in Dominican society. She had chosen to be a plastica, or an aspiring one, a real bona fide, uppity, high-class type who didn't date dark-skinned men or go to restaurants along the malecon because the seawater was brutal to the hair. In minutes, a good sea spray would expose many Dominicana's true nature: curls. For my cousin, that would be tragic.

I knew she fantasized about having roommates and giggling over lovers ala *Friends*, or having a gay best friend who was her next door neighbor, like *Will and Grace,* so she could share her deepest secrets, a man who would adore and care for her without her having to worry about sex or him trying to get at her because, for any decent-looking woman, fending off men in Dominican Republic is a full-time job. I also knew from the confessions she would make when she had one too many drinks that she secretly wished she could abandon her parents, who depended on her to pay most of their bills, and move back to New York City. So she could live alone like me, with a cat that didn't listen to her.

She liked the freedom that could come from people not knowing if she's coming or going. She had watched enough television shows set in New York City to romanticize my single lifestyle. And I never did demystify her myth. Even if shows like *Friends* or *Sex in the City* were not reflective of my life in New York at all (and I am happy about that), they still provided a contrast to all the limitations she felt as a woman living in Santo Domingo where she cared very much about aparencias.

"Com'n prima, don't get shy on me now? Is it Vagina, Vahina, or what?"

She was pissed that I was in her car; that I had come to visit D.R. for a few weeks and had to stir up the pot.

"Why do you make such a big deal about these things? When it comes up we say *down there, or tu sabes,* there is not one particular word. Can we change the subject?" She said it in English so my Tia wouldn't catch it. "This is making Mami uncomfortable."

"Mami, what? Are you talking about me?" Mi Tia wasn't born yesterday.

"Tu sabes tia . . . *The Vagina Monologues* is a show about the vagina. El cuchi, la chocha," I rattled them out as they came to me, all nasty words I would've never said as a young woman, but I was also in my thirties and still single and a writer, and from New York where I didn't know my neighbors by name and the chances of bumping into anyone I knew was unlikely. Besides, among the women in my family, I was already known as being the crazy one, mostly because I spoke my mind, because I chose to spend my time writing and globe trotting and not settling down to become a woman with responsibilities.

"Ay!" she said. "What could they possibly say in that show?"

"De todo," my mother smirked. She had seen the *Vagina Monologues* maybe more than once, and after a year's subscription to *Oprah*, dedicated with articles to motivate and empower women like my mother, she had become a bit moderna herself. She could say words like vagina without any embarrassment.

DAYS LATER, I CAUGHT MI TIA telling just about every vecina who came over to her house about the Vagina show.

"Did you know that they have a show all about esas cosas?" she said while pouring the coffee, whispering it so the men in the room couldn't hear, saying it in front of my cousin to see her blush.

"Well you know those Americans, they don't have any boundaries. So vulgar," they said.

Then they would look around the room and stare me down as if to use me as a prime example to the downfall of Latina women. In their mind, there was a time women knew how to behave. They knew not to give away the milk so the men would buy the cow. They knew to keep their legs crossed. I was la Americanita, to be blamed for the downfall of all that was pure and virtuous. In a nutshell, feminism hadn't caught on in my family's kitchen.

SO WHEN I MET MY HALF SISTERS during that trip, who were more than half my age and who defiantly wore their

hair natural, proudly showing off their thick, luscious curls, I asked them, "What do you think about feminists? Sex? Vaginas?"

My mouth was a loaded gun.

We had only been reacquainted that week.

"I'm a feminist," the oldest one proudly said. She was sixteen. "I plan to go to college and get a job."

"And what about sex, do you talk about it with your friends? And tampons, do you use them?"

"You're funny," she said and, not surprisingly, changed the subject to talk about this cute boy she liked and how much she wanted me to meet her best friend, not like the last one who she didn't talk to anymore, but this one who had a computer in her house and was teaching her to do email.

My youngest sister, who was 11, giggled even though all this time she pretended that she wasn't listening to our conversation.

While we talked, my sisters tried on the clothes I brought them from New York. I watched them scream when they recognized a label and model the clothes around like fashion models. My 16-year-old sister was piling on a ton of blue eye-shadow on her lids for dramatic effect and my younger sister started to take off her jeans when she noticed, and then I noticed, that her life was about to change. My youngest sister, shy, slight, and who only said what was necessary, covered her panties with her hands. Her inner thighs and white underwear were stained in what looked like a menstrual accident.

I immediately reached over to my luggage to look for a maxi pad and some towels so she could clean herself up. "I had no idea you were already a señorita," I said smiling.

The words came out of my mouth so easily. Señorita. The word aging women craved to hear from the lips of men, acknowledging their youth and virginal qualities. Señorita reminded me of the day I got my period and my mother said, "M'ija, you're a señorita now," and gave me a pad, having peeled off the strip so one side could stick to my panties. I remember how she had left me alone in the bathroom with the pad to think about this momentous occasion. For weeks after, that big day which became the transition from little girl to young woman, every time a woman friend came over, they congratulated me. I was no longer safe to be around the tios and friends of tios alone, especially when they were drinking. I was no longer able to nap with them or sit on their laps.

My little sister, at the young age of eleven, was a señorita. I handed over the pad to her and she pretended not to see it, or me. She pulled her pants back up and sat on the corner, looking out the window. My 16-year-old sister also pretended like she didn't see or know anything.

"Look, I don't want to embarrass her, but she's bleeding right through her pants. Give this to her," I gave her the pad. "Is this the first time?"

At this point, I was aggravated with all the silence.

"It's not my problem. That's mami's job, I can't talk to her about those things."

Again with that phrase the women in my family love to throw about to explain everything. Esas cosas. Those things.

What I wanted to say was, "You mean menstruation. The blood that comes out from your vagina every month, reminding you of your potential fertility. Esa cosa between your legs that longs to be filled, touched, and throbbed when you feel desire. Esa cosa that holds the strength and elasticity to clamp around a penis and expand to the size of a baby's head? The most vulnerable and powerful part of a woman's body, that thing, down there."

I wanted to get all, *Our Bodies, Ourselves*(1) on her, and make her look at her vagina using a mirror and say, "This is your temple. Your force."

"We'll deal with it when we get home. Mami'll know what to do," my sister insisted.

"AGH!" I yelled. They both looked at me with fear as if I was insane. They still didn't know me well enough. In their mind I could go either way. I was afraid to scare them away from me forever by being too American. It was more important to me that they trusted me and knew I was on their side, not judging them, not using this moment to reveal my politics or push my politics on them. What was right for me wasn't necessarily right for them.

I went over to my youngest sister and handed over the maxi pad and a towel. I gave her a kiss on the forehead and told her she was beautiful and that what was happening to her was something to celebrate. I walked her over to the bathroom and told her I would wait right outside just in case she needed anything. Neither of them said a word again about it. In fact it was as if it never happened.

I SPENT MY LAST FEW NIGHTS IN D.R. sitting on the porch with Mi Tia because, when it was just us, she was more open. It was as if my being an outsider made it easier for her to talk. During that conversation she admitted to having an IUD inside of her for 30 years. She told me she got it in the states when she still lived there. "Do you think it can make me sick?" she asked me.

"You have to go to a gynecologist," I said.

"For what? I'm fine. You young people make such a big deal about everything."

"If you're asking, it's because it matters to you. I'll take you to the doctor, Tia."

"Being you read so many books I figured you knew

something about that stuff. Besides, it's not like I have much use for esas cosas anymore."

She confessed to me that she hadn't had a marido in a long time.

I wanted to say, get a lover. Instead I said, "Ever think of leaving Tio?"

"I'm not moderna like your mother, who left your father. We don't leave our men. This is life. The only place I am going to is pa' vieja."

I wanted to ask if she would consider using toys. If she ever had an orgasm, if she knew what an orgasm was. What if I bought the toy and left it in the drawer in her night table. Just because my uncle was done with sex didn't mean my aunt had to close shop. She was fifty-six-years-old; too young, too beautiful, too sexy. And why was it so hard for me to talk about pleasure, the body, among the women who loved and were closest to me? My sister couldn't talk to her sister about menstruation. My cousin couldn't even say the word vagina. My aunt didn't even want to think about going to a doctor to see if everything was okay with her health.

THE NIGHT BEFORE MY DEPARTURE, my cousin and I were cruising again the downtown city streets. I had hoped I could buy some tickets for the show, *The Vagina Monologues,* for my aunt and cousin. Maybe the show would get them talking. The advertisement was gone.

In between changing the radio stations in the car my cousin said, "The teller at the bank today called me señora."

I could tell by her tone how much it upset her, this word reserved for older, married women.

"Obviously he's blind," I said. This time it was me who wanted to change the subject. I was afraid to see her cry.

"It happens overnight, you know."

"What?" I asked.

"The change in our face. One day we're young and think anything is possible; another day we are being called señora by bank tellers."

Even if to be called señora is a sign of respect, it also means off the market, no longer virginal.

She pulled the car into a parking lot. I grabbed her and held her head on my shoulder and let her cry. I wanted to tell her she was beautiful. That every woman could reinvent herself, find pleasure, love, and even more importantly, train themselves to look in the mirror and see how beautiful they truly are. I wanted to tell her that the right man would look past all the societal bullshit and celebrate the day they found a woman like my cousin who was smart and a professional, who had a secure job, who took care of her parents. I wanted to tell her that even her mother, if she really wanted to, could reinvent her life and fall in love again with a man that wanted to live life with her, not kill himself slowly by drinking himself into a stupor every day. But there were no suitable words. We were in Santo Domingo. And I was not from there. I was Americana. Just visiting. And all I could do was hold her and listen. And like a mantra, I said the words vagina, vagina, vagina inside my head, thinking how threatening and empowering that thing/ esas cosa could be. ☐

(1) Bodies Ourselves (OBOS), also known as the Boston Women's Health Book Collective (BWHBC), is a nonprofit, public interest women's health education, advocacy, and consulting organization. Beginning in 1970 with the publication of the first edition of *Our Bodies, Ourselves,* OBOS has inspired the women's health movement.

STEPHANIE AGOSTO NEGRON

Dimensions of Coqui Women

Take heed from family
stories and dreams that
died before they were born

Creating big bang funk and
judgment day protesting
generations all colors of the sun

Chanting history with abstract
words erasing lines embrace
all traces of our time

Burning oil lamps we pop
lingo and trains of thought while
hitchhikers go freedom fighting

Rolling films of yesteryear
to make sense of tribal beats that
burn the only soul you know

 Spinning salsa we dance . . .

in the wastelands
climbing ladders of perfection
into a lost horizon

 . . . we rhumba to drums

Enjoying roots a few lives back
exposing pyramids and writings
not quite understood

Erupting in cyberspace
island pride so sincere
cocktails are available to all

Beating breasts of women look
deep into their African-Taino touch
into their *arroz con gandules* thighs

 . . . and universal eyes.

New Book On Poets
Reveals Untold Stories of Poetic Souls

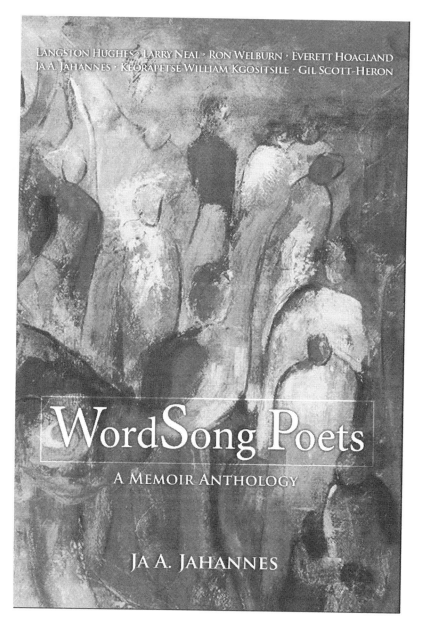

LANGSTON HUGHES · LARRY NEAL · RON WELBURN · EVERETT HOAGLAND
JA A. JAHANNES · KEORAPETSE WILLIAM KGOSITSILE · GIL SCOTT-HERON

WordSong Poets

A MEMOIR ANTHOLOGY

JA A. JAHANNES

COMING SOON
from
Turner Mayfield Publishing Company
1618 Foxhall Rd. Savannah, GA 31406

JUANA MACHO

1.

"Juana! Juana Macho!"

The husky man in the green plaid shirt, sleeves rolled up above his elbows, held four opened beer bottles in his large hands. He meandered his way between and around the throng at the bar and the stompers dancing on the small wood stage directly in front of the bar. He was glad to see Juana in the jukebox corner of the cantina and wasn't surprised that she didn't respond. The noise level could split eardrums in a matter of minutes.

"Hey, muchacha!" he tried again as he got closer to his old friend. She looked up when he plunked the bottles firmly on the small table, their clinking inaudible. He slapped her on the back and she reached out a calloused hand to shake his. She half-rose from the table, a man's gesture in the presence of a woman, but was seated again in a second.

Juana's face was pitted with scars, most of them noticeably shiny, pink patches and crinkled brown swaths across her nose, forehead, and the tops of her cheeks. Her jaw was square and firm, yet somehow feminine. Some of the scars were faint, raised welts, particularly one that ran from below her left eye to the edge of her mouth. This

(cont'd pg. 258)

ARTWORK: Lorraine Miller Nuzzo

Thelma T. Reyna

JUANA MUCHO
Thelma T. Reyna

(cont'd from pg. 257)

gave her a crooked smile, one of her well-known physical characteristics in the small, dusty Texas town she'd recently moved to and adopted as her own.

"Cabrón!" she cursed playfully at him as she slapped him on the chest and gave him a small push. "Well, there goes the neighborhood now that you're here!" Her voice was a scratchy tenor, her laugh a deep snort. She lifted one of her friend's beer bottles without invitation, and took a long swig. Her fingers around the neck of the bottle were brown and thick, wrinkled beneath the crisp sleeves of her black shirt.

"Cabrona!" he responded with a smile. He tipped his NY Yankees cap back on his head and leaned strong elbows on the table. He noticed for the first time that Juana wasn't wearing her cowboy hat. He narrowed his eyes, studied her face and head carefully, all the while drinking slowly from one of the fresh beers. He didn't remember the last time he'd seen her bare-headed. Her salt-and-pepper hair was cropped close, sideburns buzz-cut, gel making the tops and sides of her hair resemble small porcupine quills. This was a new look, to be sure. A new look for Juana. He tried to think of how many years ago he'd last seen her.

"New town, new hair, huh?" he yelled into her ear. The noise was still incredible. She hadn't changed colognes, he noticed. Still the strong musky scent she'd worn for years. He wore it, too. In fact, she'd bought a bottle for him a long time ago, then had started using the cologne herself. The thumping music from the jukebox near them reverberated in his chest as he drank slowly. Juana moved her head up and down with the music's beat, her eyes scanning the dance floor and the bar, constantly shifting and alert.

"Hey, Macho!" he said to her, hoping that this would swing her attention back to him. "Don't you want to know why I'm here? How I ran across you?"

She squinted at him, shook her head. He repeated his question in her ear, and she straightened up, squinted at him again, and shook her head. She didn't want to know.

"Well, I'll tell you anyway," he shouted. He was practically in her lap now. "I heard you were here. It's not hard to track you down." He wasn't a stalker, she knew. She wasn't concerned that her old friend had tracked her down. He kept his arm around the back of her chair, his mouth close to her ear. "I wanted to see you again."

She pulled back and stared into his face. She finished her bottle of beer and took a deep, long draught of a second one. Then she rose, swaggered to a table of women nearby, and spoke briefly to one of them. Juana took the giggling woman's hand and walked her to the dance platform. She brought the woman in close to her body, placed her head against the woman's hair, and began swaying sensually to the rhythm of the music, eyes closed.

2.

IT WAS ALMOST THREE IN THE MORNING when Juana pulled into her driveway. She was alone, having completed her carousing at the old honky-tonk after midnight and continuing at that woman's house in a nearby town. Juana stumbled a bit on the gravel in her driveway. It was especially dark tonight and, without any lighting in her yard, it was always difficult to navigate the narrow, bumpy driveway, by car or by foot. The beers she'd had weren't helping either. She fumbled with the keys and let herself into her house.

Juana had moved into this wooden shack almost two years ago. It was remote, surrounded by mesquite trees, cacti, and scrub brush. There was nothing attractive about the property, but it was ample enough for her, and it was cheap and isolated enough that it met her needs. It was a remnant of an old ranch that had flourished decades prior. Now the acre or so, with the wooden-post-and-barbed-wire fence marking its boundaries jaggedly, sat desolately at the outskirts of a God-forsaken piddle of a town called Dominguez. But living here met Juana's needs, so who could ask for more?

Her needs had dictated that she leave Laredo, a mish-mash city that cared and didn't care. Like a gypsy with too many secrets to hide, Juana had moved from her hometown, her birthplace, to three different cities, including Laredo, then eventually to smaller and smaller towns when her secrets weren't so important to hide anymore. Now, at the age of forty, she found herself in this dusty, desiccated corner of Texas: without family, without friends, without any connections from her past, which was how she liked it.

Until tonight.

Damn Manuel!

Oh yeah, she'd noticed him when he first walked in. She'd seen him despite the throng of sweating, laughing bodies massed near the doorway and throughout the cantina. She saw him as he scanned the crowds and had half-hoped he was seeking her. Her heart had slid into her stomach when he started wending his way toward

her dusky corner. He'd not spoken to anyone along the way, had not looked at any woman. He was a man on a mission, and her heart remained pitted in her stomach as she realized that she—Juana Macho—was his mission.

"Damn you, Manuel!" she said aloud now as she undressed in the dark. She'd been cool, convincingly detached . . . or so she hoped now as she wondered whether or not she'd been convincing enough. After she danced with that woman, she'd lingered in another dark corner with her, standing close to her body, her calloused hands on the woman's waist. She had the routine down pat. She knew how to deal with these women after all these years.

Manuel had waited for her at the small table for about ten minutes. He'd drunk his beer then finished off the remaining bottle. He'd glanced several times in Juana's direction but never rose from his chair until he rose to leave. He exited the back way, not looking at any woman along the way. As she saw him leaving, Juana's heart remained in her stomach. To her chagrin, it remained trapped and smothered there for the rest of the night.

In her cotton nightgown now, Juana slid into her dark bed and pulled the covers around her neck though the night was warm outside. Juana wept herself to sleep.

3.

HE DREAM WAS BRIEF. Her dreams were that way now.

When Juana Macho was a teenager, the dreams tormented her for years. Recurring dreams, scenes that shook her awake in the middle of the night, or bathed her in a dampness that shivered her awake too early in the morning. The house that she never recognized with unpainted, splintered boards bare inside and out. The emptiness that clothed the house as she floated from room to interminable vacant room. The kitchen, rocking violently back and forth as if on a ship, walls colored deep red, feeling slippery and cold. Then explosions, always two explosions, and her body lifted to the ceiling of the wretched house, glowing, glowing, sputtering and spitting, spinning in a black cloud that never settled, never opened, never cleared.

But those dreams had worn themselves away years ago, worn themselves into snapshots of those terrors. Little scenes, little horrors, explosions muffled, then poofed away, the dream ending abruptly. This was how a grown woman dreamt, a grown woman who'd used up her stock of fear, a grown woman who'd dried her eyes out pretty well in hundreds of nights. Juana Macho was grateful for the passage of years.

Yet she remembered. Of course she remembered what happened. They say that in a crisis, the body goes into overdrive, adrenaline flowing so hard that body and mind tear away from one another and maybe never reconnect. They call it shock. They call it God-given amnesia. They call it a blessing from up high that allows folks to outlive their horror. But it didn't happen that way for Juana Macho. She was eleven and shouldn't have been alone at home. But school was out and her mother had just taken a quick run to the store, just a quick run. Juanita Maria was alone at home and hungry, and it had not been the first time. She lived in the sticks, in a place that should've been torn down years ago. When the little girl named Juanita Maria Camacho put the match to that stove, neighbors in the next block heard the explosion.

4.

AS MANUEL LEFT THE CANTINA THAT NIGHT, he'd been angry, but not too angry. He'd grown accustomed to her doing that to him. Dominguez, Laredo, San Antonio, and who knows where else. Texas was a wide-open hiding place for her, had been a hide-and-seek quandary for him for years now. He'd grown accustomed to her flee-and-fetch.

Except that she didn't want to be fetched. Didn't want to be found, to be caught. As a man, he had grown to understand this.

He was just a kid when the explosion happened. Her classmate, her best friend, the little boy who sat behind Juanita Maria Camacho and twirled her long, glossy curls in his fingers while she tried to smother her giggles. The little boy who drew airplanes, boats and trains for her. The little boy who fantasized with her about how these planes and ships could take them to the land of the sphinx and to the place in Italy where houses stood on water. The little boy who also had no brothers or sisters, the little boy who also didn't live in the northeast part of town and who also didn't have nice clothes. The little boy who lived across the street from her, so near and so far. They were the proverbial peas in a pod.

Manuel knew he couldn't go to Juanita Maria's house to play. Her parents didn't let anyone in, and they didn't let her out. He knew his best friend was alone at home a lot. Knew she cleaned house, nursed her alcoholic father, hid secrets for her mother. When he allowed Juanita Maria into his heart, Manuel knew the depth of the aloneness the little girl carried in hers. He accepted her isolation and tried to mesh his isolation with hers, so that two broken child-hearts could possibly become one whole one.

And for the five years he sat in classrooms with her, Manuel and Maria Juanita slowly wove their friendship into something that could withstand the emptiness of home. Quiet and pensive, there was something spiritual about Juanita Maria that even a little boy could understand. The day the two eleven-year-olds sat underneath the giant oak tree at school, eating sandwiches from reused brown bags, reciting the ancient wonders of the world they'd see together when they grew up . . . the day of the explosion . . . Well, this was a day Manuel would never forget.

He pulled his navy blue Jeep into his apartment complex. Kingsville, his hometown now, was forty miles away from Dominguez. When he left the cantina tonight without saying goodbye to Juana, he felt abandoned, demeaned. How could she do that to him? No. How, after all these years of his protestations to her, could she still do that to him?

He entered his small but well-appointed home long before midnight, which meant he had a few hours still left for dwelling on Juana, on the tremulous joy he had felt in finding her. Dwelling on the fear in his legs and arms, and in his pulsing forehead, as he'd walked to her corner in the cantina tonight. Recalling his pleasure as he placed his mouth close to her face and wrapped his arm around her back along the edge of the chair.

He took a Pepsi from his fridge and slumped into an overstuffed chair. He drank slowly, remembering a few other things from tonight, a few more items to dwell on: the gray in her hair, the way her eyes avoided his for most of their brief encounter, the thickness in her wrinkled fingers, and especially He shifted uneasily and flicked on the TV to calm his thoughts.

The way she rubbed against that woman, how Juana held her close, her face almost lost in the woman's long brown hair. Manuel rubbed his temples in big, slow circles, his eyes closed, as he tried to erase the image from his mind. But then a bigger pain grabbed him, and the recollection of his own actions many years ago reached even more deeply, stabbed more cruelly, and he sank more heavily into his chair at the thought of it.

As a teenager, Manuel had run across Juana while visiting relatives in San Antonio, more than one hundred miles away. It was fate, he thought then. "It was fate," he said aloud now, still convinced that the gods had always meant for them to remain bonded to one another, though that first encounter after her departure was pained and horrid. Who would have guessed that two people who'd been apart, totally without communication for three years, would literally trip into one another in a place neither had visited before?

Manuel rubbed his face absent-mindedly as he recalled the faraway scene. He had not seen the effects of the fire on his beloved classmate. In truth, her parents allowed nobody but Juanita Maria's doctors near her when she returned home. The girl had been taken to a hospital in another town, far away from visitors of any sort. Her parents cloistered her more excessively than ever, and Juanita Maria became more invisible as the months wore on. The last time he glimpsed his friend was the day a brown hauling truck pulled in front of her house, and her parents piled their shabby belongings into it. Unceremoniously, they left town, Juanita Maria shrouded in a long, gray coat and floppy hat, just as she'd been when she had returned home from the hospital.

So when Manuel bounded down the grassy hill in that faraway park in San Antonio years later, he tripped on someone unknown: A boy? A girl? He couldn't tell. They tangled on the slope of the lawn momentarily, then the trampled youth stood up: baggy khakis, baggy flannel shirt, long-sleeved though it was summertime, men's shoes, baseball cap pulled low, wisps of black hair peeking timidly from underneath the canvas cap. When the youth looked up at Manuel, Manuel was stunned:

Juanita Maria Camacho. Beautiful Juanita Maria. Scarred. Disfigured. Solemn.

Manuel's silence was heart-wrenching to the girl. She had recognized him immediately and gazed at his face with clear recollections of what he had meant to her, clear remembrances of wondrous trips they had vowed to take together, lunches eaten in solidarity against the cruelties of childhood. She smiled at him with sheer joy in being with her friend again. She took a step toward him, hands outstretched. Pink, rubbery, scarred hands.

Manuel backed away stiffly, eyes glued to the girl's face, her hands. He said nothing to her. When she said his name, he remained silent, then turned quickly and ran toward the exit of the park.

In a Kingsville apartment, the forty-year-old Manuel, slouched in an easy chair by a flickering TV screen near midnight, remembered these things. He recalled all this with horror and shame, mostly shame at his horror.

5.

WOMEN ARE MY SOLACE. *My only solace. When I lost my womanhood, I knew I had to grasp for it however I could. Can you imagine what it's like to not have breasts? To have hair that stops just there, no more? Patches of skin on my head where only stubble grows? Skin no man wants to kiss?*

Juana Macho read aloud from her journal. She'd given up trying to sleep. She sat at her kitchen table, the bedcoverings wrapped around her shoulders, white nightgown scraping the floor beneath her shoeless feet. Though the bare bulb in the kitchen was too dim for proper reading, Juana had no trouble making out her words in her worn leatherette book. She had read them enough times, for many years now, these words from an alien being, from a familiar being, from someone she hated, from someone she loved.

Can you imagine a woman without softness? So the softness has to be found outside of me, beyond me, around me. I reach for it when I find it: a woman's softness, a woman's breasts, supple skin, gentle curves I've never had, pleasure denied me by flames and fury long, long ago. I reach for what I'm not. I behold and hold what I cannot find in myself.

Juana imagined herself explaining these things to Manuel. She read the words aloud, haltingly but with sincerity.

Men seek this softness as well. They won't find it in me. You won't find it in me, Manuel. Men seek beauty. You'll see none in me, Manuel.

She gazed from the book in her hand to the empty chair beside her, imagining her old friend at the table. Juana rose and set her book down hesitantly. She walked to her bedroom, let the heavy bed coverings drop away from her shoulders, and removed the nightgown slowly, letting it, too, fall to her feet. She stepped to the skinny mirror behind the bathroom door and pulled aside the curtain she had tacked over the glass. She positioned the glass so she could see all of her, head to toe, despite the fact that she had kept only the night light on in the cramped room. Courage only stretched so far.

The flames had been merciless. How she survived was a story her parents never cared to unearth. Juana recalled the excruciating pain, the chalk-faces of the men who ran to slap their jackets on her burning body, and their red, yelling mouths. As she rolled on the dirt amidst the chaos, she'd been amazed at the blueness of the sky, the brilliance of the sun, and had marveled momentarily at how the black plumes emanating from her house split the sky so neatly.

Now look at what the flames did to that little girl: her skin from forehead to toes was puckered and welted. The different colors pocked throughout her body spoke to the varying degrees of damage: deep brown across her chest, resembling a tight elastic band that obliterated any semblance of womanhood, pink across the inner thighs, coarse brown across the front and back of her legs. Her hands: permanently discolored, fingernails blunted. Her feet . . .

Juana sank to the linoleum floor and sobbed. She shouldn't have done this, shouldn't have looked. She rarely saw herself. She made a point of this. She had no other mirrors in the house and avoided all mirrors in public places. This mirror was in her home only because she had been unable to detach it from the door, and her superstitious nature wouldn't allow her to break it. So she had covered it and only now foolishly uncovered it. For what purpose?

Her head was on the bare floor now. She sobbed as she made her explanation aloud to Manuel, to her fantasy friend who had recoiled in horror many years ago and who had, from guilt no doubt, only from guilt, made feeble attempts to see her in the decades hence.

So you see now? You see why I can't have you?

She hugged herself on the floor, folded her legs as best as she could to her chest.

Do you understand now why I seek solace as I do?

She doubted that Manuel would ever come back. He had surely seen at the cantina last night that Juana was still a freak. A woman who dressed like a man, moved and spoke like a man, drank like a man, seduced like a man. A woman with a man's life but a woman's memory. How could she ever go back? How could she be what she was not for Manuel, yet continue to be what she was not for Juana?

Her keening could have awakened the dead. Only her wails the day of the fire surpassed the pain pouring forth now.

And Manuel heard it all.

Saw it all.

He couldn't sleep, so he had driven the forty miles back to Dominguez, had learned from the weary bartender where Juana Macho lived. If she wouldn't have him, at least he couldn't let the evening end without farewells.

He saw her with the book, saw from the darkness outside her window the desecrated body of his beloved friend. Saw her sink to the floor and weep. When he couldn't endure any more, he pushed the old front door open and went to retrieve her from her sorrow, as he should have done so very long ago. He picked her up and gently wrapped her in her bed coverings. He soothed her spiky hair.

He had heard her words.

Sobbing into her neck, he could only say, over and over: "Juanita Maria, Juanita Maria."

This story was published in *The Heavens Weep for Us: And Other Stories* (Outskirts Press, 2009).

"What the hell's going on here?"

The Bowery Poetry Club
308 Bowery
New York City
(ACROSS FROM CBGB)

SERVING THE WORLD POETRY SINCE 2002

www.bowerypoetry.com

Love in the time of Cornerboys

John Rodriguez

I.

WE CALLED HUH FUGLY because she had juss a lil bit a hair on huh upper lip and juss the slightest of bumps on huh chest and never told any of us as much as huh name aside from the occasional hello since we was kids.

We were in fronna Saint's building, drinking, and we saw huh with huh baby and huh husband getting inside their Lexus and driving down to Gun Hill and Mayor, my man Mayor, made us all feel better by saying "You know, I never liked that slut."

He was lyin though cuz he juss learned to dislike women type recently like the rest of us. Sayin we all been in love, young love—Puerto Rican style, ghetto style—that real sudden kinda love. We call it "First Ass Syndrome."

Like, yuh in this big building right, this tower of Love and Sex thatchu been waitin to get inside for forever—there's this long line and shit—and now you're in the lobby and ya dick's so hard that you don't even want to wait for the elevator. You go around the back and up the fire stairs straight runnin, straight blowin past all your peoples, all your family and ya don't care. All your life-shit fallin outcha pockets and it don't matter it don't. Cuz you about to get some pussy and that's all you seein and that's all you bein.

And then yuh flyin, yuh up in the clouds because nobody's having sex like y'all having sex, cuz nobody got love like y'all got love. Notcha parents, notcha friends, not even in the movies but then things change, she changes, love changes, you know?

(cont'd. pg. 264)

LOVE IN THE TIME OF CORNERBOYS
John Rodriguez

(cont'd from pg. 263)

It was one thing when y'alls was young, callin each other every night and sneakin sex in each others' parents' houses but now y'all get familiar and the woman start actin funny. Sayin you changed, you used to be different, we used to go out, we don't go out anymore and this and that when the truth is she jus feelin what you feelin and y'all feelin that y'all don't fit. That maybe y'all never fitted. That shit was hard and the both of you wanted love maybe really needed love so bad thatchu grabbed each other and didn't wanna let go for nothing.

Once that hits you, man, it's over. You are stuck like chuck out in the rain lookin for some kinda definition some kinda identification and you aint got none cuz everything fell outcha fucken pockets from runnin.

And there you are, like here we are butchu know, we betta off than that nigga wit Fugly cuz he don't know this shit yet. But he'll find out because thass life—and yo, Life, Life's not a bitch. It's not. See because if she was a bitch you would never trust huh to begin with. If shit was bad all the time, it wouldn't be bad because it wouldn't mean anything because you would never expect anything good but see sometimes it's good, and sometimes it's fucked up. So see Life is a slut, a fucken ugly slut. And you know, I never liked huh myself.

II.

I ONLY SEEN HUH TWICE. First time was New Year's Eve. Pretty little girl, sixteen maybe. Probably. Riquena, light, brown eyes, straight brown hair falling from a brown knit hat. Wide smile. Cash, I heard. Short for Casha.

At midnight she gave everyone a hug. So we hugged; she hugged me. Didn't even know my name. Didn't know that I knew huhs but we was all together in Saint's basement celebrating the New Year and so it didn't matter that we was new because we wasn't strangers, you know.

Funny how I was thinkin about huh today. Like, daydreamin that we was friends; that we was tight and that I helped her learn to respect herself so that she aint had to fuck niggas like niggas said her moms do for crack and her sister do just to feel human. Daydreamt that I saved huh. It was funny.

So I get this call from Mayor to come to the block like 10 at night. And he's out on the other corner with them younger dudes, them junior varsity corner boys from New Years and while I'm slappin hands I see huh not lookin at me so I kinda touch huh shoulder and she kinda blinks and smiles when she recognizes me and says "Yo . . . happy New Year." Pretty little girl.

A few minutes later she heads up the street with these two dudes and next thing I hear headz is debatin whether this one is gonna fuck huh or that one is gonna fuck huh or if they both gonna fuck huh. And then shit gets real weird. Like I feel something rushing inside me. And I hadn't drank. I wasn't drinkin and it wasn't even my insides it was like my head yo. Back of my head something was runnin.

By the time niggas get on some "yo what comes after sloppy seconds" shit it's type pounding type angry white cops stompin my skullpiece type native tribes doin the ghost dance on my fuckin brain yo while niggas is like "dirty thirds stinky fourfs funky fifs" I'm like YO I'M OUT don't even know if I said it out loud I couldn't hear myself over the pounding like I couldn't hear the car horns that I didn't have the light that I couldn't hear my own breathin that my mouth was open cuz my nose was runnin cuz I was cryin goin up the hill cryin that this girl pretty little girl broke my heart man that I only seen huh twice but she look like my daughter who I aint seen in too long who I don't want to grow up feelin like she need to fuck to feel love because I wasn't there for huh.

III.

I TOLD HUH I WAS AFRAID FOR HUH. "Why should you be afraid?" she said. And I wanted to be like

Porque hay monstruos, nena. Because there's monsters, like the ones that hid under your bed and in your closet. Mami made them disappear by stroking your hair and kissing your cheek. Told you they wasn't real that nothing was gonna hurtchu. Not here. Not in yuh house. Butchu can't stay home you don't stay home yuh out here. And out here hay monstruos.

You see them, nena, in your building, at the store, on the corner watching you walk. Watching you grow each time you leave home. They stare at you and hiss at you. Their eyes pull atcha clothes to steal the shape of yuh flesh. And they are so patient as to wait until they see sadness in yuh face or the weight of the world on yuh shoulders before they creep to you offering kindness.

Then they comfort you and feed your dreams, whisper names in your ear—Linda Querida Amor—until you build love and show it to them, offer it to them for them to snatch and twist into something wrong. Into something shameful that leaves you emptier than you've ever been. And I'm afraid of that, mi'ja. I fear for you.

But all that came out was cuz there's monsters out here. Didja know?

She grinned at me, from so very far. "I stopped believing in monsters a long time ago," she said, " . . . around the same time I stopped believing in heroes." And then, still grinning, she stroked my hair and kissed my cheek. ◻ .

The Last Ding-Dong of Doom

To find brotherhood in man, a stone's skip away
From my last wish to die clean, no stains left.
Drumming has been my life-long business, may my
Spirit, my ark of bones, lay square inside the one
& two, all those burning flames calling, time to
Go ya'll, the street is now playing me.

Excerpt from *The Essential Hits of Shorty Bon Bon* by Willie Perdomo.

Boogaloo Corner

Live your life by concrete, by corner store, by court, by empty
Can. Never had a Marine Tiger, mambo vacation, pero
Nada, get Shorty Bon Bon, Tony Toca Timbales, Pablo el
Negro with the hard hands, all us who have lived sea lives,
Reading our bodies, throwing congas at each other. Too
Many cats left home, came to the bandstand, spines draped
On the fence. Parts of this song can go hard blue like all
That running from the who and jumping off the ledge at the
Same time. It's true what Brother Lo used to say: It's possible
To see the future standing on the corner.

Excerpt from *The Essential Hits of Shorty Bon Bon* by Willie Perdomo.

DIANA GITESHA HERNANDEZ

Loisaida, Not The Same

Streets lined with up & coming
High risers
Yuppies turn'd guppies
Making million dollar deals/
Stolen
Chased in the quick
Rubble blowing
As Latinos rush
To hold onto their
Own
Sabor-Para LA VIDA —sabor . . .

In Loisada huddled in corners
Bodega's left barely
Shelved
Habichuelas arroz y cervesas
Conversations
In Spanglish, echoes
"the conquisodores are back!"

Stealing safety
Homes,
Tenements
By the East River
Evicted
Further
Out
Now
Past the
River
But
To where?

An exodus

 How to do it?
 Tie up *ALL* our belongings . . .

Borinquen!

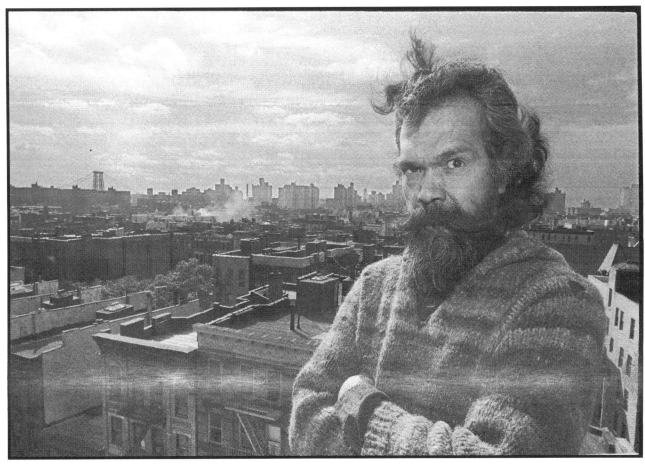

PHOTO: Marlis Momber
BIMBO RIVAS (Nov. 11, 1939 – May 21, 1982), Loisaida guardian, Vigilante, Poet, Actor, Author, and Activist. Overlooking LOISAIDA from the roof of EL BOHIO, 605 East 9 Street Headquarter of CHARAS, Community Center, Copyright © 1986

OSCAR BERMEO

When the City Ends

After Cornelius Eady's "The Dance"
with lines from the Soulsonic Force and Malcolm McLaren

When the City ends,
I will be sporting suede Pumas.
When the City ends,
I will be in a house party
 on Good Friday.
When the City ends,
I will be graffiti scrawl.
When the City ends,
I will be breath in an amber bottle.
When the City ends,
I will be a searchlight through
 a smashed windshield,
And I will pop
 like the trucks on the Cross Bronx,
And I will lock
 like the antenna
 kissed by the electric bugalú,
And I will pop;
 the apartment will pop, too.
And I will lock;
 the projects will lock, too.
And I will uprock, with the last of
 the coins and lint in my jeans pocket.
It will be Good Friday
And I will be sporting suede Pumas,
My kicks earning time-and-a-half,
My body in a windmill,
Free as double dutch girls
 round the outside,
One at last with pigeons
 and ash,
As the City burns and jerks
 down the fire escape,
The boombox searches for the perfect beat,
And the b-boys, under the awnings,
 start to reach their peak.

PEDRO LOPEZ ADORNO

Cruising

I am on the Deegan Expressway:
middle-of-the-week slo-mo
departure to oblivion.

I become a bundle of inertia.
Significant nobody
that handles the rejections of silence
as if they ever made my day.

Invidious syllables mock me as I
describe who I am. This rubble
of syllables that few (if any) will enjoy
formed by the intractable landscape
on the rear-view mirror.

A quarantined consumer. A redeemer
of sounds lost on the road.
Giving them gas so as not to lose
sight of my resemblance.

Memories of Horses

(I)
The sound of hooves atop the pavement
a path of embers.
Mango hummingbirds. Towards
a never wave the mangrove cuckoo,
the tijerillas announcing rain.
Múcaro view a childhood
where dogs barked menacingly
and ashes became recollections
of an island at noon.

(II)
The destiny of melodies in the refreshing rains. Adrift
where light simmers memory. Where
the drippings of our insomnia
battled droughts. All that
galloped swiftly out of our lives.
Pillaged exile, thunder,
mirror of oblivion.

(III)
Suspended
in the calculation
that eluded us forever
the hooves, the youngsters
gradually disappeared in flight. Casualties
of an invisible war.

(IV)
Now this emptiness
like the predatory nature of dreams
 stampedes into a forest
of vanishing images. A mythology of coral
reefs and incantations and ornate
waves wait for the wind.
And of course
rage. And music
to shield our disappointment.

NANCY MERCADO

Last Guaguancó in Puerto Rico

I am not what I am
Wandering like a lone ant
Incoherent with no direction
I find my native speech is foreign
My appearance a deception
In Puerto Rico

In the US
My mambo stifled
By freezing weather
My warm smile smothered
Under blizzards
My tears
Icicles

I try to break through
This immense space
Try to cross the endless ocean
Of Operation Bootstrap
Try to make a way home

No Island Is No Man: A Noricua of the Mind

a man—let's start a rift in the zero—make him no man, no hero. There once was no *eros*, no *number*, no easy notation. Make that no *idea*, no *focus*. There once was no *center* to a thought about *someone*, a thought about *nothing* as *someone*. An island as *someone*. There once was an entire *isolation* re-languaged as an entire *person*. An entire *beginning* reduced to an attachment. A mind shaped by a people of *no choice* where *no body* was needed. An *erasure* happening in the time of its creation, allowing *crea-sure* its time for destruction.

No territory, no land, a skin of no border. A fusion's inertia surrounded by friction. A floating meander. An out-of-reach summit. A layer traveling beside the genome. The oxygenated sideways once we turn our heads for a nostril-jump into physics. A completely unknown time as a knowable puncture into a phrase impossibly open. *Let me stop here ...*

... because you're coming in all broken up and I'm on a house phone, and I want to connect.

Once *nothing* is claimed the thought that goes with it, is suddenly framed. A refusal implied—when you say you come from *No* (as opposed to *Nowhere* which carries baggage and location). Yet this is what happens to the natives of Noricua. As inhabitants of a heightened duality, the indigenous Noricua represents the *stable/instability*, the *controlled/chaos*, the *infinite/now* in search of a form that can move *us* forward.

(cont'd. pg. 274)

EDWIN TORRES

NO ISLAND IS NO MAN
Edwin Torres

(cont'd from pg. 273)

By *us*, I am opening the portal to *you* dear No . . . holding your Zero flag in tight allegiance, perhaps this ma-*no*-festo is about form over structure. And whether there are ways to hide from failure which bring out the risk-taker and smothers him in *id*. Not *identification* but a base-below-real divison obscured by shadow resistance . . . i.e. *the party starts when the body shows up*. If *Boricua* be the body, *Noricua* be the brain—but again, my connection gets lost in my *barrio*.

Tell me about *la raza* trying to fit in, about the ways to say "we" that really mean "not you"? I can understand how similarities reflect each other—I'm thinking DNA spiral or any parade thrown by any ethnicity—but am I too ethnic for my *personal* ethnicity?

<pre>
 what city is that
 —of the ethni
 —of the ether
 a hallucinated belonging
 would call earth
 immigrant—traveling
 out of her home
 eth—ether
 ni—negate
 city—home
 is *galaxy* the home
 she wanders in
 —room to room
 are we
 in one huge *home*
 or just being kept
 in one room
 to prevent *roam*
</pre>

You don't have to understand *language* to understand *home*. My world *before* the alphabet has grown its limbs, twigs, bodies—which obscure the page, the screen, the mind, along with the reason to know where to go—so that you don't get lost. We choose our carnival, our corners, so the *structure* can survive its own inertia, i.e. we can't help but roam.

<pre>
 the indigenous father—in charge of survival
 the people of his people being the reason for his eyes
 his nose, his shoulder width, the jump of his reset button
 a new line every day—to run from, to start from—
</pre>

whose identity brings them completion
lets stand together and see how far the line goes

need, for fitting in—who tells us that we need to belong
a feral animal
 at home with his limbs
 with letting limbs dictate *charge*
gazelles run with gazelles, avoiding obstacles without thinking
Times Square shuttle during rush hour, humans
 can't help not think

close your distance by remaining next to your
 four-legged tongue
as in—*like* likes *like*
 the ability to let loose a stream of lingo and
 allow the sensory
 to gather in the creeks—has been replaced
 by fatigue at the weight of it all
the stanza in control of language will be my downfall
look at how drive has been overtaken by drivel
 style was a doorway
 but edge was the groove

Beyond border or skin, Noricua's dialogue with duality travels the byways of human interaction. And where in the tribal dance of ego-id neurosis, can we establish a ground on finality? Maybe a See Saw represents a natural slope to own: the > New/Out of the Old/York is Rich/Ricua = CEMI SAW.

An *in-the-works* Noricua, a Noricua in constant re-invention, will adapt to the changing landscape much as an *alter-ricuan* Calder mobile—a hanging collection of pun and matter . . . endlessly supported by its own, viscous membrane. A biophilic startup, a nation of continual *No*—aware of how breath and lung start from the neck and search in the mountainous nether-regions, where the poor senses live . . . somewhere over the *nobow*.

The ungraspable kinetic which defines poetry is what empowers Noricua—a language-based reality at home with syntax and modality *before* physical interference. The shadow we cast, at odds with our relation to the sun—the Caribbean sun that every true Noricua calls home. Our perspective to a larger light, a heavenly association to what *nothing* could be—Sol Power, a phenomenon *beyond* belief, the power of *Non*, of *Noh*. Noh Theater with its bare non-ideology presenting no obstacle (by the way, my exaggerated non-definition of art is exactly what this non-essay needs). Laced with faith, our belief in the grand nothing is an acceptance of *denial* over *faith*, which strengthens motion, since obstacles *redirect* while receptacles *funnel*. Could there be a funnel-shaped votive that hovers inexplicably over Noricua? A grand beacon guiding lost ships into their self-reflective flytraps?

what if I don't want to be on your team
when I was in little league
my body had yet to catch my imagination
the ball in right field and my long puppy legs
mangled any sense of balance

I tried to catch the ball, I really did
but my limbs preferred speed over physics
I was a beautiful flop
and no one else saw this

so the idea of *team*, to *this* pre-pubescent Noricua ...
was always connected
to *flop*

Let us *indigenous* Noricuas align our beginnings within
our DNA. Is there a wave-form that spins through the infinte
nada and gathers speed with every repetition of the word
No? The aesthetic of Noricua's mantra allows for a process-
oriented philosophy—a kitchen-sink approach to fringing and
flexing the Noricua mindscape, which aligns itself with Bo-
ricua's multi-versed *bochincherias*. As the alter-ricua Noricua
Judy Garland said, "*Todo, we're not in Ghetto anymore.*"

the Alter-Ricua Noricua Reachout Project
an effort to save the lost Boricuas

those who have scampered away
from whatever edge they were given
to find a new town

a citizen relocation program
where location is re-identified
as translation—a pre-dimension

surrounding the Euclidean Barrio
dimension one—TA, dimension two—I
dimension three—NO

thereby wounding liberty
with what remains of the past
 if you leave, I'll come back

 I won't take my flag
 but I do want my zero
my circular vanguard

formless ocean masquerading as manifesto
floats from tip of no island no sky
the sainted reef—blue or blame

look at the guitarist who played salsa
while we waited for grunge
or the newscaster with no accent

or the comedian who took her mother
and covered her curves with bleach—
plunge into your soft spot

with empathy *entranced* by dimension
by geography in the mangle of hybrid ...
these are the lost Boricuas

the mexican who pretends to be dominican
so that his ecuadorean visa will get him back
to cuba

this is about territory
and long legs
and how to step over tiny rocks

my embedded calling:
client, connectivity, and cloud

And where has Noricua been co-opted? Wherever we
can use Noricua's golden foci; *The Quantum No*. When a
foreigner is looking for something to spice up their *Si* ...
they look at *No*. Noricuas are co-opted by the *All* as a way
of honing their sensory attachment to extremes—*Todo*
will always be interested in *Nada*. Noricua's charge into
nothing is served with an overbite of *nofrito*, laced with
arroz y nobichuelas. Noya is the favored brand of canned
No which has been co-opted by the *Every*, those populist
noquitos that emit their endearing *noqui*, a reminder to
the natives of a land that never was.

And our vegetation, our currency, our *disambigua-
tion*? The Zero Flag—a humble reminder of our begin-
nings—a hula hoop of litmus paranoia. An empty void
that chooses our government. I remember our last non-
election, the front-runners debating with such ferocity,
allowing the non-runners to win the electorate while
chanting *"No More Years, No More Years."* And what would
such a non-people expect from their non-government? I
believe they'd want to Occupy No Street.

No money is the currency of choice. (*Dear No, are
you still there . . . can you help me decide on Tropicalia
or Nopicalia?*) Trees that need no care populate Noricua.
Not artificial, perhaps cacti shaped in tremendous hoops
mixed along the Noconut trees. Our landscape is not bar-
ren, not a dessert . . . ours is a grass that needs no water,
a beautiful colorless grass—the rare *no-grass* needing an
average rainfall of *nil*.

While the *Caribbean* becomes an existing paradigm
for Noricua's location, by way of its own indigenous sur-
vival mechanisms, the *Nuyorican* experience is a direct
influence, a sort of bizarro-migration, an earth immigrant,
a comparable doppleganger for the effects of inhabiting

a hybrid existence. Between *No* and *Si*—between *New* and *Yo*—the Ricua looks for belonging by not. No island. No man.

No Wave Music, the genre that ran post-punk in New York, is our soundtrack. A primal removal of the sound wall—the anarchic system of notes and tones which inhibits *free thought*. As a movement predicated on negation—saying *No* to its own existence—it was a blip barely lasting long enough on the music scene, yet extremely influential in its resistance to *definition*. Screeched guitar with human oratory, percussive pulsations of permanent hearing loss, radical immersions of electronic feedback, empty songwriting full of song . . . these are the benchmarks of *Noricuatory* migration—removal as meaning, as songbirds from a tangle of anthems, the blaze of reminders that fly above.

> something about a human
> who does things to be a human
> an animal
> in the guise of animal
> by wearing
> what its been given

>> *I can—yo puedo—yo soy*
>> *I want—yo quiero—yo soy*
>> *I feel—yo siento—yo soy*

> when I moved away from everything I knew
> I didn't realize the need for difficulty
> the sense of being surrounded
> by what you know you can't control

The *hoop*. The *zero*. The *not* inside. The indigenous Noricua understands circularity as homage to ancestry—a perpetual zero around their waist. When meeting a fellow native, they do an imaginary hula rotation as a handshake—their circular *oneness* representing a global ubiquity which the colorless *All* strives for, a *No* to reach through.

Noricua be 'Oricua. The mind be Noricua. The i-land of No—center of id/ego—perspective/displacement—map/edge. Noricua be desire—for understanding, for human contact, for mutual borders that consist of none.

> circulate with the earth
> and migration will skip you by
> look for new steps
> and feet will betray wonder

>> *I know—*
>> *I now—*
>> *I no—*

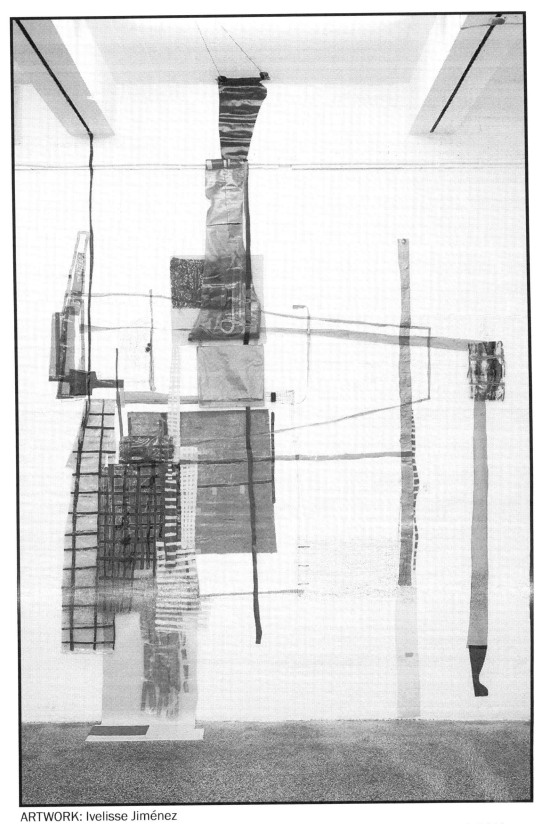

ARTWORK: Ivelisse Jiménez
"Description without place,"Mixed media installation (9' x 12' x 10'), Copyright © 2010

SAM DIAZ

it's about an old story . . .

it's about an old story
without end & no moral within
told in languages long dead,
inscribed in genotypic memories,
inherited by the wind

it's about an end at the edge
of a desert without borders,
hollow sounds drifting on sand
sketching upon the surface of time:
a story that goes on and on

it's about grains of sand
& the words written thereon
for no one to read or remember
how it began or why it ends
in questions wailing in the wind

it's about words without meaning
& the purpose therein
to recall the ancient question why
in blood we leave our tracks
& in graves our dreams

it's about beginnings
and following through
in the multiple implied choices
set upon our paths
& all the roads we cross

it's about seeking patterns
in our rambling random numbers
& the stories we choose to hear
when no one is near
to see the insights that blind us

it's about questions and answers,
and the silences
in between the voices you hear
when you thought you understood
what we were talking about

it's about coming and not going,
living & not dying, sleeping
and not dreaming impossible dreams
that require you to be awake
for your screams to be heard

it's about poems spoken to the wind,
written on sand
in all the languages we use
to obscure all we want to say
& clarify what we choose to hide.

it's about terrors of the mind
borne naked at noon,
all our deeds seen in broad daylite
silent witnesses for our trials
and silence our due sentence

it's about crying in relief
when the sun comes up
to laugh in the face of death
as it gravely stares
while you step six feet under

it's about breathing in order to live,
or living in order to dream
or dreaming without an order in mind
in the entropic disorder
of your vision spent

it's about not knowing why
but doing despite
all the reasons not to
that compel you to fill
a blank page with sounds
upon the wind into a poem

it's about a poem that
repeats itself in
an endless succession of words
striving to underline a purpose
to all your deeds & life

R. A. "Ri" ARAYA

Llueve, ven q va yo ver

En el forest q sos no vez
All you point out is the shoes on stoops
Wet complaint white leather wing street tipped feather
piedra en mi zapato y q?

La vida me trae el cafe negro irviendo
these are my drunk shoes, mi borracho muchacho en espacio
con las bolas sin fin
A grabar immortalidades mordiendo
A mascar, a no mas, tal paz

In el bosque de mi nombre
Me pierdo en mentiras queridas en pasados mercados, sudores de alma
Waiting for the exact time to cover the wares
the books on sidewalk tables or the Cafe counters so long there you'll laugh to see the original color campion
mansion marron
Soy rey de mi ser

En mi page bomba y plena fall in love with each other every other day
The day in between their busy with their theys
Work at it, send each other rhymes not even crickets combined can repeat amor amor amor dulsura pura
Ven q te creo
Amor sabor tambor your belly's my castle your noche mi pan

Me pierdo en skyscraper zurcos, me falta el chaleco moral,
me meo los viernes, los cheques me miran como perritos sin perra
Las perlas sonrisas con sus latigos sus trampas de mi compa
Vamos q va llover
The rent is wrong, the basements floods, los mares malditos me mandan, son dueños de mis duendes, cobardes alcaldes alzando banderas de miedo, yo soy tambien el estraño de mi ser
Me como lo mas facil, los postres en potreros, si pudiera me como el camello mismo de tu desierto, de camel nails of each verse burns lung holes in my songs, mi rumor mi nocion

Si supieras la sopa que tu eres, vos vosotra voz de mil luceros
the amount of your coins en Adela's on Bimbo's C
en piernas en sumos sumando lo q no puedo
Diosa de tormentas no sabes cuantas nubes te e contado
No sabes de donde te vi ni el porque de mi mal

Pero va a llover, siempre simple yo ver

JAVIER ZAMORA

Pericos Are Green Salvadoran Parakeets That Live In Igloo-Like Nests Made Of Mud Till They're Sold As Pets For Their Ability To Repeat Their Names

Walk down the hammock, Chepito—
the family parakeet name

baptized on our pericos since I was named
after Abuelito. Chepito is slang

for little José. Chepito, your name unfurls
your clipped wings,

color of unripe mangos. Your caged chirping
sequesters song into syllables,

syllables into words. Chepito, repeat our name.
Unfurl. Not for La Virgen

de Guadalupe, not for her sun-ray halo,
color of the tiny feathers

above your beak. Return to your nest.
Chepito, don't rest

till our names are Nathuatl chants.
Not Spanish bells.

Not American pop-songs. Fly, fly
if you wish.

Fly if you wish when I call your name.
Your feet tick-tick-ticking

down the hammock toward my hands
offering little pecks of dough.

RAFAEL JESUS GONZALEZ

Ave de barro negro

Un pajarito de barro negro,
la tierra dulce de Oaxaca —
ves como estira el pescuezo
y te pone el pico
como para pedir un beso.

Manos zapotecas
sabias en los encantos de la arcilla
le cavaron un gran vacío en el pecho
para que le pongas corazón de aliento.

Pone en la base los labios
y por este agujerito
sopla un resoplido redondo
para que cante bonito.

Y en una tierra lejana
donde los colores son mudos
acaricia su lustre negro
que es prisma de un dios oculto.

Bird of Black Clay (Tr.)

A little bird of black clay,
the sweet earth of Oaxaca —
see how it stretches its neck
& offers its beak
as if to ask for a kiss.

Zapotec hands
wise in the spells of the clay
carved a great space in its breast
in wait for a heart of breath.

Put your lips to the base
& through this small hole
blow a round puff
to give it its song.

& in a far land
where the colors are dumb,
stroke its black luster;
it is the prism of a hidden god.

ELIZAM ESCOBAR

Pensando

. . . desde C. Bernstein

mis gatos
mis gatos negros
mis coquíes muertos por mis gatos negros
mis lagartijas grises ayunadas
mis acerolas podridas
mis aguacates
mis dientes comiendo aguacates
mi nariz rota
mi nariz oliendo mis limones
mis toronjas con ginebra
mis ojos vegetarianos
mi correa de cuero

tu perro ladrándole al cartero
tus labios fumando
tu tabaco metiéndose en mis ojos vegetarianos
tu email
tu electricidad

mis árboles molestando al vecino
mi vecino haciendo ruido
mi vecino apestando a perro
mi pistola
mi vecindario lleno de hojas
secas, podridas, etéreas
mi carro haciendo ruido
chasqueando, estornudando, contaminando

tus gatos con sida
mi rifle de agua
que los persigue
tus uñas con hongo
tu hongo creciendo
mi hongo creciendo
mis mosquitos jodiendo
mi agua subiendo
mi luz
mi alquiler
mi sueldo bajando
mis ganas subiendo
mi navaja

mis gatos verdes
mis gatos verdes mirando a mis gatos negros
mis pensamientos
mirando, oyendo, disparando
mis estudiantes mirando oyendo
mis gatos negros pensando
mis sombreros pensando
mis anteojos pensando
mi sueño
mi pensamiento

mis árboles pensando
mis toronjas, mis limones, mis medallas
mi tijera
mi bigote
mi mosca
mi celular
mi pantalla
mis imágenes
las iguanas
los monos sueltos
los monógamos
los filántropos
los microbióticos
los chimpancés
los poddles
el dengue
el gaseoducto verde chatrés
pensando

mi navaja
mi jabón de menta
mi alcoholado
mi cubalibre
mi cuchara
mis dedos
mi pene
mi peinilla
mi dolor
mi risa

mis sarcasmos
mis orgasmos

tus jabones antibacteriales
tus leyes jodidas
tus recortes
tus despidos
tu cinismo
tu demagogia
tus martillazos
tu gordura
tu joroba
tus vivos muertos
tus ciudadanos trincos
tus trincos ciudadanos
tus comemierderías

tus democracias podridas
tus acomodos razonables
tus ejercicios
tu jodido oxígeno
tu petróleo
tu jelly
tus alkaseltsers
aspirinas, kotexs, pastillitas
tus anuncios
tus zodiacos
tus sobras
tu mierda
mi pistola
pensando

(11.IX.10)

Thinking (Tr.)

. . . from C. Bernstein

my cats
my black cats
my coquís killed by my black cats
my gray famished lizards
my rotten acerolas
my avocados
my teeth eating avocados
my broken nose
my nose smelling my lemons
my grapefruit and gin
my vegetarian eyes
my leather strap

your dog barking at the mailman
your lips smoking
your tobacco getting in my vegetarian eyes
your email
your electricity

my trees bothering the neighbor
my neighbor making noise
my neighbor reeking of dog
my gun
my neighborhood filled with leaves
dry, rotten, ethereal

my car making noise
cracking, sneezing, contaminating

your cats with AIDS
my water gun
that chases them
your nails with fungus
your fungus growing
my fungus growing
my mosquitoes fucking
my water rising
my light
my rent
my salary shrinking
my wants growing
my knife

my green cats
my green cats looking at my black cats
my thoughts
looking, hearing, shooting
my students looking hearing
my black cats thinking
my hats thinking
my glasses thinking

my dream
my thought

my trees thinking
my grapefruit, my lemons, my medalla beers
my scissors
my moustache
my fly
my cell
my screen
my images
the iguanas
the loose monkeys
the monogamists
the philanthropists
the macrobiotics
the chimpanzees
the poodles
breakbone fever
the chartreuse green pipeline
thinking

my knife
my mint soap
my rubbing alcohol
my cuba libre
my spoon
my fingers
my prick
my hair pick
my pain

my laugh
my sarcasms
my orgasms

your antibacterial soaps
your fucked up laws
your cuts
your lay-offs
your cynicism
your demagoguery
your hammers
your fat
your humpback
your living dead
your stiff citizens
your citizens stiff
your shit-eating
your rotten democracies
your reasonable accommodations
your exercises
your fucking oxygen
your oil
your jelly
your alka-seltzers
asprins, kotexes, little pills
your announcements
your horiscopes
your leftovers
your shit
my gun
thinking

(9/11/10)

Translated by Adam Wier.

The Puertoricanization of a Nuyorican

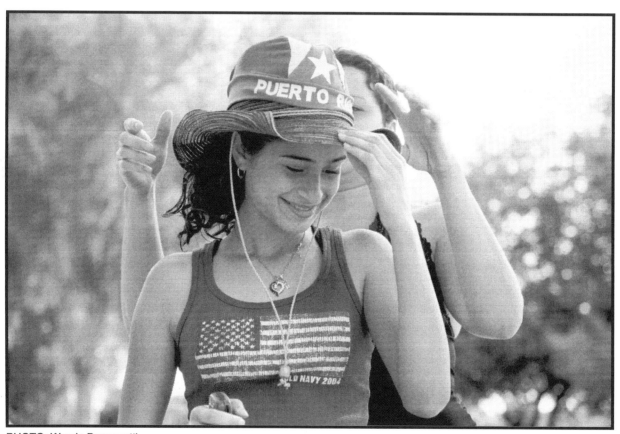

PHOTO: Wanda Benvenutti
"Two Flags," (24 x 36 in.) black and white giclée photographic print, Copyright ©2005
(The image was created in Chandler, Arizona at the annual Gran Boricua Picnic.)

I SPEAK TO YOU NOW AS A BORN-AGAIN PUERTO RICAN – not in the Biblical sense, but rather in a historical and cultural sense. Having been born and raised in El Barrio, East Harlem, New York City, I say this after visiting the island of Vieques, Puerto Rico on several occasions, most recently just two weeks ago as part of a New York delegation led by Assemblywoman Margarita Lopez of the Lower East Side. There were over 120 people in our group, representing people from various walks of life. There were, of course, several Puerto Ricans; some born here in New York City, and others born elsewhere throughout the United States. There were those who, for them this would be their first visit to Puerto Rico. Also, there were people of European descent, political activists, concerned and curious citizens, young and old, including a large number of progressive non-hispanic senior citizens. I say this to introduce you to the conglomeration of humanity that made up our delegation, which I found quite spirited and fascinating.

But this was not my first trip to Puerto Rico, nor to Vieques. In 1975, at the age of 25, I set out on that historic adventure with my good friend of many years and fellow poet, El Reverendo Pedro Pietri. Unlike me, Pedro was born in Ponce and has always been very close to his family and his cultural roots. The history of my family was immigrating to the United States and making a clean break from everyone they left behind. As a kid growing up in New York City, I never really knew many of my cousins, aunts and uncles on the island. I remember visiting my great grandmother and grandmother on my father's side that lived here in New York City. I enjoyed their company very much, but never really felt anything Puerto Rican about them, except that they were from Puerto Rico. For a variety of reasons, I didn't get to meet my relatives until February of this year, when it became my duty to escort my mother to Puerto Rico in order to identify and claim the body of my Aunt Aida, my mother's eldest sister who had died alone in her home in Rio Piedras, and whom I had never known. It seemed that everyone I knew growing up was born in the United States.

(cont'd. pg. 288)

JESÚS PAPOLETO MELÉNDEZ

THE PUERTORICANIZATION
Jesús Papoleto Meléndez

(cont'd from pg. 287)

To be sure, it's a little known fact that the Nuyorican poets' movement was by and large started by Puerto Ricans who were born in Puerto Rico and transplanted to New York City as children. Poets Louis Reyes Rivera, Sandra María Esteves, Felipe Luciano and myself are original Nuyorican poets who were born in the United States. Everyone else who lays claim to the Nuyorican experience as a poet in those days, was born, and/or to some extent, raised in some part of Puerto Rico. Pedro Pietri, Victor Hernández Cruz, Miguel Algarín, Miguel Piñero, Lucky Cienfuegos, José Angel Figueroa, Americo Casiano Jr. and others, have Puerto Rican birth certificates, giving them a direct connection to Puerto Rico. There is something that they remember, can recall, even lay claim to that Puerto Ricans born in the United States cannot do.

I've argued this point before with native-born Puerto Ricans. In fact, they resent the implication that Puerto Ricans born in the U.S. are not by definition patriots of Puerto Rico. I always believed that if we are politically conscious enough, it's up us to seek those connections and make them on our own terms.

When I was just becoming a teenager during the 1960's, I don't remember ever seeing a Puerto Rican flag. I was as American as I now dislike remembering it. I was once very proud of the sad fact that my birthday fell nearly on Flag Day (America's Flag Day), and for a great many years now, I'm glad it did not. Yet, I can say that such was the extent of my detachment from being Puerto Rican that I was disappointed to learn that the Puerto Rican flag didn't look like the Cuban flag, because I liked the placement of the colors on Cuba's flag better than Puerto Rico's flag.

My first cultural and ethnic experience growing up in El Barrio was meeting my neighbors, who were black as well as black Puerto Ricans, although back then we were all called "colored." So growing up in El Barrio was a "black" thing for me, and with the absence of my father from my life (who was also black), I had no one I could go to and ask questions about my world. There was no adult male I could turn to, perhaps in Spanish and ask, "Hey, Daddy, what's that there?" But my black friends taught me everything I needed to know, which helped define and defend myself in this society. This was my mainline into American society. This was my reality. This is how I grew up, and came to understand many things about who I am and my place in America. These loving people with skin color like me took me in, accepted me and "I" became "we."

Today I claim "Nuyoricanism" as mine because it more clearly defines my reality; the reality of a man born in a strange country, and however reluctant I may accept that — it also attaches me culturally to my people, my heritage and ancestry, which has been "infected" with American culture. This is because Puerto Ricans living on the mainland struggle with this two-world thing: Puerto Rico vs. the United States.

When I recently made the trip to Vieques, it was as a Puerto Rican born and raised in the United States, but not as an American. When I think about it, my travels to the west of this country, to Arizona, California, Colorado, as well as through parts of Mexico; Oaxaca ,Veracruz, Tijuana (where I lived for a few years), even in Amsterdam and Italy, were all conducted with this perspective as a Puerto Rican born in the U.S. I never stopped being Puerto Rican, but over the years, I found myself constantly discovering something new about myself, with my cultural heritage at different points in my life teaching me to embrace my "Puerto Ricaness."

I say that when a "Nuyorican" adopts the flag of Puerto Rico, its history, even just the flavor of being Puerto Rican, this is a big thing, a very big thing indeed. When I look at the many faces during the Puerto Rican Day Parade, and people are waving flags all over the place with so much pride – I find myself asking: "What is a Puerto Rican?" How many of those smiling, flag-waving individuals would be willing to fight to the death to protect, to liberate Puerto Rico? These are some of the many things I pondered on my last trip to Vieques, I found a lot of these ideas crashing down on me, and it was during this visit that I felt like I was visiting my long-lost aunt's house. Everyone was somehow related to me. People would come up to me and say, "¿Y de que parte eres tu?" ¿De que Meléndez's eres tu?" I was forced to recollect names of relatives whose names I haven't uttered in years. It was beautiful. And when I couldn't answer their questions because I just didn't know and felt sad and lonely like a lost child, instead of rejection there was always someone to forgive me, to hug and embrace me and make me feel like a true Puerto Rican.

Who knows, maybe one day I'll return to Vieques to live, on an island that over the years transformed from a sugar cane plantation, to a U.S. Navy Base back to its original state, a national wildlife refuge Like Vieques, I've made my own transformation, in learning about myself during different stages in my life, I've managed to get in touch with all of my roots: being black, a native-New Yorker, steeped in my newfound "Puerto Rican-ness," a reborn Puerto Rican, all on my own terms. I love being Puerto Rican! ▢

MAGALY QUINONES

Distinta Siempre

Quizás era la puesta al día del yo conmigo misma,
O el encuentro del Arte como agenda de vida,
lo que me dio, enclavada en el Caribe, carta de residencia.
O tal vez fue la unción, la ingenua ráfaga de proporciones míticas
lo que me enloqueció—siendo aún muy joven —
como un Quijote en sus novelas de caballería,
y me indujo a forjar mi propia crónica.
Quizás fueron los versos patrióticos de Julia, la piedad de Gabriela,
la insoslayable libertad en Juana, el desafío en Delmira o Alfonsina,
lo que me hizo buscar, sintiendo a América,
un nuevo modo de cantarle al mundo, una nueva cadencia.
Lo cierto es que crecí marcando rutas,
Que abandoné el discurso de Neruda y me atreví a llorar como Vallejo,
que me inventé una máscara para atraer la lluvia
y entré al Arcano de los cinco cielos rememorando a Arguedas.
Lo cierto es que escribir, como escribo,
perseguida sin tregua por el fantasma de mi propia casa,
regada por la sangre de tres razas, me garantiza la sobrevivencia.
Quizás, por eso escribo desde el recuerdo de los que se fueron,
con las mismas palabras pero, distinta siempre,
dando forma a la muerte con la vida.

Always Different (Tr.)

Maybe it was the updating of the self with my own self,
Or the encounter of Art as an agenda of life,
that gave me, buried deep in the Caribbean, a residence card.
Or perhaps it was the unction, the ingenuous burst of mythic proportions
that made me crazy—being still very young —
like a Quixote in his novels of chivalry,
and induced me to forge my own chronicle.
Maybe they were the patriotic verses of Julia, the piety of Gabriela,
the inevitable liberty of Juana, the defiance in Delmira or Alfonsina,
which made me search for, feeling America,
a new way of singing to the world, a new cadence.
The truth is that I grew by marking routes,
That I abandoned the discourse of Neruda and would dare to cry like Vallejo,
that I invented for myself a mask to attract the rain
and entered the Esotericism of the five heavens remembering Arguedas.
The truth is that writing, how I write,
persecuted without respite by the ghost of my own house,

watered by the blood of three races, guaranteed my survival.
Perhaps, because of that, I write in memory of those that have gone,
with the same words but, always different,
giving form to death with life.

El Reino De Los Pocos

Yo soy de los desangrados, traigo a un hombre de la mano,
traigo a una mujer de la mano, a un niño sobre mi corazón.
Soy de los que se rebelan.
Nací en todas las casas pobres, caminé sobre todas las carencias,
ahogada en la garra e un hambre que no me dejó leer versos.

Me desnutrí en La Perla de la Vieja San Juan,
agonicé en El Barrio de la Nueva York,
me descompuse en Las Cloacas de la eterna París,
me hice mujer en Chile, envejecí en las ruinas del Perú.
Sigo siendo de ellos, de los simples, de los irreverentes iletrados.
Huyo en cada hombre que huye tras un golpe brutal de la derecha,
en cada mercenario que deserta,
defiendo cada espacio, quiero consolar cada lágrima.

Porque yo soy de ellos, de los más, de los muchos,
y celebro la vida aún cuando me ha angustiado
que no me consultaran para traerme al mundo,
¡ al reino de los pocos!

The Kingdom of the Few (Tr.)

I am one of the bloodless, I carry a man in my hand,
I carry a woman in my hand, a child over my heart.
I am one of those who rebel.
I was born in every poor house, I walked over all paucities,
Strangled by the claw and a hunger that forbid me from read verses.

I grew malnourished in the La Perla de La Vieja San Juan,
I endured agony in El Barrio of New York,
I felt queasy in Las Cloaca of the eternal Paris,
I became a woman in Chile, I became old in the ruins of Peru.
I still belong to them, to the simple ones, to the irreverent illiterates.
I escape in every man that runs after a brutal hit from the right,
in every mercenary that deserts,
defending each space, I want to console every tear.

Because I am belong to them, to most, to many,
and I celebrate life even when it has caused me anguish
that they don't ask for me to bring me to the world,
to the kingdom of the few!

Translated by Adam Wier.

MULTICULTURALISMO E IDENTIDAD: UNA PERSPECTIVA PERSONAL

Multiculturalism and Identity: A Personal Perspective

Translated by Joanna Morales

TRES ASPECTOS DEL
multiculturalismo que me son de interés y que deseo comentar brevemente son: su importancia en las políticas culturales, educativas y electorales de Nueva York, su relación con el tema de la identidad, y mi propio trasfondo multicultural como persona y como escritora. Estos comentarios son más una declaración de mis preferencias que una intrincada exposición

(cont'd. pg. 292)

THREE ASPECTS OF
multiculturalism that I find interesting and wish to briefly comment on are: its importance in cultural, educational, and electoral policies of New York, its relationship with the issue of identity, and my own multicultural background as a person and as a writer. These commentaries act more as a declaration of my preferences than an elaborate presentation of its arguments. I have decided to write

(cont'd. pg. 294)

MYRNA NIEVES

Multiculturalismo e identidad
Myrna Nieves

(cont'd from pg. 291)

de sus argumentos. Me he decidido a escribir estas breves notas sobre el tema porque me atrae el concepto de herencias múltiples, si bien un compatriota me dijo una vez que el vocablo multiculturalismo no es para nosotros [los puertorriqueños], si no para "los otros"; "nosotros siempre hemos sido multiculturales," añadió.

A nivel actual en Estados Unidos, un aspecto del multiculturalismo que de inmediato interesa es su carácter político en Nueva York. Hay un trasfondo histórico que creo es vital al desarrollo del multiculturalismo en la experiencia latina en la Ciudad. La emigración masiva puertorriqueña en los años de 1940 y 1950 provocó una respuesta hostil del sistema de educación y el sistema social de Nueva York por la dificultad en absorber la gran cantidad de gente que llegó en esas décadas y que poseían una cultura, raza y lengua diferentes a la cultura predominante, white/black, de la Ciudad. El intercambio cultural estuvo marcado en esas décadas por la tensión y los derechos de vivienda y educación se tuvieron que luchar física (las fronteras de las gangas en los barrios) y legalmente (bilingüismo), algo que igualmente necesitaron hacer los chicanos en la costa oeste. La llegada de otros grupos en las décadas subsiguientes, en particular los dominicanos en Washington Heights y los cubanos y suramericanos, continuó la presión para que el sistema electoral y los currículos en las escuelas sean más inclusivos y las culturas latinas se vean como parte de la realidad viviente de Estados Unidos. Creo en afirmar la identidad, cualquiera que sea. El que yo afirme mi identidad no significa que niego la tuya o la de otros. Pienso que el gran reto interno de este país es la dinámica relación entre las identidades (nacionales/raciales/sexuales) y pertenecer a la vez a un todo (Estados Unidos como nación). Nueva York para mí es un gran experimento en la paz mundial, y si aquí es posible que convivamos todas las razas y culturas de la Tierra (en Queens nada más se hablan más de 100 lenguas), ello puede arrojar una esperanza de que alguna vez se pueda vivir en un mundo en paz. [Y no me refiero solamente al cese de hostilidades militares, harto obvias, sino también a detener la guerra contra los derechos de la mujer—como los derechos reproductivos y el cese de la prostitución forzada—, detener el abuso a los animales, afirmar los derechos de los niños y promover la tolerancia a las diferencias de preferencia sexual]. El multiculturalismo es un paso importante en respetar y ayudar al Otro, porque reconoce y valora lo que es diferente.

A nivel personal, me crié en un pueblo pequeño de Puerto Rico y mis tempranas influencias de otras culturas estuvieron marcadas por la familia, la Iglesia, la escuela y la música. Los santos de la Iglesia, el Papa y los almanaques de Jesús con mudras hindúes me hablaban de Roma y el lejano oriente. Los almanaques eran ilustraciones adornadas además, con ruinas de coliseos, leones y camellos en arenas de desiertos; todo ello mezclado en un cuadro indisoluble. En mi ambiente tenía así mismo su influencia la presencia norteamericana de la Base Ramey en Aguadilla, donde mi padre trabajaba y cuyo efecto era complejo: positivo y negativo a la vez; sugerían la guerra y nuestra dependencia política, pero también, por los libros que mi padre traía, conocí a Hemingway, Pearl S. Buck y Faulkner. En esta etapa las figuras femeninas del círculo familiar fueron importantes; y su influencia siempre estuvo marcada por la subversión; es decir, me interesaba lo diferente, lo que no se acomodaba al tejido que yo percibía como la cultura oficial del pueblo donde nací. Mi abuela española me hablaba de árboles, frutas y tradiciones canarias y de niña aprendí a cantar romances completos y refranes de moros y cristianos. Más interesante aún, me provocó curiosidad sus cuentos del mundo de las brujas, que eran mujeres independientes que tomaban iniciativa de separarse de la moral social y hacían viajes nocturnos: volaban y podían ir a otros sitios de noche (de ahí en parte mi interés por el mundo onírico). Muchos años después escribí la obra *Libreta de sueños,* que es un diario de mis sueños. Mi madre era maestra, una mujer bien leída, a quien le gustaba el arte y leía los escritores franceses en su idioma natal. De alguna manera la posibilidad de los viajes de las brujas y visitar otras culturas se mezcló en mi cabeza y tuvo como resultado mi dedicación al sueño, los viajes reales que he realizado y el haber venido a Nueva York a completar mis estudios.

Mi otra abuela contribuyó la herencia africana. La influencia africana, evidente a nivel físico, era más solapada en el área cultural. Mi abuela rezaba el rosario y en la pared tenía una Dolorosa y un Corazón de Jesús, pero también, en la mesa de la sala tenía una Santa Bárbara enorme y en su dormitorio una colección espiritista abierta con trozos de *El Espiritismo en su asiento* de Allan Kardec. Aprendí de ella que la cultura nunca es homogénea sino mezclada y que hay capas que permanecen soterradas por los prejuicios. La persistencia de las divinidades africanas me mostraron cómo somos capaces de transportar raíces culturales más allá de los mares, de un continente a otro, y que sobrevivan a la esclavitud y la opresión. Veía lo trágicamente hermoso de esa persistencia y gesto de voluntad. Una vez (como en los cuentos infantiles), mi abuela me

dio un gran regalo: unas oraciones para la protección y una lista de talismanes para la suerte que debía buscar. En Nueva York y Río Piedras dediqué algunos veranos a preguntar por los talismanes en las Ferias del movimiento New Age y sobretodo en las botánicas (enterándome de paso en El Barrio que eran un judío y un puertorriqueño los que los manufacturaban o importaban y distribuían). Ha sido muy interesante esta pequeña investigación, pues ella revela un origen egipcio, donde predominaba la divinidad Isis, pero también judío con Salomón; y quizás árabe por su énfasis astronómico en las constelaciones.

Otra influencia notable en mi niñez fue la música y el cine; a mi padre y mi tío les gustaba la música cubana y latinoamericana y un poco de música clásica: crecí, junto a Daniel Santos y Felipe Rodríguez, entre la música de la Sonora Matancera y el Sexteto la Playa, además de Falla y otros que no recuerdo. A mi madre le gustaba la música de Rafael Hernández y los tangos de Gardel, que cantaba constantemente. El tango "Volver" con la mención de lejanas luces de una ciudad me fascinaba, por la posibilidad de un mundo urbano cosmopolita; "Fumando espero" sugería una mujer esperando sola a un hombre en un apartamento y por lo tanto no era casada (en mi pueblo todo el mundo -por lo menos en principio-decía que las mujeres estaban casadas o eran vírgenes o eran prostitutas) y pensé en la libertad de otros modos de convivencia sexual donde la preferencia individual tuviera prioridad. Y la asocié a culturas distantes y urbanas. Las películas mexicanas que iba a ver en el único cine del pueblo—con Pedro Infante, Miguel Aceves Mejías, María Félix y Silvia Pinal—suscitaron un gran interés en el cine, la revolución y México. Siento un gran cariño por este país y su gente y lo he visitado en varias ocasiones. De ahí que haya estudiado las culturas aborígenes de América (maya, inca, azteca, taína y lakota) con persistente fascinación e interés. Mi bisabuela, madre de mi abuelo por parte de padre, era una india caraqueña de la cual lo único que supe era que era una mujer hermosa de largas trenzas, que vendía quincalla y se llamaba Irene. Recuerdo que cuando niña se descubrieron en mi pueblo algunas de las cuevas más grandes de América, las cuevas de Camuy, con sus petroglifos y río subterráneo; y mis amigos del vecino pueblo de Lares me empezaron a hablar con palabras taínas que hablaban sus abuelas y que nunca había escuchado. De Lares vino también la conciencia nacionalista, con sus historias de valor e integridad, y sus sufrimientos, pues mi madre me hablaba de los arrestos de mujeres con los niños pequeños en los brazos. Fue una experiencia de sobriedad y seriedad sin precedentes.

La literatura fue fundamental para mí: Gabriela Mistral, Palés Matos, Julia de Burgos y Clara Lair fueron mis primeras lecturas. En general mis favoritos en la adolescencia y temprana juventud fueron Clara Lair con su mundo sexual y misterioso, Palés con su irónico y rítmico lenguaje de melaza (mi pueblo era un pueblo cañero) y Luis Lloréns Torres con sus despedidas desgarradoras al terruño familiar. Una enorme influencia tuvieron en mí Edgar Allan Poe con sus mansiones tenebrosas y su fascinación con la muerte y García Márquez con su arte de contar y su mundo fantástico, no tanto porque este último fuera esencialmente irreal, sino porque el pueblo donde yo crecí era exactamente como Macondo y a mí me sorprendió que alguien de Colombia pudiera retratar a Camuy tan fielmente. Borges y su claridad intelectual para la imaginación fue siempre fundamental, pero él, así como García Lorca, Rulfo y los artistas del absurdo que luego me fascinaron, eran ya lecturas universitarias.

Actualmente, la convivencia en Nueva York me ha puesto en contacto la historia de los derechos civiles y el Black Power y el Puerto Rican Power; el movimiento de los hippies y la contracultura de los años de 1960-70, en que participé de alguna manera. De notable interés en el presente son las culturas y filosofías orientales: aquí se comenta la posibilidad de diversas evoluciones espirituales y futuras culturas galácticas; se practican yoga y meditación. Soy budista y me atraen las culturas de la India y el Japón. Por otra parte, tengo que mencionar que enseño en Boricua College y en el contacto con el mundo puertorriqueño de Nueva York he descubierto que en esta Ciudad se puede experimentar también el redescubrimiento de lo propio (que a veces se daba por sentado en el país natal), y la oportunidad para el examen crítico de los valores de mi cultura. Vivo en Williamsburg, un lugar de convergencias puertorriqueña y latina, italiana, polaca y judía hasídica y ahora están los palestinos y árabes con sus tiendas de productos naturales y sus dulces saturados de miel. En los primeros años de este siglo, pude sobrevivir el dolor y la confusión de la destrucción en el 9/11 de las Torres Gemelas que veía desde mi ventana y marchar en las protestas contra la Guerra a Iraq y la militarización de Vieques. En los últimos tiempos, soy testigo de una enorme invasión "gentrificadora" en mi vecindario: vinieron los "yuppies" con sus computadoras y sus boutiques; y veo cómo los se pasan los días enteros en los cafés con internet, mientras los protestantes del Occupy Wall Street denuncian las desigualdades obvias de este mundo que sorprende y aterra.

La migración me ha dado una pena y un gozo: por una parte la separación de toda mi familia, que cargo como

un dolorcito en el alma (a pesar de los viajes que realizo constantemente), y por otra, como decía Edward Said, los placeres del exilio: la expansión de mi vida al convivir con todas las culturas de la tierra. ¿Qué es todo lo señalado? ¿Historia personal, retrato de una época, recuento de lazos de continuidad y ruptura, identidad fraccionada o "plural"? . . . Difícil decir, por lo menos para mí, que escribo hoy bajo el refugio de esta "perspectiva personal". Recuerdo que el poeta Pedro Pietri, con todos sus rasgos surrealistas o del absurdo, cuando le preguntaban quién o cómo se identificaba, siempre decía: "Yo soy de Ponce" . . . Lo que yo sí sé, es que este conjunto me ha dado la oportunidad de explorar mi ser. Pienso, en fin, que quien se conoce a sí mismo y aprecia otras culturas, puede inclinarse a celebrar la diversidad humana y sentir cómo le crece adentro la determinación de luchar por la paz para sí mismo y para los demás. ◻

Multiculturalism and Identity (Tr.)
Myrna Nieves

(cont'd from pg. 291)

these brief notes on this issue because I am attracted to the concept of multiple heredities, although a compatriot once told me that the word "multiculturalism" was not made for our use (the Puerto Ricans), but rather for "the others"; "we have always been multicultural," he added.

Currently in the U.S., an aspect of multiculturalism that is interesting is its political nature in New York. There is an historical background that I believe is vital in the development of multiculturalism in the Latino experience of the city. The massive wave of Puerto Rican migration in the 1940s and 1950s provoked a hostile reaction in the educational and social system of New York as the city struggled to absorb the large number of people that arrived. The struggle was intensified as this wave of new immigrants brought with them a culture, race, and language different than that of the predominant culture (white/black) of the city. The cultural exchange during those decades was marked by tension. Housing rights, and education were fought for on both a physical (with gangs fighting for possession of neighborhood borders) and legal scale (bilingualism), Similar actions that also became a necessity for Chicanos on the West coast. The arrival of other immigrant groups in the subsequent decades, particularly the Dominicans that settled in Washington Heights, the Cubans and South Americans, pressured the electoral system and school curriculum to become more inclusive and to consider Latino cultures an active part of the living reality of the United States. I believe in affirming

identity, whatever that may be. The fact that I affirm my own identity does not signify that I deny yours or that of others. I think that the great internal challenge of this country is working with the dynamic relationship between affirming identities (national/racial/sexual) while simultaneously attempting to belong to a whole (the United States) as a nation. To me, New York is a giant experiment in the quest for world peace, and if it becomes possible for all races and cultures of the world to coexist peacefully here (in Queens alone over 100 languages are spoken), there is hope that world peace can be achieved on a macro scale, I am not only speaking of halting military hostilities, which is fairly obvious, but also ending the war against women's rights—including reproductive rights and forced prostitution—ending animal abuse, strengthening children's rights and promoting tolerance for different sexual preferences. Multiculturalism is an important step in respecting and aiding the "Other" since it recognizes and values which is different.

On a more personal level, I was raised in a small town in Puerto Rico and my earliest encounters with other cultures were through my family, the Church, school, and music. The saints of the Church, the Pope and the almanacs with the image of Jesus with Hindu inspired hand gestures (mudras) spoke to me of Rome and the faraway orient. They were also illustrations adorned with ruins of coliseums, lions and camels in deserts; all mixed in an indissoluble portrait. In my environment there were also North American influences particularly in the form of the Ramey Base (where my father worked) stationed in Aguadilla and whose effect was very complex: simultaneously positive and negative. The Base hinted at the effects of war and our political dependence, but it also provided books my father brought home; introducing me to Hemingway, Pearl S. Buck and Faulkner. In this stage of my life the feminine figures of the family circle were important and their influence was always marked by subversion. All that was different interested me; that which did not accommodate to what I perceived as the mainstream culture of my hometown. My Spanish grandmother spoke of trees, fruits, and traditions of the Canary Islands. As a young girl, I learned to sing entire *Romances* and proverbs about Christians and Moors. Even more interesting, my curiosity was peaked by her tales of a world of witches, who were independent women that deliberately disassociated themselves from social morality and embarked on nocturnal trips: they flew and could travel to other places during night. Hence, my interest in the dream world. Many years later I wrote the book, *Libreta de Suenos (Book of Dreams),* a diary of my dreams. My mother was a teacher; a well-read

woman, who enjoyed art and read French writers in their native language. In some way, the possibility of witches making trips and the possibility of visiting other cultures combined in my head and resulted in my dedication to dreams, the actual trips I have taken, and my trip to New York to complete my education.

My other grandmother contributed to my African heritage. The African influence, evident on a physical level, was subtler on a cultural level. My grandmother would pray the rosary and had images of the Sacred Heart and the Virgin on her wall. However, she also had on her living room table a massive statue of Saint Barbara and a spiritualist collection with snippets of *El espiritismo en su asiento* by Allan Kardec in her bedroom. I learned from her that culture is never homogenous but rather a mixture and possess layers that remain buried by prejudice. The persistant existence of African deities showed me how it is possible to transport cultural roots across the seas, from one continent to another, and survive the turmoil of slavery and oppression. I saw the tragic beauty of that persistence and gesture of willpower. Once upon a time (like in the childhood fairy tales), my grandmother gave me an amazing gift; prayers for protection and a list of talismans for luck that I had to find. In New York and Río Piedras I dedicated some summers to asking around for the talismans in fairs of the New Age movement and most of all in *botanicas* stores (finding out in passing, in El Barrio, that it was a Jew and Puerto Rican that manufactured, and/or imported and distributed them). This investigation was interesting because it revealed the talismans to be of Egyptian origin, during the time of the goddess Isis, but also Jewish in nature, with Solomon, and maybe even Arabic because of its astronomical emphasis on the constellations.

Another notable influence on my childhood was music and cinema; my father and uncle enjoyed Cuban and Latin American music, and a bit of classical as well. I grew up listening to Daniel Santos and Felipe Rodriguez, with music from "Sonora Matancera" and "Sexteto la Playa" along with Falla and a few others I cannot recall. My mother liked music by Rafael Hernandez and tango by Gardel and sang their songs constantly. The tango song "Volver" (Return), which mentioned faraway lights of a city, fascinated me because of the potential existence of an urban cosmopolitan world. "Fumando espero" ("While smoking I wait") was a song that spoke of a woman waiting alone for a man in her apartment, who was apparently not married, (in my town everyone—at least many years ago—would say that women were either married, or if not, a virgin or a prostitute) and I would think about the freedom

that could be found in other forms of sexual cohabitation where individual preferences took priority and associated it with distant and urban cultures. The Mexican movies I would watch, in the only movie theater in town—movies with Pedro Infante, Miguel Aceves Mejía, María Félix and Silvia Pinal—aroused in me a great interest in cinema, the revolution, and in Mexico. I feel great affection for this country and its people, and I have visited it on various occasions. There I have studied the aboriginal cultures of America (the Maya, Inca, Aztec, Taína, and Lakota) with great perseverance and interest. My great-grandmother (my paternal grandfather's mother), was of Indian descent (from Caracas) of who all I knew was that she possessed great beauty, with long tresses, and sold trinkets for a living. Her name was Irene. I remember that as a child, in my town, some of the largest caves of America, the Camuy Caves, were discovered, with their petroglyphs and subterranean rivers. My friends of the neighboring town of Lares began to speak using words of the forgotten Taino dialect, words once spoken by their grandmothers and consequently unknown to me. From the town of Lares also emerged the nationalist consciousness, involving tales of valor and integrity. These tales also spoke of suffering, for my mother used to speak of women being arrested with small children in their arms. It was an experience in soberness and seriousness without precedence.

Literature was fundamental for me: Gabriela Mistral, Palés Matos, Julia de Burgos, and Clara Lair were my first taste of literature. In general, my favorites during my adolescence were Clara Lair, with her world of sexuality and mystery, Palés, with his irony and rhythmic molasses-like language (my town was a sugarcane town) and finally Luis Lloréns Torres, with his heart-rending farewells to one's native land. Edgar Allan Poe, with his frightening mansions and fascination with death, and Garcia Márquez with his art of storytelling and his fantastical world were great influences on my life. Not because the latter was essentially unreal, but rather because my own town was fashioned quite like Macondo and I was rather shocked that a Colombian native could recount Camuy that accurately. Borges's intellectual clarity for the imagination was always fundamental, but like Lorca, Rulfo, and writers of the absurd movement that later fascinated me, they were primarily discovered in my college years.

Currently, living in New York has put in me contact with civil rights history, the Black Power and Puerto Rican movements, and the hippy and counterculture movements of the 1960s and 1970s. Of notable interest to me, presently, are Eastern philosophies and cultures, which focus on the possibility of diverse spiritual evolutions and future

galactic cultures. Yoga and meditation have fascinated me. I am a Buddhist and I am attracted to Hindu and Japanese cultures. Alternatively, I'd also like to mention that I teach at Boricua College and the connection with the Puerto Rican world of New York has allowed me to discover that, in this city, it is possible to experience the rediscovery of my culture, which was taken for granted in my birth place and to critically exam my culture's values. I live in Williamsburg, Brooklyn, a veritable cauldron of ethnicity, with Puerto Ricans, Italians, Polish and Jews. Now the Palestinians and Arabs can also be found here, with their stores stocked with organic products and honey-saturated sweets. Throughout the years I was able to survive the pain and confusion of the September 11 destruction of the Twin Towers of the World Trade Center, which I viewed from my window, and I marched in protests against the war in Iraq and the militarization of Vieques in Puerto Rico. In the recent years, I have been privy to the "gentrification" of my neighborhood: the introduction of the "yuppies" with their laptops and boutique shops, sitting for days at a time in cafes with Wi-Fi while protestors of Occupy Wall Street denounced the inequalities in this world that both surprise and terrify us.

Migration has provided me with both pain and happiness: on the one hand, the pain of separation from my family; a small hurt I carry around in my soul (regardless of all the trips I take to see them) and on the other, (in the words of Edward Said), "the pleasures found in exile." I found the ability to expand my life by living amongst all the cultures of the world. What is all of this that has been recounted? A personal story, a portrait of an era, a retelling of the ties of continuity and rupture, a fractured identity or plural identity . . . it is hard to say, at least for me, as I write, today, under the guise of safety found in a "personal perspective." I remember the poet Pedro Pietri, with his surrealist characteristics, would always respond when asked who or what he identified with "Yo soy de Ponce . . . (I am from Ponce . . .)." What I do know is that this amalgamation has given me the opportunity to explore myself. Overall, I feel that those that know themselves intimately while appreciating different cultures are the ones capable of celebrating human diversity and feeling within themselves the determination to fight for peace for themselves as well as for others. 🗩

MYRNA NIEVES is a Puerto Rican poet, fiction writer, essayist, cultural activist and educator. A founding member and professor at Boricua College, she was director for twenty years of its Winter Poetry Series.

JOANNA MORALES, whose parents are from El Salvador, is currently a student at Columbia University pursuing her M.A. in Hispanic Cultural Studies.

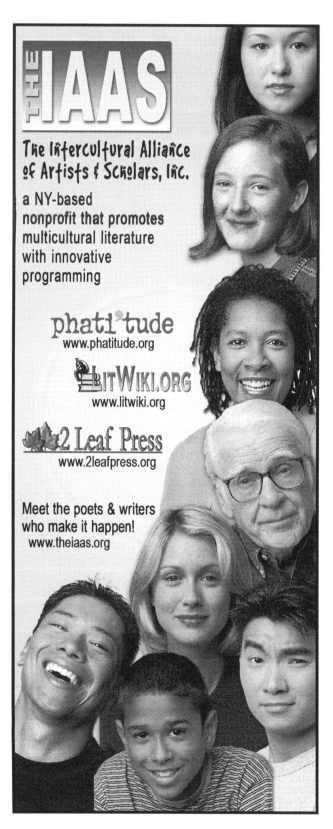

THE FINAL WORD
IT'S NOT WHO YOU KNOW
BUT WHAT YOU KNOW

What's in a Name?
Naming Ourselves

Miguel Algarin, Ph.D
Founder, Nuyorican Poets Café

Nancy Mercado, Ph.D
Guest Editor
phati'tude Literary Magazine
March 2012

Today the Hispanic [Latin@] presence has emerged, seemingly suddenly, as a pervasive fact of American life. History is filled with unintended consequences, and one of the ironies (a "latent destiny"?) of the history of a nation that expanded its influence and its "manifest destiny" into Latin America and the Caribbean is that, in significant numbers, their diverse peoples have come to the United States and themselves become "Americans."(1)

NUYORICAN IDENTITY? I'm already terrified at what I'd say. To be Latin@ is to be a cat pouncing on a mouse. All we ever know for sure is that we exist in our panic and that what is true in a name is the accuracy with which the "name" reveals about what is absolutely solid in the object being looked at. What can materialize with our naming of it, the thing we can now understand or have an understanding of, once it is named? If we do not name the external world, we remain caged in the internal body. We remain alone, isolated. We name in order to unite, to get a sense of connection to the other. Name the outside, flow from inside-out, reach to the other, and take action to become one; a community.

(cont'd pg. 298)

MIGUEL ALGARIN & NANCY MERCADO

WHAT'S IN A NAME? NAMING OURSELVES
Miguel Algarin & Nancy Mercado

(cont'd from pg. 297)

In naming, a community can emerge, take shape, function somehow. We can build for a time, create friendships, families, social structures, create art and literature. Naming captures and holds. It solidifies our ideas, whether in poetry, in paintings, in the love or hate we have for one another. Naming crafts a road for us to travel on, makes a space in which we can grow and transform. It provides a place from which we can emerge as one thing, as a whole, a place from which we can eventually generate our own histories. Naming also separates, makes someone or something more specific, gives it a distinct shape. It allows something to become familiar to the "name-er," fixes it into a place that can be revisited time and time again.

Naming is the spiritual act of living beyond the moment, of signifying something beyond the instant. Label it, and it is captured (in a particular form) for as long as it lives in that form. And when it dies, aspects of the name—as it is expressed through those individuals or objects—dies along with it. To die is to have lived. We die suddenly. We love before we die. Let us do what's important while we live. Once "goodbye" is said, there is only the future. And so, only certain characteristics of a name can outlast its original owner, for when the spiritual nature of that particular owner is no longer, that aspect or aspects of the name is gone as well. So let us say hello to tomorrow and remember what was, because some facets of "that which was named" can live beyond life in this world. Even after that person or thing we have named is no longer on this planet, we can visit some part of them or some aspect of it in pictures, sculptures, writings, film and music. We can still commune with what is named, introduce some part of it to those who come after. We can acquaint our children with a community's history, with past writers, artists, and family members. We are still able to hold objects they have left behind, contemplate their likeness in photos, paintings, read their lives in poems and books, hear their voices in recordings; the spoken word.

It is why the act of naming is so important, why possessing the name is crucial. We decide what our name will be. We are black because we decide it so. We are American because we decide it so. The act of naming is rebellious; it is the expression of power over a thing or over someone whether it is our self or someone else. And the moment in which we take possession of a name or transform a name that has been imposed on us is the moment in which we exert our control over that act and over our personhood. Naming has been and still is, used as a tool of oppression, a signifier to denote less than. So, the act of renaming, or transforming a name used to oppress, is a revolutionary one.

American writers we are—in the tradition of Walt Whitman, Allen Ginsberg, Audre Lorde, William Carlos Williams, James Baldwin, Gloria Anzaldua and Miguel Piñero. We are creators of American literature that speaks to an American life. We choose to name ourselves as such. We take the name and transform it into an expression of our lives. Through, poetry, prose, through the creation of works of art and film, through music, dance, we signify ourselves in America. What we are is what is grounded to the earth, our place in the world at this moment in time is filled because we choose it.

The 21st century will eventually find, in the Latin@ poets' verses, what it was like to enter this century. Latin@ writing will continue its rise in prominence as part of the American cannon in the 21st century. And, like past works of literature, will provide an American portrait of a nation in flux; a nation of contradictions, a nation forever in the throes of diversification.

(1) Ruben G. Rumbaut, "The Americans: Latin American and Caribbean peoples in the United States" in *Americas: New Interpretive Essays,* ed. Alfred Stepan (New York: Oxford University Press, 1992), 275.

MIGUEL ALGARIN, the founder of the Nuyorican Poets Café, is a Puerto Rican scholar and Professor Emeritus at Rutgers University. One of the most influential literary figures in the United States, Algarin has received numerous awards, including three American Book Awards, The Bessie Award for Outstanding Creative Achievement and an OBIE. A selected list of his poetry collections include; *Survival Supervivencia* (Arte Publico Pr.), *On Call* (Arte Publico Pr.), *Times Now/Ya es tiempo* (Arte Publico Pr.) and *Love is Hard Work* (Scribner). Algarin is the co-editor of the anthologies: *Nuyorican Poetry* (William Morrow) and *Aloud, Voices from the Nuyorican Poets Café* (Holt).

CONTRIBUTORS
MEET THE POETS & WRITERS
WHO MAKE IT HAPPEN!

Pedro López Adorno was born in Puerto Rico and lives in New York. The author of thirteen books, his most recent publications are *Viajes del cautivo* (1998); *Rapto continuo* (1999); *La ciudad prestada: Poesía latinoamericana posmoderna en Nueva York* (2002), *Arte de cenizas* (2004), and *Opera ardiente* (2009). He received his Ph.D. from New York University, and has been a professor in the Department of Africana and Puerto Rican/Latino Studies of Hunter College since 1987.

Carlos Aguasaco is a poet and video artist born in Bogotá who immigrated to New York in 1999. He recently coedited the anthology, *Ensayos sin frontera (Estudios sobre narrativa hispanoamericana)* (2005); and published the poetry collection *Nocturnos del caminante* (2010). Aguasaco's poetry has been published and translated in the U.S. and throughout Latin America. His videos have been featured at Camaguey International Video Art Festival and Region 0, and won the India Catalina prize for best video in the art category at the Cartagena International Film Festival. He received his Ph.D. at Stony Brook University (SUNY) and is currently an assistant professor of Latin American Cultural Studies at the Department of Interdisciplinary Studies of The City College of CUNY

Miguel Algarín is a Puerto Rican poet, writer, co-founder of the Nuyorican Poets Café, and retired Rutgers University professor of English. He has published several poetry collections and co-edited three anthologies and is the recipient of three American Book Awards, and the Larry Leon Hamlin Producer's Award at the 2001 National Black Festival.

Steven Alvarez has published poems in journals throughout the Americas. He recently published his first book, *The Pocho Codex: Piercing an Amurkan Poetic Historiography* (Editorial Paroxismo, 2011), a novel in verse. His poetry has appeared in *Fence, Drunken Boat, EAOGH, Shampoo,* and *Acentos Review.* His poem "& So Tio & Chaley" won the Poetry Society of America's "Bright Lights, Big Verse: Poems of Times Square" 2008 competition. Alvarez currently resides in Jackson Heights, New York. www.stevenpaulalvarez.com

Miguel Ángel is an artist whose medium is photography.

Maria Aponte, born and raised in New York City's East Harlem (El Barrio), has performed in various theatre and film productions. She has written and performed her one-woman show "Lagrimas de Mis Madres," a biography of the women in her family, and "I Will Not Be Silenced," based on the life of Sor Juana Ines de la Cruz. She performs nationally at conferences, colleges and universities, and has published in the *Marymount Review* and *Caribe Revista de Cultura y Literatura.* She received her B.A. in English Literature at Marymount Manhattan College and studied at Iowa University Summer Writer's Workshop. Aponte currently works at Fordham University in Career Services and is pursing her Masters in Latin American and Latino Studies.

R. A. "R!" Araya writes, reads and hosts poetry programs in New York City.

Carmen Bardeguez-Brown is a poet and educator born in Puerto Rico who migrated to the U.S. in 1984. Her work is showcased in "Latino Poets in the United States," an award-winning documentary filmed and produced by Ray Santiesteban. She has read at many venues, including the Nuyorican Poets Café, The Fez, Mad Alex Foundation; and has published in *Tribes, Long Shot, Fuse, School Voices,* and the anthology, *Aloud Voices from the Nuyorican.* Bardeguez-Brown also produced the poetry CD, "Straight From the Drum," a collection of poetry that encapsulate her Afro Caribbean poetic rhythm. cbbpoetry@tumblr.com

Sandra C. Barreras del Río, having lived in New York City for many years, has returned to Puerto Rico where she was born. She was a college professor at Boricua College (NY) and is currently teaching at the University of Puerto Rico at Arecibo (UPRA). Her literary essays and poetry has published in *Guaíza* (Boricua College), and in *Amauta* and *Cuarto Propio*, internet journals of the UPRA. Her awards include First Prize in Essays at the Ateneo Puertorriqueño (1997), and

Honorary Mention at the Ateneo for "Para leer a Nietzsche en puertorriqueña" (1998). Her poetry appears in the anthology, *Breaking Ground; Anthology of Puerto Rican Women Writers in New York 1980-2010* (2011) edited by Myrna Nieves.

Nestor Barreto is from Puerto Rico where he studied comparative literature at the University of Puerto Rico in Rio Piedras. He is the author of six books, recently *la actual fantasía de nosotros@s y otros poemas* (colección maravilla 2010); *si* (terranova editores, 2006); and *legión, poema pánico* (editorial de la Universidad de Puerto Rico 2001).

Rosebud Ben-Oni, a former Rackham Merit Fellow at the University of Michigan and Horace Goldsmith Scholar at the Hebrew University of Jerusalem, is a playwright at New Perspectives Theater in New York City. She has written the plays "Shamhat," "Drawn from Water," "Untouchable," "Quimera on the Storm," "Don't Call it Returning," "Owless of Santa Clara" and "The Amaranthine Thread." Her work has appeared in numerous publications including *Structo Magazine,* and *Maggid: A Journal of Jewish Literature.* Her short story, "A Way out of the Colonia," won the Editor's Prize at *Camera Obscura: A Journal of Contemporary Literature and Photography,* and was nominated for a Pushcart Prize.

Wanda Benvenutti is a Seattle-based freelance photojournalist and first-generation mainland born Boricua. She received a B. A. in English and Latin American Studies from Oberlin College, and an M.S. from the Columbia University Graduate School of Journalism. Her photographs are featured in the book, *100 New York Photographers* by Cynthia Maris Dantzic, and her work has been featured in solo and group exhibitions, including *Beggars and Choosers: Motherhood is Not a Class Privilege in America,* and *Wanda Benvenutti, Boricua: Puerto Rican Life in the American West* at the University of Washington Jacob Lawrence Gallery. She is currently working on "American Boricua," a visual history of Puerto Rican life in the U.S. www.americanboricua.com

Oscar Bermeo, born in Ecuador and raised in the Bronx, is the author of four poetry chapbooks, his most recent, *To The Break of Dawn.* His poems have appeared in *Achiote Seeds, BorderSenses, CrossBRONX, In the Grove, 12 Ways: An Anthology of the 2007 Intergenerational Writers* Lab (Kearny St. Workshop Pr., 2007), *Points Not Found: Writings on the Meaning of Place* (Kearny St. Workshop Pr., 2006), among others. He has taught creative writing workshops to at-risk youth in the Bronx, fosters teens in San Jose, mentors bilingual elementary school students in Oakland, and works with adults through the Oakland Public Library's Oakland Word program. He currently resides in Oakland. www.oscarbermeo.com

Susana Cabañas is a poet and cultural activist. Born in Puerto Rico, she migrated to the United States at a young age where she lived most of her life. She self-published *Poemario* (1984), a bilingual collection of her early work, and *La Hora de la Yautía: Poemario 7* (2009), a collection of poetry written in Spanish. She co-edited and published *Breaking, An Anthology of Latina Writers* (1985), and her poetry has published in numerous publications in the U.S., Spain, Mexico, and Puerto Rico. A recipient of the First Books Award in Poetry from the National Writer's Voice Project of the YMCA of the USA (1992), she directs poetry workshops and coordinates weekly poetry readings.

Christopher Carmona was born and raised in Donna, Texas. He was a nominee for the Alfredo Cisneros de Miral Foundation Award for Emerging Writers in 2011, and has published in *The Writers' Block, Beatlick Art & News, World Audience Literary Journal, The Houston Poetry Festival 2011 Anthology* and other publications. Carmona published his first poetry collection, *beat* (Slough Pr., 2011), and is working on an anthology of Beat Texas writings for UT Press with Chuck Taylor and Rob Johnson. He is currently pursuing his Ph.D. at Texas A&M University, and is an organizer of the Annual Beat Poetry and Arts Festival.

Karen Chau is an editor of *phati'tude Literary Magazine.* She is originally from Allentown, Pennsylvania, and recently graduated from Brandeis University. She has previously been published in *Racialicious.*

Lydia Cortes is a Puerto Rican born and raised in Williamsburg, Brooklyn. She has published two poetry collections, *Lust for Lust* and *Whose Place;* and her poetry, fiction and essays have published in anthologies such as *Through the Kitchen Window; Teaching With Fire; In Praise of Our Teachers* and *Monologues On the Road,* and online zines such as *Press1.* Cortes was awarded residencies at Virginia Center for the Creative Arts (VCCA), Valparaiso in Mojacar, Spain, and at the MacDowell Colony for artists.

Marithelma Costa was born in Puerto Rico, and has been living in New York since 1978. She is the author of three poetry collections, the novel *Era el fin del mundo,* three books of interviews, and several studies of Spanish and Caribbean Literature. She has published in *Revista de Occidente, 80 Grados, Frontera D, Claridad, LL Journal,* and *American Letters & Commentary.* Costa is a professor of Spanish Literature at Hunter College and the Graduate Center of the City University of New York.

Angie Cruz, a Dominican born in New York City's Washington Heights, graduated from New York University with an M.F.A. She co-founded WILL: Women In Literature & Letters with Adelina Anthony and Marta Lucia, an organization that produced readings, workshops, and a conference. Cruz has published two novels, *Soledad* and *Let It Rain Coffee,* and her work has appeared in numerous periodicals including *Latina Magazine, Callaloo* and *The New York Times.* She is the

recipient of The New York Foundation of The Arts Fellowship, Barbara Deming Award, Yaddo, and The Camargo Fellowship, and currently teaches creative writing at Texas A&M University.

Mairym Cruz-Bernal, a Puerto Rican poet and essayist, is president of PEN-Puerto Rico. She recently edited *Ejército de rosas* (2011), and published her latest poetry collection, *Ese lugar bajo mi lámpara* (2010). She directed the Grupo Puertas: Artistic-Literary End of Century Movement (1993-1999), and presided over the V International Meet of Writers in Puerto Rico (2003). Cruz-Bernal received her B.A. in psychology at Loyola University, and completed her Masters in creative writing at Vermont College. She is the advisor of International Encounters of Writers, an honorary member of the Circle of Writers of Venezuela, and resides in San Juan, Puerto Rico.

Amanda A. Cunniff, a translator, is a junior at New York University, studying History and Romances, with a focus on Spanish and French. She has recently pursued a career in literary translation. Besides being proficient in Spanish, having lived in Spain and Miami, she is currently translating oral histories regarding the U.S./Mexican border wars from Spanish to English.

Gabrielle David, Editor-in-Chief of *phati'tude Literary Magazine,* is a multimedia artist that has worked as a desktop publisher, photographer, artist, video editor and musician. David has published several essays on multicultural literature and published the poetry collections: *this is me, a collection of poems & things* (CCI Books, 1994); and *spring has returned & i am renewed* (CCI Books, 1995). Her work has published in *Paterson Literary Review, Journal of New Jersey Poets, AIM Magazine,* and *phati'tude Literary Magazine*. She is the Executive Director of the Intercultural Alliance of Artists & Scholars, Inc. (IAAS), a NY-based nonprofit organization that promotes multicultural literature and literacy, which publishes *phati'tude Literary Magazine*.

Pablo Delano, born in San Juan, Puerto Rico, holds an M.F.A. degree from Yale University School of Art. His photographs have been exhibited in galleries and museums throughout the world. He is the author of several books of photography, including *Faces of America* (Smithsonian Institution Pr., 1992) and *In Trinidad* (Ian Randle Pub., 2008). He teaches photography at Trinity College in Hartford, CT.

Sam Diaz is a Puerto Rican poet and writer born in the South Bronx. While working as a chemist, he participated in meetings that led to the founding of the Nuyorican Poets Café, New Rican Village and other venues. Over the years, he has coordinated poetry and reading series, and managed theatrical events for Pedro Pietri and the Nuyorican Poets Café. He also served as a coordinator for the Puerto Rican-based Bienal de la Poesia Puertorriqueña and subsequent events for La Muestra de la Bienal. He currently heads Computer and Administrative Office Services (BxCAOS), which assists small businesses and non-profits in the Arts and Housing fields.

Lyn Di Iorio, born and raised in Puerto Rico, is a professor at The City College of New York and The Graduate Center of the City University of New York. She pursued a bachelor's degree at Harvard University, and later acquired a master's degree from Stanford University's Creative Writing Program, and a Ph.D. in English literature from The University of California at Berkeley. She is the author of *Killing Spanish: Literary Essays on Ambivalent U.S. Latino/a Identity* (Palgrave Macmillan 2004); and coeditor of *Contemporary U.S. Latino/a Literary Criticism* (Palgrave Macmillan 2007).

Marcos Dimas was born in Puerto Rico and raised in New York City. An artist, advocate and former member of The Art Workers Coalition, he earned his B.F.A. from the School of Visual Arts, and is one of the original founders of Taller Boricua/The Puerto Rican Workshop. As the Artistic Director of that organization, Dimas has curated and organized over 240 exhibitions in the past 30 years. He has also won several awards for painting, graphic work, and video.

Elizam Escobar is a Puerto Rican poet, author and visual artist. A former member of the underground group, The Armed Forced of Puerto Rican National Liberation (FALN), Escobar was charged with seditious conspiracy and sentenced to a prison term of 68 years in 1981. During his incarceration, he produced a series of artwork and poetry, and after he was granted clemency by President Clinton in 1999, he became Dean of the Painting Department of the School of Fine Arts (Escuela de Artes Plásticas) in San Juan, Puerto Rico. He has published his work and poetry in *Beginnings, Currents, Left Curve, De Pie y En Lucha, Polvo* and *the Anthology of Latino Poets;* and his paintings have been exhibited in New York, Chicago, Philadelphia and Puerto Rico. Escobar has also authored two books, *Speech in the Night* and *Sonia Semenovena,* published by Quinera Books.

Sandra María Esteves, a Dominican Boricua Nuyorican poet has published several collections of poetry which include her self-published collections *DivaNations* (audio cd, 2010), *Wildflowers* (audio cd, 2009); *Portal* (2007), and *Poems In Concert* (2006). She is the recipient of numerous awards and fellowships including a Pregones Theater/NEA Master Artist Award (2010), and the Con Tinta Award from the Acentos Poetry Collective (2007). Her poems have published in prestigious anthologies such as *The Afro-Latin@ Reader, History and Culture In the United States* (Duke Univ. Pr., 2010); and *Understanding the Latina/o Experience in the United States: Readings in Ethnic Studies* (Pearson Education Co., 2007). A teaching artist for over thirty years, Esteves has conducted literary programs for the New York City Board of Education, Teachers & Writers Collaborative, the Bronx Council on the Arts, the Caribbean Cultural Center and El Museo del Barrio. www.SandraEsteves.com.

José Angel Figueroa is a poet, actor, playwright, editor, journalist, activist and professor was born in Mayaguez, Puerto Rico, and came to the U.S. at the age of seven. He received a B.A. in English Literature from New York University, and a Writing Fellowship and M.A. from SUNY at Buffalo. His poetry collections include *East 110th Street* (Broadside Pr., 1973), *Noo Jork* (Instituto de Cultural Puertorriquena, 1981), *Hypocrisy Held Hostage* (UPR-RUM/CEPA 2006). He has published in many anthologies, notably *Bum Rush the Page: A Def Poetry Jam* (2001), *Papiros De Babel: Antologia de la poesia puertorriquena en Nueva York* (1991), and *Puerto Rican Writers at Home in the USA* (1991). He is currently a professor of Puerto Rican, Latin American and Caribbean Literature at Boricua College in New York City.

Jaime "Shaggy" Flores is a new generation Nuyorican, Massarican Poet/Writer/Cultural Revolutionary hailing from Spanish Harlem, Cupey, Puerto Rico, and Springfield, MA. A graduate and scholar from the University of Massachusetts with a Bachelors degree on the African Diaspora and a Masters in History from Virginia State University, he has published in numerous anthologies and journals, such as *Centro Journal of the Center for Puerto Rican Studies at Hunter College; Bum Rush the Page A Def Poetry Jam Anthology; Role Call An African-American Intergenerational Literary Anthology; The Bandana Republic;* and *Hostos Review: New Rican Voices.* Flores published his first collection of poetry, *Sancocho — A Book of Nuyorican Poetry* (2001). His second book of poetry, *Obatala's Bugalu: A Nuyorican Book of Sights and Sounds,* is forthcoming. www.shaggyflores.com

Tammy Melody Gomez is a Mexican-American Texas-born writer, performance artist, and media producer that specializes in literary performance events. She curated the Poetry Tent readings for the Texas Book Festival, and produces Palabrazos, a festival of multimedia literary performance. Her poems and essays have been widely anthologized in publication such as the *Brooklyn Review, Conjunctions, the Yellow Medicine Review, Hecho en Tejas* (Univ. of New Mexico Pr., 2006), and *Bicycle Love* (Breakaway Books, 2004). She has edited two anthologies, *Yoniverse: In a Loud Kitchen* (Tejana Tongue Pr., 1997) and *North Texas Neruda Love* (Tejana Tongue Pr., 2005); and will be reprising her first full-length play "She: Bike/Spoke/Love" at the Mexican American Cultural Center (Austin) in May 2012. www.unitedstatesartists.org/user/tammygomez.

Rafael Jesús González was raised in the bicultural/bilingual environment of El Paso, Texas and Cd. Juárez, Chihuahua, Mexico. Having joined the U.S. Navy in the hospital corps and served in the Marine Corps with the rank of Staff Sergeant, he attended the University of Texas, El Paso (then Texas Western College of the University of Texas) in pre-med and the Universidad Nacional Autónoma de México where he studied archaeology and Mexican literature. He completed his graduate studies at the University of Oregon and founded the Department of Mexican and Latin-American Studies at Laney College. His poetry and academic articles have appeared in reviews and anthologies in the U.S., Mexico, and abroad. González's recent poetry collections is *La musa lunática/The Lunatic Muse* (2009). In 2005, he named featured poet by the San José Poetry Center, and currently sits on the Latino Advisory Council of the Oakland Museum of California. http://rjgonzalez.blogspot.com

Ysabel Y. Gonzalez is a Puerto Rican born in the Bronx and raised in Newark, New Jersey. She received her bachelors in Latino and Hispanic Caribbean studies, and has been published in online journals such as *Race-Talk.org, Writers Bloc, LatinaFatale, Struggle Magazine* and in the upcoming second volume of *El Centro's Letras* at Hunter College (NY). www.ysabelgonzalez.com

Paula Hayes is a poet, scholar, and educator. She holds a Ph.D. in Textual Studies/English from the University of Memphis and teaches Professional Writing, English Composition, and World Religions. Her poetry has published in *Hispanic Culture Review, Black Magnolias, Dead Mule,* and *Taj Mahal Review.* Hayes' articles and book reviews have appeared in *The Griot: The Journal of African American Studies, Rupkatha Journal on Interdiscplinary Studies in the Humanities,* and *Rougarou* (Louisiana Univ. at Lafayette). Her book on Robert Lowell and his confessional movement in poetry is forthcoming in 2012 from Peter Lang Publishing.

Diana Gitesha Hernandez, a poet, singer and painter/print maker, is a Nuyorican transplant from her native San Juan, Puerto Rico. She has performed in poetry venues throughout the New York City, as member of Barry Harris Jazz Chorus Ensemble, and her own band, Orgasmic Orchestra. Her works have appeared *in Long Shot, Aloud!; Voices from the Nuyorican Poets Cafe Anthology, BE Magazine, Sound of Water, Heal; between the pages of these folks we seek a panacea,* Farid Bitar's CD Poetry collection "Fatoosh" and Brant Lyon's collection "Beauty Keeps Raising Her Sharp Knife Against Me." She is the author of two chapbooks, *Slingshot Luv; Love Poems From a Nuyorican Princess Dreaming of Rimbaud* and *Raw Lips Melao, a Nuyorican Rhapsody.* Hernandez is a school counselor, yoga instructor, and massage therapist.

Andrea O'Reilly Herrera, poet and author, is a Professor of Literature and Director of the Women's and Ethnic Studies Program at the University of Colorado at Colorado Springs. Her publications include *ReMembering Cuba: Legacy of a Diaspora* (Univ. of Texas Pr., 2001); a novel, *The Pearl of the Antilles* (Bilingual/Review Pr., 2001); an edited collection of essays, *Cuba: Idea of a Nation Displaced* (SUNY Pr., 2007); and the coeditor of textbook *The Matrix Reader: Examin-*

ing the Dynamics of Oppression and Privilege (McGraw Hill, 2008). Her most recent work is a monograph titled *Cuban Artists across the Diaspora: Setting the Tent Against the House* (Univ. of Texas Pr., 2011).

Elvis Irizarry was born in Puerto Rico and raised in the Bushwick section of Brooklyn, New York. Since childhood, he has been recognized for his work in the genres of comic book, graffiti and German expressionist art. He is also an art critic for the *International Examiner,* an Asian-American news journal based in Seattle, Washington.

Ivelisse Jiménez, born in Santurce, Puerto Rico, is a painter that works in installations and constructions. She received an M.F.A. in Studio Arts from New York University, and has exhibited her work in international venues such as the ARCO art fair, Art Basel Miami and the Prague Bienniale. She is a grant recipient for the Joan Mitchell Foundation in 2009, and currently works at Escuela de Artes Plásticas de Puerto Rico as Head of Painting Department, and as an adjunct at University of Puerto Rico.

Jennifer-Crystal Johnson, Managing Editor of *phati'tude Literary Magazine*, is originally from Germany, but was raised all over. She has published one novella, *The Outside Girl: Perception is Reality* (Publish America, 2005) and the poetry collection, *Napkin Poetry* (Broken Publications, 2010). Her poetry has appeared in various anthologies including *The Lightness of Being* (Int'l Library of Poetry, 2000), *Theatre of the Mind* (Noble House, 2003), *Invoking the Muse* (Noble House, 2004), and *Our 100 Most Famous Poets* (Famous Poets Pr., 2004). She is a freelance writer and editor, and is based in the Pacific Northwest. www.soulvomit.com

Rebecca Kaye, Associate Editor of *phati'tude Literary Magazine*, is in her second year of the Masters in Creative Writing program at Oxford University. As an undergraduate, she attended Durham University where she mastered in English Literature and French. She is the former editor of *Etcetera Magazine,* literary supplement to *The Cherwell,* an Oxford-based student newspaper. She is currently a house contributor to the online journal, *The Fabelist.*

E.K. Keith, originally from Texas, currently resides in California. Her work has published in *Sparring with Beatnik Ghosts Anthology, The 16th & Mission Review,* and *The Panhandler.* She is one of the founding organizers of "Poems Under the Dome," an annual celebration of National Poetry Month inside San Francisco's City Hall.

Marilyn Kiss, an Associate Professor of Spanish, teaches language and literature classes at Wagner College, Staten Island, NY. For seventeen years, she coordinated the Study Abroad Program there. Her research interests include Spanish and Latin American film and Latino(a) literature of the U.S. She has published two books of poetry: *Pacharán Dreams: The Pamplona Poems* (2011) and *Signal Moments: Poems of Loss and an Antidote* (2007), both with Plain View Press, Austin, TX. She travels widely in the Spanish-speaking world and is an avid photographer.

Bethany M. Korp-Edwards, translator for Lourdes Vasquez, is an American Translators Association Certified Translator (Spanish to English), a federally certified Court Interpreter and president of the New Mexico Translators and Interpreters Association. She received a Master of Arts in Spanish Translation from Rutgers University and is currently the owner of Running Dog Translations, a Spanish translation and interpreting service.

Jane Losaw translates from Spanish and Catalan. She is a graduate student in Latin American and Iberian Cultures at Columbia University.

Tato Laviera was born in Puerto Rico and has lived in New York City since 1960. A writer, poet and playwright, he has been called a "chronicler of life in El Barrio." He has served as an administrator, artist-in-residence, consultant, and educator in numerous venues. His volumes of poetry include *Mixturao and Other Poems* (Arte Público Pr., 2008-09), *Mainstream Ethics-Etica Corriente* (Arte Público Pr., 1988), *Enclave* (Arte Público Pr., 1985), *AmeRícan* (Arte Público Pr., 1985), and *La Carreta Made a U-Turn* (Arte Público Press, 1979).

William Luis received his Ph.D. at Cornell University. He has taught at Dartmouth College, SUNY-Binghamton, Washington University in St. Louis, Yale University, and is currently the Chancellor's Professor of Spanish at Vanderbilt University in Tennessee. His has published numerous papers, written, edited and co-edited several books, notably, *Lunes de Revolución: Literatura y cultura* (2003); *Culture and Customs of Cuba* (2001); and *Dance Between Two Cultures: Latino Carribean Literature Written in the United States* (1997).

Sheryl Luna was born and raised in El Paso, Texas and earned her Ph.D. in Contemporary Literature from the University of North Texas. Her first poetry collection, *Pity the Drowned Horses* (Univ. of Notre Dame Pr., 2005), which received the Andres Montoya Poetry Prize for emerging Latino/a poets. Her work has appeared in *Puerto del Sol, Prairie Schooner, Georgia Review* and elsewhere. She received the Alfredo Cisneros del Moral foundation award funded by Sandra Cisneros, and fellowships at Yaddo, Ragdale, the Anderson Center and is a Canto Mundo fellow. http://sheryl-luna.blogspot.com/

George Malave is a photographer born in Puerto Rico and raised in New York City. He holds a degree in Photography/Painting from SUNY, Empire State. An original member of En Foco, he has taught at the New School, Educational Alliance

Photography Institute and privately; and was awarded a Creative Artist Public Service Fellowship and a National Endowment Survey Grant. Malave has photographed for major corporations, publications, non-profit groups, and educational institutions and his work have been used in magazines, CD covers, newspapers, book jackets, and other publications. His works are also in the collections of The New York Public Library, The Alternative Museum, Museo De Puerto Rico and Museum of the City of New York and private collections. He has published the photography books *The Tourist* (2008) and *Third Avenue El* (2004), and recently co-edited *Poetic Visions: Contemporary Latino Words and Images* (2012).

Sheila Maldonado is a Honduran who grew up in Coney Island, NY. She recently published her first poetry collection, *one-bedroom solo* (Fly by Night Pr., 2011) and is the recipient of a 2012 Northern Manhattan Arts Alliance Artist Grant. She holds degrees in English from Brown University and poetry from The City College of New York. Maldonado teaches creative writing for the City University of New York and the Teachers & Writers Collaborative.

Soraya Marcano is a visual artist born in Puerto Rico and based in New York City. Her mixed media artwork has been exhibited internationally and it is represented in public and private collections, including the Museum of Contemporary Art of Chamalieres, Center for the Humanities, The New York Public Library, Rockefeller Library, and Institute of Puerto Rican Culture, among others. Marcano has participated in international artist-in-residence programs and she is the recipient of several recognitions and awards. She studied at the University of Puerto Rico and completed her M.F.A. at Pratt Institute.

Reggie Marra, translator for Marianela Medrano is the author of two volumes of poetry, *This Open Eye* and *Who Lives Better Than We Do?,* and two works of nonfiction, *The Quality of Effort* and *Living Poems, Writing Lives.* He spent 21 years as a teacher, administrator and basketball coach in secondary and higher education, and 16 years as a teaching poet. Marra is currently an Integral Coach, working with leaders who want to excel amid the complexities of 21st-century life.

Tony Medina, born and raised in the South Bronx, is the author of 17 books for adults and children, his most recent, *An Onion of Wars* (2012), *My Old Man Was Always on the Lam* (2010) and the award winning children's book, *I and I: Bob Marley*, with illustrator Jesse Joshua Watson (2009). His young adult book, *The President Looks Like Me and Other Poems* is forthcoming in 2012. Medina earned his M.A. and Ph.D in Poetry and American and African American Literature from Binghamton University, SUNY, and is currently Associate Professor of Creative Writing at Howard University in Washington, D.C.

Marianela Medrano is a Dominican writer and poet living in Connecticut since 1990. Her recent poetry collections are *Diosas de la Yuca* (Torremozas, 2011), and *Curada de Espantos* (Torremozas, 2002). She has published in literary magazines and academic journals such *Letralia, Journal of Poetry Therapy, Sandplay Therapy Journal, The Afro-Latin@ Reader,* and *Kacike,* among others. Medrano holds a Ph.D. in psychology and is a licensed professional counselor and certified poetry therapist. Her literary work has earned two fellowships and several awards, including the Distinguished Award prize from the National Federation for Poetry Therapy (2009). She currently works as a consultant and has a psychotherapy private practice in Connecticut. http://marianelamedrano.com

Jesús Papoleto Meléndez, a proud Puerto Rican born in New York, is one of the original founders of the Nuyorican poets' movement. He is a recipient of a New York Foundation for the Arts Fellowship in Poetry (2001); an Artist for Community Enrichment (ACE) Award from the Bronx Council on the Arts, New York (1995); and a COMBO (Combined Arts of San Diego)-NEA Fellowship in Literature (1988). Meléndez has spent the past 30 years working as a poetry-facilitator working in the public schools, during which time he has coordinated many successful poetry/creative writing workshops, impacting the lives of tens of thousands of young people. The author of the poetry collections, *Casting Long Shadows* (1970), *Have You Seen Liberation* (1971), *Street Poetry & Other Poems* (1972), and *Concertos On Market Street* (1993). http://papoleto.com/

Gizella Meneses was raised in Chicago and Quito, Ecuador. She recently published, "El diablo de la montana: raza e identidad en las tradiciones orales andinas" in the journal *Hipertexto*. Her documentary entitled "Second Generation Stories: Growing Up Latino/a in Chicago" premiered at the International Chicago Latino Film Festival in 2010. Meneses is the 2011 recipient of Lake Forest College's William Dunn Award recognizing scholarly promise and outstanding teaching. She is currently an Assistant Professor of Spanish at Lake Forest College.

Judith Mercado is a fiction writer and essayist. Her short stories have been published in *Nassau Review, North Atlantic Review,* and other literary reviews; and has published essays in *Latina Voices* and *Being Latino.* Mercado's poems about disability have appeared in *The Barefoot Review* and in her other blog "Peace Be With You" (http://lapazconvos.blogspot.com/). She blogs about culture, religion, and fiction at "Pilgrim Soul" (http://judithmercadoauthor.blogspot.com/)

Nancy Mercado, Guest Editor of this issue of *phati'tude Literary Magazine,*'was most recently featured on the PBS NewsHour Special: *America Remembers 9/11.* She is also featured in *The Encyclopedia of Hispanic American Literature* (Facts on File) and inducted into *The Museum of American Poetics.* Profiled in *Latino Leaders Magazine,* as "one of the most celebrated members of the Puerto Rican literary movement in the Big Apple," Mercado is the author of *It Concerns the Madness* (Long Shot Productions) and the editor of, *if the world were mine;* a children's anthology published by the

New Jersey Performing Arts Center (NJPAC). She was an editor of Long Shot for 11 years and the publication's editor-in-chief for one of those years. The author of 7 theatre plays, Mercado's writing has been extensively anthologized. She has toured throughout the US, Europe and Canada as a featured poet and conference panelist. Mercado received her Ph.D. from Binghamton University- SUNY and is currently an Assistant Professor at Boricua College in New York City. www. thelatinoauthor.com/authors/M/Mercado-Nancy/

Oscar Mireles has been writing poetry for the past 25 years. He is the editor the anthologies, *I didn't know there were Latinos in Wisconsin: 20 Hispanic Poets* (Focus Comm.,1989); and *I didn't know there were Latinos in Wisconsin: 30 Hispanic Writers* (Focus Comm.,1999). He has published in numerous anthologies and magazines and among his many awards for community service and activism, was selected the Advocate of the Year by Wisconsin Literacy (2011); and the Dane County Martin Luther King Recognition Award (2009). Mireles is currently Principal/Executive Director of Omega School, an alternative school in Madison, Wisconsin.

Renny Molenaar has been exhibiting in New York City and elsewhere since the early 1980s. He has created numerous installations and interventions in the streets and other alternative locations. Molenaar was the founder and director of the Black and White in Color gallery in the Bronx and is currently working on the IMPERFECT gallery in Germantown, Philadelphia. His work has appeared at the Neuberger Museum, Artists Space, Fashion Moda, and the Nuyorican Poets Café.

Marlis Momber was born in Berlin, Germany and has lived in New York City since 1966. She initially bean working as a fashion photographer before becoming a documentary photographer. Her 1978 documentary film, VIVA LOISAIDA, became a classic through her many local, national and international lectures and exhibitions. Her work was inaugurated into the Hunter College Library and Archives of the Puerto Rican Diaspora at EL CENTRO, Center for Puerto Rican Studies, 2009, and was included in the "Images of America PIONEROS II: Puerto Ricans in New York City 1948-1998." http://eastvillage.thelocal.nytimes.com/2011/01/21/viewfinder-marlis-momber/

Joe Montoya, Jr., poet and artist, was born and raised in California, and currently lives in Sacramento. While working as a supplier and business owner in the automotive electrical industry for nearly thirty years, he has been writing, performing and publishing in literary magazines, books and journals. He created the award winning series, "Poetry Unplugged," now enjoying its 17th year at Luna's Café in Sacramento.

Joanna Morales, a native New Yorker whose parents are from El Salvador, is a translator. She is currently a student at Columbia University pursuing her M.A. in Hispanic Cultural Studies. Having completed her undergraduate education at a woman's college in Virginia, she maintains a strong connection with her Spanish roots by visiting El Salvador annually.

Rafael Colón Morales is a painter and artist, born in Puerto Rico and raised in the Bronx. He studied art at the San Fernando School of Fine Arts in Madrid, The University of Puerto Rico in San Juan and The American University in Washington, D.C. A former member of The Taller Boricua who now lives in Cataño, Puerto Rico, Morales' art work has been exhibited in Puerto Rico, the United States, Spain and the Dominican Republic. He has held over 25 individual exhibitions, and has been included in over 35 collective exhibitions; and has lectured on art and Caribbean myths at many institutions, including El Museo del Barrio, The Metropolitan Museum of Art, Cooper Union School of Science and Art, Pratt Institute, Georgetown University and Columbia University.

Amina Muñoz-Ali is a Puerto Rican Arab American who was born and raised in New York City. She has read at the Nuyorican Poets' Cafe, Bluestocking Books, Nkiru Books, Brooklyn Public Library, the Bronx Museum of the Arts, Bowery Poetry Club, Bar 13, Tribes Gallery, WBAI-FM, WNYC-TV and many other venues. Muñoz-Ali has published in *Essence Magazine, AM NY, Long Shot* and *Tribes* magazines. She currently lives in Brooklyn and was a recent participant in the Community Word Teaching Artist and Internship program.

Stephanie Agosto Negron is a Boricua poet/activist. She received her A.A. from Queensborough Community College, attended Hunter College and Film & Video Arts in New York City to study Film Production; and went on to produce and host the poetry series, "Universal Beats," a weekly series on Manhattan Neighborhood Network (MNN). Her poetry has published in numerous poetry compilations, anthologies, art books and periodicals; and she has performed at numerous venues throughout New York City and Florida. She serves as a board member of the Intercultural Alliance of Artists & Scholars, Inc., and was instrumental in distributing *phatLiterature, A Literary TV Show* to public access and college television stations across the country.

Myrna Nieves is a Puerto Rican poet, fiction writer, essayist, cultural activist and educator. Her recent poetry collection is *Viaje a la lluvia, poemas* (2002) and recently edited the anthology, *Breaking Ground: Anthology of Puerto Rican Women Writers in New York 1980-2012* (Editorial Campana, 2012). Nieves received the Pen Club Award in 1998 for her work *Libreta de sueños (narraciones)*. Her work has been anthologized in groundbreaking literary collections and included in many literary journals and internet magazines. Nieves received her Ph.D. in Latin American and Caribbean Literature at New York University and is a founding member and professor at Boricua College, where she served as director of its Winter Poetry Series for twenty years.

Urayoán Noel is a poet originally from San Juan. He recently published the artist's book and website, *The Edgemere Letters* (2011), a collaboration with visual artist Martha Clippinger, and the poetry collections *Hi-Density Politics* (BlazeVOX Books, 2010), and *Boringkén* (Ediciones Callejón, 2008. His work has appeared in various anthologies, and he has translated a number of Latin American and U.S. Latino/a poets. He is currently a Bronx Council on the Arts Poetry Fellow and a Ford Foundation Postdoctoral Fellow at the Center for Puerto Rican Studies, where he is completing a book on Nuyorican poetry. Noel has also recorded a CD and a DVD of his poetry in collaboration with musician and composer Monxo López, with whom he occasionally performs. He is Assistant Professor of English at the University at Albany, SUNY.

Lorraine Miller Nuzzo has been Curator, Art Director of *phati'tude Literary Magazine* and "phati'tude-related" projects since 1997. While pursuing her professional career, Nuzzo studied painting with Mary Nagin and Carole Jay in New York; and with Tim Holden in Italy. She has held exhibitions at MIB and BJ Spoke Gallery; and is also a former partner of "hotshots unlimited photography," which held an exhibit at the Langston Hughes Library. She holds a Master's degree in Industrial/Organizational Psychology from Hofstra University and a Bachelors degree in Psychology with a minor in Art from SUNY, Empire State. www.rainynuzzo.com

Henry Ignacio Padrón-Morales was born in Brooklyn, New York of Puerto Rican parentage. His work has appeared in a variety of formats, and he performs with Salmorejo, a percussion ensemble that he founded and directs. Padrón-Morales participates in local poetry events, the International Poetry of Resistance Festival celebrated annually in Toronto, Ontario, and currently writes poetry with migrant farmworkers in the upstate region of New York. He also writes an education column for the newly established Spanish language magazine, *IMAGEN NY.*

Dylcia Pagan was born in the Bronx and raised in El Barrio-East Harlem. She is the first Puerto Rican woman to serve as a TV producer and filmmaker in New York City, developing investigative documentaries and children's programs at NBC, ABC, CBS, and PBS. She was arrested in 1980 and was charged with Seditious Conspiracy for fighting for the Independence of Puerto Rico and was sentenced to 63 years of imprisonment in state and federal facilities in the U.S. During her incarceration, she developed educational and cultural programs, as well as three documentaries. When President Clinton gave her a Presidential Conditional Clemency in 1999, Pagan relocated to Puerto Rico where she continues to work as a producer and director of multimedia productions in film, video and the internet. http://www.dylciapagan.com

Adriana Páramo, a Colombian nonfiction writer, is a cultural anthropologist currently pursuing a graduate degree in Creative Writing at the University of South Florida. Her work has appeared in *Alaska Quarterly Review, The Los Angeles Review, Consequence Magazine, Fourteen Hills, Magnolia Journal, Line Zero, SoToSpeak, Thumbnail Magazine, Waccamaw Journal, Latina Voices Anthology,* and other journals. She volunteers as a transcriber for Voice of Witness, a nonprofit book series founded by author Dave Eggers, and does extensive work among undocumented women farmers in Florida. She also co-produces LOL, Life Out Loud, a nonfiction reading series held quarterly in Tampa Bay. http://www.paramoadriana.com/

Willie Perdomo is the author *Where a Nickel Costs a Dime,* which was a finalist for the Poetry Society of America Norma Farber First Book Award; and *Smoking Lovely,* which received a PEN Beyond Margins Award. He has published in *The New York Times Magazine, The Harlem Reader* and *Poems of New York.* He is also the author of two award-winning children's books, *Visiting Langston* and *Clemente!* He has been a Pushcart Prize nominee, a Woolrich Fellow in Creative Writing at Columbia University and is a three-time Fellow in Poetry from the New York Foundation for the Arts. Perdomo has been on the faculty at the VONA Writing Workshops, NEH Summer Seminar and currently teaches at Fordham University. He is founder/publisher of Cypher Books. www.willieperdomo.com

Kevin Tobar Pesántez, an Editor of *phati'tude Literary Magazine*, is a writer, spoken word poet and facilitator. He was born in Queens, New York to immigrant parents from Ecuador. He has put together a literary magazine for his university, performed poetry at various international venues, and has produced various spoken word poetry and theater of the oppressed workshops. He recently participated in Festival Sudaka, an international alternative young Latin American theater festival, in Quito, Ecuador as a playwright representing the United States. www.inkejaculate.tumblr.com

Meg Petersen is the Director of the National Writing Project in New Hampshire. Her work has appeared in *Concrete Wolf, English Journal, The Leaflet, The International Journal for Teaching Writing, Revistapingpong,* among other publications, and she recently published the essay, "Shadow People and Shared History" in *Sargasso Quisqueya: La Republica Extended.* Petersen is a former New England Teachers of English Association poet of the year, and a featured poet on the NH Poets Showcase. She is a founding editor of the *Plymouth Writers Group Anthologies of Teachers' Writing.*

Yolanda Arroyo Pizarro was born in Puerto Rico. She is the author of *Caparazones* (Editorial Egales, 2010), the first Puerto Rican lesbian fiction novel; and directed the *Anthology Cachaperismos* (2010), the first Puerto Rican lesbian

anthology from the island. Her work has appeared in *Seasons African Edition, a Periodic Journal of the International Centre for Women Playwrights in South Africa* and Pirene's *Fountain Japan Anthology* (2011). Her awards include the Woman Latino Writer Award Residency from National Hispanic Culture Center in Albuquerque, New Mexico (2011), and the PEN Club Prize (2010 and 2006). Pizarro currently serves as a radio host for cultural and literature program "Cooltureate" at Bonita Radio, a Puerto Rican radio station on the internet, and serves as Chief Editor of the literary magazine journal *Revista Boreales*.

Magaly Quiñones, born in Ponce, Puerto Rico, has published 15 books of poems, stories, essays, book critiques and travel reviews. She received her Master's degree from the University of Puerto Rico in Comparative Literature and foreign languages. Her many literary distinctions include the Mairean Prize, PEN Club Prize, Alejandro Tapia Prize, Home of the Poet Prize and the medal of the Institute of Culture. Recently published books are *Pasión y Libertad /Passion and Liberty* (2008) and *Nana al Niño Jesús / Nana to the Child Jesus* (Tiempo Nuevo, 2008).

Thelma T. Reyna is the author of *The Heavens Weep for Us and Other Stories* (Outskirts, 2009), which has received four national honors. Her stories, poems, essays, book reviews, and other nonfiction have been published in literary and academic journals *PALABRA* and *Chicana/Latina Studies: Journal of Mujeres Activas en Letras & Cambio Social;* textbooks such as *New Voices in Literature, Language, & Composition;* anthologies, such as *Vwa: Poems for Haiti;* blogs; and in regional media. Her first chapbook, *Breath & Bone* (FLP, 2011), was a Semi-Finalist in the 2010 National Poetry Chapbook Competition by Finishing Line Press. Reyna is an adjunct professor at California State University, Los Angeles, and an editor, ghost writer, and writing consultant. www.TheWritingPros.com); www.ThelmaReyna.com

John Riofrio, the son of Ecuadorian migrants, earned his Ph.D in English from the University of Wisconsin-Madison and teaches Latino studies at the College of William and Mary where he is an Assistant Professor in the Department of Modern Languages and Literatures. He has published on the confluence of Latin American and Latino studies, is at work on a book-length manuscript entitled "Continental Shifts: Hemispheric Migrations and the Struggles over Latin@ Identity in the Americas," and occasionally publishes opinion pieces in *Huffington Post.*

Etnairis Rivera, born and living in Puerto Rico, has published a book of short stories, *MAR* (SEA, 2011) and twelve poetry books, among them, *Ariadna del Agua / Ariadne of the Water (*2011), *Los pájaros de la diosa / The birds of the goddess* (2009), and *Return to the sea* (bilingual ed. 2007). Her work has been translated and published in international anthologies and reviews; and she has presented her poetry in cities across Latin America, Spain and the United States. Rivera is a Professor of Hispanic Literature at Universidad de Puerto Rico and leads Workshops of Creative Writing. She lived for several years in New York City and frequently visits.

John Rodriguez holds a Ph.D. from the CUNY Graduate Center. His writing has recently appeared in *PALABRA, One Word: Contemporary Writers on the Words They Love or Loathe,* and *Obscura.* He is part of The Acentos Foundation and a frequent member of their writers' workshop. He teaches English at Queensborough Community College, and lives in the Bronx.

Floyd Salas is the author of four novels, a memoir and two volumes of poetry. His first novel, the award-winning *Tattoo the Wicked Cross* (1967) and his memoir *Buffalo Nickel* (1992) are featured in Masterpieces of Hispanic Literature (HarperCollins 1994). His poetry books include, *Color of My Living Heart* (1996) and *Love Bites: Poetry in Celebration of Dogs and Cats* (2006). He was a staff writer for the NBC drama, *Kingpin* (2003), and a 2002-2003 Regent's Lecturer at University of California, Berkeley. Salas' papers are archived at the Floyd Salas collection in the Bancroft Library, University of California, Berkeley. He has taught creative writing at numerous colleges, universities, conferences and at San Quentin, Folsom and other correctional institutions. He is also a founder and president of the multicultural writing group PEN Oakland.

Yrene Santos, a poet and actress, was born in Villa Tapia, Dominican Republic. She has published numerous books, including, *Después de la lluvia* (2009), *Por si alguien llega* (2009); and co-author of the book *Desde la Diáspora: Cuentos y poemas de niños y niñas dominicanas* (2005). Her work has been translated to Italian and English. She has participated in numerous international book fairs, festivals and conferences.

Terry Sanville is a retired urban planner and an accomplished jazz and blues guitarist who once played with a symphony orchestra that backed up jazz legend George Shearing. He writes full time, producing short stories, essays, poems, an occasional play, and novels. Since 2005, his short stories have been accepted by more than 120 literary and commercial journals, magazines, and anthologies including the *Fifth Wednesday Journal, Birmingham Arts Journal* and *Boston Literary Magazine.* He was nominated for a Pushcart Prize for his story "The Sweeper." Sanville currently resides in San Luis Obispo, CA.

Amy E. Savage, a translator, is originally from Central New York. She holds a Master's degree in Hispanic Linguistics from the University at Albany and teaches Spanish at area colleges in Albany, New York. She has also participated in several fiction workshops, including a Community Workshop with the New York State Writers Institute.

Noel Shafi is a first generation American of Dominican and Pakistani descent, born and raised in New York City. He is an aspiring Speech-Language Pathologist, Neuroscientist and poet, and has published in the *Graduate Student Journal of Psychology* and the *Journal of Poetry Therapy.*

Danny Shot was the longtime publisher and editor of *Long Shot* arts and literary magazine, which he founded along with Eliot Katz in 1982. Shot's poetry has appeared in: *bum rush the page* (Def Poetry Jam) *Aloud: Voices from the Nuyorican Poets Cafe* (Henry Holt), *In Defense of Mumia* (Writers and Readers), *The Outlaw Bible of American Poetry* (Thunder's Mouth), and *Changing America: U.S. Poems of Protest 1980-1995* (Le Temps des Cerises). Shot has read his poetry throughout the United States, also appearing on television (WNBC, New York) as part of Felipe Luciano's Wordchestra. He is proud to have his poetry included in the *Occupy Wall Street Poetry Anthology*. He lives in Hoboken, NJ (home of Frank Sinatra and baseball).

Suzie Dod Thomas is Assistant Managing Editor for *Social Justice,* a refereed quarterly journal. An activist, she is a founding member of Bay Area Women Against Rape (1974); worked as an organizer in the San Francisco Latin American community; and from 1976 to 1985, was active in solidarity work in Central America and Cuba, organizing, leading, and translating for fact-finding delegations to Nicaragua and Cuba. She coedited the book, *Immigration, A Civil Rights Issue for the Americas* (with Susanne Jonas for Scholarly Resources, Wilmington, Delaware, 1999); and executive produced two CDs of music and poetry by Piri Thomas, "No Mo' Barrio Blues" and "Sounds of the Streets." Thomas also translated her husband's novel, *Down These Mean Streets* (1967), into Spanish.

Edwin Torres is a bilingual Nuyorican poet, born in the Bronx and a longtime resident of New York. He is the author of several poetry collections and his latest is *In the Function of External Circumstances* (2010). As a member of Real Live Poetry (formerly Nuyorican Poets Café Live) from 1993 to 1999, he has led workshops and performed in the U.S. and abroad. He is recipient of poetry fellowships from The Foundation For Contemporary Performance Art, the New York State Foundation for the Arts, and The Poetry Fund. He has served as coeditor of the journal, *Rattapallax* and has been writer-in-residence at the Lower Manhattan Cultural Council. Torres is currently coediting *POeP!* an eJournal, and *Cities Of Chance: An Anthology of New Poetry from The United States and Brazil,* both from Rattapallax Press.

Ida N. Torres was born in Cabo Rojo, Puerto Rico and migrated with her family to the Bronx, New York when she was eight years old. She has a B.S. degree from the City University of New York and an Ed. D. from Teachers College, Columbia University in New York City. She is an educator and college professor whose research is focused on the adult learner, the nontraditional student, organizational leadership and the Puerto Rican community in New York City.

Sonia Rivera Valdés was born in Cuba, lived in Puerto Rico for eleven years and has resided in New York for the past thirty-four years. She is a writer, literary and film critic and professor of Literature, Spanish Language and Puerto Rican Studies at York College, City University of New York; and is the president and founder of Latino Artists Round Table (LART). In 2000, *The Daily News Magazine* selected her as one of the New York's Grassroots Latino Influentials, and in 2004 she was selected as a Distinguished Honoree Latino by the Comptroller of the City of New York and Hispanic National Bar Association, NY Region.

Carlos Cesar Valle was born in Lima, Peru. He majored in Arts and Human Sciences in Pontifical Catholic University and currently lives in New York. He has published three works that have each been divided into three parts: three untitled poems, three poems about sex and more sex, and three poems on loneliness and enlightenment, which is part of a conceptual project, *Useless Pornography (and other New York poems).*

Richard Vargas received his M.F.A. (with distinction) from the UNM Creative Writing Program in 2010. He has published the books, *Mclife* (Main St. Rag Pr., 2005) and *American Jesus,* (Tia Chucha Pr., 2007). He received the Editor's Choice Award for poetry anthologized in *New Poets of the American West* (MVP Pr., 2010); the 2011 Hispanic Writers Award at the Taos Summer Writers' Conference; and a community scholarship from the 2011 National Latino Writers Conference. He currently resides in Albuquerque, NM, where he edits and publishes *The Más Tequila Review.* http://www.wix.com/rvargas54/rvargas54

Jose Antonio Vazquez (Tontxi) is a Puerto Rican film producer, artist/curator, mentor and a photographer. He has exhibited at the New Museum for Contemporary Art, the Catskills Center of Photography, Bronx Museum, Carnegie Mellon, the Schomburg Collection and the Newark Museum, including numerous private collections. He is the recipient of a National Endowment for the Humanities; and was chosen for the prestigious 2009 and 2010

Cannes Producer's Network Select. He currently working on the monographs, "MEET YOU AT THE CODA/A Latin Jazz Portrait" and "THE NOISE OF TIME/My First Twenty Years of Memory," where he continues to explore issues of first world people, post-colonialism and omissions in history. He resides in London, UK. www.goldenfleecefilms.co.uk, www.gihonrivercollective.com

Lourdes Vazquez has widely published her short stories, essays, poetry and interviews in journals and newspapers in the U.S. and abroad, among the latest, *Carátula and ANIDE* (Nicaragua), *Tsé, Tsé, Gaceta Virtual* (Argentina), *Revista Actual* (Venezuela), and *Kaledoiscope* (Canada). Her work also appears in numerous anthologies, including, *L'altra Penelope* (Italy, 2008); and *El hacer poético* (México, 2008). Her recent poetry collection is *Bestiary: Selected Poems 1986-1997* (Bilingual Rev. Pr., 2004). Her latest novel is, *Not myself without you* (Bilingual Rev. Pr., 2012). Some of her work has been translated to English, Swedish, Portuguese, Italian, Rumanian, Catalan, Galician and Mixtec.

Kukuli Velarde is a Peruvian painter and ceramic artist. The recipient of many awards, she recently received the Leeway Foundation's Transformation Award for Visual Arts (2011); a USA Knight Fellow (2009); and the PEW Fellowship for Visual Arts (2003). She has held solo and group exhibits around the world, recently at Garth Clark Gallery (NY); John Michael Kohler Arts Center (WI) Bellevue Museum of Arts (WA); Museum fur Angewandte Kunst (Frankfurt, Germany); and Society for Contemporary Craft (PA). Velarde, who received her B.F.A. from Hunter College CUNY, *magna cum laude,* has been featured in several publications including *Art in America* (2008); *American Ceramic* (2006); and *Postmodern Ceramics* (2001). http://www.kukulivelarde.com

Mónica González Velázquez has published the poetry collections *Tríptico de desamor* (Fundación Cultural Pascual y Trabajadores del Arte, A.C., 2001), *La luz y las sombras altas* (Fósforo, 2006), *Poesía Reunida* (miCielo ediciones, 2007), *Las cosas últimas* (Fridaura, 2008) *y Gran mal* (miCielo ediciones, 2010). Her poetry has appeared in various poetry anthologies in Mexico, Spain and Argentina. Velázquez has studied graphic design at Escuela Nacional de Artes Plásticas (UNAM), and creative writing in the school of the Society General Writers of Mexico (SOGEM). In 2010, she was granted a scholarship by the Spanish International Cooperation Agency in the area of literature. She works as Director of miCielo editions, a project specializing in the publication of poetry in format of Object-Book.

Manuel Adolfo Villalobos is a musician, painter, and writer, and is currently an Art Studies major at Nassau Community College. He is a founding member of the hip-hop group A Side Of Darkness (A.S.O.D). They have a self-titled album, various music videos and their own recording studio at Music Farm in Elmont, NY. Through the live performances under the stage name The O.G Manny-G, he displays his artwork. He currently lives in Long Island, NY.

Adam Wier, a translator, recently graduated as valedictorian of the Winter 2012 class of Hunter College, where he majored in Spanish-English Translation and Interpretation and Interdisciplinary Honors Studies. He is also a graduate of the American Musical and Dramatic Academy's theatre and film program, in 2004. He currently works translates for the Diocese of Brooklyn, and as a freelance translator. He is also putting the finishing touches on his rendering of Chema Rodriguez's play, *Nubes Frente Un Espejo (Clouds in Front of a Mirror)* for Haberdasher Theatre, of which he is a co-founder. http://www.haberdashertheatre.com

Ted Wilson is a cultural worker that produces and promotes cultural events in the NY/NJ area. He is the author of the poetry chapbook, *Senses & Shadows,* and the poetry/prose collection, *Slo Dance* (2003). He has published poetry, essays and interviews in numerous anthologies, journals and publications, including *The Bandanna Republic, Tribute: A Rainbow of Praises, Bum Rush the Page, Racing & (E)Racing Language: Living with the Color of Our Words, New Rain* (Vol. 9), *Black Renaissance Noire,* and *Callaloo,* among others.. In 2009, Wilson edited and published a 500-page anthology in tribute to poet/playwright Amiri Baraka for his seventy-fifth birthday.

Emanuel Xavier is author of the novel, *Christ Like,* the poetry collections, *If Jesus Were Gay & other poems, Pier Queen, Americano,* and editor of *Bullets & Butterflies: queer spoken word poetry, Mariposas: A Modern Anthology of Queer Latino Poetry,* and *Me No Habla With Acento: Contemporary Latino Poetry.* He has appeared on Russell Simmons' *Def Poetry Jam* and on his spoken word/music collaboration album, *Legendary,* which is available for download on iTunes. He recently curated El Museo del Barrio's "Speak Up!" spoken word poetry series and continues to perform regularly throughout the country and abroad. He lives in New York and works for Random House. www.emanuelxavier.com

Javier Zamora was born and raised in La Herradura, La Paz, El Salvador, and immigrated to the U.S. at the age of nine. He attends UC Berkeley, majoring in Latin American history and minoring in creative writing. In 2011, he attended the Frost Place, Southampton, and Napa Valley writer's conferences as a scholarship student. In 2010, he was a Breadloaf waiter and attended Squaw Valley and Napa Valley writer's conferences with scholarships. Zamora's poems have appeared in *Interrupture, The Homestead Review, Mitali's Fire Escape,* and *Spillway Magazine* who nominated him for the *2011 Best New Poets Anthology.* He is the winner of the 2011 Organic Weapon Arts Chapbook Contest.

C O V E R A R T

Goñi Montes

BORN AND RAISED IN PONCE, PUERTO RICO, Goñi Montes did not discover art until his junior year in college. Up until that point he had very little drawing and absolutely no painting experience whatsoever. Shortly after studying fine arts and receiving his Bachelor of Arts degree at the University of Puerto Rico at Mayagüez, he began his career at the Puerto Rico Sea Grantas as a scientific illustrator. After acquiring his Master of Fine Arts degree from the Savannah College of Art and Design (SCAD) in Atlanta, he switched to editorial and advertising illustration, occasionally teaching classes at SCAD. Montes has certainly come a long way in a very short period of time to become one of the most sought after digital artists in recent years.

While Montes is building up a reputation as a digital artist, he also works with traditional media. Artists as diverse as Henri de Toulouse-Lautrec, Lord Frederic Leighton, Alphonse Mucha, Norman Rockwell and J.C. Leyendecker, have influenced Montes' work. He also admits to having a heavy infatuation with old Korean prints.

Some reviewers have noted that "Montes portrays sceneries with impact. Very into the desaturated color palette, very French, yet Japanese too." Montes is very open about his work and occasionally shares his process on his blog (www.goniart.com/blog), from sketches to final inking.

His work has been featured in professional and student shows for both Society of Illustrators Los Angeles and New York. His recent client list includes *Tor Books, Oz Magazine,* and *Work Style Magazine.*

Montes currently lives and freelances in Decatur, a nice little artistic oasis in the outskirts of Atlanta, Georgia. His website is at www.goniart.com.

COVER: "Helix," Copyright © 2012, digital media

Made in the USA
Lexington, KY
21 April 2012